Daniels' Running Formula

SECOND EDITION

Jack Daniels, PhD

The State University of New York at Cortland

**HUMAN
KINETICS**

Library of Congress Cataloging-in-Publication Data

Daniels, Jack, 1933-
    Daniels' running formula / Jack T. Daniels.-- 2nd ed.
        p. cm.
    Includes index.
    ISBN 0-7360-5492-8 (soft cover)
    1. Running. 2. Running--Training. I. Title.
    GV1062.D36 2005
    796.42--dc22   2004007091

ISBN: 0-7360-5492-8

Acquisitions Editor: Martin Barnard; **Developmental Editor:** Julie Rhoda; **Assistant Editor:** Carla Zych; **Copyeditor:** John Wentworth; **Proofreader:** Annette Pierce; **Indexer:** Betty Frizéll; **Permission Manager:** Toni Harte; **Graphic Designer:** Nancy Rasmus; **Graphic Artist:** Kim McFarland; **Photo Manager:** Dan Wendt; **Cover Designer:** Keith Blomberg; **Photographer (cover):** Andy Lyons/Getty Images; **Photographer (interior):** Photos courtesy of the author except where otherwise noted; **Art Manager:** Kareema McLendon; **Illustrator:** Tom Roberts; **Printer:** Versa Press

Human Kinetics books are available at special discounts for bulk purchase. Special editions or book excerpts can also be created to specification. For details, contact the Special Sales Manager at Human Kinetics.

About the cover photo: 2000 and 2004 U.S. Olympian Alan Culpepper races in the 2000 U.S. Olympic trials.

Printed in the United States of America   10   9   8   7   6   5   4   3   2

Human Kinetics
Web site: www.HumanKinetics.com

United States: Human Kinetics
P.O. Box 5076
Champaign, IL 61825-5076
800-747-4457
e-mail: humank@hkusa.com

Canada: Human Kinetics
475 Devonshire Road Unit 100
Windsor, ON N8Y 2L5
800-465-7301 (in Canada only)
e-mail: orders@hkcanada.com

Europe: Human Kinetics
107 Bradford Road
Stanningley
Leeds LS28 6AT, United Kingdom
+44 (0) 113 255 5665
e-mail: hk@hkeurope.com

Australia: Human Kinetics
57A Price Avenue
Lower Mitcham, South Australia 5062
08 8277 1555
e-mail: liaw@hkaustralia.com

New Zealand: Human Kinetics
Division of Sports Distributors NZ Ltd.
P.O. Box 300 226 Albany
North Shore City
Auckland
0064 9 448 1207
e-mail: info@humankinetics.co.nz

To my daughters, Audra Marie and Sarah Tupper,
who keep me youthful and zealous about the future,
and my loving wife, Nancy Jo,
whose presence is a blessing from God.

Contents

Part III Training for Fitness

Part IV Training for Racing

Foreword

Ten steps easy…ten steps hard…twenty steps easy…twenty steps hard…one hundred steps easy…one hundred steps hard—this has been one of my most effective training mantras, and it was taught to me by Jack Daniels.

If the best measure of good training techniques is staying power, then Jack Daniels has set the gold standard. I continue to employ his simple training techniques twenty-four years after meeting Jack in 1980 at Nike's first research lab in Exeter, New Hampshire.

"Jack Daniels?" I questioned, thinking that his name was a set-up for a punch line. I learned differently soon enough. A gentleman and a scholar, Jack Daniels is the epitome of an exercise physiologist, athletic researcher, and coach, who does it the right way—with scientific data, organization, simple explanations, and heart. Jack deserves all the accolades and praise that he receives from his colleagues in the field of exercise physiology and from those in the running community.

All serious athletes endure periods of subpar performance or injury, and believe me, these periods can be filled with nothing less than self-doubt and panic. How wonderful it has been to know Jack and to have the opportunity to listen to a voice of calm and reason during such times. More often than not, Jack would lay out a sound strategic and proactive plan to overcome the hurdles and obstacles I was facing. Waking up from arthroscopic surgery 17 days before the Olympic Marathon Trials in 1984, I was an emotional wreck. Although I reached out to a number of professionals to help speed my physical recovery, it was Jack Daniels who eased my nerves and provided me with creative and practical techniques to maintain my fitness level—both physical and emotional. Were it not for the bicycle that Jack mounted on his treadmill for me to pedal with my hands, I would not only have gone berserk, but I would probably have snuck out for a run the day after surgery, thereby ruining my slim chance of healing properly before the upcoming Trials.

I'm thrilled that Jack has decided to share his insights and knowledge in this book. I can only hope that others benefit from his expertise as much as I have during my career. You're in for a comprehensive and easily understood lesson in running, coaching, and exercise physiology.

And when I'm passed on the roads by someone mumbling "ten steps easy…ten steps hard," I'll know that the circle has been completed. Enjoy!

Thank you, Jack!

—*Joan Benoit Samuelson*

Preface

My main purpose for writing a book on running was to try to simplify the terminology and workouts so that the same types of training could be used for all categories of runners, from relative beginners to the elite. My motivation, during the 15 years I spent working on the first edition of *Daniels' Running Formula*, was the seeming lack of general training advice that could be used with beginners as well as more accomplished runners.

When I decided to become a runner, after spending my high school and college years as a swimmer, I found that most of the advice I heard and read about came from a coach telling other coaches how his star runner trained. The programs of these stars didn't really seem applicable to runners who were just getting started, or to serious runners who were not yet at a high performance level. More often than not, though, the practice was to train everyone the same way, often too hard, and hope that some would survive (the prevailing attitude being that anyone who couldn't keep up might as well give up on the sport).

I was not an elite runner, nor were the runners I was coaching when I first began my college coaching career, so I decided that I would study the science of exercise and training and see what could be applied to training runners. This took me to Sweden, where I was lucky enough to have some top physiologists as teachers (P.O. Åstrand and E.H. Christensen, to name two who influenced me greatly). After that I decided to pursue my PhD in Exercise Physiology at Wisconsin, where Bruno Balke served as my major professor. In addition to being an outstanding physiologist, Balke had been a good athlete in his native Germany, and he was also a specialist on exercise and altitude. Together we did several years of altitude research, leading up to the 1968 Mexico City Olympics, and this put us in contact with the top distance runners of that era. Interestingly the 26 runners who were the subjects of my dissertation all returned for follow-up testing 25 years later; this was one of the most encouraging research studies I have ever been involved in, and it made me feel that I had been on the right track in training my elite runners.

These elite-runner subjects from the 1960s and '70s were followed by more elite runners during the 1980s and '90s. If you are willing to listen, you can learn a great deal from successful runners, and something they all seemed to agree on is that a major key to success is to avoid injury and to immediately take care of the injuries that occur despite all precautions. In a sense, the runners we send to the Olympics are not necessarily our top runners, but they are very good runners who have avoided injury at critical times. With this in mind, I have designed programs that optimize the benefits of different types of training and avoid placing too much stress on the runners.

Many of the elite runners I worked with did not start out to be runners. Often they took up running when they were cut from another sport or while they were doing some running as conditioning for another sport; by chance, they found that they had a special ability for running and stuck with it. Many said they wish they had received more information about how to train and how to compete.

One important thing I've learned as a coach of distance runners is that no one has all the answers about how best to train and that no single system suits every runner equally well. Therefore, I decided I would take what some great scientists and great runners had passed along, toss in what I learned as a college coach, and try to put it all down in a way that would be easily understood. I wanted to make it simple enough that a runner could learn some basic principles about training and even write his or her own training plan based on those same training principles. Clearly, even the training programs I suggest, although good for many runners, will not be ideal for every runner; therefore I provide some leeway in my recommendations.

After finishing the first edition of *Daniels' Running Formula*, I promised myself that I wouldn't spend another 15 years preparing a second edition. I have been well pleased with the first edition of my book, and comments I've received from runners and coaches from many parts of the world indicate that many readers have found it to be useful. Still, coaching is a never-ending search for better ways to succeed and for better ways to convey what may be useful information about our sport. As a result of my continued evaluation of my work, and in response to input from coaches and runners who have let me know what they want to know more about, comes this second edition of *Daniels' Running Formula*.

In part I of this new edition, I present some basic principles of training, discuss the physiology of running, and retain the practice of using "VDOT" as a performance-based measure of running ability and fitness, from which you can accurately determine appropriate intensities for all types of training. I have added a new approach to monitoring and logging training (time spent training at a variety of "zone" intensities); runners convert fractions of known VDOT values or monitored heart rates and durations at specific intensities into training "points." This point system can be used to monitor weekly or seasonal involvement in each type of training as well as total training stress, information that may be useful in tracking progress in training over consecutive seasons. Part I concludes with a description of how to plot out a season training plan.

In part II I describe in some detail various intensities of training, from easy runs and marathon-pace runs to threshold, interval, and repetition intensities. I explain the use of continuous (tempo) and broken (cruise-interval) runs at threshold pace, and I introduce a new table showing how to adjust the pace for tempo runs that last longer than the pace prescribed for steady 20-minute threshold runs. I conclude part II with a chapter on supplemental training, nonrunning workouts that can be used along with regular running workouts or during times when runners must curtail or abandon their running training.

Part III is a new section of my book addressed to individuals who want to use running as a means of achieving better aerobic fitness and achieving or maintaining good body composition. I identify four different levels of training and fitness by color code, starting with a level of white fitness for complete beginners and progressing through red and blue levels to an ultimate gold category, which demands some high-quality training sessions.

Part IV, as in the first edition, presents some specific training programs for a variety of race distances. New to this part of the book are chapters on training for the 800 meters and specific workouts for the cross country season.

I am confident that I have introduced enough new information in this second edition of *Daniels' Running Formula* to justify the time and effort put into the project. I recommend that readers first look through the table of contents and the brief introduction to each of the four parts of the book, and after reviewing these more general components, move to those chapters that are of particular immediate interest. When time permits, look over all the chapters because often you learn something about training for different events that you can apply to your own program. I continue to welcome comments, and in the meantime, may you run beyond your expectations.

Acknowledgments

The number of people who have helped me better understand distance running is far too great for me to include all their names, but some deserve special thanks because they either played a major role in my formal education, gave unselfishly of their time to help in one of my research projects, or were serious (many elite) runners who were happy to share what they had learned about training and racing. These people deserve a great deal of credit for any success I have had as a coach, and some helped me to put my thoughts into words.

Certainly, Bruno Balke, and Per-Olaf Åstrand were instrumental in sparking my interest in the science of endurance exercise, and I thank them for their encouragement. In the 1960s many of our top distance runners let me conduct numerous tests on them to study the effects of altitude. Some participated with special commitment, and to them I am particularly thankful—Jim Ryun, Tom Von Ruden, Chris McCubbins, Dave Chisholm, Conrad Nightingale, and John Mason. Carl Foster kept me on my toes with research, and Penny Werthner made coaching rewarding for me in the 1970s. In the 1980s there were many Nike runners who were extremely supportive of my ongoing research, and Joan Benoit Samuelson and Alberto Salazar were frequent visitors to the lab. Thanks to Brian Diemer, Doug Padilla, Bob Williams, and Gerry Lindgren, who provided me with some interesting insights into training and racing that have been very useful in shaping my training philosophy—I appreciate their confiding in me. Thanks to Ken Martin and Lisa Martin, who trusted me with their training and certainly substantiated some of my suspected thoughts about marathon training.

For some outstanding performances and for having confidence in me as a coach in the 1990s, I thank Jerry Lawson and the many runners at SUNY Cortland who confirmed that my ideas about training were sound. I also thank coaches Bob Sevene and Frank Gagliano, both of whom have had a positive influence on my coaching career, and the many Farm Team runners who placed their trust in me, especially Magdalena Lewy, Lori Riedy, Heather Tanner, and Peter Gilmore. For over 20 years of loyal support I want to thank Jeff Johnson, a true friend of runners. Thanks to Jimmy Gilbert for the VDOT tables, and to Graham Covington and Harry Turvey for their encouragement. Thank you all, and thank you Nancy Jo, Maro, Gerd, Carlos, and the Chasquis.

Finally, I want to offer special thanks to Julie Rhoda, whose editing expertise and understanding of the sport of running has made the task of finalizing this second edition of *Daniels' Running Formula* far easier than could have ever been anticipated.

Introduction:
The Ingredients of Success

There are four key ingredients for success in distance running—or for any other pursuit in life, for that matter. They are, in order, inherent ability, motivation, opportunity, and direction.

Inherent Ability

Nearly anywhere you look in sports you can see the important role that genetics (inherent ability) plays in success. When you imagine an Olympic female gymnast, a male shot-putter, an NBA center, and a jockey, you almost certainly see a petite, trim girl; a large, powerful man; an extremely tall man; and a short, lightweight man or woman. These are the necessary body types for success at the elite level in women's gymnastics, shot putting, the center position in the NBA, and horse racing. Such athletes don't achieve their anatomical structure through training; they're born with bodies that perfectly suit their sport.

Now think of a successful distance runner. What do you see? Someone who is short, tall, muscular, or very lean. There have been, and still are, outstanding runners of many body types, but physiologically they are as similar in their design as female gymnasts or NBA centers are. You can't see the physiological characteristics that make some distance runners great and others not so great, but there are inherent qualities that separate one runner from another, just as surely as body size and composition are factors in shot putting or horse racing.

Genetic ability is the first ingredient of success. You have a certain amount given to you at birth on which you can, of course, improve, but the top end of your potential is set for you, and it's up to you to do what you will with your gifts.

Motivation

Motivation to use your God-given talent is the second ingredient of success, and this must come from within. It's easy for a basketball coach to be motivated for a seven-foot high school player, but if this seven-footer wants to be an artist rather than a basketball player, chances are he won't fulfill his full potential on the court.

I believe there are four kinds of distance runners:

1. Those who have inherent ability and the motivation to use that ability
2. Those who have the ability to do well but aren't motivated to use their ability

3. Those who lack much ability but have great motivation to achieve success

4. Those who lack ability and aren't motivated

The first group of runners is made up of champions—they almost always perform well. The second group contributes significantly to coach frustration. The coach sees the potential, but there's little or no desire on the part of the athlete to use it. "If you wanted it enough, you could be a champion," you hear the coach lament. Runners who fall into the third group satisfy the coach but frustrate themselves. These runners have the will it takes to be a champion, but they lack the genetic makeup. They do exactly what their coach says; they try every workout imaginable and run as much mileage as they can fit into a day. They are candidates for overtraining and for being beaten by type-2 runners. You've probably seen these two types in action—the "natural" athlete, who seldom trains, eats, or sleeps right but who still manages to beat the highly motivated, nongifted, frustrated runner. It's sad to see, but it happens all the time.

In my view, coaches shouldn't nag type-2 runners about their lack of motivation—not any more than they castigate type-3 runners for their lack of ability (which is almost never). It's very possible that the type-2 runner is running only because of coach, family, or peer pressure. The coach should talk to the runner about the possibility that running might not be the right place for him or her, despite the obvious talent. Coach support can go a long way toward converting a type-2 runner into a type 1, a transformation that's impossible for a type-3 runner.

I don't think we should discourage high-motivation, low-ability runners (type 3) from running; their perseverance might lead to considerable personal satisfaction in the sport. Plus their enthusiasm might provide type-2 runners with just the influence they need. Type-3 athletes are fun to coach and deserve your appreciation and attention.

Finally, there are the no-ability, no-motivation runners. These people seldom even try running; if they do give it a shot, they probably won't enjoy it or be any good at it. Of course, type-4 runners are likely type-1 people in other aspects of their life: both gifted and motivated.

Opportunity

The third ingredient for success is opportunity, which includes many factors, perhaps the most prominent being the environment in which you grow up or live. Someone born with outstanding ability for downhill skiing but who lives in a warm, southern climate with no mountains might never have the opportunity to develop in the sport or even recognize his or her aptitude for it. Even if highly motivated (through movies and videos, for example), he or she might fail because of a lack of access to facilities.

Swimming pools aren't available to many individuals; this fact likely precludes many of them from becoming good swimmers. Equestrian events, yachting, and skating are other sports unavailable to most individuals. Similarly, a talented and motivated golfer or tennis player might see success as unattainable because a warm geographic location (or indoor training facility) isn't available during the important years of development.

In one way or another, some people can break away from a prohibitive environment or overcome other obstacles and achieve unexpected success in a sport. Still, the opportunity to participate in an activity is an important ingredient of success. In addition to having the climate, facilities, and equipment necessary for the pursuit of a sport, for many sports, athletes also need enough time and money. Living in a hotbed of golf, for example, doesn't guarantee access to the sport.

Finally, the opportunity to compete in a chosen sport is also important. A young fencer who truly loves the sport of fencing, has a good teacher, and possesses adequate time for training might still find the road to success a long one if there are no other fencers around to compete with.

Opportunity is an important ingredient of success, yet in our affluent society it's difficult for us to perceive it as a limiting factor. But that's often how it is. In the United States, the business of providing opportunity in the sport of running is left primarily to high schools and colleges. Schools with adequate finances have track facilities, good equipment, and travel expenses. Perhaps the greatest obstacle many aspiring runners face is the lack of opportunity outside the framework of the schools.

The lack of clubs for postschool competition hurts American runners at the very time when they need the most support—in their early 20s. Another drawback of a school-based support system is the lack of continuity of coaching. A high school athlete might have more than one coach during early development, and then might attend a community college before finishing at a four-year university; such an athlete might run for three or four different coaches before reaching his or her best running years. American runners face a difficult task: Consider the fact that learning a new training system often takes a full season to accomplish, and many athletes aren't in a stable coaching environment for more than a couple of years at a time. Without steady, consistent guidance, many American runners falter before reaching their physiological peak and never have the opportunity to develop their full potential.

Direction

Direction, the final ingredient of success, involves a coach, a teacher, or a training plan that can be followed. Of the four ingredients of success, direction is probably the one of least significance. I say this because direction is the only ingredient that can have either positive or negative influence on the athlete.

If you consider inherent ability, you'll realize that everyone has some degree of this basic ingredient. The same can be said for motivation and opportunity. However, an absence of direction is usually better than bad direction. Examples of bad direction might be telling a beginning runner that anything less than 150 miles of running per week won't lead to success in distance running, or that one must do repetition work every day for the final two weeks leading up to an important marathon race.

When I think of all the great runners I've known who had to suffer at one time or another through a tough coach–athlete relationship, it's amazing to me that they reached the degree of success they did. What we all tend to overlook more than we should is the importance of positive individual attention given to each athlete on the team. Nothing can replace the encouraging comments or understanding words of support from a quality coach. To become an elite runner, an individual needs a support system, and this support system must have his or her best interests in mind. A coach must sometimes simultaneously attend to the best interests of 20 or more aspiring runners, and he or she must also be able to manage the individuals as a collective group, helping them come together as a team.

The Coach's Role

It's easy to misinterpret the effectiveness of coaching when we reward or recognize major university coaches primarily for the level of performance of their athletes. A coach who uses all available scholarship aid on distance runners and wins a cross country championship has a good chance of being voted coach of the year, even if the team is made up of newly recruited athletes who had no improvement in performance from the previous year when they each had a different coach.

If the term "coach" refers to the person who directs the improvement or refinement of running performance, then a good coach can always answer the question, "Why are we doing this workout today?" A good coach produces beneficial reactions to training, creates positive race results, and transforms the athletes he or she brings into the program into better runners (and, one hopes, better human beings). In many large universities, however, the head coach is actually more of an administrator than someone who directs the training of the athletes. Even though the head coach reaps the glory when the team does well, and is probably deserving of some praise, it's often the assistants (or a written training system) who have guided the athletes through the season.

Far-Reaching Results of Positive Direction

Talented athletes who have motivation and opportunity can usually perform well enough to mask the job being done by a poor coach. On the other side, good coaches aren't always recognized for positive results when the available talent is not high caliber. Actually, a coach who provides good direction can do a lot to instill motivation and often has a good deal to do with providing opportunity as well, which in turn increases motivation.

One could say that the four ingredients of success really boil down to two—ability and motivation, the latter being derived from one's intrinsic desire plus the drive fanned by opportunity and direction from the coach.

Of course, there are no clear-cut categories into which all athletes can be sorted. Differing amounts and various combinations of ingredients give runners their individuality. Whether you're a coach or a runner, be happy with what you have. Use your ability, or the ability of your runners, to its fullest. There are basic principles of training for you to consider, but don't be afraid to take some chances now and then. There are as many individual pathways to success as there are individual runners. Discovering what works best for you is a large part of the challenge and of the fun.

Training Essentials

Here in part I, I provide general thoughts about running and some basic principles of training that apply to developing middle- and long-distance runners. In chapter 1, I summarize basic physiology of performance as it relates to middle- and long-distance runners and discuss how systems of the body are related to a runner's ability to train and race. Specifically, I describe what's meant by maximum oxygen consumption ($\dot{V}O_2max$), a running economy curve (determined by $\dot{V}O_2submax$ data), velocity at $\dot{V}O_2max$ ($v\dot{V}O_2max$), and lactate threshold.

In chapter 2, I discuss types of training that can optimize the physiological systems or components of running fitness. I provide a definition of each type of training; a range, or zone, of intensities associated with each type; and a new way of prescribing and logging training sessions based on intensity and duration of exercise. You can use this method of monitoring training stress with either fractions of maximum heart rate (HRmax) or fractions of current $\dot{V}O_2max$.

In chapter 3, I provide a version of the VDOT tables that Jimmy Gilbert and I developed and presented in detail in the book, *Oxygen Power.* You can use these VDOT tables to identify both current running ability and ideal training paces for each type of training you'll use in your training programs.

Chapter 4, which concludes part I, includes information on how to set up a season of training. This prepares you for understanding the in-depth discussion of types of training detailed in part II.

CHAPTER 1

Training Focus

The transition from running for fitness or as a member of a school team to approaching the sport as a serious, competitive athlete is not always easy to negotiate. When runners decide to get serious about training and competing, they usually make several adjustments.

- They increase their mileage (total distance run or time spent running each week).
- They run more regularly (progressing to six or seven days a week or adding a second run to their daily training routine).
- They introduce some (or more) quality work into their current program of regular steady runs.

But a danger in changing your training schedule in any of these ways is that you increase the likelihood of injuring yourself. A sudden and overenthusiastic dedication to running often leads to an injury that makes you give up running permanently. Or an injury might convince you that competitive running isn't for you and that you'll never be a serious runner, so you might as well return to your previous approach to running and hope to avoid another setback.

Instead of jumping into a commitment with reckless abandon, what you need at this point is firm guidance. You need a plan to follow, a teacher, a coach. Probably what you need least of all is to discover the fantastic

If winning is the only thing that rescues athletes from "wasting their time training," then there are a lot of unhappy people wasting their time running.

training program followed by a recent winner of the Boston Marathon. Throwing yourself headlong into such a program is usually a recipe for great disappointment.

The fact that distance running requires minimal technical skill yet a high level of conditioning shouldn't prompt coaches and runners to escalate the stress of training too rapidly. Everyone has different physical and mental strengths and weaknesses, and each runner must be treated according to his or her own mix. Take the time to evaluate in detail the factors, past and present, that influence a training program.

In this chapter, I present principles of training that can serve as the basis for any training system you develop. These principles are based on a combination of the physiology of the body's reactions to training and the environment, the many training responses I've seen in my 40-plus years of coaching, and the experiences passed on to me by other runners and researchers. Being a very good teacher usually boils down to common sense, along with a willingness to experiment a little now and then.

Get to Know Your Training Needs

The one question regarding training that any athlete (or coach) needs to answer on a regular basis is, "What's the purpose of this training session?" I wonder how many athletes and coaches ask this question for every session and answer it in a way that makes sense. I think I can answer just about any question you might have about your training and racing (if racing is part of your plan). For example, I might tell you that the purpose of today's easy run is to get in some running while recovering from yesterday's demanding interval session, or that today's repetition session will include long recoveries between workbouts so that you can practice good mechanics while running fast. However, I'm not so naive as to believe that I (or anyone else) have all the answers for everyone who takes up a running career. Sometimes what works well for one person might not work for another. That said, some sound scientific principles do apply to everyone, and there are some ways of doing things that work far better than others.

Runners who train together often forget that they might not all be training for the same event. Further, even if they're shooting for the same goal and same event, they might react differently to the same training. Tom Von Ruden, my friend and a great middle-distance runner, was in the final weeks of preparation for the 1968 U.S. Olympic Trials, to be held at altitude in South Lake Tahoe, California. He and the other finalists for the trials had been training together for several weeks in Tahoe, and Tom was feeling a bit down about his chances, possibly because he'd watched the others seemingly float through their workouts. Tom asked me what I thought might be the best thing to do for his final preparation, and I suggested that he fly out to Leadville, Colorado (elevation nearly 10,000 feet), for a week or so and have some time to himself at an altitude a fair bit higher than what he'd be facing just outside Tahoe (about 7,300 feet) in his Olympic Trials race. Out of trust in my scientific knowledge of the effects of altitude, or simply out of desperation for something different to try, Tom made the trip. On his return, he not only made the U.S. team but was also a finalist in the 1,500 meters at the Mexico City Olympics, where he finished ninth.

Chris McCubbins leads Jim Ryun through a workout in Alamosa, Colorado, during preparation for the 1968 Olympic Trials.

I believed in what I was advising, based on sound scientific knowledge about training. I also had spent time with Tom at altitude research camps and felt I understood his psyche to some degree. In any case, at that time, for that athlete, training at higher altitude was the right thing to do. Would it have been the right thing for all the finalists training in Tahoe? Probably not. Certainly it might not have been right for the other finalists who ended up making the U.S. team by staying in Tahoe to train.

More recently, one of my female collegiate runners entered the cross country season running personal-best times, but as we added more quality to our program (to which everyone else on the team responded favorably), her performances started to decline. It didn't take us long to realize that she responded better to the steady distance running she'd done in the summer; with a change back to that training, she went on to have even better-than-usual seasons during her final two years in college. The point is that each runner has unique personal strengths and weaknesses—you need to get to know your *own* training needs. When I was coaching Lisa Martin, she got a positive feeling about doing fairly fast repetition 400s, although the marathon was her primary event, whereas other marathoners I've coached seldom included repeat 400s in their program because they felt better doing more threshold-pace training. Lisa's craving for short, fast running probably dated back to her early years of competing as a 400 hurdler. Jerry Lawson, another great marathoner, always relied on high mileage to get him through.

SET YOUR OWN PACE

I'd like to emphasize that each runner and coach should abandon the "copy the current champion" approach to training and instead challenge the runner's own body with training based on scientific principles. With your understanding of the runner's body, and with some common sense and a little creativity and boldness, you can set up a program that might well make you the next wonder of distance running or coaching.

On the other hand, don't ignore what current champions are doing, because they might be supporting a training scheme that you've believed in but been unable to prove effective. When you hear of a new approach to training, don't try to copy it—try to *analyze* it. Evaluate what systems of the body are reaping the benefits, and why and how they're doing so.

Keep in mind that what you read about an athlete's training might not be his or her regular or daily training regimen. For instance, I'm sure every runner has been asked at some point how much he or she runs. The answer might be, "I do five miles a day," in hopes that the person asking interprets this to mean 35 miles a week. But, in fact, the runner might run only three days a week, and his or her longest run recently (or ever) was a 5-miler. In other words, to gain some respect from others or to get an ego boost, the runner might want to give the impression of a more demanding training schedule than is actually the case.

When weekly training logs of champion runners are made public, what you usually see is a particularly great week of training, not a typical week in the runner's training period. Or you might see a week during the strenuous phase of training, which is not at all the same as a week during a competitive phase of training. Some runners speak of their 150-mile weeks as if they're normal, when really they've accomplished only one such week.

By the way, for those who think that high weekly mileage is a new approach to improved performance, let me relate the answers that one of my research subjects (a U.S. Olympian at 10,000 meters and a national high school record holder at 5,000 meters) gave to the following questions in the late 1960s.

"What's the single longest training run you ever took?" *Answer:* 66 miles, on more than one occasion.

"What was your greatest week of running?" *Answer:* 360 miles.

"What was your greatest weekly mileage for a six-week period?" *Answer:* 300 miles per week.

"What was the greatest weekly mileage you averaged for an entire year?" *Answer:* 240 miles.

For all of you who like to copy what the great ones do, try to resist replicating the accomplishments of this runner; you might not have the same body type or the ideal mechanics to handle that much running. Or your mental attitude toward the sport might be different. We're all individuals and must train with this in mind to achieve success.

The same principles apply to runners with little experience who are serious about reaching their potential and to runners who have had some success but think there's room for improvement: Know your own body, identify your strengths and weaknesses, establish priorities, and try to learn more about why you do what you do and why you might consider trying something new in your approach.

The great miler Jim Ryun used to tell me of youngsters who wrote him asking about his training program. They wanted to do what he was doing so they could run like he ran. They didn't want to wait until they were his age or until they had progressed to a particular performance level before launching into his program—they wanted to get the workouts and start doing them right away. I receive similar letters and calls: "How should I adjust my (or my team's) training to have the success that you're having with your runners?"

Although I appreciate these calls and letters and hope that I provide some help, it's difficult to work with only part of the picture. To suggest a workout without considering such details as current fitness level, experience level, goals, and available time makes it hard for training advice to have a positive effect. When I receive such requests, I initially find myself asking more questions than I answer because I need to figure out what type of individual or team of individuals I'm dealing with. I go through a mental checklist of questions about each athlete before coming up with what I hope is a reasonable answer. Here are some of the questions that I consider important in assessing any athlete's individual training needs:

1. What is the runner's current level of fitness? What is his or her readiness for training and competing?

2. How much time (in weeks) is available for a season's best performance?

3. How much time (in hours per day) is available for training?

4. What are the runner's strengths and weaknesses, in terms of speed, endurance (lactate threshold), $\dot{V}O_2$max (aerobic capacity), economy, and reaction to different amounts (mileage) of running?

5. What types of training does the runner like to do? To what types of training does the runner respond well psychologically?

6. For what specific event is the runner preparing?

7. How should periodic races fit into the training program? That is, what are the race commitments?

8. What are the environmental conditions (season of the year), facilities, and opportunities that must be taken into account?

Most coaches and runners consider all these questions at some level of conscious or subconscious thought, but it's not a bad idea to list the questions and their answers for reference when you need help setting up a program. The principles of training presented in this chapter provide the answers to many of these questions. In chapter 4, I show you how to put everything together into a comprehensive training program.

Understand the Training Principles

As I've mentioned, you should resist copying a coach's or champion's training regimen just because it works great for him or her; each runner's training schedule should be based on sound principles of training. Of course it's possible that through pure luck the coach or champion you're copying follows a schedule that's ideal for you, but this is rare. It's best to know and understand why you're doing what you're doing.

Runners should understand exactly what each day's training is designed to accomplish. Ideally, they should also know how long it might take before they realize the benefits of their training. Further, understanding how the body reacts to various stresses can help prevent overstressing and allow runners to maximize all the systems of importance in achieving their running goals. Here are some principles of training that answer often-asked questions regarding how the body reacts to the stress of training.

Principle 1: The Body Reacts to Stress

There are two types of reactions to the stress of exercise. The first is an acute reaction, such as you would experience if you got up from your seat, went outside, and ran to the corner. Your heart rate speeds up, your stroke volume (the amount of blood your heart pumps with each beat) increases, your ventilation rate and depth of breathing increase, your blood pressure rises, and your muscles feel some fatigue. If you perform an exercise on a regular basis, you experience regular reactions to the activity. The second type of reaction to the stress of exercise is the training effect, which results from repeated, chronic exercise.

Training produces changes throughout your body that over time allow you to perform the daily run to the corner with less discomfort (and probably in less time, as well). The muscles that you stress with this exercise become stronger, and blood flow to the muscles is increased. Changes inside the muscle cells provide more energy for the muscles, and less lactic acid accumulates during the bout of exercise. Your resting heart rate undoubtedly becomes slower (because a stronger heart can pump more blood per beat it and thus requires fewer beats to deliver the needed blood). You probably also develop a lighter, springier step (because your leg muscles are more fit), lower resting blood pressure, lower body weight, and less fat under the skin. All of these reactions to the stresses you impose on your body lead to improvements in how you react to stress, the increases of stress you can tolerate, and how prepared you'll be to handle new stresses and competitive efforts.

Principle 2: Specificity of Training

The system you stress during exercise is the one that stands to benefit from the stress. Training for one sport usually has little or no beneficial effect on your ability to perform a second sport; in fact, in some cases there might be a detrimental effect, such as the negative effect that long-distance running has on performing explosive leg activities, such as sprinting and jumping. It works the same way for bodybuilding and distance running: The extra muscle mass developed through bodybuilding can act as dead weight and interfere with distance-running abilities.

The principle of specificity means that to become accomplished at an activity, you must practice *that* activity and not try to achieve gains through performing another activity. Doing another activity takes time away from your primary interest and might produce results that limit performance in your main activity. You must give considerable thought to every aspect of your training, and you must know what everything you do is doing for you and to you.

Please don't take the specificity principle so literally that you limit *all* your training to running (although if you have limited time for training, you might be best off spending what time you do have on running). Most runners can realize definite benefits through some nonrunning (supplemental) training sessions—because flexibility and strengthening exercises can help ward off running injuries common among runners who spend all their available training time running. I address supplemental (support-system) training in chapter 10.

Specificity of Overtraining

The specificity of overtraining is a corollary to principle 2. Just as training benefits those body systems that are properly stressed by the exercise, overtraining has a negative impact on the systems that are overstressed.

It's possible for a single, overstressed system to affect a variety of activities other than just the activity that caused the damage. For example, a stress fracture in the leg, caused by too much or improper running, can prevent a runner from performing other activities that stress the injured extremity. Too much running doesn't always mean you become overtrained in other types of physical activity, and it might be beneficial to limit running for periods of time in favor of other types of training. When you have an injury that eliminates running for a while, this might be a good time to do some deep-water running or to work on an elliptical trainer, either of which might work some leg and hip muscles even better than running would. Keep in mind that when you've been away from running for a period of time, you should work your way back into it with reduced intensity (see chapter 4). We quickly learn to appreciate the frailty of our bodies when we depend on everything to go right at all times as we try to reach our goals.

Specific Stress Produces a Specific Result

This corollary to principle 2 might be somewhat obvious, but its importance makes it worth mentioning. The benefits that you can expect from doing three one-mile runs at eight minutes each, with five minutes recovery between runs, three times a week, are specific to that frequency (three times each week), amount (three miles of running per session), intensity (eight-minute pace), and recovery between runs (five minutes). Someone who performs this training regimen regularly will reach a level of running proficiency that will remain stable (and that will differ from the proficiency level reached if the training program consisted of five one-mile runs at seven minutes per mile). Figure 1.1 shows how a new level of fitness is reached over time.

Adding a new level of stress on top of your current training further increases your fitness level. If you have performed this training regimen regularly and reached a stable level of proficiency, many training modifications are possible. You could increase the training frequency from three to four (or more) days per week, you could increase the amount of training from three to four miles per session, or you could increase the distance of each interval from one mile to one and a half miles each. Another possibility is to increase the intensity (the speed of each mile) from 8:00 pace to 7:40 pace, for example. A final possibility is to change the recovery time allowed between the mile runs within a workout. Any one of these changes in training (frequency, duration, intensity, or recovery) or any combination of these changes will affect the result of the program, leading to a new level of fitness (see figure 1.2).

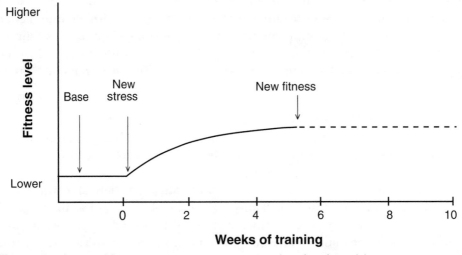

Figure 1.1   Increased fitness as a response to a new stress introduced to training.

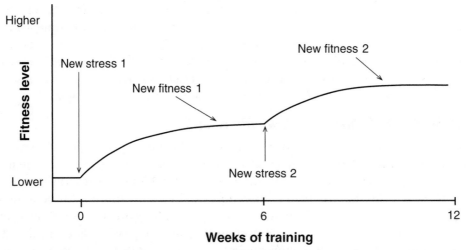

Figure 1.2   Increased fitness as a response to adding a new level of stress (new stress 2) onto prior training (new stress 1).

Principle 3: Rate of Achievement

Notice in figures 1.1 and 1.2 that the rate of achieving the benefits of a training program is rapid at first and then tapers off over time. If you look at the time scale on these two figures, you see that most of the benefits of a particular training regimen are adequately realized within about six weeks. Sticking with a training program for longer than six weeks, however, can produce more benefits. Without an increased stress of training, changes in body composition (loss of unnecessary fat, for example) can continue, leading to better performance.

You might realize adequate benefits within a matter of weeks; however, if you want to increase training, a good time to do so is after six weeks of adapting to the previous training stress. Changes you impose after fewer or more than six weeks of a program would follow the curves shown in figures 1.3 and 1.4, respectively. The primary danger of increasing training too often is an escalated risk of injury and overstress caused by taking on too much too fast. It's difficult to get a feeling of what a particular training

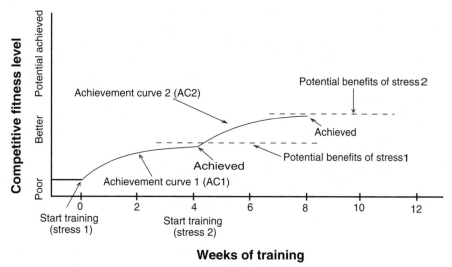

Figure 1.3   Changing the training stress you're doing within a phase of your program too soon prevents you from achieving the maximum benefits from that phase.

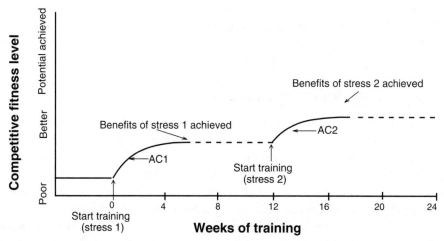

Figure 1.4   To progress beyond any achieved level of fitness, the training stress must be increased or you'll reach a fitness plateau and never exceed it.

load is doing for you if you don't stay with it a while. You might be ready to increase your training stress after fewer than six weeks, and on occasion that's perfectly acceptable, but I think you should give any particular amount of stress at least three, preferably four, weeks before increasing training. I prefer that my runners feel that one amount and intensity of training is getting easier before they try running more or faster.

Principle 4: Personal Limits

Another principle of training related to the curves presented in figures 1.1 through 1.4 is that each individual has unique limits. In fact, you could probably say that every system in a person's body has limits. For example, there's a limit on how tall you will be, how strong a particular muscle in your body can get (including the heart), how much air you can breathe in and out of your lungs, how much blood can be transported to your running muscles, how much oxygen your running muscles can use in converting fuel to energy, and how fast you can run a mile, a 10K, or a marathon. Different people will reach different degrees of success, which are greatly dictated by personal limits. The good news is that few people *realize* their limits, relative to running, and improvement is almost always possible.

Having limits presents us with the dilemma of testing the "no pain, no gain" theory. Let's say you've been gradually increasing your training every six weeks for the past six months, and your performances are steadily improving. After several weeks of even more difficult training, you feel tired and can't do the workouts very well. When a race comes along, your performance is subpar. Your reaction is likely to be, "I need to train harder," but it should be, "Maybe I have reached a personal limit and need to reassess my training program." Something has to be done, and the train-harder approach, although quite common, is usually not the answer. Often the limit is seasonal, and the next year your performances will begin to improve again, to a new limit. I often see limits varying among college runners, largely because of changes in class schedules, work, and personal relationships. When an athlete's results don't meet expectations, the athlete might be the victim of the personal (perhaps temporary) limit principle. On the other hand, the principle is also often at play when runners achieve a breakthrough season. In most cases, physiological performance should and usually will continue to improve over many years; a subpar season is often the result of outside influences, which are usually temporary.

Principle 5: Diminishing Return

As training increases in duration and intensity, the benefit—or return—from the training decreases. This doesn't mean that increasing training decreases fitness; it means that the fitness increases later in training aren't as great as they were earlier in training. To clarify this principle, the benefits of increasing weekly mileage are shown in figure 1.5, with an all-inclusive term, competitive fitness (or percent of potential achieved), plotted against weekly mileage. Take the example of someone who starts training at 10 miles per week, doubles the weekly mileage to 20, doubles it again to 40, and finally reaches 80 miles per week, allowing a couple of months at each level.

Regardless of how gradually the runner progresses from 20 to 40 to 80 weekly miles of training, the benefits reaped from 40-mile weeks are not double those realized at 20-mile weeks, nor are the results of 80-mile weeks double the return of 40-mile weeks or quadruple the benefit of 20-mile weeks. Adding more and more mileage to your weekly training doesn't produce equal percentages of improvement in competitive fitness. The same principle of diminishing return applies to increasing the amount of faster quality training. The difference between this principle and the rate-of-achievement principle (principle 3) is that the rate of achievement applies to each degree of achievement along the curve of diminishing return, shown in figure 1.5. It still takes an equal amount of time to reach the benefits of a new level of training, but each new level achieved will be less of an improvement than the previous one was.

It's a sad but true fact that harder and harder training results in less and less improvement; even so, improvement *will* continue as long as the accelerating setback principle (number 6) doesn't become too large a factor. Still, even small improvements, which might be associated with greater-than-ever increases in stress, might pay off, especially when only a second or two separates runners at the end of a race or when an athlete is contending for an Olympic medal.

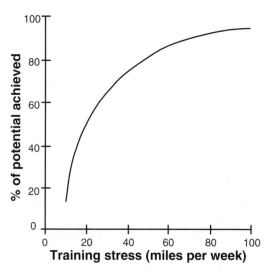

Figure 1.5 The principle of diminishing return states that as you continue to increase the amount of stress in your training, you get less benefit from the increase. This is why beginning runners make vast improvements in their fitness and elite runners don't.

Principle 6: Accelerating Setbacks

The setback principle states that low levels of training cause few setbacks (such as injury, illness, or reduced interest in training), whereas high levels of training increase the risk of setbacks occurring. The curve that depicts this principle is a reverse image of the diminishing returns curve (figure 1.5). In figure 1.6, increases in training stress are plotted against the chance of encountering a setback.

A setback is a setback and must be avoided at nearly all costs. Thus, this principle is one to be wary of, especially in more important seasons. It's very difficult to say what's too much for any particular runner, and it might take several seasons of working together before a coach and an athlete can arrive at what's enough and what's too much. It's particularly important to log your responses to different amounts and intensities of training so that you can refer to earlier seasons, how much you did, and how you responded to various types of training. I hope the new point system presented in chapter 2 is useful in this regard.

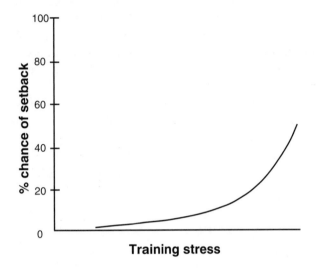

Figure 1.6 Increasing your training stress increases your chance of setback caused by injury or illness.

Principle 7: Ease of Maintenance

This principle applies to maintaining a level of competitive ability, which is at least partly a function of reaching a particular level of confidence. Although I'm referring primarily to physiological fitness, it's no secret that psychological factors play an important part in how fast you can race. Once you break the barrier of the five-minute mile, or any other personal goal, the training effort required to repeat the task is usually well short of what it took to reach the goal in the first place.

The maintenance principle is important when planning a long-term training program. It allows you to shift your training emphasis from one system (e.g., development of cellular adaptations that respond favorably to long, easy mileage) to another system (e.g., repetition work for the enhancement of economy) and still maintain the original benefits through less frequent attention (to the longer runs). The ability to improve a system and then maintain it while building up another system relies heavily on the maintenance principle.

This principle can be of particular importance for runners involved in another sport between cross country and outdoor track season. Basketball, for example, helps a runner maintain some impact–stress conditioning that will be of benefit when returning to running as the primary sport. By taking advantage of previous conditioning maintained through less-than-major involvement in running, you can make it easier on yourself when it comes time to set up for a new running season. Whereas some runners might have to start from scratch each new season, those who retained some fitness while away from running can take on more demanding workouts earlier in the season and perhaps progress to a greater level of achievement.

Be Flexible in Your Training

Education is a never-ending process, as is the search for improvement in any endeavor. I continue to learn about coaching and training by talking to other coaches and runners and trying to answer their questions. Sometimes I don't have the answer, but the question prompts me to evaluate the situation and come up with what I consider a logical response—often a new approach to training.

Some local high school coaches asked me how their cross country teams could get in some training when they were required to compete every Tuesday and Saturday. I don't like training (other than easy running) for two days before a competition, so that left only Wednesdays as the day for training. Further, because racing 5,000 meters provides benefits similar to those of a good interval session, it wasn't necessary to add an interval session to the weekly schedule. Thus, by treating Tuesdays (race days) as interval days, I opted for a threshold session (a few miles of comfortably hard running; see chapter 7 for details) on Wednesdays, creating back-to-back quality days each week. If a Tuesday race wasn't too demanding, the teams did some fartlek running (mixing fast and slow runs of various distances; see chapter 2) over the race course following the race, making Tuesday a full-blown, quality interval day.

After a season or two, so many high school coaches reported success with this approach (back-to-back quality days on Tuesdays and Wednesdays) that I incorporated the same approach into my cross country training system and have stayed with it ever since. Of course, we don't all have Tuesday races, so that becomes a good long-interval quality day, which I follow with another quality (threshold) day on Wednesday. I continue to follow this system to some extent during track season because the back-to-back training has at least three advantages. (1) It allows my runners to adapt to racing on consecutive days. (2) Muscle soreness is often greater the second day after a stressful session than it is the very next day, so the follow-up quality day comes before the negative effects of the first day have occurred. (3) For younger, overzealous runners, the knowledge that tomorrow brings another quality day might calm their enthusiasm somewhat and make overtraining less likely.

As I've discussed in this chapter, my approach to training runners is getting to know their individual needs and applying the principles of training to those needs. I've arranged the chapters that follow to apply this training focus to the demands of the event being trained for and to finding the proper mix of training that best meets the event's demands, thus optimizing a runner's performance.

Sara Bei

Sara Bei was born in San Mateo, California, and started running at age 12, having concentrated on soccer and basketball in her earlier years. Sara's junior high English teacher was also the cross country coach. He immediately spotted her obvious talent for running, and he has been very supportive of her running career ever since. Making it to the Foot Locker cross country nationals as a freshman at Montgomery High School in Santa Rosa, California, prompted Sara to drop her other sports and concentrate on running. As a result of her early success, Sara set her goals at the national level and accomplished some outstanding achievements along the way. She became the first California high school runner to win four state cross country championships, on the way to winning the Foot Locker nationals in a record time of 16:51. As a high school sophomore, she set a national indoor record for 2 miles (10:21).

Photo courtesy of Sara Bei

Sara made her first international appearance during her freshman year at Stanford University when she ran in the Junior World Cross Country championships in Ireland. As a member of Stanford's cross country and track teams, she gave strong performances on outstanding track relay teams as well as in individual track and cross country events. Sara's most recent achievement was an 11th place finish in the 5,000 meters at the 2004 U.S. Olympic Trials. Sara's ability to graciously accept both success and disappointment, her resolve to take one day at a time, and the faith we both share make me a fan of hers.

Personal bests: mile—4:36; 3,000m—9:05; 5,000m—15:36.

CHAPTER 2

Physiology of Training Intensities

The physiological components of most importance in distance running are the cardiovascular system, the muscular system, lactate threshold, aerobic capacity (or maximum oxygen consumption), speed, and economy of running. I refer to these components as systems, but only the first two are body systems in the true sense of the word. Each of the six components involves the functioning of one or more of the traditional body systems (neuromuscular or metabolic, for example). Although it might be technically incorrect, the word "system" is useful when referring, for instance, to training the "lactate system" or lactate component of performance, rather than to break this difficult-to-define phenomenon into the multiple functions that lead to the production of lactic acid and its removal from the muscles and blood. Thus, throughout this chapter, I sometimes refer to the six physiological components as systems in order to avoid long and tangential discussions of the body's complex functions.

After describing the components and the types of training that improve them, I explain how to create a personal profile to help you get the most out of each workout. I then describe how to formulate your training goals and the types of training that help you attain those goals and to become a faster and stronger runner in your desired event.

We all get more practice losing than winning, so it is as important to learn to be a good loser as it is to be a graceful winner.

Improving Each Component of Running Performance

When a runner is at a low level of fitness, easy running produces benefits to most of the components of running performance. To optimize the contribution of the components, however, you need to understand how the components function and be aware of the factors that affect their role and capacity.

Developing the Cardiovascular System

The cardiovascular system refers to the heart (cardiac) muscle and the network of vessels carrying blood to and from the parts of the body. For runners, the part of the body that needs a large blood supply is the part of the muscular system that does the running.

The function of the cardiovascular system is to provide an adequate supply of oxygen to the running muscles and to meet the increasing demands for oxygen as the runner becomes more fit. The delivery of oxygen depends on how powerful the pump (heart) is, how much oxygen a unit of blood can carry, how well the blood flows through the vessels, and how efficiently blood is diverted from less crucial areas of the body to the exercising muscles.

The Heart As a Pump

Cardiac output (the amount of blood that the heart pumps in a given period of time, abbreviated $\dot{Q}$) is determined by heart rate (HR) and stroke volume (SV, the volume pumped by each beat):

$$SV \times HR/minute = \dot{Q}$$

At rest, the heart of a typical nontrained adult pumps 70 milliliters of blood at a rate of 70 beats per minute (bpm). Thus, at rest cardiac output is 70×70, which equals 4,900 milliliters (4.9 liters) pumped per minute. After a runner has trained for a month or two, his or her heart's stroke volume might increase to over 80 milliliters because training strengthens the heart and allows it to squeeze more blood with each beat. Now the same 4,900 milliliters (4.9 liters) of blood needed to accommodate the resting metabolism of the body can be met with a heart rate of 61 beats per minute: $61 \times 80 = 4,880$ milliliters (about 4.9 liters). Further increases in stroke volume would result in an even slower resting heart rate.

Easy, steady exercise is the best type of training for desirable cardiovascular adaptations with the least discomfort. Think of time spent running as more important than intensity of training. You'll spend more time running if the intensity isn't too great.

The maximum heart rate (HRmax) that a runner can reach doesn't necessarily change with training, but the stroke volume does, at least up to a point. The intensity associated with easy runs best accomplishes the desired results. Thus, the heart rate associated with any submaximal exercise task, such as an easy distance run, decreases following training, just as heart rate at rest is decreased. Stronger heart muscle is a desirable result of regular exercise and separates many athletes from their more sedentary counterparts.

Oxygen-Carrying Capacity of the Blood

The amount of oxygen that blood can carry is expressed in milliliters of oxygen carried per 100 milliliters of blood and is a function of the hemoglobin concentration of the blood. Each gram of hemoglobin can transport 1.34 milliliters of oxygen; a person with a hemoglobin count of 15 (that is, 15 grams per 100 milliliters of blood) can carry 15 × 1.34 (about 20 milliliters) of oxygen per 100 milliliters of blood, provided the blood is 100 percent saturated with oxygen. At sea level, blood is usually about 96 to 97 percent saturated, which, for the person just mentioned, would permit over 19 milliliters of oxygen to be carried by each 100 milliliters of blood. So, for this person, the arterial blood (the blood that travels from the heart to the running muscles) has an oxygen content of 19 volumes percent (100 volumes of blood carry 19 volumes of oxygen).

If the hemoglobin concentration falls below normal for any individual (often a result of a diet low in iron), it's not difficult to calculate the difference in arterial oxygen content. Even small changes in the hemoglobin concentration can lead to significant performance discrepancies. In fact, the primary negative effect of running at altitude is that the lower atmospheric pressure results in a drop in the oxygen content of the arterial blood, which reduces its oxygen-carrying capacity. Both altitude and a reduced hemoglobin concentration have the same effect—a drop in maximum oxygen consumption ($\dot{V}O_2$max)—but for different reasons.

Hemodynamics: The Characteristics of Blood Flow

Blood flow is determined by the diameter of the vessel through which the blood moves, the pressure difference between the heart and the destination of the blood, and the viscosity or thickness of the blood. The viscosity of the blood stays pretty constant, but vessel diameter varies considerably depending on the tone of the muscular walls of the vessel, the nature of the tissue (particularly muscle tissue) surrounding the vessel, and the presence of deposits within the vessel that inhibit flow. Basically, vessel diameter is the primary determinant of flow.

When exercise commences, the most desirable situation is for the vessels feeding the exercising muscles to relax and open up, which decreases the pressure in that area, increasing the pressure difference between the source of the blood and its destination. Blood flow to the needy muscles, therefore, increases. Increased pressure of the blood leaving the heart as a result of faster and more powerful beating also increases the pressure difference, further enhancing flow. It's nice to be able to get large flow increases through drops in peripheral pressure (drops in resistance to blood flow) and moderate increases in central pressure (blood pressure as it leaves the heart) because this lowers the overall pressure in the system and reduces the energy expended by the heart to send blood, and oxygen, to the muscles during exercise.

Also, blood flow to the exercising muscles increases as a result of a diversion of blood from areas of lesser need—the organs of digestion lose blood during exercise, as does the skin (unless weather conditions are so warm that large quantities of blood must be sent to the skin to help with body cooling).

EFFECTS OF ALTITUDE TRAINING

The two areas of running research in which I've done the most work relate to running economy and altitude training and racing. Many articles in journals address the altitude issue, and here I summarize the more important aspects of altitude as it relates to distance running.

Altitude affects distance running by lowering the amount of oxygen that can be delivered to the running muscles, which is the result of the blood's reduced saturation of oxygen. Hemoglobin acts as the carrier of oxygen from the capillaries in the lungs, through the left side of the heart, and then to the rest of the body. The amount of oxygen carried by the blood—through its association with hemoglobin—is a function of the partial pressure of oxygen in the blood, which reflects the pressure in the lungs and in the atmosphere.

Because atmospheric pressure gets lower as altitude gets higher, the effects of higher altitudes are a lower pressure of oxygen in the blood and a diminished oxygen–hemoglobin association—that is, less oxygen is carried by the all-important hemoglobin. The percentage of oxygen in the air doesn't change with changes in altitude, but the pressure does change, which means there's a lower partial pressure of oxygen available to drive it into association with hemoglobin. The higher the altitude, the greater the problem.

Actually, because of the characteristics of the relation between oxygen pressure and hemoglobin association and dissociation (that is, how easily oxygen is freed from hemoglobin in order to enter the exercising muscles), the effect of lowered air pressure (high altitude) and oxygen saturation of the blood is not a linear one. The effect of altitude on endurance performance starts at an altitude of about 1,000 meters (around 3,000 feet). For practical purposes, I'd consider the altitudes from about 1,000 to 2,500 meters (3,280 to 8,202 feet) to be moderate; these are the altitudes most frequently encountered by runners. These are also the altitudes at which training produces good acclimatization. I prefer the 2,000- to 2,500-meter (6,562- to 8,202-foot) range for reaping the benefits of altitude training.

Keep in mind that being at altitude has a direct negative effect on distance-running performance. You can't run as fast at altitude (for races of 1,500 meters and longer) as you can at sea level. This applies to both sea-level residents and to those who live at altitude. Of course, training at altitude improves performance at altitude, and the body acclimatizes to a certain degree, but not to the extent that performance at altitude will ever equal what you can do at sea level. As you go up in altitude, the atmospheric pressure gets lower, and the lower the atmospheric pressure, the lower the pressure of oxygen. Because oxygen pressure determines how much oxygen is carried by the hemoglobin in the blood, the result is that a given amount of hemoglobin carries less oxygen to the exercising muscles at altitude. This drop in oxygen delivery also lowers your $\dot{V}O_2$max at altitude. However, altitude doesn't affect performance as much as it affects exercising muscles at altitude. This is because economy improves at altitude as a consequence of the decreased air resistance encountered in the less dense altitude air. Further, aerobic capacity doesn't represent the only available energy source, and anaerobic power isn't negatively affected by being at altitude.

Improvements in performance through altitude training aren't necessarily temporary in nature, provided training back at sea level is adequate to maintain the fitness achieved at altitude. What I'm saying is that altitude training often allows for—or stimulates—a better fitness level in an athlete, just as serious training does anywhere. The fitness level achieved through altitude training might be better than that previously reached at sea level, but not necessarily better than what could be reached with continued sea-level workouts. It's certainly possible that proper sea-level training under ideal conditions might produce just as much improvement in performance as that achieved through altitude training.

Altitude training seems to permit runners to reach their potential more quickly. Some runners experience a breakthrough as the result of increases in weekly mileage or through a more structured program. I've observed many breakthroughs following altitude training of only a few weeks' duration, and seldom have the athletes involved had any trouble maintaining their new-found success, even if they return to sea level for entire seasons, or years, of performance.

Not all endurance runners thrive at altitude. Some benefit little, and others have significant breakthroughs. Again, it's best to compare altitude training to other types of training. Not everyone responds well to 100-mile weeks, and not everyone benefits from training at altitude. I'm sure there are many reasons for this, involving both physical and mental factors. The success, or lack thereof, of altitude training is most certainly a function of how you train at altitude and the confidence you have in your program or coach. In chapter 3 I provide more details about how to adapt training intensities at altitude.

Although benefits of altitude training can differ, most bodies go through a fairly predictable reaction to going to altitude. Unless you have a week or more of acclimatization time available to you, the first day at altitude is often the best time to race. Somewhere around the third to fifth day at altitude, newcomers feel their worst, though with normal training, performances are usually better by the end of the first week. From that point on, confidence and acclimatization improve, and workouts and races go much better.

As I've mentioned, the viscosity of blood doesn't change much under normal conditions. It does, however, change under conditions of dehydration, when the blood thickens because of a partial loss of plasma (water) from the blood. Viscosity also changes when the red blood cell count changes; a lowered red cell count (usually associated with reduced hemoglobin concentration, as in the case of anemia) results in thinner blood, which to some degree allows for easier flow, though usually not enough to offset the loss of oxygen-carrying capacity caused by the lower hemoglobin concentration.

Maintaining optimal blood volume is very beneficial for races and daily training sessions. Doing so depends on maintaining good nutritional and hydration (fluid intake) habits. See chapters 6 and 15 for more details concerning hydration and nutrition.

Building the Running Muscles

The cells (fibers) of the running muscles are the beneficiaries of the labors of the cardiovascular system. They make up the peripheral portion of the system, to which the heart delivers fuel and oxygen and from which carbon dioxide and lactic acid are removed.

Many adjustments take place in and around the muscle cells as a result of training, and as with adaptations to the heart muscle, relatively slow, easy running does an excellent job of promoting the desired results. Of particular importance is an increase in the number, size, and distribution of the mitochondria, the sites of aerobic metabolism within the muscle fibers. Another cellular adjustment is an increase in oxidative enzyme activity, which improves the rate at which the delivered oxygen can be processed. A third peripheral adjustment is greater perfusion of the exercising muscles with blood vessels—more capillaries become active and distribute blood to the muscle cells (an increased number of vessels distributing blood means a greater cross-sectional area of vessels, indicating enhanced flow; thus, more oxygen can flow to more parts of the muscle). These adaptations to training improve the muscles' capacity for receiving and processing oxygen. The muscles also can become better at conserving stores of glycogen (their key stored carbohydrate fuel), metabolizing fat for energy, and dealing with lactic acid.

I've described quite a few central and peripheral benefits to comfortable training—speeds associated with 59 to 74 percent of an individual's aerobic capacity (65 to 79 percent of maximum heart rate). For most people, this is a good 45 to 60 seconds per mile slower than their marathon race pace, or one and a half to two minutes per mile slower than their 5K race pace. The benefits of slow, easy running are so important that I set aside an entire phase of training just for them (see chapter 4). At this point I would like to discuss components that benefit from more demanding (quality) types of training, which you'll also need to develop to improve your running performance.

Increasing Lactate Threshold

Runners must be able to work increasingly close to their maximum oxygen consumption without suffering from high accumulations of lactic acid in the blood. Blood-lactate accumulation is a function of how much lactic acid is being produced by the exercising muscles and the rate at which it's being cleared by the muscles, heart, and liver. Being able to hold down blood-lactate accumulation and minimize its effects for longer at faster and faster running speeds is a desirable attribute for a distance runner, and one usually acquired better through threshold (**T**) training (see chapter 7) than other methods. Although the importance of threshold training increases with longer

| Threshold training offers multiple physiological benefits to middle-distance and long-distance runners.

races, even middle-distance runners can use it with success because it provides quality training with limited stress. Threshold training also aids in recovery from the higher intensity training that often makes up much of a middle-distance runner's program.

Measuring blood-lactate accumulation became popular among athletes and coaches in the 1980s. The idea was to quantify threshold training intensity by using a specific blood-lactate value (4.0 millimoles of lactic acid per liter of blood is commonly accepted as a desired threshold value). What's really being sought is an intensity of effort (identified as a running pace known as "threshold pace") associated with a constant blood-lactate value. The constant blood-lactate value is produced during a steady training run of 20 to 30 minutes at a pace that most runners can maintain for about one hour in a race situation. For trained runners, this speed corresponds to about 88 percent of maximum oxygen consumption ($\dot{V}O_2$max) or 92 percent of maximum heart rate (HRmax) and 92 percent of velocity at $\dot{V}O_2$max ($v\dot{V}O_2$max).

For a large group of runners, the lactate value associated with this intensity might average about 4.0 millimoles per liter (blood-lactate accumulation, or BLa), but individuals show vast variations from this 4.0 value. One runner might maintain a steady blood-lactate concentration of 2.8 and feel the same degree of stress as another runner who has a steady BLa of 7.2. They both might be at their lactate thresholds, although the actual lactate values differ (and neither is 4.0 millimoles). To ask these runners to train at a BLa of 4.0 would overwork the former and underwork the latter, if the idea was to perform threshold training. It's much more valuable to use a given percentage of each runner's VDOT value (an estimate of an individual's aerobic capacity based on actual race times; see chapter 3) to calculate threshold pace rather than to try for a constant lactate value. Of course, if you have the equipment and time to do a thorough job of identifying the actual lactate threshold for each athlete, that's fine. Most coaches have neither the equipment nor the time. Improper use of equipment is another potential roadblock to getting an accurate reading.

Improving Aerobic Capacity ($\dot{V}O_2$Max)

Improvements in the cardiovascular system and in the peripheral components just discussed enhance the body's capacity for consuming oxygen. Oxygen consumption can be specific to a muscle or a group of muscles. The amount of oxygen someone consumes when performing a particular activity, such as running, depends directly on how much oxygen can be delivered to the muscles involved in the activity, how well the muscles process the delivered oxygen, and how easily the muscles can deal with the carbon dioxide and lactic acid produced during exercise. Exercising arm muscles trains the heart but does little at the peripheral level to benefit the leg muscles needed for running. This is one of the main arguments supporting the principle of specificity of training (see principle 2 in chapter 1, pages 8-10).

To optimize $\dot{V}O_2$max, the runner must stress the oxygen delivery and processing system to its limit while running. To accomplish this, I assign a phase of interval (**I**) training, which is the most demanding phase of training for most people. Interval training involves repeated runs of up to five minutes each, at about 3,000- to 5,000-meter race pace, with relatively brief recoveries between runs (see chapter 8).

Developing Speed

I've heard coaches say, "Speed kills—all those who don't have any." It's true that many races from 800 meters to the marathon are won during a final kick to the finish line. Those runners who win with a kick, however, are often the ones in a position to use the kick when the time comes. In other words, having a great kick does you no good if you can't stay with the pace during the bulk of a distance race. And staying with the pace means having a high aerobic capacity ($\dot{V}O_2$max), a high lactate threshold, and good economy (discussed in the next section).

Still, I agree that speed wins many races. Bob Schul, the gold medal winner at 5,000 meters in the 1964 Tokyo Olympics, had good speed. It paid off, particularly in the finals of the 5,000 meters, when the pace was slowed by track conditions (this was before the days of artificial track surfaces, when rain could slow things down on cinders and crushed stone) and allowed some runners to stay in the race when normally they would have dropped back. This was a race for kickers, and Schul was the best of them. Others can only wonder what they might have done had conditions been different. I'm sure that Bob Schul would have had his kick under any conditions, but the slow track emphasized his advantage. Even today, with many all-weather tracks, runners with a good finishing kick look forward to slow early paces so they're able to stay with the pack until the time comes to use their speed.

Many coaches feel that speed is inborn but that endurance is earned through hard work. I believe that you're born with a certain gift for speed and a certain gift for endurance and that both can be improved with work. Sure, some people are physiologically more gifted than others in one area or another, but a would-be 800-meter runner shouldn't give up on the 800 meters in favor of longer races just because the first attempt isn't particularly fast.

Everyone has fast-twitch muscle fibers that respond better to faster training than they do to endurance-type running; slow-twitch fibers are better suited for endurance running. Still, all muscle fibers respond to different types of training. You can find your particular strengths and weaknesses by putting your body through many different types of training.

Type of muscle fiber is only one factor in determining the ability to perform well at a particular distance. Runners with less desirable physiological makeups often keep up with others who have more desirable physiological makeups through superior biomechanical characteristics or a tougher mental attitude. Many things determine success. Speed, however, is important for distance runners to train for. Fortunately, the type of training that best addresses speed also improves running economy; the intensity of training might sometimes be the only variable from runner to runner (see the discussion of repetition workouts in chapter 9).

Improving Running Economy

Running economy involves the amount of oxygen being consumed relative to the runner's body weight and the speed at which he or she is running. If one runner uses 50 milliliters of oxygen per kilogram of body weight per minute (usually written 50 $ml \cdot kg^{-1} \cdot min^{-1}$) to run at 6:00 pace and another runner uses 55, the first runner is more economical. If the first runner, as a result of training, can change oxygen consumption ($\dot{V}O_2$) at 6:00 pace from 50 $ml \cdot kg^{-1} \cdot min^{-1}$ to 48, then he or she has improved economy to an even greater level. This is a highly desirable result of training because the runner can now race at a faster speed than before without using more energy to do so. Repetition (**R**) training (see chapter 9) improves economy by helping the runner eliminate unnecessary arm and leg motion, recruit the most desirable motor units while running at or near race pace, and feel comfortable at faster speeds of running.

I've found that runners often have trouble linking the concepts of $\dot{V}O_2$max, economy, and lactate threshold to performance. The easiest way to bridge the gap between these physiological characteristics and running performance is to go through the steps that occur when runners evaluate economy, aerobic capacity, and lactate response to different intensities of running. Evaluating these physiological aspects of your running is part of creating your aerobic profile.

Creating Your Aerobic Profile

At any given time during your running career, whether you're in top shape or following a break in training when your fitness is not so good, you'll have a $\dot{V}O_2$max, economy curve, and lactate profile that relates your running velocity to your blood-lactate accumulation and aerobic demand. With the proper equipment, you can measure these variables and use the resulting information to describe your current capabilities and identify all the training speeds necessary for optimizing your $\dot{V}O_2$max, economy, and lactate threshold. The following discussion summarizes how you would determine and plot $\dot{V}O_2$submax (running economy), $\dot{V}O_2$max (aerobic capacity), and lactate threshold (threshold) for any distance runner. Should you have the opportunity to be tested, you would display a profile similar to those illustrated in the following pages.

| Testing on the track.

$\dot{V}O_2$Submax

Let's say we have a runner who has reached a steady state by running for about six minutes at a submaximal speed (marathon race pace, for example), and we collect a bag of expired air from this runner during the final minute or two of the six-minute run. Analyzing this expired air will tell us the aerobic (oxygen) demand of running at a certain pace for this particular runner. Heart rate (taken during the final minute or two of the run) and a small, finger-prick blood sample (drawn immediately after the run is completed) will provide information on the pulse rate and blood-lactate accumulation, respectively, associated with this velocity of running for this particular runner.

If the same procedure is repeated several times at increasingly faster (but still submaximal) running velocities, then you can plot the $\dot{V}O_2$, heart rate, and blood-lactate accumulation responses against running speed. Figure 2.1 shows the data collected on one of the elite athletes whom I have tested. Notice that the $\dot{V}O_2$ response is relatively linear, as is heart rate. Blood-lactate accumulation, on the other hand, shows a

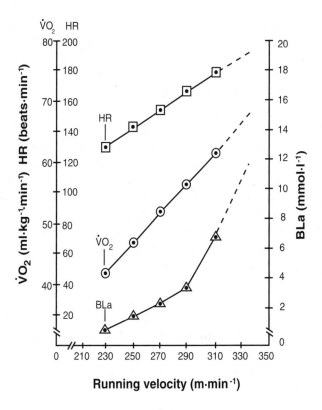

Figure 2.1 Increases in heart rate (HR), oxygen consumption ($\dot{V}O_2$), and blood-lactate level (BLa) in an elite runner as running speed is increased.

different picture. Easy running speeds show little change in BLa, but as the speed of running becomes more intense, a dramatic increase in blood lactate occurs. This lactate-response curve is typical for any runner. The better the runner, however, the faster the running pace at which the lactate-response curve demonstrates the change from a gradual to a steep slope; a better runner's lactate curve is displaced farther to the right on the horizontal axis. The intensity at which the transition from a gradual to a steep lactate curve takes place is referred to as the runner's lactate threshold intensity.

If the runner being tested completes three or four submax tests (at increasingly faster speeds, up to about 10K race pace or a little faster) and then performs a "max" test, the resulting response picture is useful for determining current training, and even competitive intensities of running.

$\dot{V}O_2$Max

In the max test, the runner starts running at the same pace as the final submax test (about current 10K race pace). He or she holds this speed constant for two minutes on a treadmill (or for one lap on a 400-meter track). After the initial two minutes (or lap on the track), the treadmill grade is increased by 1 percent each subsequent minute (or the pace is increased to 5K race pace if the test is on a track). In a treadmill test, when the intensity of the ever-increasing treadmill grade becomes so great that the runner can't continue, the test is over. In the case of a track test, after two or three laps at 5K race pace, the runner performs a final 400 meters at all-out speed to complete the test.

In either case, expired air samples are continually collected, starting with about the third minute of the max test and ending when the runner stops. Heart rate is taken at the end of the test (or recorded during the final 30 seconds of the test, if using a monitor). The final blood sample (used to detect maximum lactate accumulation) is drawn two minutes after completion of the max test (when blood lactate has reached its peak).

By adding the $\dot{V}O_2max$ (the highest $\dot{V}O_2$ measured during the max test), the maximum heart rate (HRmax), and the maximum blood-lactate accumulation (BLamax) data points to the submax data shown in figure 2.1, we get what I refer to as a runner's aerobic profile (see figure 2.2). $\dot{V}O_2max$ is placed on an extension of the economy curve (the line drawn through the previously calculated $\dot{V}O_2submax$ data points that show how much oxygen the runner consumed at different speeds), and this permits you to determine the velocity at which $\dot{V}O_2max$ would first be realized. This velocity is called $v\dot{V}O_2max$ (velocity at $\dot{V}O_2max$) and is used to calculate a VDOT value, which, in turn, determines training paces and race potential (see chapter 3).

By now it should be apparent that the measurement of $\dot{V}O_2max$, by itself, provides limited information in terms of discriminating among groups of good runners. As a result, when I hear that some runner was found to have a $\dot{V}O_2max$ of 90 ml·kg^{-1}·min^{-1} or higher, I have two immediate reactions. First, the tests might have been poorly controlled (perhaps inaccurate reference gases were used for the gas analyzers, or maybe faulty equipment mismeasured ventilatory gas volumes). Second, if the tests were well controlled, why doesn't this runner outperform everyone else?

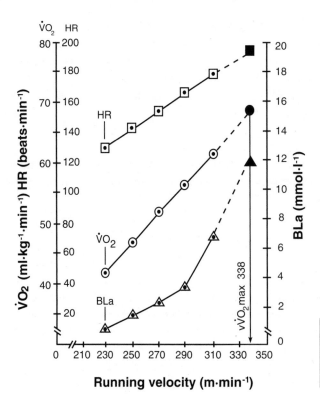

Figure 2.2   An elite runner's aerobic profile, which includes submax (open symbols) and max values (solid symbols) for HR, $\dot{V}O_2$, and BLa.

Assuming that the runner with the high $\dot{V}O_2$max does have an accurate assessment of his aerobic capacity, the most logical reason that he doesn't outperform everyone else is because his economy is poor. When a runner with a value of 70 for his $\dot{V}O_2$max runs a 2:10 marathon and outperforms a 90-$\dot{V}O_2$max runner, imagine how poor the latter's efficiency must be. And who is to say that the 90-$\dot{V}O_2$max runner can improve efficiency (economy) any more than the 70-$\dot{V}O_2$max runner can improve his $\dot{V}O_2$max? Learning your $\dot{V}O_2$max value can be useful for monitoring changes in your response to training, but without supporting information concerning your economy, the data could be misleading. Of course, there's another possible explanation for why a runner with high test results might not always beat runners who score less well—a simple lack of determination (guts).

Differences in Aerobic Profile

If the results of $\dot{V}O_2$ tests performed on different individuals or groups of runners are plotted, as seen in figure 2.2, some interesting information becomes apparent. Figure 2.3 compares three female 3,000-meter runners, all of whom I tested during the same week a few years ago. Notice that two of the runners have similar $\dot{V}O_2$max values (69.6

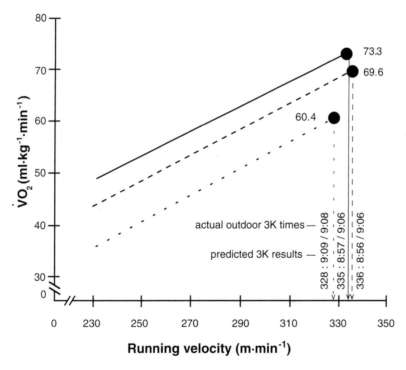

Figure 2.3   Three female runners with different aerobic profiles that produce similar predicted and actual 3,000-meter times.

Adapted from Daniels, J. et al. 1986. "Elite and sub-elite female middle- and long-distance runners." In *Sport and Elite Performance— 1984 Olympic Scientific Congress Proceedings,* Vol. 3, ed. D. Landers. Champaign, IL: Human Kinetics. First published in Daniels, J. 1985. "A case for running economy, an important determinant of distance running," *Track Technique* (92) Spring, 2937-2938, Track & Field News. Los Altos, CA.

and 73.3); the third has a relatively low $\dot{V}O_2$max (60.4) but is much more economical than the other two runners (she has a lower economy curve, or a lower oxygen cost of running at submax test speeds). These facts suggest that if the three runners ran a 3K race at their $\dot{V}O_2$max, they would all finish in times of just about 9:00. In fact, their actual outdoor 3K times were in the predicted range, as shown in figure 2.3.

Figure 2.4 shows a comparison of many of the elite men and women distance runners whom I've tested. You can see that the typical elite male runner has a higher $\dot{V}O_2$max and is slightly more economical than the typical elite female runner (at comparable absolute running speeds). When running at the same absolute speeds, women are working at a higher intensity, relative to their $\dot{V}O_2$max, than their male counterparts are. When running at the same relative intensities (at the same percent of their $\dot{V}O_2$max), however, elite males and elite females don't significantly differ in economy. Still, the difference in aerobic profiles suggests that the men should outrace the women by about 14 percent, which is just a little greater than the typical percent difference turned in by these elite distance runners.

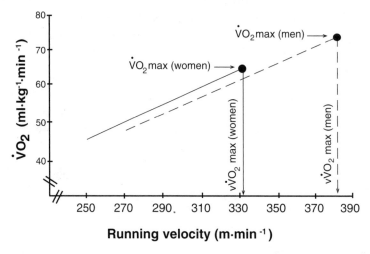

Figure 2.4   Comparison of aerobic profiles of elite male and elite female runners.

Adapted, by permission, from J. Daniels and N. Daniels. 1992, "Running economy of elite male and elite female runners." *Medicine and Science in Sports and Exercise* 24 (4): 483-489.

A great overlap is present in the $\dot{V}O_2$max and economy data for elite men and women, but the combination of the two (v$\dot{V}O_2$max) tends to favor the men. For example, two elite marathoners (one male and one female) I tested both had $\dot{V}O_2$max values of 78 ml·kg^{-1}·min^{-1}, but the woman's best marathon was over 10 minutes slower than the man's. The difference in performance was a consequence of economy—the man was a fair bit more economical. On the other hand, I tested a woman whose economy was so good that her times were almost always better than the times of any man with a comparable $\dot{V}O_2$max. When I've compared elite male and female runners of equal aerobic profiles, performances have also been equal.

Figure 2.5 shows data collected on a runner at two different times of the year: early season, before the runner was fit, and midseason. Figure 2.5 shows that $\dot{V}O_2$max,

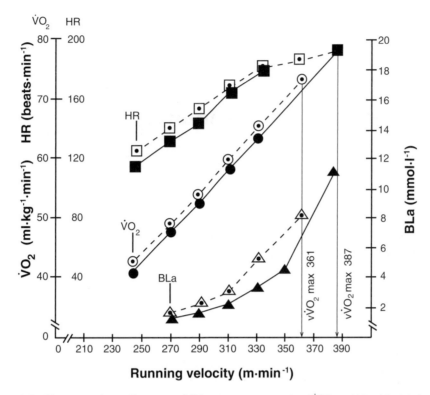

Figure 2.5 The comparison of heart rate (HR), oxygen consumption ($\dot{V}O_2$), and blood-lactate level (BLa) of an elite runner during the early season and midseason. The open symbols delineate early-season measurements, and the solid symbols delineate midseason measurements.

economy, and lactate accumulation all responded well to training. As I show in the following section, specific types of training are necessary to optimize each of these components of performance.

Using Race Performance to Determine Training Needs

An important relation exists between $\dot{V}O_2$, HR, BLa, and $v\dot{V}O_2$max. The configuration of the economy curve (which plots $\dot{V}O_2$ against running velocity) is such that a 1 percent change in velocity is also nearly a 1 percent change in $\dot{V}O_2$. Further, an intensity of 70 percent $\dot{V}O_2$max is equal to about 75 percent of both $v\dot{V}O_2$max and HRmax, and an intensity of 88 percent $\dot{V}O_2$max is equal to about 92 percent of $v\dot{V}O_2$max and HRmax. Both intensities are important, and I refer to them in detail in part II.

The relationship between velocities and intensities is extremely useful; it signifies that if $v\dot{V}O_2$max can be identified, there's no need for $\dot{V}O_2$max or economy testing for the purpose of setting training intensities. Fortunately, current $v\dot{V}O_2$max can be closely estimated from knowing the race performance capabilities of a runner.

What I'm saying is that you can use current race information as well as your goals to determine how hard to train and how to get to the next level of performance. I believe this works better than relying on laboratory tests. There's a place for laboratory testing, but such testing is simply unnecessary for the many runners and coaches who should be using more concrete information to plan training intensities. After all, what's better than using how good you are as a measure of how fast you should train? In chapter 3, I show you how to use race information to set training intensities.

Achieving the Goals of Training

Based on the six components highlighted at the beginning of the chapter, the tasks a runner is really trying to accomplish through training are the following:

- Improve the body's ability to transport blood and oxygen
- Increase the ability of the running muscles to effectively use their available oxygen (to convert carbohydrate and fat fuel into useful energy)
- Shift lactate threshold to correspond to a faster running speed
- Increase aerobic capacity ($\dot{V}O_2max$)
- Improve speed
- Lower the energy demand of running (improve economy)

There are other goals of training—improving race tactics, elevating self-confidence, changing body composition, and bettering self-image—but these less tangible factors often result from improvement in one or more of the six areas just listed.

The way a runner achieves these physiological goals of training is to apply the right type of training for the job at hand. It seems that every once in awhile someone comes up with a new training technique, something destined "to change the way runners perform." But all too often these "new" methods of training are just old methods with new names. I'm as guilty as anyone else in this regard. For example, I've referred to what I like to call "nonstructured interval training," which is nothing more than fartlek training. I should be ashamed of myself, after studying sport for a year in Sweden and understanding fartlek training about as well as any coach outside that country's borders. I can still remember my Swedish classmates encouraging me to "öka fart" (increase speed) when running in class relay events. Fart (speed) and lek (play) go well together, and I think it's still a great type of training to include in almost any running program. I guess I got tired of explaining fartlek as a sort of nonstructured interval session and started calling it just that. I'd like to take it back at this point and use the right terminology. When I spoke of nonstructured interval training in the past, what I meant was fartlek training, and that's what it will be for me from now on.

It's not only the term "fartlek" that confuses people—many aren't sure what interval training or repetition training are, either. A few years ago I wrote an article for a scientific journal on the topic of interval training. As I did my research and interviewed some elite runners and coaches, I was amazed to discover that nearly everyone had his or her own understanding of what intervals were. Some said in an interval workout, workbouts had to last at least two minutes. Others said if workbouts were longer than two minutes each, the session was no longer an interval workout in nature. Some said recovery intervals had to last until a particular heart rate was reached, whereas others claimed that the duration of the recovery depended on how long the preceding workout lasted.

One of my goals since that time has been to try to associate types of workouts with desired benefits of the workout in question. This led to my coming up with the now often-used term, "$\dot{V}O_2$max intervals." It has always seemed to me that the commonly accepted duration, intensity, and recovery of a typical interval session are meant to stress an individual's aerobic power ($\dot{V}O_2$max), so I tacked "$\dot{V}O_2$max" onto the already existing word, "intervals," for clarification. Now it would be nice if we could standardize the understanding of the term "intervals" to mean exactly what they are: workouts that optimize $\dot{V}O_2$max.

Many people call intervals what I refer to as "repetitions." So what is the difference between an interval and a repetition session? Generally, the only point of agreement is that both these terms mean "intermittent," as in the alternating occurrence of two things (such as stress and recovery, or workouts and recovery bouts). Because I've always looked to interval training as the best approach to maximizing aerobic capacity (and because I like to categorize types of training according to benefits reaped), I had to come up with something different for repetition training, and I did. Repetitions are repeated bouts of work and recovery, as are intervals, but with a different purpose, so the two types of training are performed differently. "Reps" are not designed to best improve $\dot{V}O_2$max. Rather, they're meant to enhance speed and running economy (good mechanics and reduced energy expenditure at important running paces).

Really, the same thing goes for "sprint training" (a faster version of repetition training), "threshold" training, and "easy" running. All of these types of training have a purpose, something they're meant to accomplish for the runner, and each type of training should have a specific intensity and duration that best accomplish that purpose.

Before I carry on further, I'd like to present some definitions of terms I use in my coaching. These definitions are from a dictionary, and I'm happy to report that they all fit my perception of what they mean to me as a coach of runners.

easy—free from trouble, care, worry, constraint, pain

hard—laborious, fatiguing, something that's difficult to endure (this suggests rather intense running, with limited recoveries, when performed intermittently)

fast—movement that's rapid; quickness of motion (not necessarily *hard* in terms of effort, if adequate recoveries are allowed)

sprint—to run at top speed (among runners this is more often at top "effort" than at true top speed)

threshold—the point at which a physiological effect begins to be produced (i.e., in the case of lactate threshold, the point at which the accumulation of blood lactate rises rapidly)

comfortable—giving the appearance of comfort (note that this could be *fast* but probably not *hard* running)

interval—a space of time between recurrent events or conditions (so, interval training refers to repeated workouts separated by recovery intervals, which get particular emphasis)

repetition—the act of repeating (in running it would be nice for repeated runs—**workbouts**—to be identical in terms of stress and efficiency of movement, which require longer recoveries between workbouts than intervals do)

intermittent—alternating occurrence of two things (this term fits both intervals and repetitions)

Training Zones

Now that you know some of the basic terminology used for training, let's look at specific types of training (or training intensity zones) that help a runner elicit the desired physiological response to help him or her improve performance. It has become more apparent to me in recent years that there's some variation in applicable training intensities (mostly based on how different running abilities determine appropriate fractions of $\dot{V}O_2max$), and thus I now refer to various training zones that offer a range of intensities. Table 2.1 summarizes each of these training zones.

Easy pace running. I refer to all warm-ups, cool-downs, and long runs as "easy" in nature; they are, or should be, free from trouble or pain. Easy running pace (**E** pace), although typically in the range of only 59 to 74 percent of $\dot{V}O_2max$ (65 to 79 percent HRmax), elicits desirable physiological benefits that build a solid base from which higher-intensity training can be performed. The heart muscle is strengthened, muscles receive increased blood supplies, and the working muscle cells increase their ability to process the oxygen delivered through the cardiovascular system. **E**-pace runs make up the vast majority of a week's training schedule.

Be advised that the benefits of **E** pace (or "**E**-zone running") are more a function of the time spent exercising than the intensity, and the low running intensities (percentages of $\dot{V}O_2max$ stated above) are as hard as you need to go to get the benefits you want at the cellular level and in the heart muscle. Chapter 5 provides a little more information on **E** pace and long runs, which are most often performed in the **E** zone of intensity.

Marathon-pace running. Although marathon pace (**M**) running for any runner is a fairly predictable intensity (speed of running), there's a range of intensities that applies to runners of different ability levels. Naturally, **M**-pace running is particularly useful for runners training for a marathon, but this pace might also provide nonmarathon runners an alternative to some of their easy runs, especially when conditions are good and there's adequate time to recover for a subsequent quality session. Elite male marathoners can race at about 84 percent of $\dot{V}O_2max$ (about 89 percent of HRmax), and these relative intensities drop to about 75 percent of $\dot{V}O_2max$ and 80 percent of HRmax for runners who have been training regularly but who take about 5 hours to run the event. Marathon pace varies from about 10 to 15 seconds per mile slower than threshold pace for elite runners to about 30 seconds slower than threshold pace for slower marathoners.

Threshold training. This type of training falls in the "**T**-zone" of intensity and comes in two varieties (steady, prolonged runs, also called tempo runs, and intermittent runs, also called cruise intervals) both of which are run at the same relative intensity.

Table 2.1 **Types of Training, with Purpose, Intensity, and Duration per Session**

Zone	Purpose	Intensity % $\dot{V}O_2$max % HRmax	Varieties	Duration (min or % week's mileage)
E (easy)	Promote desirable cell changes and develop cardio-vascular system	59-74% 65-79%	Warm-up Cool-down Recovery run Recovery within a workout Long run	10-30 min 10-30 min 30-60 min Up to several min Up to lesser of 150 min and 25% of the week's total mileage
M (marathon race pace)	Experience race-pace conditions for marathoners; as an alternative easy pace for others	75-84% 80-90%	Steady run or long repeats	Up to lesser of 90 min and 16 miles
T (threshold)	Improve endurance	83-88% 88-92%	Tempo runs or cruise intervals	Tempo runs: 20-60 min Cruise intervals: repeated runs of up to 15 min each with 1/5 run time for rest; total lesser of 10% week's mileage and 60 min
I (intervals)	Stress aerobic power ($\dot{V}O_2$max)	95-100% 98-100%	$\dot{V}O_2$max intervals	Repeated runs of up to 5 min each with equal or less time of jog recoveries; total lesser of 10K and 8% of the week's total mileage
	Stress aerobic system at race pace	Race pace	Race-pace intervals	Repeated runs of up to 1/4 race distance, equal or less time for rests; total lesser of 10K and 2 to 3 × race distance
R (reps)	Improve speed and economy	Mile race pace	Pace reps and strides	Repeated runs of up to 2 min each, full recoveries; total lesser of 5 miles and 5% of week's total mileage
		Fast and controlled (race pace or faster)	Speed reps and fast strides	Repeated runs of up to 1 min each, full recoveries; total up to 2,000m

HR cannot be used in **R** zone because it's not possible to record heart rates greater than 100% of HRmax.

Threshold-pace (**T**) training is great for improving endurance. Being at the same intensity doesn't always mean being at the same speed (due to headwinds, hills, poor footing, for example, which all affect the speed without changing intensity), but you would like it to be the same speed when conditions make it possible. The intensity of choice here is a speed of running, *beyond* which blood lactate progressively accumulates to a point where activity must be terminated. Subjectively, threshold intensity is "comfortably hard," or 24 to 30 seconds per mile slower than 5K race pace. Objectively, threshold intensity is in the area of 83 to 88 percent of $\dot{V}O_2$max, or about 88 to 92 percent of maximum heart rate. In chapter 7, I go into more detail about **T** training.

Interval training. As I've already mentioned, the purpose behind interval pace (**I**) training is to stress the runner's $\dot{V}O_2$max (aerobic capacity)—more through a single session of intermittent running than could be accomplished in a hard continuous run. Remember the definition of interval: a space of time between recurring events. Also remember that the time between repeated workouts is important, especially if the duration of the workouts is relatively short (under three minutes). It takes about two minutes for the system to gear up to functioning at $\dot{V}O_2$max, so the ideal duration of interval workouts is about three to five minutes each. The reason for not going over the five-minute limit is to prevent too great an anaerobic involvement, which can result in a pretty stressful blood-lactate buildup. The intensity of power interval training should be between 95 and 100 percent of $\dot{V}O_2$max or 98 to 100 percent of HR max, rather than always demanding a 100 percent value. This is because if maximum heart rate coincides with 5:00-mile pace, for example, then a faster pace, such as 4:50 pace, will also elicit maximum heart rate, but it's too fast for the purpose of the training session (which is to obtain the optimal result with the least possible stress). Race-pace interval training would be performed at race pace for a runner's particular event.

I training is demanding (I refer to it as "hard" running), but it isn't all-out running. In the case of **I** pace, the harm of going too fast in an interval session is that you obtain no better results, and the excessive pace will probably leave you overstressed for the next quality training session. In addition, going too fast in the early part of a series of interval workouts is that you might be too fatigued for subsequent workouts to be performed at the appropriate aerobic intensity. For example, if **I** pace is 3:20 for repeated 1,000-meter runs, running 3:10 might be possible for a couple, but the additional speed (associated with undue accumulation of blood lactate) may cause subsequent 1,000s to be run slower than 3:20, which is not taxing $\dot{V}O_2$max. I go into more detail about interval training in chapter 8.

Repetition training. This type of training (**R** training) involves repeating a particular workout a number of times for the purpose of becoming comfortable running fairly fast, feeling light on the feet and efficiently running at race pace—or sometimes even faster than the pace used in longer races. The intensity for repetition training is typically race pace or a little faster for a given distance.

Unlike slower training intensities, "rep" training paces aren't directly associated with $\dot{V}O_2$max. For example, a miler and a 10K runner who share the same v$\dot{V}O_2$max, based on similar economies and $\dot{V}O_2$maxes, would have the same training intensities for **I**, **T**, and other slower training runs. However, their rep (**R**) paces might differ because one is training to run efficiently at a faster race pace than the other is. The purpose of **R**-pace training is to improve economy and speed (and it's always prudent to remember the purpose of every workout you perform). I discuss **R**-pace running in chapter 9.

Figure 2.6 displays the various types of training and the associated intensities needed to stress the systems of importance to a distance runner. Degree of intensity is represented by the height of the peak as well as the amount of time spent at peak relative to the amount of time spent at rest (indicated by troughs). Note that it's sometimes okay, even desirable, to mix various types (intensities) of training into a single session, as we do in a fartlek workout.

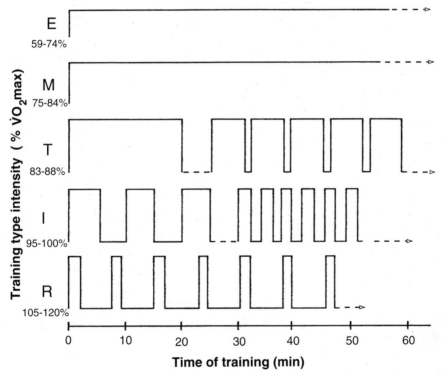

Figure 2.6 Types of training and their levels of intensity.

Adapted from J. Daniels and N. Daniels, 1984. "Interval training and performance," *Sports Medicine* 1(4): 327-334.

Using Mileage Training Points

You have already learned how to represent various types of training with an intensity fraction (percentage or multiple of a runner's $\dot{V}O_2$max) that is tied to an intensity zone (see table 2.1, page 35).

You also know that the time you spend performing at different intensities and the amount of rest you take between workouts affects the overall stress of a training session (or race). Different intensities are designed to challenge different systems of the body, and a combination of the intensity and duration of exercise determines how much stress is enough or too much for that particular system.

It's generally accepted that runners can handle more time doing easy running than they can tolerate at higher intensities of stress. For example, it's not unusual for a runner to complete more than 100 miles of easy running in a single week—but it's doubtful that any runner would try 100 miles of fast (mile race pace) running in a single week. Maybe that's possible to do, but doing so would neglect other important systems that require training, which is why we include several types of training in a program.

A big question is, Can the various intensities of stress be evaluated in such a way that they can be compared relative to total training stress? For example, in terms of how much the body can (and should be able to) handle, how much time spent at threshold (**T**) pace equates to the amount of time spent at an easy (**E**) pace? How do the other intensities fit into the picture? I've designed a system for comparing the various intensities of training in a way that allows you to monitor overall stress and to determine the desired amounts of each type of stress.

A common way of logging how much running you do is to keep track of your weekly mileage, and this is certainly a good way to monitor your own training (and that of other runners similar to you in ability and experience, over time). Possibly a better way of logging your total training is to add up the *amount of time* you spend training each week, month, or year. The advantage of this time-associated method is that it does a better job of equating the amount of stress placed on runners of various abilities. For example, running for a total of six miles at **T** intensity for an elite runner might take no more than 30 minutes, but a not-so-fast runner might take over 40 minutes to accumulate six miles at **T** pace. Both might be working at nearly the same relative intensity, but given that the less-talented runner takes 30 percent longer at this intensity, he or she experiences more stress. Thus, it would be better for the slower runner to shoot for 30 minutes of **T** running, which would be more like four miles at his or her threshold pace, whereas the faster runner would achieve the same effects running six miles at his or her **T** pace (still 30 minutes).

When looking over a month of training, a slower runner trying to log the same mileage as an elite runner will find doing so has taken a great deal more time, which often means that the slower athlete is subjected to a greater risk of injury.

To alleviate this problem I've designed a table of training intensities from which a runner of any ability level can convert his or her runs of different intensities into training points (table 2.2). Simply put, this method gives more points, per minute, for runs at higher relative intensities; the athlete can then base the intensities on a current VDOT value (a performance-based $\dot{V}O_2$max, see chapter 3) or by using heart rate data. The table corresponds to the same intensity zones described earlier as well as a 10K training zone, which covers intensities of running typical of 10K race paces for different ability levels. In addition, as you'll notice in table 2.2, there's a 2 percent overlap in the **M**- and **T**-pace zones, which accounts for the fact that marathon pace for very good runners is at a relative intensity equal to threshold pace for slower runners (or for better runners not currently in top form).

Table 2.2 Intensity Training Table

Points awarded per number of minutes shown

% VDOT	% HRmax	HR	1 min	5 min	10 min	20 min	30 min	60 min
			E zone (easy running)					
59	65		.100	.500	1.00	2.00	3.00	6.00
60	66		.110	.550	1.10	2.20	3.30	6.60
61	67		.122	.610	1.22	2.44	3.66	7.30
62	68		.135	.675	1.35	2.70	4.05	8.10
63	69		.150	.750	1.50	3.00	4.50	9.00
64	70		.167	.835	1.67	3.34	5.00	10.00
65	71		.183	.915	1.83	3.66	5.50	11.00
66	72		.200	1.000	2.00	4.00	6.00	12.00
67	73		.217	1.085	2.17	4.34	6.50	13.00
68	74		.233	1.165	2.33	4.66	7.00	14.00
69	75		.250	1.250	2.50	5.00	7.50	15.00
70	75.5		.267	1.335	2.67	5.34	8.00	16.00
71	76		.283	1.415	2.83	5.66	8.50	17.00
72	77		.300	1.500	3.00	6.00	9.00	18.00
73	78		.317	1.585	3.17	6.34	9.50	19.00
74	79		.333	1.665	3.33	6.66	10.00	20.00
			M zone (marathon pace)*					
75 (5:00)	80		.350	1.750	3.50	7.00	10.50	21.00
76 (4:40)	81		.367	1.835	3.70	7.40	11.10	22.00
77 (4:20)	82		.392	1.960	3.90	7.80	11.70	23.50
78 (4:00)	83		.417	2.090	4.20	8.40	12.60	25.00
79 (3:40)	84		.442	2.210	4.40	8.80	13.20	26.50
80 (3:20)	85		.467	2.340	4.70	9.40	14.10	28.00
81 (3:00)	86		.492	2.460	4.90	9.80	14.70	29.50
82 (2:50)	87		.517	2.590	5.20	10.40	15.60	31.00
83 (2:20)	88		.550	2.750	5.50	11.00	16.50	33.00
84 (2:05)	89		.583	2.920	5.80	11.60	17.40	35.00
			T zone (threshold/tempo)					
83	88		.550	2.750	5.50	11.00	16.50	33.00
84	89		.583	2.920	5.80	11.60	17.40	35.00
85	89.5		.600	3.000	6.00	12.00	18.00	36.00
86	90		.617	3.090	6.20	12.40	18.60	37.00
87	91		.650	3.250	6.50	13.00	19.50	39.00
88	92		.683	3.420	6.80	13.60	20.40	41.00
			10K zone**					
89 (60:00)	92.5		.700	1.400	3.50	7.00	14.0	21.00
90 (50:00)	93		.723	1.450	3.60	7.20	14.4	21.70
91 (40:00)	94		.763	1.530	3.80	7.60	15.2	22.90
92 (35:00)	95		.800	1.60	4.00	8.00	16.0	24.00
93 (30:00)	96		.840	1.68	4.20	8.40	16.8	25.20
94 (27:00)	97		.883	1.77	4.40	8.80	17.6	26.50

(continued)

Table 2.2 **Intensity Training Table,** *continued*

% VDOT	% HRmax	HR	1 min	2 min	5 min	10 min	20 min	30 min
			I zone (interval)***					
95 (21:00)	97.5		.900	1.80	4.50	9.00	18.00	27.00
96 (18:00)	98		.917	1.83	4.60	9.20	18.40	27.50
97 (15:30)	98.5		.940	1.88	4.70	9.40	18.80	28.20
98 (13:30)	99		.960	1.92	4.80	9.60	19.20	28.80
99 (12:15)	99.5		.983	1.97	4.90	9.80	19.60	29.50
100 (11:00)	100		1.000	2.00	5.00	10.00	20.00	30.00
			R zone (repetition)***					
105 (7:02)	100		1.25	2.50	3.75	6.25	12.50	25.00
110 (4:40)	100		1.50	3.00	4.50	7.50	15.00	30.00
115 (3:00)	100		1.75	3.60	5.25	8.75	17.50	35.00
120 (1:43)	100		2.10	4.20	6.30	10.50	21.00	42.00

* **M**-pace times are approximate marathon times associated with % VDOT.
** **10K** zone times shown are approximate 10K times associated with % VDOT.
*** **I** and **R** zone times are race times associated with given % VDOT; distance is irrelevant.

In contrast to the clear-cut training intensities that I've presented in the past, table 2.2 now reflects the way the training zones sometimes overlap. One reason for wider ranges of appropriate training intensities is that runners of different ability levels have different variations from one intensity to the next because the same ranges of relative intensities relate to different ranges in absolute speeds. Using various training zones all but eliminates what I used to call "quality junk" training areas. Now I think a better term applies—misplaced quality training—but primarily to training performed outside the zone selected as the appropriate one for the workout being performed. Remember to have a purpose for every training session. Ask yourself, "What system do I hope to improve by doing this workout?" and "What am I really trying to accomplish?"

To keep track of the points accumulated in a workout, simply multiply the number of minutes you run at any particular intensity by the appropriate points-per-minute "point factor." You can simplify this by using an easy to work with value representative of the zone in question. For example, warm-up and cool-down runs might be at 1 point for every 5 minutes, recovery runs between interval or rep workouts could be considered worth 0.1 points per minute, and steady **E** runs could be in the area of 2 to 3 points for each 10 minutes of running (12 to18 points per hour). An easy-to-work-with point factor for the **M** pace might be 25 per hour, and 6 points for every 10 minutes at **T** pace might be a useful estimate. I prefer to use 1 point per minute when doing **I**-intensity training, and the 1.5 point per minute factor will usually suit most distance runners when in the **R** zone. The 2.1-point-per-minute **R** factor applies better for runs in the 800-meter race pace category. Table 2.2 presents points associated with different intensities of training, from 59 to 120 percent of $\dot{V}O_2$max (65 to 100 percent of HRmax).

If you're keeping more precise track of training intensity, using table 2.2, or if you're monitoring heart rate carefully, then the exact point factor is appropriate. Chances are your percentage of heart rate will vary a good deal depending on weather conditions, so unless you're particularly interested in keeping track of HR on a regular basis, I think the percent $\dot{V}O_2$max (or VDOT, as explained in chapter 3) is the way to go. Of course, the percent HR factor is very useful when doing other types of training (swimming, cycling, rowing, skiing, skating, and so on).

Clearly, the faster the training pace, the more points you get per minute of running, but it's more difficult to accumulate as many fast minutes as slower ones. My best estimates, based on training schedules I've known runners of different ability levels to follow, are that fairly new runners, including most high school novices, will want to consider a weekly total of about 50 points. More advanced high schoolers will be in the 100-point-per-week range, and typical collegians will be around 150 points per week. Elite runners with adequate time for training will undoubtedly be around 200 points per week. For example, an elite distance runner doing nothing but easy running during a base phase of training might spend in excess of 15 hours a week running. At an average of 74 percent HRmax, this would be 14 points per hour, or 210 points for the week. Table 2.3 lists some weekly training intensities and amounts that might represent the four different point levels just referred to (50, 100, 150, and 200 points per week).

Table 2.3 **Examples of 50-, 100-, 150-, and 200-Point Weeks**

~50-point weeks	300 min (5 hours) **E** @ 70% HR (64% VDOT)	= 10 × 5 = 50
	180 min (3 hours) **E** @ 70% HR (64% VDOT)	= 10 × 3 = 30
	60 min (1 hour) **M** @ 80% HR (75% VDOT)	= 21 × 1 = 21
		= 51
	120 min (2 hours) **E** @ 70% HR (64% VDOT)	= 10 × 2 = 20
	60 min (1 hour) **M** @ 80% HR (75% VDOT)	= 21 × 1 = 21
	20 min **T** @ 88% HR (83% VDOT)	= 11
		= 52
~100-point weeks	300 min (5 hours) **E** @ 70% HR (64% VDOT)	= 10 × 5 = 50
	60 min (1 hour) **M** @ 80% HR (75% VDOT)	= 21 × 1 = 21
	20 min **T** @ 88% HR (83% VDOT)	= 11
	7 min **R** @ 100% HR (110% VDOT)	= 10.5
	10 min **I** @ 100% HR (100% VDOT)	= 10
		=102.5
	300 min (5 hours) **E** @ 70% HR (64% VDOT)	= 10 × 5 = 50
	60 min (1 hour) **M** @ 80% HR (75% VDOT)	= 21 × 1 = 21
	30 min **T** @ ~88% HR (83% VDOT)	= 17
	17 min **R** @ 100% HR (105% VDOT)	= 21.25
		=109.25
~150-point week	360 min (6 hours) **E** @ 75% HR (69% VDOT)	= 15 × 6 = 90
	30 min **T** @ 90% HR (86% VDOT)	= 18.6
	20 min **I** @ 100% HR (100% VDOT)	= 20
	16 min **R** @ 100% HR (110% VDOT)	= 24
		=152.6
~200-point weeks	480 min (8 hours) **E** @ 75% HR (69 VDOT)	= 15 × 8 = 120
	50 min **T** @ 89.5% HR (85% VDOT)	= .6 × 50 = 30
	25 min **I** @ 100% HR (100% VDOT)	= 25
	16 min **R** including strides @ 100% HR (110% VDOT)	= 24
		199
	480 min (8 hours) **E** @ 75% HR (69 VDOT)	= 15 × 8 = 120
	90 min **M** @ 88% HR (83% VDOT)	= 49.5
	50 min **T** @ 89.5% HR (85% VDOT)	= 30
		199.5

Using Supplemental Training

Supplemental training produces few direct benefits but can mean the difference between success and failure. Such training includes flexibility, muscle strengthening, and mental and psychological approaches to performance enhancement (see chapter 10). Runners benefit to differing degrees from the different types of support-system training. If you're considering supplemental training, be sure that what you choose to do helps satisfy your needs and doesn't merely add unproductive activity to your training program. Keep your goals foremost in mind. For example, are you doing stretching exercises to improve your running, or just to become more flexible? Often, the only way to see if something works for you is through trial and error. When you're trying a new approach to training, give the approach a fair trial—more than just a few days.

When choosing from among the many different training methods, apply the same considerations as you would in evaluating support training. Ask yourself, "Am I doing this type of training because I like it and I'm good at it? Or am I doing it because it will produce the results I want in races?" If you're clear and realistic about your goals and expectations, you'll almost always be happy with your performance.

You might need to regularly review the information in this chapter so that you can keep in touch with what you're trying to accomplish and the types of training that work best in helping you reach your goals. Attend to matters often taken for granted, such as proper nutrition, rest, and total body conditioning. It's sometimes easy to get so involved in one aspect of your training that you overlook other important areas.

In the next chapter, I discuss how to use these training intensities to establish benchmarks in your training so that you know how to perform each intensity in the right amount.

Brad Hauser

Brad Hauser was born in Danville, Pennsylvania, and initially participated in soccer as a youngster. When an older brother experienced some success as a high school runner, Brad took up running at the age of 11, developing an immediate interest in distance events. As he continued running, he became more and more successful, especially as a high school athlete at Kingwood High School in Texas. He set his sights on a collegiate running career with goals of winning an NCAA national title and making an Olympic Team.

His high school success led to a college career at Stanford University, where he continued to improve and to achieve his early goals. It was during his sophomore year at Stanford that Brad realized he was truly capable of performing at the national and international level. In 1998 and 1999, Brad won NCAA 5,000 meter titles at the indoor nationals. He took outdoor NCAA titles in the 10,000 meters in 1998 and 2000, and won the NCAA 5,000 meter outdoor title in 2000. In addition to his collegiate accomplishments, Brad competed for the U.S. in the 10,000 meters at the 1999 World Championships and in the 5,000 m at the 2000 Sydney Olympic Games. His cross country achievements include running in the World Championships in both 2000 and in 2001. As has often been the case for me and the runners I know and work with, I became acquainted with Brad because he was willing to participate in some lab testing I was doing—this time during my year with the Farm Team in Palo Alto, California.

Personal bests: 3,000m—7:51; 5,000m—13:27.31; 10,000m—27:58; marathon—2:14:13.

CHAPTER 3

Fitness and Intensity Benchmarks

The physiological needs a distance runner should address are $\dot{V}O_2max$ (through central and peripheral adaptations), lactate threshold, speed, and economy. In chapter 2, I discuss the types of training that best meet these needs (easy runs, marathon-pace runs, intervals, threshold running, and repetitions). The next logical step in setting up a good training program is to determine your current level of fitness so you can match your intensity to your training needs.

You could go to a lab somewhere and get a series of tests run on yourself to measure your $\dot{V}O_2max$, running economy, and lactate threshold, but that would probably cost a lot of money, and such a lab might not even be available. Or, as I discussed in chapter 2, you could use another measure of your current fitness—recent race performances—to establish how hard to train. As the result of many years of research involving runners of all ability levels, a former runner of mine, Jimmy Gilbert, and I came up with a comprehensive book of tables that associate race performances with a common measure of distance-running fitness. The book, *Oxygen Power*, allows runners of different abilities and event specialties to identify where they are in their running fitness by determining their aerobic profile.

In this chapter, I expand on the idea of using race performances and their associated VDOT values to give you an idea of your current fitness with no lab testing

A great coach is the result of a coach and a great athlete getting along well.

45

required. I also provide accurate and practical ways of determining how fast to perform the types of training (intervals, reps, and threshold runs) that you'll be doing in your quest for improved performance. I note how altitude training and acclimatization affect training intensities and how you can adjust for these. Finally, I present a few useful "test session" workouts that you can use to compare your progress at various stages of a season.

VDOT—A Measure of Your Current Running Ability

As discussed in chapter 2, an aerobic profile involves identifying a $v\dot{V}O_2max$ (velocity at $\dot{V}O_2max$) that represents the speed of running a race that lasts about 10 to 12 minutes. This $v\dot{V}O_2max$ reflects the runner's economy and $\dot{V}O_2max$ and will be the same for all individuals of equal race ability—although one runner might accomplish his or her $v\dot{V}O_2max$ with great economy and a relatively meager $\dot{V}O_2max$ and another runner with not-so-great economy and a high $\dot{V}O_2max$. It doesn't matter how the components vary if they combine to provide the same result. Basically, Gilbert and I placed every runner of equal performance ability onto a common economy curve, which meant they would also have the same mathematically generated $\dot{V}O_2max$ and a similar lactate-response curve. Equally performing runners are assigned equal aerobic profiles, which means they would also have an identical pseudo$\dot{V}O_2max$ but not necessarily the $\dot{V}O_2max$ they would show in a laboratory test.

Instead of referring to this pseudo$\dot{V}O_2max$ (the one based strictly on performance) as $\dot{V}O_2max$, we use the term "VDOT." $\dot{V}O_2max$ is properly stated "V-dot-O_2max." By placing a dot over the V, we're identifying the rate of oxygen uptake—that is, the volume of oxygen consumed per minute. We shortened V-dot-O_2max to VDOT. This way, each runner has a reference VDOT value: a single number that's easy to work with when comparing performances. This system is also ideal for setting training intensities because intervals, threshold runs, and even easy long runs and marathon-pace runs are best performed at specific fractions (or percentages) of each runner's VDOT.

When you know your VDOT value, you can eliminate a great deal of guesswork from training and can avoid overtraining. I'll go so far as to say that your VDOT takes into account your psychological input into racing, because instead of using lab tests to determine your ability level, we're using your race performances, which are affected by your motivation and willingness to deal with discomfort. VDOT reflects everything that an individual calls on to perform in a race.

In addition to a generic economy curve we use to fit a variety of runners (figure 3.1), Gilbert and I came up with another curve that represents the relative intensity at which a runner can race for various durations (figure 3.2). Duration, not distance, is the key here because the intensity (percentage of current VDOT) at which any race can be run is a function of how much time it takes to complete the race. For example, one runner might complete a 10,000-meter race in 50 minutes; another runner might race 10 miles in 50 minutes. Both runners race at about the same intensity for 50

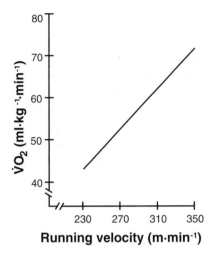

Figure 3.1 Relationship between running velocity and $\dot{V}O_2$ demand.

Adapted, by permission, from J. Daniels, R. Fitts, and G. Sheehan, 1978. *Conditioning for distance running: The scientific aspects.* New York: John Wiley and Sons, 31.

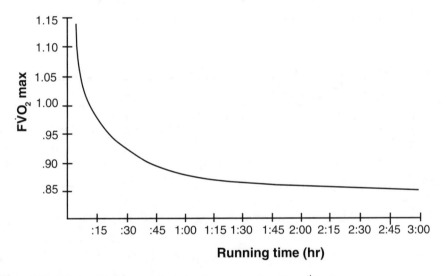

Figure 3.2 Relationship between race duration and fraction (F) of $\dot{V}O_2$max.

Adapted, by permission, from J.Daniels, R. Fitts, and G. Sheehan, 1978. *Conditioning for distance running: the scientific aspects.* New York: John Wiley and Sons, 31.

minutes. Intensity is of utmost importance; the intensity that you can maintain reflects the various reactions occurring inside your body, based on how long you're expected to be running in a race.

Runners learn to deal with a certain level of discomfort for a certain period of time, regardless of how many miles they can cover in that time. For example, blood lactate accumulates at a certain rate, based on how fast you're running. At a fairly hard intensity (as in a 5-mile or 10K race), lactate accumulation is slow enough to allow you to go on for 30 minutes or so; at a higher intensity of effort (as when racing 3,000 meters or 2 miles), lactate accumulation is more rapid, and you might be forced to stop after only 10 minutes of running. All runners learn to identify the intensity of effort they can tolerate for different periods of time; of course, better runners can cover greater distances than lesser runners in the same amount of time. By using the equations that generate the curves in figures 3.1 and 3.2, along with a few other calculations, Jimmy Gilbert and I developed the VDOT tables that have been used very successfully since the 1970s.

These VDOT tables can relate performances over an unlimited number of distances and can be used to predict performances in races of any distance from a known performance in a race of any other distance. In addition, the formulas associated with the development of the VDOT tables allow runners to identify the pace associated with a desired training intensity (such as $\dot{V}O_2$max intervals, threshold, or marathon pace).

Table 3.1 presents a condensed version of the VDOT tables found in *Oxygen Power* (which details VDOT values for over 40 distances and in smaller increments). Use table 3.1 when you want to find a VDOT value that's associated with either your race performances or with examples presented throughout the rest of this book. A VDOT value can be generated for virtually any performance over any race distance but is

Table 3.1 VDOT Values Associated With Times Raced Over Popular Distances

VDOT	1,500 m	Mile	3,000 m	2-mile	5,000 m	10,000 m	15K	Half-marathon	Marathon	VDOT
30	8:30	9:11	17:56	19:19	30:40	63:46	98:14	2:21:04	4:49:17	30
31	8:15	8:55	17:27	18:48	29:51	62:03	95:36	2:17:21	4:41:57	31
32	8:02	8:41	16:59	18:18	29:05	60:26	93:07	2:13:49	4:34:59	32
33	7:49	8:27	16:33	17:50	28:21	58:54	90:45	2:10:27	4:28:22	33
34	7:37	8:14	16:09	17:24	27:39	57:26	88:30	2:07:16	4:22:03	34
35	7:25	8:01	15:45	16:58	27:00	56:03	86:22	2:04:13	4:16:03	35
36	7:14	7:49	15:23	16:34	26:22	54:44	84:20	2:01:19	4:10:19	36
37	7:04	7:38	15:01	16:11	25:46	53:29	82:24	1:58:34	4:04:50	37
38	6:54	7:27	14:41	15:49	25:12	52:17	80:33	1:55:55	3:59:35	38
39	6:44	7:17	14:21	15:29	24:39	51:09	78:47	1:53:24	3:54:34	39
40	6:35	7:07	14:03	15:08	24:08	50:03	77:06	1:50:59	3:49:45	40
41	6:27	6:58	13:45	14:49	23:38	49:01	75:29	1:48:40	3:45:09	41
42	6:19	6:49	13:28	14:31	23:09	48:01	73:56	1:46:27	3:40:43	42
43	6:11	6:41	13:11	14:13	22:41	47:04	72:27	1:44:20	3:36:28	43
44	6:03	6:32	12:55	13:56	22:15	46:09	71:02	1:42:17	3:32:23	44
45	5:56	6:25	12:40	13:40	21:50	45:16	69:40	1:40:20	3:28:26	45
46	5:49	6:17	12:26	13:25	21:25	44:25	68:22	1:38:27	3:24:39	46
47	5:42	6:10	12:12	13:10	21:02	43:36	67:06	1:36:38	3:21:00	47

Table 3.1

VDOT	1,500 m	Mile	3,000 m	2-mile	5,000 m	10,000 m	15K	Half-marathon	Marathon	VDOT
48	5:36	6:03	11:58	12:55	20:39	42:50	65:53	1:34:53	3:17:29	48
49	5:30	5:56	11:45	12:41	20:18	42:04	64:44	1:33:12	3:14:06	49
50	5:24	5:50	11:33	12:28	19:57	41:21	63:36	1:31:35	3:10:49	50
51	5:18	5:44	11:21	12:15	19:36	40:39	62:31	1:30:02	3:07:39	51
52	5:13	5:38	11:09	12:02	19:17	39:59	61:29	1:28:31	3:04:36	52
53	5:07	5:32	10:58	11:50	18:58	39:20	60:28	1:27:04	3:01:39	53
54	5:02	5:27	10:47	11:39	18:40	38:42	59:30	1:25:40	2:58:47	54
55	4:57	5:21	10:37	11:28	18:22	38:06	58:33	1:24:18	2:56:01	55
56	4:53	5:16	10:27	11:17	18:05	37:31	57:39	1:23:00	2:53:20	56
57	4:48	5:11	10:17	11:06	17:49	36:57	56:46	1:21:43	2:50:45	57
58	4:44	5:06	10:08	10:56	17:33	36:24	55:55	1:20:30	2:48:14	58
59	4:39	5:02	9:58	10:46	17:17	35:52	55:06	1:19:18	2:45:47	59
60	4:35	4:57	9:50	10:37	17:03	35:22	54:18	1:18:09	2:43:25	60
61	4:31	4:53	9:41	10:27	16:48	34:52	53:32	1:17:02	2:41:08	61
62	4:27	4:49	9:33	10:18	16:34	34:23	52:47	1:15:57	2:38:54	62
63	4:24	4:45	9:25	10:10	16:20	33:55	52:03	1:14:54	2:36:44	63
64	4:20	4:41	9:17	10:01	16:07	33:28	51:21	1:13:53	2:34:38	64
65	4:16	4:37	9:09	9:53	15:54	33:01	50:40	1:12:53	2:32:35	65
66	4:13	4:33	9:02	9:45	15:42	32:35	50:00	1:11:56	2:30:36	66
67	4:10	4:30	8:55	9:37	15:29	32:11	49:22	1:11:00	2:28:40	67
68	4:06	4:26	8:48	9:30	15:18	31:46	48:44	1:10:05	2:26:47	68
69	4:03	4:23	8:41	9:23	15:06	31:23	48:08	1:09:12	2:24:57	69
70	4:00	4:19	8:34	9:16	14:55	31:00	47:32	1:08:21	2:23:10	70
71	3:57	4:16	8:28	9:09	14:44	30:38	46:58	1:07:31	2:21:26	71
72	3:54	4:13	8:22	9:02	14:33	30:16	46:24	1:06:42	2:19:44	72
73	3:52	4:10	8:16	8:55	14:23	29:55	45:51	1:05:54	2:18:05	73
74	3:49	4:07	8:10	8:49	14:13	29:34	45:19	1:05:08	2:16:29	74
75	3:46	4:04	8:04	8:43	14:03	29:14	44:48	1:04:23	2:14:55	75
76	3:44	4:02	7:58	8:37	13:54	28:55	44:18	1:03:39	2:13:23	76
77	3:41+	3:58+	7:53	8:31	13:44	28:36	43:49	1:02:56	2:11:54	77
78	3:38.8	3:56.2	7:48	8:25	13:35	28:17	43:20	1:02:15	2:10:27	78
79	3:36.5	3:53.7	7:43	8:20	13:26	27:59	42:52	1:01:34	2:09:02	79
80	3:34.2	3:51.2	7:37.5	8:14.2	13:17.8	27:41.2	42:25	1:00:54	2:07:38	80
81	3:31.9	3:48.7	7:32.5	8:08.9	13:09.3	27:24	41:58	1:00:15	2:06:17	81
82	3:29.7	3:46.4	7:27.7	8:03.7	13:01.1	27:07	41:32	:59:38	2:04:57	82
83	3:27.6	3:44.0	7:23.0	7:58.6	12:53.0	26:51	41:06	:59:01	2:03:40	83
84	3:25.5	3:41.8	7:18.5	7:53.6	12:45.2	26:34	40:42	:58:25	2:02:24	84
85	3:23.5	3:39.6	7:14.0	7:48.8	12:37.4	26:19	40:17	:57:50	2:01:10	85

most desirable and accurate for races lasting from about three and a half minutes to about three and a half hours. Because the race duration of the 800 meters is typically shorter, training intensities for these runners are presented in chapter 16.

To use the VDOT table, look up a recent time under any of the distances presented and then read across that row to find the corresponding VDOT. If you have more than one recent race distance to work with, the one with the highest VDOT is the one that describes your current state of fitness.

Make sure that the race from which you're predicting the VDOT was run on a flat course, with good footing, and under good weather conditions; when using a race run in difficult weather or terrain conditions, time is affected negatively, and the VDOT will be lower than it should be. If, however, you're determining a VDOT on a cross country course that you'll also use for regular training sessions, then it's fair to use the VDOT value from that adverse course to set training intensities for the same type of adversity. You can use a time from a recent, moderate-distance road race to predict an upcoming marathon time, but for the prediction to be accurate the conditions of the two races must be similar; you can't expect to accurately predict a hot-day marathon time from a half-marathon time run under cool conditions.

Of course some runners might find that they have different VDOT values depending on the distance of the race. For example, a runner might have a best time of 4:31 for the 1,500 meters (VDOT 61) but a 9:33 for the 3,000 meters (VDOT 62) and a 15:54 for the 5,000 meters (VDOT 65). In such cases, select your highest VDOT value for your training intensity.

Using VDOT to Establish Training Intensities

Once you have established your VDOT, the next thing you need to do is to set training intensities, which can be done using the information in table 3.2. To use table 3.2, find the VDOT value from table 3.1 that best applies to you and move across table 3.2 to see the various paces for the different kinds of training you'll be doing. For example, a runner with a best VDOT of 50 (based on a 5,000-meter time of 19:57 in table 3.1) would shoot for the following paces:

Easy (**E**) and long runs—5:18 per 1,000 meters (or 8:32 per mile)

Marathon (**M**) pace—7:17 per mile

Threshold (**T**) (tempo or cruise-interval pace)—1:42 per 400 meters, 4:15 per 1,000 meters, and 6:51 per mile

Interval (**I**) pace—93 seconds per 400 meters, 3:55 per 1,000 meters, and 4:41 per 1,200 meters

Repetition (**R**) pace—43 seconds per 200 meters and 87 seconds per 400 meters

In the 50-VDOT example cited above there's no mile pace noted for **I** training. A single bout of work in an interval session shouldn't last longer than about five minutes, and with a VDOT of 50, interval mile pace would be 6:12, which would be too demanding. In this case, interval 1,200s or 1,000s would be the recommended distances for long intervals (4:41 per 1,200, in this example).

Again, chapter 16 provides more precise training intensities for 800-meter runners who specialize more in the 400 to 800 meters or the 800 to 1,500 meters.

Daniels' 2.2 + Six-Seconds Rule

As a result of constantly dealing with VDOT values and their associated training intensities (paces) for distances between 1,500 meters and marathons, it has become clear to me that an alternate rule can be applied to training intensities for runners who specialize in races longer than 1,500 meters without referring to the VDOT tables.

Refer to table 3.3 on page 56, a table I devised in the late 1960s to associate the times for 400-, 800-, 1,500-meter, or mile-race performances. If you put a mark by your recent race times for these distances, a straight line across the row will probably connect the three performances. This line might slope down to the right, indicating better speed than endurance, or it might slope up to the right, indicating better endurance than speed. A horizontal line suggests equal current ability in speed and endurance, which fits the profile of a surprising number of well-trained runners. Mathematically, times that fit a horizontal line are associated by a factor of 2.2 (multiplying a 400-meter time by 2.2 gives the corresponding 800-meter time, and multiplying an 800-meter time by 2.2 produces the corresponding 1,600-meter time).

If you compare your times from table 3.3 and look them up in table 3.2, you'll notice that 1,500-meter and mile-race pace is essentially the proper speed for repetition (**R**) training, which is about six seconds faster per 400 meters than proper interval (**I**) pace. In fact, runners who can race a mile in 5:30 or faster can identify threshold (**T**) pace as being about six seconds slower per 400 meters than **I** pace. Using the six-seconds rule produces a **T** pace that's too aggressive for runners whose best mile time is slower than 5:30; these runners should stay with the VDOT tables all the way.

Adjusting Training Intensities

I suggest staying at a training intensity for at least three weeks, even if a race performance suggests that you've moved to a higher VDOT reference value. During a period of prolonged training, without races for evaluating improvement, it's safe to increase your VDOT value by a single unit after four to six weeks at the same value—if all's going well and workouts seem to be getting easier.

On a related note, a VDOT based on your best 1,500-meter race, for example, doesn't necessarily mean that you can race a 10K at the equivalent VDOT value. It will tell you what an equivalent 10K time would be provided you adjust your training to prepare for a 10K race.

Table 3.2 Training Intensities Based on Current VDOT

VDOT	E pace		M pace		T pace		
	Mile	Km	Mile	Km	400m	1,000m	Mile
30	12:40	7:52	11:01	6:51	2:33	6:24	10:18
31	12:22	7:41	10:45	6:41	2:30	6:14	10:02
32	12:04	7:30	10:29	6:31	2:26	6:05	9:47
33	11:48	7:20	10:14	6:21	2:23	5:56	9:33
34	11:32	7:10	10:00	6:13	2:19	5:48	9:20
35	11:17	7:01	9:46	6:04	2:16	5:40	9:07
36	11:02	6:52	9:33	5:56	2:13	5:33	8:55
37	10:49	6:43	9:20	5:48	2:10	5:25	8:44
38	10:35	6:35	9:08	5:41	2:07	5:19	8:33
39	10:23	6:27	8:57	5:33	2:05	5:12	8:22
40	10:11	6:19	8:46	5:27	2:02	5:06	8:12
41	9:59	6:12	8:35	5:20	2:00	5:00	8:02
42	9:48	6:05	8:25	5:14	1:57	4:54	7:52
43	9:37	5:58	8:15	5:08	1:55	4:49	7:42
44	9:27	5:52	8:06	5:02	1:53	4:43	7:33
45	9:17	5:46	7:57	4:56	1:51	4:38	7:25
46	9:07	5:40	7:48	4:51	1:49	4:33	7:17
47	8:58	5:34	7:40	4:46	1:47	4:29	7.10
48	8:49	5:28	7:32	4:41	1:45	4:24	7:02
49	8:40	5:23	7:24	4:36	1:43	4:20	6:55
50	8:32	5:18	7:17	4:31	1:42	4:15	6:51
51	8:24	5:13	7:09	4:27	1:40	4:11	6:44
52	8:16	5:08	7:02	4:22	98	4:07	6:38
53	8:09	5:04	6:56	4:18	97	4:04	6:32
54	8:01	4:59	6:49	4:14	95	4:00	6:26
55	7:54	4:55	6:43	4:10	94	3:56	6:20
56	7:48	4:50	6:37	4:06	93	3:53	6:15
57	7:41	4:46	6:31	4:03	91	3:50	6:09

Times are listed in seconds up to 99, then in min:sec.

| VDOT | I pace | | | | R pace | | |
	400m	1,000m	1,200m	Mile	200m	400m	800m
30	2:22	--	--	--	67	2:16	--
31	2:18	--	--	--	65	2:12	--
32	2:14	--	--	--	63	2:08	
33	2:11	--	--	--	62	2:05	--
34	2:08	--	--	--	60	2:02	--
35	2:05	--	--	--	59	1:59	--
36	2:02	5:07	--	--	57	1:55	--
37	1:59	5:00	--	--	56	1:53	--
38	1:56	4:54	--	--	54	1:50	--
39	1:54	4:48	--	--	53	1:48	--
40	1:52	4:42	--	--	52	1:46	--
41	1:50	4:36	--	--	51	1:44	--
42	1:48	4:31	--	--	50	1:42	--
43	1:46	4:26	--	--	49	1:40	--
44	1:44	4:21	--	--	48	98	--
45	1:42	4:16	--	--	47	96	--
46	1:40	4:12	5:00	--	46	94	--
47	98	4:07	4:54	--	45	92	--
48	96	4:03	4:49	--	44	90	--
49	95	3:59	4:45	--	44	89	--
50	93	3:55	4:41	--	43	87	--
51	92	3:51	4:36	--	42	86	--
52	91	3:48	4:33	--	42	85	--
53	90	3:44	4:29	--	41	84	--
54	88	3:41	4:25	--	40	82	--
55	87	3:37	4:21	--	40	81	--
56	86	3:34	4:18	--	39	80	--
57	85	3:31	4:15	--	39	79	--

(continued)

Table 3.2 **Training Intensities Based on Current VDOT, *continued***

VDOT	E pace Mile	E pace Km	M pace Mile	M pace Km	T pace 400m	T pace 1,000m	T pace Mile
58	7:34	4:42	6:25	3:59	90	3:45	6:04
59	7:28	4:38	6:19	3:55	89	3:43	5:59
60	7:22	4:35	6:14	3:52	88	3:40	5:54
61	7:16	4:31	6:09	3:49	86	3:37	5:50
62	7:11	4:27	6:04	3:46	85	3:34	5:45
63	7:05	4:24	5:59	3:43	84	3:32	5:41
64	7:00	4:21	5:54	3:40	83	3:29	5:36
65	6:54	4:18	5:49	3:37	82	3:26	5:32
66	6:49	4:14	5:45	3:34	81	3:24	5:28
67	6:44	4:11	5:40	3:31	80	3:21	5:24
68	6:39	4:08	5:36	3:28	79	3:19	5:20
69	6:35	4:05	5:32	3:26	78	3:16	5:16
70	6:30	4:02	5:28	3:23	77	3:14	5:13
71	6:26	4:00	5:24	3:21	76	3:12	5:09
72	6:21	3:57	5:20	3:19	76	3:10	5:05
73	6:17	3:54	5:16	3:16	75	3:08	5:02
74	6:13	3:52	5:12	3:14	74	3:06	4:59
75	6:09	3:49	5:09	3:12	74	3:04	4:56
76	6:05	3:47	5:05	3:10	73	3:02	4:52
77	6:01	3:44	5:01	3:07	72	3:00	4:49
78	5:57	3:42	4:58	3:05	71	2:58	4:46
79	5:54	3:40	4:55	3:03	70	2:56	4:43
80	5:50	3:32	4:52	3:01	70	2:54	4:41
81	5:46	3:35	4:49	2:59	69	2:53	4:38
82	5:43	3:33	4:46	2:57	68	2:51	4:35
83	5:40	3:31	4:43	2:56	68	2:49	4:32
84	5:36	3:29	4:40	2:54	67	2:48	4:30
85	5:33	3:27	4:37	2:52	66	2:46	4:27

Times are listed in seconds up to 99, then in min:sec.

VDOT	I pace				R pace		
	400m	1,000m	1,200m	Mile	200m	400m	800m
58	83	3:28	4:10	--	38	77	--
59	82	3:25	4:07	--	37	76	--
60	81	3:23	4:03	--	37	75	2:30
61	80	3:20	4:00	--	36	74	2:28
62	79	3:17	3:57	--	36	73	2:26
63	78	3:15	3:54	--	35	72	2:24
64	77	3:12	3:51	--	35	71	2:22
65	76	3:10	3:48	--	34	70	2:20
66	75	3:08	3:45	5:00	34	69	2:18
67	74	3:05	3:42	4:57	33	68	2:16
68	73	3:03	3:39	4:53	33	67	2:14
69	72	3:01	3:36	4:50	32	66	2:12
70	71	2:59	3:34	4:46	32	65	2:10
71	70	2:57	3:31	4:43	31	64	2:08
72	69	2:55	3:29	4:40	31	63	2:06
73	69	2:53	3:27	4:37	31	62	2:05
74	68	2:51	3:25	4:34	30	62	2:04
75	67	2:49	3:22	4:31	30	61	2:03
76	66	2:48	3:20	4:28	29	60	2:02
77	65	2:46	3:18	4:25	29	59	2:00
78	65	2:44	3:16	4:23	29	59	1:59
79	64	2:42	3:14	4:20	28	58	1:58
80	64	2:41	3:12	4:17	28	58	1:56
81	63	2:39	3:10	4:15	28	57	1:55
82	62	2:38	3:08	4:12	27	56	1:54
83	62	2:36	3:07	4:10	27	56	1:53
84	61	2:35	3:05	4:08	27	55	1:52
85	61	2:33	3:03	4:05	27	55	1:51

Table 3.3   Time Associations Among 400-, 800-, 1,500-Meter, and Mile Runs

400m	800m	1,500m	Mile	400m	800m	1,500m	Mile
46.0	1:41.2	3:27.6	3:44.1	78.0	2:51.6	5:51.5	6:19.8
47.0	1:43.4	3:32.0	3:48.9	79.0	2:53.8	5:56.0	6:24.7
48.0	1:45.6	3.36.5	3.53.8	80.0	2:56.0	6:00.5	6:29.6
49.0	1:47.8	3.41.0	3:58.6	81.0	2:58.2	6:05.0	6:34.4
50.0	1:50.0	3:45.5	4:03.5	82.0	3:00.4	6:09.5	6:39.3
51.0	1:52.2	3:50.0	4:08.3	83.0	3:02.6	6:14.0	6:44.2
52.0	1:54.4	3:54.5	4:13.2	84.0	3:04.8	6:18.5	6:49.1
53.0	1:56.6	3:59.0	4:18.0	85.0	3:07.0	6:23.0	6:53.9
54.0	1:58.8	4:03.5	4:22.9	86.0	3:09.2	6:27.5	6:58.8
55.0	2:01.0	4:08.0	4:27.7	87.0	3:11.4	6:32.0	7:03.6
56.0	2:03.2	4:12.5	4:32.6	88.0	3:13.6	6:36.5	7:08.5
57.0	2:05.4	4:17.0	4:37.5	89.0	3:15.8	6:41.0	7:13.4
58.0	2:07.6	4:21.5	4:42.4	90.0	3:18.0	6:45.5	7:18.3
59.0	2:09.8	4:26.0	4:47.3	91.0	3:20.2	6:50.0	7:23.1
60.0	2:12.0	4:30.5	4:52.2	92.0	3:22.4	6:54.5	7:28.0
61.0	2:14.2	4:35.0	4.57.1	93.0	3:24.6	6:59.0	7:32.8
62.0	2:16.4	4:39.5	5:02.0	94.0	3:26.8	7:03.5	7:37.7
63.0	2:18.6	4:44.0	5:06.8	95.0	3:29.0	7:08.0	7:42.5
64.0	2:20.8	4:48.5	5:11.7	96.0	3:31.2	7:12.5	7:47.4
65.0	2:23.0	4:53.0	5:16.6	97.0	3:33.4	7:17.0	7:52.3
66.0	2:25.2	4:57.5	5:21.5	98.0	3:35.6	7:21.5	7:57.2
67.0	2:27.4	5:02.0	5:26.3	99.0	3:37.8	7:26.0	8:02.0
68.0	2:29.6	5:06.5	5:31.2	1:40.0	3:40.0	7:30.5	8:06.9
69.0	2:31.8	5:11.0	5:36.0	1:41.0	3:42.2	7:35.0	8:11.8
70.0	2:34.0	5:15.5	5:40.9	1:42.0	3:44.4	7:39.5	8:16.6
71.0	2:36.2	5:20.0	5:45.7	1:43.0	3:46.6	7:44.0	8:21.5
72.0	2:38.4	5:24.5	5:50.6	1:44.0	3:48.8	7:48.5	8:26.4
73.0	2:40.6	5:29.0	5:55.5	1:45.0	3:51.0	7:53.0	8:31.3
74.0	2:42.8	5:33.5	6:00.4	1:46.0	3:53.2	7:57.5	8:36.1
75.0	2:45.0	5:38.0	6:05.2	1:47.0	3:55.4	8:02.0	8:41.0
76.0	2:47.2	5:42.5	6:10.1	1:48.0	3:57.6	8:06.5	8:45.9
77.0	2:49.4	5:47.0	6:14.9	1:49.0	3:59.8	8:11.0	8:50.8

Adjusting for Altitude

Two kinds of acclimatization occur with altitude training. The body makes some physi-ological adjustments within a month or two that result in better altitude performance (see chapter 2, pages 20 to 21), and a certain degree of competitive acclimatization takes place as a result of racing at altitude—that is, you learn how to race under the stress of altitude. The net result of these two acclimatizations is that on returning to altitude, even after months or years spent at sea level, overall performance won't be so adversely affected the second time around. This is primarily because the competitive acclimatization pretty much stays with you. You have remembered how to race at altitude even though your body is a little out of tune physiologically. You can train as hard and as much at altitude as you did at sea level.

It's not uncommon for athletes to travel to altitude for a few weeks of altitude training and either take it too easy at first (hoping to ease into the new environment gradually) or increase the training load and intensity in order to make the most of the time spent at altitude. Really, there's no need to follow either approach. The proper way to go about it is to simply press on with training as usual, using your normal loads and intensities.

Load If your normal training program calls for 70 miles of running per week, there's no reason to vary from that, unless it's time for a change anyway. If your current program calls for 3 miles of repetition (**R**) training and 5 miles of interval (**I**) training once each week, these amounts are also appropriate at altitude, with the adjustments outlined in the following sections. There's no problem keeping up a 17-mile long run at altitude, if that's been a normal long run for you. Please keep in mind that I'm talking about training at *moderate* altitude, which falls in the area of 1,500 to 2,500 meters (4,900 to 8,200 feet).

Intensity Remember that as you go up in altitude, the atmospheric pressure gets lower, and the lower the atmospheric pressure, the lower the pressure of oxygen. Because oxygen pressure is what determines how much oxygen will be carried by the hemoglobin in the blood, the result is that a given amount of hemoglobin carries less oxygen to the exercising muscles at altitude. This resulting drop in oxygen delivery also lowers your $\dot{V}O_2$max at altitude. However, altitude doesn't affect performance as much as it affects $\dot{V}O_2$max. This is because economy improves at altitude as a consequence of the decreased air resistance encountered in the less dense altitude air. Further, aerobic capacity ($\dot{V}O_2$max) doesn't represent the only available energy source, and anaerobic power isn't negatively affected by being at altitude.

Running intensity can be identified in absolute terms or in relative terms. A relative intensity is expressed in relation to an individual's $\dot{V}O_2$max. For example, I have recommended running at 83 to 88 percent of $\dot{V}O_2$max for threshold training. On the other hand, an absolute intensity is a specific running velocity (pace), such as six minutes per mile.

When you train at altitude for races at sea level, some training must be geared to sea-level race paces, or absolute intensity. This principle applies to **R** training, which is primarily related to race intensity, not to $\dot{V}O_2$max. This means that reps run at altitude would be run at the same speed as they would be run at sea level. However, intervals and threshold training (including cruise intervals and tempo runs) will actually be slower at altitude than at sea level to accommodate the lower VDOT value that dictates training intensities at altitude. Remember, though, that the loss in VDOT is not as great as the loss in $\dot{V}O_2$max because of a gain in economy at altitude. In effect, upon exposure to an altitude of 2,000 meters (6,562 feet), $\dot{V}O_2$max is diminished by about 12 percent, but performance is only about 6 percent worse (as is VDOT) because of improved economy. Most runners would perform about 10 to 20 seconds per mile slower at this altitude depending on their state of acclimatization, compared to recent sea-level times. Figure 3.3 shows how various altitudes affect training and race performances, depending on performances at sea level.

Naturally, as anyone acclimatizes to altitude, his or her altitude $\dot{V}O_2$max and VDOT increase, becoming a greater percentage of the former sea-level values. All in all, there's no need to plan adjustments in training intensities—they'll pretty much occur as you become acclimatized.

One way of monitoring the relative intensity of workouts is to be aware of breathing patterns. If you can handle threshold runs comfortably at sea level with a 2-2 breathing rhythm (see chapter 7), then use this same rhythm and associated subjective feelings for altitude threshold (**T**) training.

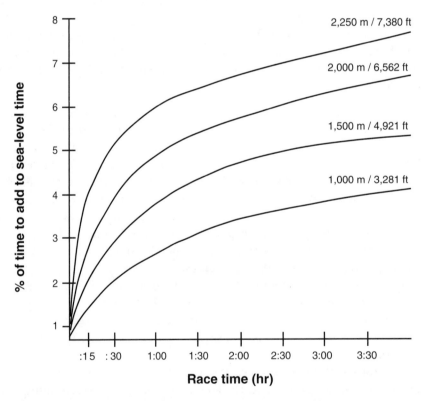

Figure 3.3   The effects of altitude on running performance, shown as a percent of sea-level time to add to running time for races of different durations at various altitudes for acclimatized runners. Nonacclimatized runners may expect to add up to double these amounts.

Adapted, by permission, from J. Daniels, 1975. "Equating sea-level and altitude distance running times," *Track and Field Quarterly Review* 75(4): 38-9.

The same applies to interval (**I**) training. By shooting for the same subjective ratings during this type of training, you can be pretty accurate in adjusting intensities to remain the same at altitude, relative to your new lower $\dot{V}O_2$max. Insofar as training effect goes, the slower training speeds for **I** and **T** runs at altitude will be as effective as the faster relative speeds at sea level.

You might have to change your repetition (**R**) workouts if your altitude training is geared toward upcoming sea-level races. To maintain desired speed, economy, and sense of pace, normal **R** intensity (speed) must be retained at all costs. This might mean taking longer recoveries during an **R** workout, or it might mean using shorter **R** workouts (300s instead of 400s, for example). Also keep the usual total amount of reps. To perform three miles of reps, for example, which might normally be accomplished by doing 12 × 400, the 400s could be replaced by 16 × 300. Both sessions produce the same amount of work at the desired pace.

When altitude training is geared toward an altitude race, then you can adjust **R** pace to coincide with the demands of the anticipated altitude race pace. Usually, though, altitude residents venture to sea level for a fair number of races, and for this reason their training should incorporate sea-level performance **R** intensities.

Other Factors You need to take in more than normal amounts of fluids at altitude, where the effects of dry air on body fluids are deceiving. Furthermore, some altitude newcomers tend to feel sleepy and yet find it difficult to sleep. Naps are beneficial, and early-morning runs are easier to do at altitude than at sea level.

It's normal to increase your ventilation at altitude, an adjustment that carries over to sea level for a few days. Some runners find it somewhat frightening to hear themselves breathing so hard the first few days back at sea level, but if you ignore how it sounds, your performance should be fine. Eat a well-balanced diet with adequate iron-rich foods, or use supplements, if necessary. This allows your body to take advantage of its desire to build more red blood cells at altitude.

I've always found altitude training enjoyable. I'm sure that where you go and with whom makes a big difference in performance; certainly being happy is an important part of performing well, either at altitude or sea level. Runners who make substantial alterations to their lifestyles, especially to their social or financial circumstances, just to train at altitude, often end up not doing well because of the psychological stresses involved. If the shift to altitude is going to wear you down mentally, you're better off training at sea level.

Many runners choose to adjust their altitude training sojourns so that they can live at a relatively higher altitude than that at which they train, thus using a "live-high-train-low" approach. Reports of positive results when using this technique have led to runners living at sea level, under altitude conditions (in an "altitude house" or sleeping in "altitude tents" and so forth). An unfortunate result of elite runners using one or more of these approaches or devices has led to a general feeling that no runner can be successful without altitude. Of course we don't typically hear of attempts to follow one of these approaches in which the runner fails to improve (or gets worse), but we do hear many of the success stories.

I suggest that you consider the African runners, who now dominate distance-running events around the world. They don't follow a live-high-train-low approach. Sure, they live and train at altitude, and that might (or might not) be why they're so dominant. I, for one, hope that they never adopt the live-high-train-low approach, if indeed it's advantageous. They're already pretty good at what they're doing, and it would be scary to see them even better.

Runners who can work altitude training into their regimens without undue strain on other aspects of their lives are more likely to enjoy it and to benefit from it.

Gauging With Heart Rate

In addition to using VDOT values, can knowing how fast your heart is beating be useful in reaching athletic excellence? As with any of our body's physiological functions, there are many interrelated factors at play. Heart rate (HR) is affected by blood flow, aerobic fitness, and the amount of oxygen being transported by the circulating blood. In addition, the temperature of the air around you, the clothing you wear, your state of health, and body-fluid status also affect your heart rate.

Because cardiac output (the amount of blood pumped per minute) is the product of heart rate and stroke volume (amount of blood pumped with each beat of the heart), it's useful to understand what affects the flow of blood around the body.

At any given time, your body needs a particular amount of blood flowing to its parts. During exercise, blood flow increases dramatically to the exercising muscles and also possibly to the skin. Muscle demand is a function of how hard the muscle is working, and skin demand depends on the body's need to hold down a rise in body temperature associated with exercise and climate.

Blood flow to any particular area is determined by cardiac output and resistance in the vessels that supply that area with its blood, and resistance is a function of where the body wants to divert blood by constricting some vessels and dilating others.

With this in mind, here are some of the reasons you might notice a change in heart rate:

- A change in blood volume, often associated with the degree of hydration or dehydration
- A change in blood available to be sent to the exercising muscles, which depends on the amount routed to other areas (e.g., to the skin for cooling)
- A change in overall fitness level
- A change in the oxygen-carrying capacity of the blood, which often depends on nutritional status.

Given the many conditions that affect HR, you must pay close attention to what exactly you're evaluating when monitoring your HR. Consider some of the times that athletes monitor their HR.

Morning (Resting) Heart Rate   Some athletes use their "wake-up" HR to measure fitness, but keep in mind that resting heart rates can vary a great deal, even among highly trained runners. A world-record holder I tested on many occasions never had a heart rate below 60; for others, resting HRs drop well down into the 30s. Monitored on a regular basis, a slower morning HR than usual can indicate improving fitness. Conversely, a consistent increase in wake-up HR can indicate overtraining, dehydration, or poor nutritional status. In any case, you can easily measure resting HR by placing a finger on a pulse point and looking at a watch or clock with a second hand. Be sure to do this while you're still lying down in bed, before sitting up.

Exercise Heart Rate   Most people assume that measuring heart rate during exercise tells you precisely how hard you're working. As I mentioned earlier, the problem with this assumption is that heart rate is influenced by many factors other than just how hard the body is exercising (working).

Thus, if you adjust your work intensity to produce the same HR today that a previous workout suggests that it should, you actually could be working harder (or more easily) than you have set as a goal. Is your goal in training to produce a particular HR or to subject a system of the body to a certain amount of stress?

For example, if you've been performing particular workouts for a couple of months at sea level, will you try to reach the same HR in similar workouts at altitude? If so, you're surely understressing the exercising muscles because at altitude less oxygen is being delivered with each beat of the heart, and to get the same oxygen delivery, HR must increase. Otherwise, you'll undertrain the muscles you're targeting in your workout.

It's not uncommon for an exercising HR to be higher on stationary exercise equipment (particularly indoors, where there's little air movement) than when exercising at the same stress outdoors, where movement of air can lead to better body cooling. The body's reaction to increased heat stress is to send blood to the skin, which usually leads to a higher HR. Setting up a fan that faces indoor exercise equipment can help in such a case.

Needing to wear more clothes during winter running can also affect the HR associated with a particular speed of running. Of course, running against (or with) the wind, over hilly terrain, or on poor footing can also affect HR as it might relate to a desired running pace.

Recovery Heart Rate Athletes often monitor recovery HR after both aerobic and anaerobic events. As with resting HR, recovery values are also subject to contamination by factors other than those directly associated with the bout from which you're recovering. So, given that under different conditions the same HR might reflect different degrees of recovery, it might be better to subjectively measure when you've had enough recovery.

Further, using a particular HR as a guide for recovery must be geared to each individual. You need to know your own resting HR as well as maximum HR (HRmax). For example, a HR of 120 beats per minute reflects a different degree of recovery for a runner with a resting HR of 70 beats per minute and an HRmax of 200 beats per minute than it does for a runner with a resting HR of 40 beats per minute and an HRmax of 160 beats per minute.

Another area in which using a specific rule-of-thumb HR can get a runner into trouble is using a particular formula for determining HRmax (220 – age, for example). I once tested a 30-year-old elite athlete who had an HRmax of 148 beats per minute; 220 minus age for this runner would suggest an HRmax of 190 beats per minute. Certainly, any training based on percentages of an estimated HRmax of 190 would greatly overstress this athlete. In fact, telling him to shoot for an HR of 160 in a certain workout would be unreasonable. I've also seen several world-class 50-year-old runners with HRmax in excess of 190. In these cases, 220 minus age would suggest a max of 170, and targeting 153 beats per minute as the appropriate HR to represent 90 percent of these runners' max would be inappropriate.

Benefits of Heart Rate Monitoring As you can see, heart rate monitoring can be of benefit if you understand its limitations and train accordingly. Some athletes don't have measured courses over which to monitor training pace, and HR can aid them in performing a series of repeated exercise bouts at similar intensities. Heart rate can help determine relative stress when running against the wind, up and down hills, or over difficult footing. Possibly the greatest use of HR monitoring is to help avoid over-training. When standard workouts under ideal conditions produce HR values higher than usual, it's often an indication that something is wrong and further evaluation should be made.

In general, when it can be adequately monitored, pace itself tells the best tale. But when pace isn't easily monitored, HR can be useful in controlling intensity. See chapter 2 regarding the association between relative VDOT ($\%\dot{V}O_2max$) and percent HRmax. Often the best approach is to learn to read your body based on your own perceived exertion scale and to train within the constraints that you monitor by using a device you have with you at all times—the built-in computer in your head.

Test Efforts

There are several workouts that you can use as test efforts, with the idea of repeating the workouts later in the season to compare either performance times in the workout or your subjective feelings while repeating the same performance times. These test workouts aren't set up to tell you how fast to train but rather to give you a feeling of how your training is going if you're in a period during which you're not racing regularly.

Warm up for these test efforts just as you would warm up for a race. At a minimum, do 10 minutes of easy running, followed by stretching and four to six strides.

> **Repeated 400s (8 to 10) with one-minute recoveries.** After a good warm-up, run the 400s with the fastest possible average for the total number run. The best approach is to run the first few 400s at your current one-mile race pace. After the first three or four 400s, try to speed up the pace a little, and keep going as best you can until you're finished. Don't put on a kick for the final 400; keep the same steady effort. Complete 10 runs if your pace is 70 seconds or faster; do 9 if you're running between 71-second and 80-second pace; do 8 if you're slower than that.
>
> If your 400-meter times are slower than 70 seconds, use the one-minute recoveries; if they're faster than 70 seconds, start a 400 every two minutes, which permits the remainder of the time for recovery (e.g., running 400s in 65 seconds allows 55 seconds of rest between each).
>
> When done properly, this is a demanding session because it's faster than interval pace but is performed with short, interval-type recoveries.
>
> The average pace that you can run for this test set is probably the pace at which you can race one mile or 1,500 meters. In fact, your race pace might be faster than your average pace for this set, so don't start out too fast or the short recoveries will catch up with you, and the overall average time won't be the best estimate of your mile fitness. I recommend doing this workout only a couple of times in a season, when you need a test. Ideally, you would do it in one of the middle phases of the season.

Repeated 200s (16 to 20) with one-minute send-offs. With this test session, a 200 is started every minute if the pace is 40 seconds or faster; if the pace is slower, take a 30-second break between 200s. This is similar to the repeated 400s test but with shorter runs, less rest between runs, and same total distance run (16 repeats if going slower than 40 seconds, 18 repeats if running between 35 and 39 seconds each, 20 repeats if running faster than 35 seconds).

Three-mile-plus tempo test. After a good warm-up, run a steady three-mile tempo run at your proper threshold pace, followed immediately by a test-effort 1,000 meters or mile. If your typical tempo run is four miles, add one mile to the end of the three-mile tempo run; if three miles is your tempo distance, add 1,000 meters.

This test is best run on a track, but you can do it on a flat road if you always use the same course. Run at threshold pace for the initial tempo effort and see how much better you can go for the final 1,000 meters or mile. Hold a hard, solid pace throughout the final few minutes.

Three- to four-mile tempo run. Conduct your usual tempo run at your proper threshold pace and record your reactions to this run. Evaluate your fitness subjectively or objectively (by testing heart rate or blood-lactate values). If you use subjective measures, try to rate the effort at the end of each mile, starting with mile two.

Cruise-interval test. Run four to six miles of cruise intervals with one-minute recoveries. Record your subjective feelings or your heart rate and blood-lactate values after each mile, starting with mile two. Do as many miles of cruise intervals as you would normally run in a workout based on current training levels. Be honest with your evaluation of how you feel. Use your prescribed threshold pace.

Cruise-plus test. This test is similar to the three-mile-plus tempo test; it lets you see what kind of mile you can add to the end of a cruise-interval workout. To perform this test, run one fewer than your normal number of cruise intervals, and, following the usual one-minute recovery, see what kind of mile you can add on. For example, if your usual cruise-interval session involves five miles at six-minute pace, do four cruise intervals at six-minute pace, take the one-minute rest, and then see what you can do on the fifth interval, which is the true test.

Along with knowing your starting point and keeping on top of your training intensities, you should also evaluate other aspects of your overall training situation. Write down your long-term and immediate race goals. Determine how many days each week you can train and how much time each day. Are you able and willing to train twice on some days? Include the conditions that you expect during various phases of your season, such as the weather and the availability of a track, grass, or trails to train on. Is a treadmill available for training sessions? Is there a pool you can use for deep-water running? When setting up a season of training, address all these concerns in addition to the paces that you'll apply to your quality workouts and how much total mileage you expect to run. In the next chapter, I help you determine how to set up a weekly plan. The programs presented in parts III and IV provide additional program guidance depending on your race goals and event specialty.

Magdalena Lewy Boulet

Magdalena Lewy Boulet was born in Poland and began her athletic career as a swimmer. She escaped with her family from Poland in 1989 and eventually ended up in Southern California, finishing high school at Lakewood High. She recalls that she took up running at the age of 18 because she "realized I was a lot more competitive as a runner than I ever was as a swimmer." Her initial goal as a runner was to earn a scholarship to go to college, and the event that most interested her was the 1,500 meters.

© Victah Sailer

After a start at Long Beach Community College, Magda attended the University of California at Berkeley on scholarship and in 1997 placed third in the 5,000 meters at the NCAA Division I national championships. She earned her MS in Exercise Physiology from Cal State at Hayward in 2001. Magdalena was sworn in as an American citizen on September 11, 2001. She married mile standout Richie Boulet in 2002, the same year I became her coach while working with the Farm Team in Palo Alto. Chewy (nick name I have borrowed from a Cal teammate) went on to place 5th in the 5,000 meters at the 2003 U.S. Outdoor Championships, to compete in the World half-marathon championships in Portugal in 2003, and to place 5th at the 2004 Olympic Trials in the marathon. Magdalena feels her future in running is in the marathon; I agree. What continues to impress me about Chewy is her complete dedication to family and friends coupled with her ability to work and still never waver from her commitment to success as a runner.

Personal bests:1,500m—4:23; 3,000m—9:25; 5,000m—16:04; 10,000m—32:41; marathon—2:30:50

CHAPTER 4

The Season Plan

No one has all the answers to what works best for any individual runner. Plus, everyone reacts differently to each type of training. The amount of feedback from a coach that runners need also varies tremendously. The approach presented here for planning a season of training is as simple and effective as possible; it works both for runners who want to coach themselves and for athletes under the firm control of a coach.

In this chapter I present the concept of breaking a season down into phases of training, with four phases being the ideal model but with consideration also given to shorter or longer seasons. For athletes who don't have time for four full phases of training, I provide a way to decide how much of each phase to keep or what might be eliminated altogether. After considering the season's training scheme, I discuss how to arrange quality days of training within each week of the season, taking into account weeks with no competition as well as weeks with races.

Any time that you set up a running training program—be it for yourself, an athlete you're coaching, or a team—you must answer several questions relating to each runner in the program. I present a list of these questions in chapter 1 (see page 7), including such considerations as available time, strengths and weaknesses, the athlete's likes and dislikes, and current fitness level. Once you've answered those questions, you can develop your seasonal plan.

No one has all the answers to running success, but it sure seems that way when a talented athlete and an understanding coach get together.

Step 1: Map Your Season

Start mapping your season by drawing up a block of time on a sheet of paper (see figure 4.1). Start at the far right of the time block and mark this as your goal or peak performance date. This is the period of time when you want season-best performances, such as in a single championship meet or at the beginning of a series of competitions lasting several weeks. The training that you perform during this final quality (FQ) phase is geared to prepare you for your best performances of the season.

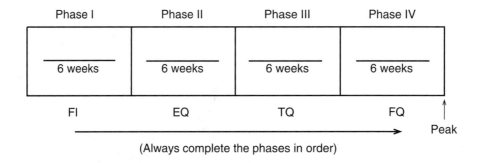

Figure 4.1 Sample plan for setting up a 24-week training program. Insert the dates (into the four boxes) that you want to train in each phase. Start with your peak-performance date and work backward.

This time plan is influenced by many factors. For example, many high school runners participate in different sports during different seasons. The amount of time available for running training varies greatly from person to person, from school to school, and from one region of the country to another. For all runners, weather and facilities are two big factors that dictate, at least to some degree, how the various training blocks can be set up.

Runners training for a marathon usually have a simpler situation to plan for than do runners training for a series of middle-distance races. Marathoners know the exact date of their competition and can focus all their training on the one race; they don't need to worry much about races prior to or following the marathon. Still, there are various schemes of training that can be used successfully to prepare for a marathon as well; an approach that's useful this year might not be as useful next time around. The blocks of training shown in figure 4.1 can be set up for any marathon and are quite manageable.

Unlike the marathoner, the typical high school and college runner has many important races to contend with on the way to the peak period. If you can work the races into your training program, you can still follow the general plan with success.

In figure 4.1, I show four 6-week blocks of training leading up to the peak period. This is a desirable amount of time to set aside for preparation, but it isn't always workable within the framework of a school program. School seasons are often more likely to operate within a 12-week program (some might be shorter and some slightly longer).

Step 2: Break Your Program Into Phases

My preferred approach to a generic 24-week season of training, which I believe is the ideal length, is four 6-week phases. The first phase is a foundation and injury prevention (FI) phase. For most runners, the second phase, early quality (EQ), is for working on mechanics, running economy, and some speed—so, this is primarily a rep phase. Phase three, transition quality (TQ), is the toughest and concentrates primarily on long intervals. The fourth and last phase, final quality (FQ), involves a fair amount of threshold running along with fewer reps or intervals, and, of course, races. A good deal of what goes into this phase depends on the events of primary importance.

In other words, my ideal approach to a 24-week program is 6 weeks each of easy running, followed by reps, then intervals, and finally threshold running and racing. Obviously, such a program wouldn't be the same for every type of runner but would suit most middle- and long-distance runners. As I say, a 24-week program is my ideal approach, but because things rarely work out ideally, we often have to make adjustments. I've prepared a way to fit the best possible training scheme into the time available for any individual, outlined as follows.

Figure 4.2 shows four blocks of training, progressing from phase I at the left to phase IV at the right. Within each block 6 numbers are listed, 24 in all. Consider these numbers to indicate "priority" weeks of training. I arrived at this prioritization by asking myself, "If someone who has logged no training whatsoever up to this point has only one week available to prepare for the final race of the season, what should he or she do for training?" My answer is that this athlete should perform only FI running that week—so place this one-week priority number (1) in the phase I column. I hold the same view for any runner who has only two or three weeks available before racing in the last race of the season—that only phase I training should be performed—so place 2 and 3 in the far-left column as well.

If a runner has six weeks available before his or her last race, allocate three weeks of phase I training (priority weeks 1, 2, 3) and three weeks of phase IV training (priority

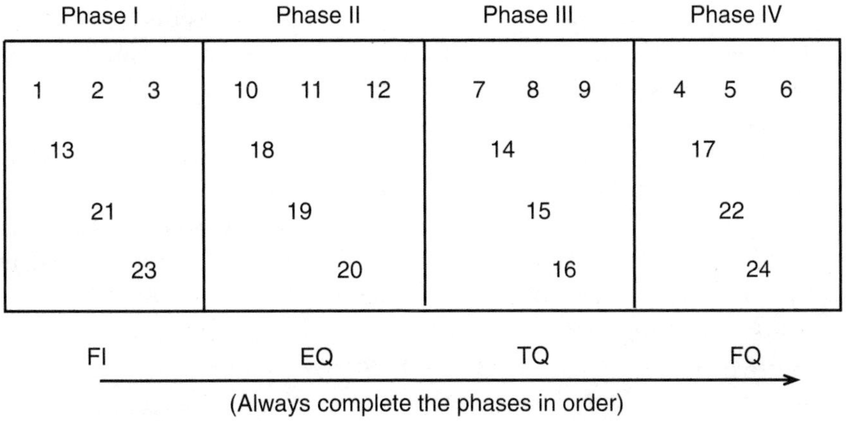

Phase I	Phase II	Phase III	Phase IV
1 2 3	10 11 12	7 8 9	4 5 6
13	18	14	17
21	19	15	22
23	20	16	24
FI	EQ	TQ	FQ

(Always complete the phases in order)

Figure 4.2 Priority weekly numbering system to determine the number of weeks of training per phase according to how many weeks you have available.

weeks 4, 5, 6). A practical way to identify the weeks of training for each phase is to circle the numbers 1 through 6. In the event of ten weeks of training being available, circle numbers 1 through 10, which gives you three weeks of phase I, one week of phase II, three weeks of phase III, and three weeks of phase IV. If you think that only one week of phase II is not worth the change in training, you can push that week into phase III and skip phase II. Whatever the number of weeks assigned to each phase, and regardless of the priority numbers, the number of weeks set aside for phase I must be performed before going to phase II, which must be done before moving to phase III, and so on. If the one week of phase II is moved to phase III, then the runner would have three weeks of phase I, followed by four weeks of phase III, and a final three weeks of phase IV. Once you identify how many weeks you have available for training, simply circle the numbers in the blocks that correspond to the number of available weeks and then progress through the phases in order, spending the specified amount of time on each.

If you have more than 24 weeks in your season or have more than this amount of time to train, extend the phase that makes most sense for you. One way would be simply to extend phase I, allowing yourself more time to gradually build up your mileage to the amount you desire. This is often the best approach because it lets you build a solid base before getting into faster running; this approach is common for runners preparing for a longer race or for a marathon.

On the other hand, with extra weeks available, it might also be a good idea to pay a little more attention to an area you're weak in. This will likely mean extending phase II—a good quality phase, but not the most demanding. In other cases when you're preparing for a season that goes longer than six weeks without a competition, you might extend phase IV, using care to schedule races carefully so they continue to complement each week's training. You'll be least likely to want to extend phase III because it's usually the most demanding phase, but you could even extend this phase if you take care to reduce the amount of primary quality work every other week of the phase.

Sometimes you have fewer than 24 weeks available. In such cases, when determining where your priorities should be, I believe you should consider the FI phase first and the FQ phase, which is associated with final race preparation training, second. If either phase II or phase III must be sacrificed, get rid of phase II. Phase III is more likely to prepare you for FQ than phase II is.

Of course some coaches and runners feel that the ideal season is not 24 weeks, and I agree in certain cases. When a longer or shorter season seems optimal, you can still use the same type of approach. Ask yourself, "If I have only *X* weeks available, how will I prepare?" "*X*" can be any number of weeks. Once you've decided the ideal amount of time to prepare, map out your program, then go through each phase of training completely before moving to the next phase (that is, complete all of the weeks circled for a particular phase before you progress to the next phase).

Up to now, I have presented two concepts:

1. A way to look at a season in terms of phases of training: phase I (FI)—easy, steady running for cell adaptation, foundation, and injury prevention training; phase II

(EQ)—in which the focus is on mechanics, running economy, and some speed development; phase III (TQ)—the most demanding phase, emphasizing long intervals; and phase IV (FQ)—which includes threshold running, some reps or intervals, and races in which best performances are attained.

2. A way of determining how many weeks of attention each of the four phases of training should receive, taking into account the total number of weeks available for the season

Some of what I've discussed stems from my personal coaching philosophy. Obviously, there's more than one approach to the number of phases of training that should make up a season, the length of each phase, the type of training that you should emphasize in each phase, and the order in which you should perform the various types of training. I present different approaches to a season for runners preparing for different events when I discuss how to structure full training seasons in parts III and IV of this book.

That said, I'll now analyze further my four phases of training, with some suggestions regarding what you might accomplish with each. Overall, set up the season with phases of training that will

- build resistance to injury,
- prepare you for different types of training yet to come,
- develop the systems that are beneficial to the races of primary importance, and
- bring you into races with confidence and a feeling of freshness, not fatigue.

Each phase of training should include a quality training session designed to accommodate a primary training focus (I call them Q1 in workouts, which stands for "quality 1"), which develops the component of fitness of greatest importance at the time. There's usually enough time available each week for a secondary emphasis (Q2), and occasionally, some maintenance (Q3) work can also be performed. Seldom do I believe in trying to include every type of training pace (**M, T, I,** and **R**) into a single week of training, unless they're done in limited amounts and in combination with each other (such as in a fartlek workout).

When setting up your phases of training, arrange them to build on each other. Some coaches might require (and some events dictate) that reps precede intervals (I usually do); others demand the opposite, always going from slower to faster training. Have a plan in which you have confidence, and follow that plan. My suggestion is that you focus first on planning the workouts that will be part of your final phase of training (FQ) because this is the period of time during (or immediately following) which you plan to perform at your best. From there you can work backward to phase III, II, and I training.

Phase IV: Final Quality Training

Gear the final phase of training toward preparing for actual race conditions. There are two main issues to consider for this phase: accounting for the elements and focusing on your strengths.

© Empics

Train under conditions as similar as possible to the conditions you'll be racing under.

Make your phase IV preparations as specific as possible to the conditions of the coming races. If the peak race will be in warm weather, include heat acclimatization as part of this phase. If the all-important race will be at altitude, spend time at altitude during this phase (see chapter 3 for details on altitude training). If your race is in a faraway time zone, consider the time change and plan accordingly. If an important race is to be in the morning hours, perform quality workouts (if not all workouts) early in the day.

The next thing to consider relative to the FQ block of training (and possibly the first thing for those who won't have to travel far from their training site) is the type of training you'll perform. First, consider your strengths and weaknesses. In general, you want to attend to weaknesses early in the season and take advantage of your strengths during the final weeks of training. For example, a distance runner weak on speed should work on developing speed early in the season. If the same runner is well known for endurance and tenacity in a race, then this type of training should be emphasized during FQ training. In other words, focus your FQ training on what you do best when the chips are down—at this critical time of the season don't spend a lot of time on aspects of your personal arsenal that don't serve you well.

In addition to concentrating on what works best for you, give some thought to the events of importance during this racing phase. For example, FQ training usually differs among runners preparing for a marathon and those concentrating on racing a fast 1,500 meters. The marathoner most likely will have left faster, rep-type training behind in favor of more threshold and long runs, whereas the 1,500-meter specialist might be doing just the opposite during his or her final preparations.

Take into account your likes and dislikes during FQ training. Some marathoners might like to continue doing some reps or intervals this late in the season because it builds their confidence or because a particular fast workout serves as a reference point to help evaluate fitness. Muscle makeup might partly determine how some runners treat their final weeks of preparation. Some find that faster training leaves them with little spring in their stride; others like what fast strides do for their psyche.

Phase III: Transition Quality Training

Because TQ training involves the most stressful, event-specific training, and because it also sets you up for the less stressful FQ phase, I like to focus on it next. During this phase emphasize workouts that build on what you've already accomplished in earlier weeks of training and that provide a good transition into the final phase of training.

During this phase your goal is to optimize the components of training (that is, stress the proper systems) that apply to your event of primary interest. For example, $\dot{V}O_2$max training (intervals) usually demands your primary attention when training for a 5K, 10K, or similar distance. On the other hand, 800-meter and 1,500-meter runners might be better off with more anaerobic training, accomplished via primary emphasis on repetition training. The type of training to which each individual responds best (some 1,500-meter runners respond better to intervals than to reps, for example) is of primary importance during phase III.

By the time they reach phase III, many runners have enough FI and EQ training under their belts that they feel very fit and sometimes invincible. But this is not a good time to show how tough you are by training faster or more than the program has scheduled you to do. It's a good time to pay particular attention to hitting the proper training paces and taking good care of yourself. It's late enough in the season that you want to avoid injury or illness at all cost. Good nutrition and adequate rest are of utmost importance now. Also, because phase III is usually the most stressful in terms of quality training sessions, it's not a good idea to further stress yourself by increasing mileage at this time. Presumably, you have had adequate time to reach your mileage goal by the time you move into the TQ phase of training.

Phase III challenges a runner's mental and physical toughness. It's tempting to slack off on some of the tough workouts you'll face in this phase. I believe in being flexible, even to the extent of rearranging the days on which you perform various quality sessions. For example, Tuesday's session might be moved to Monday or Wednesday to avoid nasty weather. But make every effort to get in all scheduled training some time during each week.

Races during this phase can produce performance breakthroughs and confidence boosts, often because a serious race can replace a dreaded training session and might produce a surprisingly good result at a time when you're not peaking for a top performance. This is a good time to race distances that are either shorter or longer than your primary event of interest. Off-distance races can stress you in a way that makes a normally difficult workout seem much more tolerable. For example, racing 1,500 meters or a mile, when your primary event is 3,000 or 5,000 meters, will often make subsequent interval and repetition sessions seem easier than before.

Running a race during phase III can bring about a change in perspective by elevating your perceived level of fitness and building your confidence.

Phase II: Early Quality Training

When I approach EQ training, I generally ask two questions: What type of training can the athlete handle considering what has been done so far? And what will best prepare the runner for the next phase? This means that the type of running that you feel is most important in the TQ and FQ phases of training must be prepared for in this EQ phase. In a rather short season, some runners might find that there's not enough time to include an EQ phase in the overall scheme of the season. A formal phase II, however, can go a long way in making your season's goals more attainable.

Early quality training is designed to introduce faster workouts into a season's program after the initial FI phase. During phase II, I like to include strides and reps in the weekly schedule. Reps (primarily 200s and 400s at current mile race pace, with plenty of recovery time between runs) and strides (20- to 40-second runs at about mile race pace, using a light, quick leg cadence) go a long way in building good mechanics early in the season. Improving mechanics (which improves running economy) and strength (which is associated with faster running) also reduces the chance of injury. I usually recommend five or six strides as part of at least two or three workouts each week (during warm-ups and cool-downs and in the middle of or at the end of long runs).

The faster, usually **R**-pace, running used for most phase II programs prepares the muscles mechanically for the more stressful **I** training that's typical of phase III quality workouts. Phase II reps are not very taxing on the cardiovascular and aerobic systems, so the overall stress imposed on the body is not great. During phase III, when more demanding intervals are involved, the new stress will be primarily limited to the aerobic systems of performance. On the other hand, if intervals are performed in phase II, then mechanical and aerobic stresses will be introduced at the same time, with a good chance of overload. In this type of situation, coaching philosophy, tempered by the needs of each runner, should ultimately determine the type of training that goes into a particular phase of the season's overall plan.

Phase I: Foundation and Injury Prevention Training

The steady, easy running that produces many desirable cellular benefits while minimizing the chance of injury (as long as the amount of running isn't increased too rapidly) makes the FI phase the ideal type of training for early in the season. As the season progresses, the benefits of steady, longer running are maintained physiologically even with reduced emphasis on this type of training.

During this phase take care not to increase stress too rapidly, which is a real temptation because you have yet to do any really stressful training, in terms of intensity, and it's common to want to increase mileage quickly. Stick with my recommendation not to increase weekly mileage more often than every third week, and you'll seldom run into trouble in this regard. Learn to recognize signs of fatigue or too much running too soon, and don't be afraid to take a day off now and then to keep yourself feeling in control of your running.

It's a mistake to get caught up in letting mileage become so important that it dominates your training, especially if you maintain this attitude when moving into subsequent phases of training when various types of quality running are your primary emphasis. Of course, marathoners and ultramarathoners often view long runs as being of primary importance during most of their season, and, keeping with the priorities I set for determining types of training, I'd say in many cases they're right. As I've mentioned, the benefits of high mileage are well preserved once attained, so don't fear dropping some mileage later on during the season while you're emphasizing other types of training.

Phase I is the time to get yourself into a good daily schedule of running, eating well, and sleeping regularly. If morning runs are to be a part of your overall program, schedule some, even if they're very short, just to get in the habit.

Step 3: Determine How Much Quality Training

The next step in introducing details into a season of training is to determine how much of each type of training to include in each of the chosen phases. I try to include two or three types of quality training in each week of each different phase of the overall program. This usually means I give primary emphasis to one type of training, secondary emphasis to another, and, occasionally, maintenance emphasis to a third. In many school situations, one of these emphases (and sometimes more than one) is, by necessity, a race, which still should be worked into the overall scheme of training.

Many runners keep track of their weekly mileage, and some also add up the amount of faster quality running they do week by week. A factor that often gets little or no consideration is how different types (and intensities) of training fit into the overall training plan. I feel it's important to monitor not only mileage but also the amount of faster running you're performing. In chapter 2, I presented a new concept in keeping track of quality running, an approach that I hope will provide runners and coaches with a new and useful instrument in their bag of training tools.

Step 4: Plot a Weekly Schedule

When plotting out each week's schedule, consider the workout of primary emphasis first. If, for example, you're in phase III, where interval training is of primary concern and midseason races limit you to just one quality session for the week, then that workout should be at **I** pace (unless, of course, the races you're performing replace or offer the same benefits as interval training offers). When possible, do the primary emphasis (Q1) workout in desirable conditions so that you have a good chance of completing it on a positive note. It's also usually best to schedule the primary workout for earlier in the week, so that you're more likely to get it done and don't have to worry about poor weather spoiling your plans later in the week.

When your competitive schedule permits, each week you'll usually include another session (Q2) on the system of secondary emphasis. For example, when **I** running is of primary emphasis, a secondary emphasis might be on **T** runs, which are a different stress but still of good quality and of importance to another component of fitness. In addition, a long run or some reps added to the end of a **T** session can help maintain the benefits of an earlier emphasis on easy running or an **R** phase of training.

If you follow the idea that you'll do one primary and one secondary workout each week and a maintenance workout every other week, this means that in a six-week block of training, you'll have six primary, six secondary, and three maintenance sessions—15 quality workouts over a six-week phase of training. You can also view it as having three quality sessions one week, followed by two quality sessions the next week, and so on. In effect you're alternating harder and easier weeks of training. When there's a weekly competition during this type of training scheme, then the (usually Saturday) competition replaces the scheduled Saturday training session.

Mix In Competitions With Quality Training

Another approach is to schedule three quality sessions each week, with the primary emphasis being the first quality day, the secondary emphasis being the second quality day, and a maintenance day, or an additional primary day (Q3), scheduled for Saturday of the week. The advantage of this scheme is that each week has a primary and a secondary session, and some weeks also have an additional primary or maintenance emphasis, again depending on whether a competition is scheduled for that week. In fact, to ensure both a primary and a secondary session each week, in the event of a midweek competition, the secondary quality session could replace the usually scheduled Saturday session to free up the midweek date for competition.

The key factor is to always give top priority to a primary quality workout and then to include a secondary and, possibly, an additional quality workout in that order, with competitions first replacing the maintenance or second primary session, as desired. However, keep in mind that the competition events might better replace one type of training than another, which can also dictate the type of training session that you can best afford to drop for that week. Figure 4.3 shows some possibilities regarding the placement of easy, primary (Q1), secondary (Q2), and maintenance (or additional primary, Q3) sessions in weeks with and without a Saturday competition.

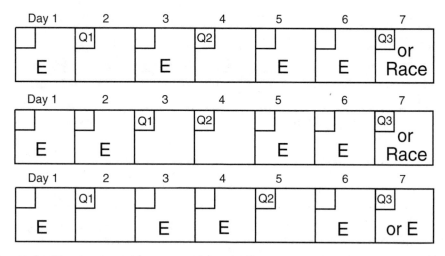

Figure 4.3 Three possible weekly schemes for quality 1 (Q1), quality 2 (Q2), and quality 3 (Q3) workouts.

In looking over figure 4.3, notice that one of the examples I've provided involves back-to-back quality days on Tuesday and Wednesday each week. I've found this to be a particularly good way of arranging a schedule when you want two quality sessions in the same week and you also have a Saturday competition to end the week. The advantages include the following:

- You get two easy days of training after a Saturday race and before another quality session.
- You get two easy days before a Saturday race.
- Knowing you have to come back with a good session on Wednesday keeps you from getting carried away with Tuesday's workout and trying to set a workout record of some kind.
- Having finished a solid day of training on Tuesday tends to keep you from over-training on Wednesday.

What I've been describing refers mainly to weeks of training when competitions aren't a high priority ("high priority" meaning qualifying and championship meets). Figure 4.4 shows a few examples of a weekly training scheme when the weekend competition is particularly important. Remember that even though you might continue with a good quality session in the week leading up to an important competition, the usual tactic is to lower the weekly mileage and amount of quality training (but not necessarily the intensity). On the other hand, it's not wise to increase intensity (speed) of running in the final week before an important race, because increased intensity often leads to muscle soreness. An important rule to follow in the days (or even the couple of weeks) leading up to important races is not to do anything you're not used to doing regularly.

Sometimes it's best for your one quality day of the week leading up to an important competition to be on the day four days before the race; other times, it might be better

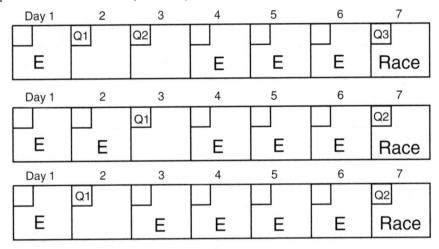

Figure 4.4 Three sample weekly training schemes when preparing for an important competition.

to go with the final quality session five days before race day. In either case, you can still include a few quality strides or 200s up to three days before the important race, but be especially careful not to run anything that's faster than normal for you—not even a small amount. Keeping some light, quick strides as part of the final days can be particularly useful if the coming important competition is a meet lasting several days. On the other hand, you can approach a single-day effort (such as a cross country national or state championship) very nicely with more days of just easy running.

Keep Long Runs In Perspective.

Throughout these weeks of training, I assume that Sunday is probably a long run, but this run is still considered an easy day in terms of intensity. On the other hand, if you specialize in distances of 10K or longer, there are definitely times when you can count a long run as a quality day.

Let me say something about replacing workouts with races. In general, you can consider a race that lasts from about 8 to 30 minutes to stress aerobic capacity greatly enough that races within this range of distances would normally replace a good interval workout for the week in question. For races shorter than 3,000 meters, and particularly when a runner competes in several races in the same meet (say the mile, 800 meters, and a leg on a 4 × 400 relay), then this type of session would replace a rep workout. Sometimes when you're using a meet to replace a workout you can add some extra running to the races, making the day a full-blown workout. For example, you might race a mile and run a leg on a relay. After the formal racing, you might want to get in a set of six or so repeat 200s at **R** pace. This makes a full **R** session out of the day. For an interval day, you might follow a 3,000-meter race or maybe a shorter cross country race (5,000 meters or less) with a trip around the course doing one-minute or two-minute **I**-pace runs or a light fartlek session. Too often the tendency is to say, "We didn't do much at that meet today, so we better try to get in some quality training tomorrow and avoid missing out on our scheduled training this week." I prefer to extend a race day's demands a little by having athletes follow the race with some additional quality running. This helps fill out a full session, thereby eliminating the need to add another quality day to the week.

Put It All Together

Once you decide which days of each week will receive special attention in terms of quality training, as shown in figures 4.3 and 4.4, the next step is to indicate what type of workout goes with which day. For example, if you're in phase II of training, with primary emphasis on **R** running, place an "**R**" on the calendar where there's a "Q1" in the schedule. If your current secondary emphasis is at threshold pace, then simply place a "**T**" in each day marked with "Q2." Do the same thing for any other day identified as a Q day.

When your program switches to a new phase of training, you merely change what Q1, Q2, and Q3 stand for and go on to the new schedule. In part IV I provid sample training programs that follow this plan for events from 800 meters to the marathon.

Keep in mind that this is where coaching philosophy plays a major role in setting up a program. Different coaches like different system emphases during various phases of a season's program. Following the plan outlined here helps keep the coach (and runner) focused on the idea that particular systems are receiving different degrees of priority for determined periods of time throughout the season.

I base part of my coaching philosophy on the premise that it takes a long time to attain greatness and that skill should come before conditioning. By this I mean that it's better to develop speed (skill) before endurance (aerobic conditioning). I should clarify, though, that I believe in this approach over a number of seasons of training, not necessarily within every season. So, what I really believe in is helping runners to

- learn good technique as youngsters,
- work toward speed development without high mileage during the developmental years of high school and college, and
- progressively carry out more endurance work later in their careers.

I consider this an ideal approach. Unfortunately, in our scholastic-based athletic system such an approach can rob young runners of athletic scholarships because the endurance needed to demonstrate good distance times might not be adequately developed by the time the runner reaches college age. But there can still be some compromises made in today's scholastic coaching by high school coaches working more for speed in early years and adding some endurance as the runners move into their final year or two of high school competition.

You can also use this ideal approach (of moving from speed to endurance training) as a model for seasonal programs, which for some runners and coaches might appear to throw the training components out of order (according to traditional training ideas). For example, faster training is often understood as requiring increased emphasis later in the season. However, it usually takes several weeks to rebound from a phase of fast workouts, and better races often come after the bulk of fast training has been discarded or reduced for the season. One of the real keys to taking advantage of repetition work is to reduce total weekly mileage as well as the amount of quality work being done. A program of some fast running (but not faster than usual) coupled with threshold training works well at the end of a season for distance runners who like to maintain some quality running with minimal stress and good day-to-day recovery.

For long-term development, future distance runners are sometimes better off alternating sports rather than simply performing more and more running. This can be true because muscle weakness often leads to injuries, and performing only easy, long-distance training does little for muscle strength. Without good strengthening programs (which often come with participation in other sports and which should always accompany a physical education program), aspiring distance runners are set up perfectly for injuries. Add to this the desire of young runners (and often their coaches and parents) to reach outstanding performances as soon as possible, and it's no wonder that young distance runners (particularly females) have a high incidence of injury, leading to a high dropout rate from the sport. Athletes who take up running after they've reached physical maturity usually avoid injuries that plague young beginners; the more mature runners are physically stronger and often aren't unreasonably driven (by themselves or by a coach) to try to peak in performance before they're ready.

Most beginning runners fall into one of three categories:

1. Runners who start running before reaching physical maturity
2. Runners who begin running in their early years of physical maturity
3. Runners who take up running well after reaching physical maturity and after they've completed their years of formal education

Young beginners would do best to follow the 1,500- to 3,000-meter program (see chapter 17), possibly downgrading interval training to nothing more than maintenance emphasis during any phase of training. These youngsters need reps and threshold training to learn good mechanics and to get in good quality with limited stress. More mature youngsters can handle a slightly tougher approach, but they're still better off in a 1,500-meter to 3,000-meter program. On the other hand, older beginners might find the marathon approach—but with limited mileage—to be a good start to formal training. This latter group might also want to extend phase I training or consider one of the fitness programs presented in chapters 11 through 14.

For runners who participate in another sport during the winter, consider the demands of the other sport and figure a way to work it into your overall running plan. Many runners who do another sport in the winter are involved in basketball, which demands fast running and jumping. From a physiological point of view, these activities accomplish some of the same things as rep training. A runner involved in basketball can spend less time on reps and more time on other systems once formal running training commences. Some runners get involved in cross-country skiing or ice hockey in the winter. The explosive, speed training of hockey and the endurance required in cross-country skiing are useful in determining what to include in (or leave out of) an upcoming outdoor track season.

Again, I want to stress that athletes who have only a few weeks of running training available to them (because of participation in other sports) must scrutinize the final phase of training because that might be their only chance to get in some event-specific training. Under such circumstances, other desirable aspects of an ideal season might have to be scrapped for lack of time. Often, multisport athletes miss out on a good muscle endurance base. But if running is an important long-term goal for an athlete, it's often better to ignore endurance at an early age than it is to neglect speed.

Programs for Less Experienced Runners

A few words for those of you who take up running later in life. I've geared most of this chapter's discussion toward younger runners, particularly in regard to spending the early years focusing on developing technique and speed. But if you're coming to running as an adult, what works for young runners might not work best for you. In your case, starting with easy, aerobic running often works best, primarily because racing is probably not your top priority; more likely, your motivation for running is getting good, healthy, aerobic exercise. This is why I recommend considering one of the fitness plans in part III (chapters 11 through 14) as a starting place.

Once older runners have reached a reasonable level of fitness, however, many want to test themselves in a race of some kind. This often leads to wanting to run faster, and it's at this time that the idea of quality workouts starts to become a reality. I still think some repetition training can be beneficial, but I've found that there's more enjoyment (and still desirable results) in a program that minimizes intervals and repetitions and focuses more on threshold training as the main quality emphasis.

Table 4.1 gives examples of how training might be broken down for runners interested in different events. Always keep in mind that it's important to adjust to individual differences, which might alter the way different phases of training are arranged. I encourage coaches and potential runners to work on general body conditioning, basic leg speed, and good running mechanics, particularly during early phases of each season.

Table 4.1 **Training Emphases for the Four Phases**

Training phase	Emphasis	800m to 3,000m	5K to 15K and cross country	Marathon
I		Easy runs/strides	Easy runs/strides	Easy runs/strides
II	Q1 Primary	Reps or hills	Reps or hills	Reps or interval
	Q2 Secondary	Threshold	Threshold	Threshold
	Q3 Maintenance	Interval	Interval	Long or threshold/long
III	Q1 Primary	Interval	Interval	Interval or threshold/long
	Q2 Secondary	Reps	Reps or hills	Threshold
	Q3 Maintenance	Threshold	Long	Marathon pace
IV	Q1 Primary	Reps	Threshold	Threshold/marathon pace
	Q2 Secondary	Threshold	Interval/reps	Threshold/long
	Q3 Maintenance	Interval	Reps/interval	Marathon pace/long

Step 5: Include Planned Breaks

Runners should take a few weeks off occasionally as scheduled breaks from training. Of course, some runners experience forced breaks because of illness or injury (unplanned setbacks are discussed in chapter 10), but here I'm concerned with breaks that are planned as part of the season's training.

Although runners are often reluctant to take breaks, most breaks are beneficial in terms of overall development. A break gives both the body and the mind some time to regroup from what might have been a pretty strenuous period of training and competition. Good health, both mental and physical, is more likely to occur when a runner is training moderately and leading a low-stress lifestyle. Continuous exhaustive training can place too much wear and tear on runners' bodies and have an adverse psychological effect.

It's true that some runners pick up new habits—such as overeating—during a break from training. However, these habits can sometimes be productive. Overeating, for example, can actually enable some runners to build up depleted iron stores that will serve them well when strenuous training is resumed. Breaks in training also allow little injuries to heal, ones that might not have been serious enough to interrupt training but that could have become much worse had hard workouts continued.

Another benefit to taking a planned break is that when you return, you approach your running program with renewed enthusiasm. After a break, you're fresh physically and mentally; in most cases, you're eager to work toward new goals you've set for yourself. Although fitness has been reduced during the break, big improvements can occur once training resumes. Remember the principle of training that says maintaining fitness is easier than achieving it in the first place (principle 7, chapter 1)? A similar principle applies to regaining a previous level of fitness—it's easier to regain a level of fitness than it is to attain it in the first place. You've been there before, so experience is on your side.

Depending on interests and lifestyles, the best time for a planned break varies for runners. It also depends somewhat on the type of training program being followed. For example, some runners don't train very much during the winter, especially if they live in adverse climates and have limited facilities for indoor training. For them, winter is a good time to take a planned break. Other distance runners have little or no interest in cross country, so for them the competitive cross country season might be a good time for a planned break. Many high school and college runners use early summer as their downtime from regular training after competing in cross country in the fall, indoor track in the winter, and outdoor track in the spring.

You should plan your breaks as part of plotting out your season of training. Simply work back from the most important part of your upcoming season and see where a break best fits. Don't just take a break because it's the end of a particular season or because friends and teammates are goofing off for a while. Each runner should have his or her own plan. Of course, if your plan is the same as a whole group of other runners, you might all have the same break time. In any case, I recommend a serious break of a few weeks from training at least once per year, and it might also be wise to take other shorter breaks at different times in the same year.

How Long a Break Lasts

The length and timing of a break depends on how hard your training has been and how many unplanned setbacks you've endured over the past year. If there's been a lengthy setback or two or a few smaller setbacks during the season, they might have provided the physical and mental recovery you need so that a planned break is unnecessary. In such a case, you should be able to go right into the next season without taking a planned break.

In the case of a female runner who's having a baby, the break might last a year or more; the same might be true for a runner who wants to devote a significant amount of time to pursuing a career. At the other extreme, a break might last only a few weeks. Sometimes, a couple of two-week breaks fit into an annual schedule quite well, but eventually a more prolonged break (four to six weeks) is probably a good idea.

Many coaches and runners don't want to take time away from running, especially when things are going well, for fear of losing fitness. Such individuals tend to be pessimistic types who figure there will eventually be an unplanned setback that will serve the same purpose. I don't think you should ever plan on unplanned setbacks, because that's a pretty sure way for a serious setback to occur. In any case, don't look at a planned break from training as a setback in your progression toward better times. Look at breaks as important, useful steps toward reaching your long-term goals. Convince yourself that the break is an actual phase of training, a stepping-stone toward better training and superior performances.

What to Do During a Planned Break

A planned break might include small amounts of running or might be a complete furlough from running. If it takes place during the winter, the break might consist of fairly extensive cross-country skiing or other sports, depending on interests, climate, and conditions during the break time. It's also okay for the break to involve no special physical activities at all; some runners like to escape a structured lifestyle for a while. Yet, other runners might be comforted to know that a break can still involve some light running. For someone who has been running regularly for a long time, daily running has become no greater stress than a typical nonexercise lifestyle for a sedentary person. For experienced runners, light running can be part of a "sedentary" lifestyle.

In the hierarchy of training, breaks rank right up there with threshold runs, intervals, reps, and steady running. Each has a function, and when placed in proper sequence, they each build on one another. If it makes you feel any better about taking breaks, add "break training" to the other types of workouts I've described earlier, and then plan a program to follow during this phase. The program might involve, for example, walking two hours a day, reading an hour each day, or visiting friends for six hours on weekends. Often, a training break offers a great opportunity to carry out a strength program or to learn more about stretching and relaxation. In whatever way you visualize your break, remember to look at it as a positive part of your overall plan. Your breaks play an important part in helping your body and mind rebuild for the next season or phase of training.

Returning to Running After a Planned Break

When a break ends and you're ready to start working out seriously again, follow this advice:

1. Refer to tables 4.2 and 4.3 and review the associated information.
2. Don't race until you've completed at least one phase of training.
3. Refer to the early pages of this chapter to review the procedure used in designing a new or revised program.
4. Long breaks can be associated with substantial changes in body composition (for better or for worse) or might have been accompanied by serious illness, injury, surgery, or pregnancy, so regain normal, healthy strength and body weight before progressing to quality phases of training (to accomplish this, you might have to extend the initial steady run phase of training). Don't let a

break cause concern that time has been lost and that training should thus be accelerated to make up for lost time. If you follow appropriate training rules, your previous level of competitive fitness will return, probably more quickly than you expect.

5. Have confidence in what you're doing; you have a sensible plan of training, and it will produce excellent results.

In an attempt to take some of the guesswork out of the return to training following a break or setback, I provide some guidelines in tables 4.2 and 4.3. But keep in mind that you need to make two basic adjustments in your training program—one in intensity of running and the other in amount.

Adjusting Intensity

Table 4.2 is a guide for adjusting intensity of training based on your time away from normal training. Remember how I've presented the idea of using a VDOT value to determine training intensities? Current VDOT drives the speed at which you do each type of training—steady, long runs, marathon-pace runs, threshold runs, intervals, and reps. As you improve your fitness with training, your VDOT improves, as do the various training intensities. The same thing applies when your fitness deteriorates, as invariably occurs with a setback. If you haven't engaged in cross-training, multiply the FVDOT-1 value in the table by your pre-setback VDOT to determine your new VDOT. If you've done cross-training while away from running, multiply FVDOT-2 by your pre-setback VDOT.

Table 4.2 **VDOT Adjustments for Time Off From Running**		
Time off from running	**FVDOT-1**	**FVDOT-2**
Up to 5 days	1.000	1.000
6 days	.997	.998
7 days (1 week)	.994	.997
10 days	.985	.992
14 days (2 weeks)	.973	.986
21 days (3 weeks	.952	.976
28 days (4 weeks)	.931	.965
35 days (5 weeks)	.910	.955
42 days (6 weeks)	.889	.994
49 days (7 weeks)	.868	.934
56 days (8 weeks)	.847	.923
63 days (9 weeks)	.826	.913
70 days (10 weeks)	.805	.902
72 days or more	.800	.900

For example, if you've taken two weeks off training, table 4.2 indicates that your return-to-training VDOT should be 97.3 percent of the pre-setback VDOT (multiply the pre-setback VDOT by 0.973 to get a new training-intensity VDOT). If during the break you cross-trained, use an adjustment of 0.986 instead of 0.973. Table 4.2 also indicates some extremes. You might notice that with five or fewer days missed, no adjustment is needed. Once you've missed 72 days (usually in the case of injury or illness; see chapter 10) you have just about reached the end of possible deterioration. This adjustment (0.800) is representative of the fact that optimal training can improve VDOT by about 20 percent (0.200), so it stands to reason that you can't deteriorate more than you could improve in the first place.

If you lost or gained weight during your time off, you'll need to adjust your VDOT to account for your weight change. Use the following method to figure your adjusted VDOT:

Enter your pre-setback weight in kilograms in A

(weight in kilograms = weight in pounds × 0.454)   (A)_____

Enter pre-setback VDOT in B   (B)_____

Multiply A × B to get C   (C)_____

Divide C by current weight in kilograms to get D   (D)_____

D is your weight-adjusted VDOT. Apply the appropriate FVDOT value from table 4.2 to D to determine the VDOT on which you should base your comeback training. Once you resume racing, use race times to establish an updated VDOT.

Adjusting Mileage or Duration

Just as table 4.2 addresses the issue of intensity adjustment, table 4.3 provides a guide for adjusting the amount of training (mileage) following a break from training, whether planned or unplanned. Table 4.3 also provides recommendations and examples for the time spent at reduced amounts of weekly mileage.

In addition to the formula for mileage reduction shown in column four, I've given the time (column two) at various reduced loads that would apply for one or more examples in that category. For a category II setback, for example, the first half of the return time is easy running at 50 percent of the pre-setback weekly mileage. A runner who had been doing 40 miles per week prior to setback, and who missed two weeks of training, would total about 20 miles the first week back (50 percent of pre-setback weekly mileage) and 30 miles the second week back (75 percent of original mileage). Both of these return weeks would involve nothing more than steady, easy running. Easy pace would be driven by 97.3 percent of original VDOT, shown in table 4.2 as 0.973 for two weeks off.

Another runner who missed six weeks, but who cross-trained diligently, would take 94.4 percent of his or her original VDOT to determine training intensity (0.944 in table 4.2) and would determine load adjustments from category III in table 4.3. If this runner was doing 60 miles per week pre-setback, then the first third of the return time (two weeks) would be at 20 miles per week (one third of 60 = 20) of easy running, which would be followed by two weeks at 30 miles per week (50 percent load) of easy running. The final two weeks of return would allow for 45 miles per week (75 percent load) of easy running plus some strides to start to regain a feeling for moving a little faster than easy pace.

Table 4.3 **Adjustments to Training Following a Setback**

Category	Time off from running *or* time at adjusted intensity	Adjustment to make (pace at % pre-setback load)	% of pre setback VDOT
I	Up to 5 days	**E** @ no more than 100% load	100%
	5 days	5 days **E** @ no more than 100% load	100%
II	6 to 28 days	First half: **E** @ 50% load Second half: **E** @ 75% load	See table 4.2
	6 days	3 days **E** @ 50% load + 3 days **E** @ 75% load	99.7%
	28 days	14 days **E** @ 50% load + 14 days **E** @ 75% load	93.1%
III	4 to 8 weeks	First third: **E** @ 33% load Second third: **E** @ 50% load Final third: **E** @ 75% load with strides	See table 4.2
	29 days	9 days **E** @ 33% + 10 days **E** @ 50% + 10 days **E** @ 75 % with strides	93.1%
	8 weeks	18 days **E** @ 33% + 19 days **E** @ 50% + 19 days **E** @ 75% with strides	84.7%
IV	8 weeks or more	3 weeks **E** @ 33%; not greater than 30 miles per week 3 weeks **E** @ 50%; not greater than 40 miles per week 3 weeks **E** @ 70% + strides; not greater than 60 miles per week 3 weeks **E** @ 85% + strides + **R**; not greater than 75 miles per week 3 weeks **E** @ 100% + strides + **T** + **R**; not greater than 90 miles per week	See table 4.2

Notes: The shaded boxes show examples of each category. Refer to table 4.2 for a detailed list of percentage of VDOT to use on return to running, based on days off. Go to normal training (see phases of training in this chapter) after at least six weeks of return training. With serious cross-training (see chapter 10), reduce VDOT by only half the amount shown in the table. Adjustments to VDOT might be needed because of weight change, explained on page 86.

Following whatever time frame, mileages, and intensity that the return formulae dictate, the runner is then free to return to the full pre-setback values and to follow normal procedures for increasing load and intensity, as described in earlier chapters. I want to reiterate the possible need to revalue VDOT as dictated by changes in weight or body composition.

———

Whatever type of training program you decide on, follow one that's enjoyable enough (or at least rewarding enough) that you'll stay with it long enough to find out how good you're capable of becoming. Train in such a way that you are able to look back and say you enjoyed the training as much as you enjoyed the outcome of a well-run race. That is the real sign of a good training program.

Ryan Hall

Ryan Hall was born in Kirkland, Washington, and started his athletic career playing T-ball, baseball, basketball, soccer, and football. He started running when he was 15 years old and was not particularly fond of it until one day on the way to a basketball game, while gazing at a peaceful lake, he felt God had a future for him in running. Ryan immediately turned from hating to run to having a passion for the sport. From the time he started running, his main event interest has always been the 1,500 meters and the mile. Asked when he first realized he was capable of performing at a national or international level, he responded "Day 1," referring to the day he realized running was for him. Ryan attended Big Bear High school in California, and his initial running goals were to earn a college scholarship, break four minutes in the mile while in high school, go to the Olympics, win an Olympic gold medal, and set a world record.

Photo courtesy of Ryan Hall

He admits that he is now more focused on the process of getting to his goals (rather than the goals themselves) and that it is important to him to set a good example with his faith. I first met Ryan when I was a counselor at one of Jim Ryun's running camps and later when he was a runner at Stanford and I was working with the Farm Team. It's amazing how favorably his lab test results compare with those of Jim Ryun. Ryan has been a member of two Stanford University NCAA cross country championship teams, and in 2003 he was the individual second-place finisher at the NCAA cross country nationals. In the summer of 2004 Ryan and I met again, this time both as counselors at a Jim Ryun running camp.

Personal bests: 1,500m—3:42.7; 5,000m—13:45; 10K cross country—29:15

PART II

Training Levels

In this part I discuss intensities of training in some detail, moving from relatively slow and comfortable speeds to hard and eventually fast speeds of running. I've set aside separate chapters for easy running, marathon-pace running, threshold intensity, interval training, and repetition training. I include a new table on training speeds for tempo runs longer than those typically associated with threshold-intensity running.

Photo courtesy of Mark Smith

Each type of training has its particular place in a training program, and you should always be able to answer the question, "What is the purpose of this workout?" In a progression of running velocity associated with the different types of training presented in this part of the book, easy (**E**) runs are of course "easy," marathon-pace (**M**) runs are "relatively easy," and threshold (**T**) running is "comfortably hard." Interval (**I**) training is "hard," and repetition (**R**) is "fast" but not necessarily hard. You need to learn to recognize how each of these training intensities feels so you won't always have to rely on specific distances in predetermined times to get the most out of your training.

I conclude part II with a description of supplemental training and the ways various nonrunning exercises might benefit your training. I also discuss injury and illness, and how they can be dealt with. After reading part II, you should be well prepared to take on a training program of your choosing, be it for fitness or for competition at the elite level of performance.

CHAPTER 5

Level 1: Base Building

Regardless of the phase of training you're in, always know why you're doing what you're doing. Have some goals in mind. If you haven't been running very long, start out with only easy running. As I mentioned in chapter 4, I call this initial period of **E**-pace training "foundation and injury-prevention training." This is a good time to develop a regular stretching and muscle-strengthening routine to supplement your more formal running regimen.

Participants in any sport need to spend some time subjecting the body to low-intensity stress, mainly to prepare the body for more quality training, but also to develop those components of fitness that respond well to low-stress training. In this chapter I address the types of training that fall into the category of relatively low-intensity stress—training that could be called "conversational" because you can carry on a conversation with another runner while running. I also explain how to keep track of the amount of running you're doing and how to increase mileage.

How much time you spend in this foundation phase might vary a good deal, but unless you're starting this phase following some serious running associated with another sport, I recommend setting aside at least 6 weeks for this phase, and it could be a fair bit longer if you have more than 24 weeks of preparation time for important races.

Training is often demanding and not necessarily fun, but it should always be rewarding.

Determine Your Weekly Mileage

A good measure of how much work you're doing as a runner is how much distance you're covering. It costs just about the same amount of energy to run eight miles in 40 minutes as it does to run eight miles in 60 minutes; you're doing the same amount of work—only the rate is different. However, the amount of work (mileage) that you're performing represents only part of the stress to which you're subjecting yourself. Slower runners spend more time accumulating the same mileage covered by faster runners, and more time on the road means more footfalls, more landing impact, and a greater chance for increased fluid loss and elevated body temperature. Thus, although mileage achieved is a logical starting point, it's also useful to keep track of total time spent running.

Keep track of your weekly mileage so that you can use this record as a basis for how much of the various types of quality work you do and so that your training is consistent. Just as you use your current VDOT or (based on current racing ability) to guide your training intensities, you can use your current weekly mileage to set limits on quality sessions—but use time spent running to log points accumulated at various intensities of running.

In the case of weekly mileage, remember the principles of stress and reaction (principle 1, page 8) and diminishing return (principle 5, page 12) I discussed in chapter 1. Stay with a set amount of mileage for at least three weeks before increasing your mileage. This gives your body a chance to adjust to and benefit from a particular load before moving on to a more demanding one. When it's time to increase your mileage, add to your weekly total as many miles (or one and a half times as many kilometers) as the number of training sessions you're doing each week, up to a maximum of a 10-mile (15-kilometer) total adjustment. For example, after at least three weeks of 20 miles per week spread over five training sessions, your maximum increase should be 5 miles or 7.5 kilometers—1 mile (or 1.5 kilometers) for each of the five sessions you're doing each week. In this case, you would be moving from 20 to 25 miles per week.

A runner who's doing 10 or more workout sessions per week could increase his or her weekly total by 10 miles, after spending at least three weeks at the previous amount. Let a 10-mile (15-kilometer) weekly increase be the maximum mileage change, even if you're running two or more daily sessions seven days a week. Another way of dealing with increases in weekly training load is to add to the weekly total the lesser of 60 minutes per week or 6 minutes multiplied by the number of training sessions you undertake each week.

I think that two hours a day of running is quite a lot, and it's unusual for even elite runners to run more than three hours a day (about 30 miles a day for an elite distance runner). Remember that stress is a function of time spent doing something, and that's why a 20-mile run is more stressful for a slow runner than for a faster one. It's not just the 20 miles but the time spent completing those 20 miles. The increased number of steps can wear you down, and the extra hour in the heat or on slick roads can take its toll. To avoid overtraining and injury, slower runners might have to run less total mileage than faster runners.

STRIDE RATE: A STEP IN THE RIGHT DIRECTION

One of the first things I teach new runners is some basics about running cadence, or stride rate. Almost all elite distance runners (both men and women) tend to stride at about the same rate: 180 or more steps per minute. This means that they're taking 90 or more steps with each foot each minute, a rate that doesn't vary much even when they're not running fast. The main change that occurs as runners go faster is in stride length; the faster they go, the longer the stride becomes, with little change in rate of leg turnover.

The stride rate many beginning runners take is quite different from that of elite runners. When I have new runners count their own stride rates, I find that very few (sometimes none out of a class of 25 or 30) take as many as 180 steps per minute. In fact, some turn over as slowly as 160 times per minute. The main disadvantage of this slower turnover is that the slower you take steps, the longer you spend in the air, and the longer you're in the air, the higher you displace your body mass and the harder you hit the ground on landing. When you consider that many running injuries are the result of landing shock, it's not surprising that experienced runners tend to turn over faster than beginning runners do.

If a group of beginners were required to start running 100 miles a week, two things would probably occur: Many runners would hurt themselves, and many who didn't get hurt would adjust to taking quicker, lighter steps. I try to save runners a lot of grief by encouraging them to convert to a stride rate associated with less landing shock and more efficient use of energy.

Several studies have been conducted on the energy demands of different stride frequencies, and it turns out that experienced runners are most efficient at their chosen rate of turnover; longer or shorter strides (which mean slower or faster stride rates) result in greater energy demands. However, when working with less-experienced runners, running economy can often be improved by converting slow-turnover runners into runners who use a faster rate.

My wife and I spent most of our time at the 1984 Olympics counting and measuring stride rates and stride lengths of male and female runners competing in distance events from 800 meters up to the marathon. The results were convincing—the fastest turnover rates were among the 800-meter specialists, and next fastest were the 1,500-meter runners, but from the 3,000-meter distance on up to the marathon there was little variation in turnover rate. In fact, the women took only a few steps more per minute than did the larger men, who were often running considerably faster as a result of longer stride length.

Next time you watch a marathon race on television, count how many times the right arm of one of the runners swings forward in 20 or 30 seconds. Use the recorded number to calculate a one-minute rate (of course you're accepting the probability that the runner is swinging his or her right arm as often as he or she is taking steps). Try counting steps of the same runner at various stages

(continued)

(continued)

of the race. Chances are good that strong runners won't lose the cadence they began with. We often talk about getting into a good running rhythm, and the one you want to get into is one that involves 180 or more steps per minute.

If you count your own stride rate and find it's considerably slower than what I'm suggesting, try to work on a shorter, lighter stride. Imagine that you're running over a field of raw eggs and you don't want to break any of them—run *over* the ground, not into it. Try to get the feeling that your legs are part of a wheel that just rolls along, not two pogo sticks that bounce along.

If you feel that you need practice improving your stride rate, focus on this during easy runs. Rate usually goes up for slower-turnover people when they race shorter distances, so you may not need to think about it during faster quality training. When practicing turning over faster on easy training runs, don't let the fact that you're taking quicker steps force you to run faster. Try to run at your normal training speed, but do it with a shorter, quicker stride rate. With practice, you'll find it becomes quite natural and comfortable.

The number of right-arm swings, and thus the number of steps, taken by elite marathoners such as Paula Radcliffe varies little over the duration of a race.

Account for Individual Limits

The principle of personal limits (principle 4, page 12) advises you not to increase your training stress just because a three-week period at current mileage has elapsed. You must have a purpose for everything you do, and you must judge things by how you feel and how you perform in training and in races. You might find that 45 miles a week is ideal for you, based, for example, on your goals, available time, and injuries. This means that a mileage increase is not appropriate after three weeks. Also, you might not want to increase mileage as often as every third week, or by as many miles or kilometers as there are training sessions. That's fine; simply make smaller adjustments. Use the guidelines I've mentioned in this chapter and continue to follow the principles presented in Chapter 1 to avoid making too great a demand on yourself.

When is it time to put a cap on the workload you're imposing on yourself? This is an individual matter that each runner should consider prudently while keeping set goals in mind. A mileage total that works for one runner might be not enough, or might be too much, for another. Certainly a new runner shouldn't copy a veteran runner's training program. In addition to daily and weekly considerations, think of training in blocks of weeks, and even in yearly cycles. Weeks totaling 100 miles, or 10 to 15 hours of running, might be good for you, but usually only after a few years of lesser weekly mileage that gradually builds up to this amount. Besides the daily stresses imposed by training, there are more gradual long-term stresses that take their toll (and can produce adaptations, as well). What you're able to handle next year is a function of the stress you placed on yourself this year and the adaptations your body has made during the current season. Again, the principle of personal limits applies in this case.

Another factor that determines limits of weekly mileage is the event for which you're training. A marathoner needs more total mileage than an 800- or 1,500-meter specialist. Some people overlook this obvious fact. It's true that a 1,500-meter runner might reap considerable benefit by undergoing a period of high-mileage training, and that a marathoner can benefit from periods of lesser mileage while working on a specific system, but basically the marathoner should get in more distance than the shorter-distance specialist. The principle of specificity of training (principle 2, page 8) applies in this case.

Still, all marathoners shouldn't necessarily run 120 miles per week—not even if you polled the top 50 marathon men and women and found that they all run between 100 and 150 miles per week. Consider how many years they've been running; it might have taken them eight years to build up to what they're currently doing. Or maybe some of these top marathoners were once running higher mileage totals and have cut back to 120 miles per week. Also, remember that some of the top 50 marathoners might not be running as well as they could be on less (or more) mileage; they might have bodies that can handle more mileage stress than most people's bodies (the genetic factor); or they might have more time and financial backing to support the demands of the training program that they're following.

I wish I could simply say, "You must run *X* miles per week to be a good marathoner" or that there's a magic number of weekly miles needed for optimal development of an 800 runner—but I just don't believe the picture is clear enough to make statements like that. I feel comfortable saying that you should probably average somewhere between 70 and 150 miles (112 to 240 kilometers) per week to optimize your performance as a marathoner, but, then again, even 70 miles (112 kilometers) might be too much for some people, particularly during their first year or two of running. And some people might be able to go beyond 150 miles a week, such as the elite runner I knew (not a marathoner, by the way) who over 30 years ago ran an average of 240 miles per week one year, including a 300-mile weekly average for one six-week stretch. I think we see some pretty wide ranges in the weekly miles of 800-meter runners, from about 50 to over 100 miles a week among those I've been associated with.

The impossibility of laying out training loads that can be effectively applied to each and every runner is the very reason we'll never be able to do away with coaches. Runners need someone to say, "You're starting to look really good running," or, "You're looking sort of dead-legged—better cut back on the mileage for a while before an injury sets you back."

Include Rest Periods

Longer-term adaptations depend partly on how you treat your body. As I mentioned in chapter 4, you might need a full six-week rest period somewhere during the year. In fact, more than one planned "rest-from-running" period might be more appropriate for you than continuous training.

As with any type of training, monitor your results as you increase mileage and as you increase intensity. It's a long road to reaching your potential; rushing along that road too fast might send you on a detour and prevent you from taking the shortest path. Overtraining (see chapter 10), or hypertraining, shouldn't be your most common type of training. If you're doing well on a given amount of training and are eager to move up in mileage, it's okay to try an increase. If results are negative after several weeks, however, realize that an increase in mileage might not have been the right move for you at that time. Don't train harder for the sake of training harder; train harder to achieve better fitness and better performance. If you're not performing better after four to six weeks of more demanding training, or if your workouts aren't feeling easier, then admit that the harder work you're doing is not producing the desired results.

I'm a strong believer in avoiding overtraining rather than spending lots of time and money on researching at what point a runner is overtrained. The more we try to identify overtraining, the more likely we'll try to use the indices of overtraining as goals to shoot for. One of the best goals you can have is to race better by running faster times or to race well and recover more easily. Trying to drive your body fat down to 4 percent or running on the brink of overtraining are not desirable goals.

Runners' and coaches' egos can get in the way of optimal training. Sometimes it seems to mean more to talk about the great workouts you or your athletes have been doing than to watch the great race results come in. I'm not impressed by the guy who brags about doing 150-mile weeks but can't hold a competitive marathon pace for 20 miles, nor by the guy with the lab-determined 90 ml·kg^{-1}·min^{-1} $\dot{V}O_2$max who drops out at the 20-mile mark of a marathon because the pace was too fast. Both have been misled somewhere along the line.

Your training should bring you a certain degree of enjoyment and satisfaction. Don't let training performance be your goal, but do enjoy the training and the satisfaction of being fit and healthy. It's disheartening to hear someone say "I wasted four years of training" because he or she didn't make the Olympic team. If you carry that reasoning to the extreme, you could say that an Olympian wasted four years because he or she didn't win a gold medal (or three gold medals, or three gold medals plus three world records and a million-dollar endorsement). If winning is the only thing that rescues athletes from "wasting their time training," then a lot of unhappy people are wasting their time in sports. It's true that you train to improve performance, but many other benefits come from training as well.

Consider Your Terrain

Some runners live in flat areas, whereas others inhabit hilly terrain. Some runners have only paved streets and paths on which to run; others see only dirt, sand, grass, or rocky trails. Most runners have a nearby running track, be it all-weather or natural material in composition. Some runners have a treadmill at their disposal, which in itself constitutes another terrain feature to account for (see chapter 9 for details about treadmill training).

Regardless of the type of terrain you face, it's important to feel that no one has any advantages over you because of where they train and where you train. Certainly,

A demanding terrain can prove beneficial to runners who adopt the appropriate mind-set. These runners benefit from sea-level training in their native Lima, Peru, as well as training at the higher altitudes of the surrounding mountains.

given all the resources possible, an ideal terrain could be concocted for any runner, and chances are that this ideal would vary considerably depending on personal taste.

A hilly terrain might seem downright obnoxious to some runners, but others might feel that the constant challenge of hills makes them tougher competitors. Whatever terrain you're working with, find the good things about it. Think of running hills as a positive because afterward flat races will seem easy. Think of flat terrain as allowing for easier speedwork or steadier tempo runs. Think of rough footing as helping you develop greater resistance to injury, not as producing injuries. In other words, try to take what the terrain has to offer and work with it, not against it.

Easy Runs

Easy (**E**) runs are often run in the morning or as second runs in a two-a-day schedule. They also are used in the early phase of warm-up and cool-down sessions and during recovery between high-intensity training bouts. An **E** run means running easily, and on many days that's all a runner needs to do. I suggest a minimum of 30 minutes for most **E** runs; the stress isn't great, and the benefits are substantial. With **E** runs shorter than 30 minutes you're likely to spend more time changing clothes and showering than actually running. An **E** day of training could mean anything from no running (obviously easy) to two (or even more than two) different runs lasting up to an hour or so each. The important point is that the intensity is easy.

Long Runs

The long (**L**) run is a steady run performed at **E** pace (based on your VDOT). If you have no basis for determining a VDOT—if you haven't run any races recently or if you're unable to guess your current fitness—just make your **E** pace a comfortable, conversational pace. Set a long-run goal of 25 to 30 percent of your total weekly mileage or weekly duration of running, and place a two-and-a-half-hour limit on this run. Less-talented, less-fit, or less-experienced runners shouldn't necessarily set a specific distance for their **L**-run goal because they stand a greater chance of overstressing themselves (for example, a 20-mile run might take three hours or more to complete). Runs of three hours or more aren't popular for elite runners, so why should less experienced runners try them? Ultramarathoners and some marathoners will benefit from runs in excess of 23 miles, but the improvement in performance for races such as a marathon, half-marathon, 15K, and 10K is likely to be very slight (if it exists at all) in a physiological sense.

When I refer to setting the distance of the **L** run at 25 to 30 percent of weekly mileage, I'm talking about the long run for any runner, not just a marathoner. If you're doing 40 miles a week, your **L** run would be about 10 miles (25% of 40 = 10). The 30-percent value is more likely to be used by runners who train fewer than seven days per week at relatively low mileage. After all, someone who runs only four days a week is already averaging 25 percent of his or her weekly mileage per training session.

For many runners, marathon-pace (**M**) running is at a comfortable enough intensity that it fits in the category of base building. On the other hand, **M** pace is not always that comfortable and does require concentration to maintain for extended periods of time. For this reason, I've added a separate chapter (chapter 6) on **M**-pace training; I believe training at this pace will become a more important part of many runners' training programs, and justifiably so.

Easy runs, long runs, and (for some runners) marathon-pace runs are all beneficial to the development of important physiological attributes that stay with you and don't demand high-intensity stress to achieve. These types of training produce direct benefits and also contribute to the overall building of resistance to injury and to a solid foundation (base) on which to build faster training sessions in the weeks, months, and years ahead. Probably 80 to 85 percent of the running any runner does will be at an intensity associated with these types of runs. These runs are good opportunities to reap substantial benefits from relatively low-stress training. They're also almost always enjoyable to do.

Don't let total mileage dominate your training thoughts to the extent that you overlook other types of training. The benefits of easy and long runs stay with you; profit from them, then move on to other training, carrying the earlier benefits with you.

Shayne Culpepper

Shayne Culpepper was born in Atlanta, Georgia, and spent 10 of her early years pursuing gymnastics. Her dad started running when he was 30 years old, trained about 50 miles a week, and ran the Boston marathon in 2:30. His dedication and success prompted Shayne to give running a try. Her initial running interest was in cross country and the 800 meters on the track, and her initial goal as a competitive runner was to make it to her state championships, something that she never achieved.

© Victah Sailer

Shayne continued her running at the universities of Vermont and Colorado, and in the late 1990s had a series of successful performances at NCAA and USA national championships in the 1,500- and 3,000-meter distances. She first realized that she was capable of performing at the national and international level when she ran the 1,500 meters in 4:10 at the U.S. Nationals. In 2000, she placed 4th in the U.S. 4K cross country championships, 7th in the 5,000 meters and 4th in the 1,500 meters at the Olympic Trials, which earned her a place on the team. Following a maternity leave during the winter and spring of 2002, Shayne was the U.S. cross country 6K champion by fall and in 2003 won the 4K cross country championship. Success continued during 2004, with a win at the U.S. indoor nationals and a bronze medal at the World Indoor Championships in the 3,000 meters. During the outdoor season of 2004, Shayne scored a dramatic win in the U.S. Olympic Trials in the 5,000 meters, which earned her a trip to the Athens Olympic Games.

Personal bests: 800m—2:02.1; 1,500m—4:06.3; 3,000m—8:55.3; 5,000m—15:01.3

CHAPTER 6

Level 2: Marathon-Pace Training

I got the idea of marathon-pace (**M**) runs from one of my former subjects, Bob Williams, a very successful runner who is now a successful coach. Marathon-pace runs allow runners to spend time running at the pace at which they hope to race in upcoming marathons.

I like the duration of an **M** run to be between 90 and 150 minutes without exceeding 16 miles. (Runners who race 800 to 1,500 meters might find this pace appropriate for durations of 40 to 60 minutes.) Fairly long runs at this pace can be demanding, and sometimes it's a good idea to perform this type of training session in a race situation. Find a half-marathon race you can run at **M** pace or a marathon race in which you can run partway. Being around other runners makes this type of training run much easier to handle. When you do an **M** run as part of an official race, make sure you officially enter the race. Don't interfere with others, and don't get caught up in the excitement and go too fast or too far. For marathoners, an **M** run is a great opportunity to practice taking in water and gels or carbohydrate and electrolyte drinks while on the run and otherwise preparing for an impending marathon race.

In recent years, and with more involvement in training marathon runners, I've come to believe that training at marathon pace (**M**) has a definite place in many marathoners' training programs. I've also become convinced that **M** running can be useful in the programs of other

Completing your first marathon can change your outlook on the sport of running forever

distance runners not particularly interested in running a marathon. This pace is not very strenuous when used for runs of even an hour or longer, and being a little faster than a typical easy run, the pace provides many runners with an alternative to an easy run on a day when conditions are good and going a little faster might even be a relatively comfortable pace. Naturally marathon runners will schedule this type of training more often and for longer durations than shorter-distance specialists will, but I encourage the use of **M** runs as an occasional different stress for all runners. Most runners have days when things are just clicking, and a little faster than **E**-run pace (which might be **M** intensity) comes with relative ease.

With many of my slower runners, I find that some of their easy runs get so slow that technique suffers, which can lead to injury. The answer might be running a little faster. To prescribe a pace for this "faster than easy" run, I just use **M**, as shown in the VDOT tables. When doing this, I remind my runners to imagine themselves maintaining this pace for longer than the run is actually scheduled to last, which keeps them from going too fast.

Choosing Your Proper Pace

Usually, for a marathon runner—or runners who are experienced in other distances and are planning their first marathon—determining the proper marathon pace is not too difficult. By using the VDOT tables in chapter 3, it's quite easy to get a pretty good idea of the pace that you can handle for a marathon. On the other hand, first-time marathoners, shorter-distance specialists who aren't planning to run a marathon, or others who have minimal racing experience in running might have a real problem determining the pace they should try for an upcoming marathon. Actually, this is the ideal time to include some marathon-pace training in their program.

One approach is to look over the relative training intensities presented in chapter 2 (see tables 2.1 and 2.2). Here you can get an idea of the relative heart rates and percent $\dot{V}O_2$max (or VDOT) values that fall in the **M**-pace zone of training. Start off with an intensity at the lower end of the **M**-pace zone and use that for your initial **M** runs. Over a few weeks' time you can try moving up in that **M**-pace zone and monitor your body's reaction to the slightly more intense effort. Try to do the various test runs on days of similar climatic conditions and when you're in a similar state of readiness so that change in pace is the primary variable. Obviously, if several weeks have gone by you might have reached a better level of fitness, and a slightly faster **M** pace might not feel any more demanding at all. This is a good sign that you're progressing.

If you're planning to run a marathon and have based your **M** pace on a projected marathon time (or chosen **M** pace) and on several test runs of an hour or so, try the following workout. Plan this workout to total 2 hours or 20 miles, whichever comes first. After a couple of easy miles to get warmed up, move into a pace that's about three or four VDOT values slower than the marathon pace you think is reasonable for you. After about 20 to 25 minutes of this pace (30 minutes for faster runners), move up to the next faster VDOT **M**-pace intensity and run at this pace for the next 20 to 30 minutes. Arrange the run so that you end up using four different (increasingly faster)

© Human Kinetics

| Practicing runs at your projected marathon pace gives you extra confidence on the day of the race.

marathon paces for the total run, with the final one at a pace that's as fast as you would consider racing at. The advantage of this approach is that the fastest pace you'll use in this session comes late in a fairly long run at a pace you're considering for an upcoming marathon. This gives you a much more realistic idea of what your chosen marathon pace will feel like toward the latter stages of the actual marathon race.

It's not too difficult to handle 10 or 12 miles at **M** pace, but that same pace often gets to be a struggle in a longer run. One of the reasons for this is that as you start to deplete energy stores, you lose fluid and build up heat. The key to running a good marathon is to handle your chosen pace under these adverse conditions. With this in mind, it's desirable to see how that feels without having to hold that pace so long, and even running at a somewhat slower pace can help you achieve this.

Even on a long run at a comfortably slow pace you subject yourself to fluid loss, likely core temperature increase, and use of stored glycogen. Thus earlier, slower paces will accomplish much of what a long run at an even faster pace would accomplish. The feeling you want to achieve is how things will go later in the marathon, and without running too long at that pace, you experience that feeling with the incremental run I've just described. By the time you're running at the fastest **M** pace of those selected, you'll get a reality check on what lies ahead.

I have used this incremental **M**-pace run with some of my marathoners with good success. The change of pace challenges them, especially mentally, and this provides them with a good confidence boost as the marathon race approaches. There's no doubt that there can be variations of this **M** pace run—some with even faster pick-ups throughout the run, as you'll find in the marathon program presented in chapter 20.

The main point about **M**-pace runs when preparing for a marathon is to get periodic checks on how the pace(s) you're considering will feel and monitor your reactions to that pace in terms of prolonged work, fluid loss and replacement, and the clothing and shoes you choose to wear.

Training in the Heat

The exercising human body is far better designed to handle cold than heat. When you exercise, you add internal heat to any heat being imposed by the external environment. With the proper clothing we can exercise and perform quite well when the ambient temperature is many degrees below our own body temperature, but our bodies have a difficult time surviving in an environment that's just a few degrees above normal body temperature. For a runner, particularly a distance runner, heat is enemy number one. You can dress for the cold or for the rain, and you're forced to slow down at altitude, but heat sneaks up on you even if you slow down, which is about all you can do to survive under hot conditions. This is especially true during longer duration runs and **M**-pace training.

The two big problems in running in the heat are an increase in body temperature, which immediately affects performance, and dehydration, which steadily erodes your ability to function. Both increased body temperature and dehydration must be held to a minimum or you just won't be able to continue running.

Normal body temperature is 37 °C (98.6 °F), but exercise, even under cool conditions, can lead to an increase in body temperature of a few degrees. Actually, an increase in body temperature of a degree or two can aid performance (one of the purposes of a warm-up), but as body temperature reaches about 39 °C (102 °F), performance begins to suffer, and you definitely start to feel worse. When training, runners usually learn to recognize this limit subconsciously and back off when increased temperature makes them feel bad. In a race, on the other hand, runners don't like to back off, which makes trouble more likely. This is why heat acclimatization is so important—the body learns to recognize limits and to adapt to allow for optimal performance within those limits. You can't perform as well in a distance race in the heat as you can in a cooler environment.

As soon as the body starts to heat up, blood is diverted to the skin, where cooling (through evaporation of sweat from the skin's surface) takes place. A greater portion of the body's blood volume is at the body's surface to facilitate cooling, leaving less blood available for carrying oxygen to the exercising muscles. In effect, to prevent overheating, the body reduces the amount of blood available to enhance performance. It's fortunate that we can't usually override the life-preserving functions of the body in favor of the performance-enhancing functions. Still, the body can overheat (even without exercise), and we must learn to adapt.

Staying Hydrated

Staying properly hydrated (having an adequate amount of water in the body) is a necessity. When fluid levels drop, the cooling mechanisms are affected, and temperature goes even higher. Keep in mind that you can overheat without being dehydrated, and dehydration can take place in the absence of overheating. A negative side of lowering your carbohydrate intake, as some runners do during the depletion phase of a "carbohydrate depletion/loading" regimen, is that body fluid levels go down when carbohydrate intake is reduced, and you can actually become dehydrated, even when you think you're not sweating that much.

Dehydration can also occur through a lack of attention to fluid intake. When loss of fluid causes body weight to drop 3 to 5 percent, adverse effects on performance will occur. Certainly, people have had greater fluid losses, but they're getting into dangerous territory when they lose more than about 5 percent of body weight in fluid. Runners who perspire a great deal must monitor their body weight closely.

The perceived desire for fluid replacement (thirst) doesn't keep up with the body's needs, and it's easy to get behind in replenishing lost fluids. Failure to replace enough fluids becomes a particular problem in dry climates. It becomes even more of a problem at altitude, where it's typically very dry and you don't notice you're sweating because sweat evaporates as fast as it's produced and water doesn't drip off your body as it does in more humid conditions.

Runners need to understand the effects of humidity on fluid loss. Remember that skin is cooled (which allows circulating blood to also be cooled) as a result of moisture evaporating from the surface of the body. Evaporation rate is a function of relative humidity; when humidity is low, the evaporation rate increases, and the skin is an effective site for cooling the blood. On the other hand, when humidity is high, evaporation and cooling can slow to a standstill. No wonder you feel miserable on a warm, muggy day. The warm weather heats your body, exercise produces more body heat, and high humidity prevents cooling. If the sun is not blocked by clouds, things become even worse. And if you're running with a tailwind, which further hampers cooling, you'll feel even worse, and your chances of overheating will increase even more.

When it comes to fighting the effects of heat and dehydration, runners respond in many different ways. In a study involving heat-acclimatized runners, we found that under identical conditions, some runners perspire twice as much as others, although their body composition, weight, and running speeds are identical. During a 25K race, two of our subjects ran within a few seconds of the same time and both consumed exactly 1 liter (about 2.2 pounds) of fluid during the race. One of them lost water at the rate of 200 milliliters per kilometer of running, whereas the other lost water at a rate of 100 milliliters per kilometer. The net effect was a 4-liter loss for the first runner (5.6 percent of his body weight) and a 1.5-liter loss for the other runner (a 2.1 percent drop in body weight). Clearly, the one runner was on the edge of serious dehydration, whereas the other could probably have continued for some distance without much difficulty.

What if these two runners had gone on to finish a full marathon (42 kilometers), both losing and taking in fluid at the same relative rate? The second runner would have been able to make it okay, but the first runner probably wouldn't have because he would have had greater than a 14-pound net loss, which is right at 9 percent of his body weight. A 9 percent loss is extremely dangerous, and this runner probably would have been forced to withdraw from the run before finishing the marathon.

Runners tend to have a particular amount of fluid they feel comfortable consuming at any given time. If runners are given two opportunities for fluid intake during a race, they'll take in about half as much fluid as they would if given four opportunities to drink. Good hydration is related to the number of opportunities available for drinking, which makes the situation more difficult for the average (relatively slower) distance runner. When you realize that net fluid loss is a function of fluid intake and time spent running (more than distance run) and that slower runners take longer to reach each fluid station, it becomes a bigger problem to care for the mass of average runners than for the elite athletes.

Our research showed that in the absence of required amounts of intake at fluid stations, some runners drink very little (we had a runner who consistently drank less than 100 milliliters in each 25K race that he ran), whereas others manage to gulp down a great deal (one runner took in 2,000 milliliters in a 25K race). The only way to properly replace lost body fluids is to be aware of your own needs under various conditions. If you can't influence race directors to provide more fluid stations along their race courses, then you must learn to ingest more when you do get the opportunity to drink. You can easily improve in this area with practice.

In recent years, the problem of hyponatremia (a significant loss in sodium concentration of the blood) has become of considerable concern, especially among marathon runners who aren't particularly fit and who take many hours to complete their runs. Much has been written about remaining hydrated and drinking as much water as you can, but many people don't understand that drinking only plain water can lead to a serious drop in the sodium concentration of the blood. This condition can reach dangerous levels, even causing disorientation and convulsions, especially if the affected individual is encouraged to take in more plain water. The solution to this problem for distance runners is two-fold—first, consider a little more salt in your regular diet and find a good sport drink to consume during runs instead of drinking only plain water. Second, for additional salt, snack on pretzels, or add tomato juice, tomato soup, or chicken noodle soup to your training diet.

Testing Your Own Fluid Loss

All athletes are concerned about fluid loss and fluid replacement. Runners and coaches often ask me how much and how often fluid should be taken in during workouts and longer runs. You can check your unique reaction to running under various environmental conditions pretty easily through prerun and postrun weigh-ins.

Every time you go for a steady run that lasts 60 minutes or longer, collect the following data:

1. The air temperature (and humidity level, if available) at the time you start your run

2. Your nude body weight (to the nearest 0.1 pound if possible), just before starting your run

3. Total ounces of fluid you take in during your run (record 0.0 ounces if you drink nothing)

4. Your nude body weight (to the nearest 0.1 pound, if possible) on finishing the run (before any postrun food or fluid intake)

5. The air temperature (and humidity, if available) when you finish the run

6. An estimation in ounces of fluid lost during any pit stops you took during the run (0.0 if no pit stops)

7. Your total run time in minutes

Weigh yourself nude so that you don't weigh any fluid that might have collected in your clothing or shoes. To get an accurate reading of fluid intake, use water bottles on which you have marked off two-ounce lines with a magic marker (or bottles that already indicate various volumes). Now, record and calculate your results (for each test run) using table 6.1

Table 6.1 **Worksheet for Calculating Fluid Loss**

Prerun weight (**W1**)	_____ lb
Postrun weight (**W2**)	_____ lb
Net loss (**NL** = W1-W2)	_____ lb
Any pit-stop loss (**P**) = __oz ÷ 16	_____ lb
Sweat/respiration loss (**S**) = (NL − P)	_____ lb
Fluid intake (**F1**)	_____ oz
Gross sweat/respiration loss (**G1**) = (**S**) × 16 + **F1**	_____ oz gross loss
Gross sweat/respiration loss (**G2**) = G1 ÷ 16	_____ lb gross loss
Duration of run in min. (**M**) or hours (**H**)	_____ min ÷ 60 = _____ hour
Distance or run in km (**DK**) or miles (**DM**)	_____ km or _____ miles
Sweat rate 1 (**SR1**) = G1 ÷ M	_____ oz per min
Sweat rate 2 (**SR2**) = G2 ÷ H	_____ lb per hour
Sweat rate 3 (**SR3**) = G1 ÷ DK	_____ oz per km
Sweat rate 4 (**SR4**) = G1 ÷ DM	_____ oz per mile

From *Daniels' Running Formula, Second Edition* by Jack Tupper Daniels, 2005, Champaign, IL: Human Kinetics.

Next, record the temperature and humidity and the date for each run you take under various weather conditions. You can use this information to predict how much fluid you can expect to lose during a marathon based on the weather forecast for the day of the event. These data also allow you to estimate how much you need to consume to keep from losing more than a few percentage points of your body weight. Record data from all test runs (by date) using a spreadsheet, such as the one shown in table 6.2. You can copy this table and use it to predict fluid needs for any distance or duration of a run you're taking. Calculate your needs so that you won't lose more than 4 or 5 percent of your body weight by the time you have completed your run.

Table 6.2	**Worksheet for Determining Fluid Needs**					
Date	Temperature	Humidity	SR1 oz/min	SR2 lb/hour	SR3 oz/km	SR4 oz/mile

From *Daniels' Running Formula, Second Edition* by Jack Tupper Daniels, 2005, Champaign, IL: Human Kinetics.

If 60 minutes of running under a certain set of environmental conditions results in a two-pound weight loss, you can figure what will happen after an hour or more under similar conditions. You can also go a step further and learn to consume fluids at various rates and frequencies to counteract the fluid loss that you have reason to expect. Use tables 6.1 and 6.2 to monitor your fluid loss and requirements under various weather conditions and for predicting your fluid needs in upcoming events.

If you use consumer gels or high-energy products during your races or long training runs, understand that these substances shouldn't be taken with energy drinks but rather with plain water so that the energy can be optimally diluted in the stomach and be well absorbed.

Acclimatizing to Heat

The body does acclimatize to heat after a couple of weeks of training in warm conditions, but you need to learn when to train under these conditions. Early morning is the coolest time of day, but it's usually also the most humid. Evening, after the sun goes down, is the least humid, but it's hotter than morning. If you train twice a day, there's no better choice than early and late in the day. When training for an important race that's likely to be run under hot conditions, do some training, and even some competition experiences, under those conditions and at the appropriate time of day. However, don't train in particularly hot weather or at the hottest time of day because your quality of training will suffer and your fitness level might deteriorate.

When training in warm weather, learn how to minimize the effects of the heat by dressing appropriately. The general rule is to wear as little clothing as possible; what you do wear should fit loosely. Porous materials tend not to stick to your skin and thus allow the movement of heat away from the body. Wearing a cap with a sun-protecting bill might help, but a cap usually makes the head much hotter. Make sure that whatever you wear, air can flow freely to and from the parts of the body being covered.

Although I've used marathon-pace (**M**) running for several years, it's new for me to suggest this pace as an independent part of a training program. Let me summarize the most useful comments about this intensity of training.

- **M** runs of up to 15 or 16 miles are a valuable part of a marathon training program because they add reality to the training, including an opportunity to practice taking in fluids at race pace.

- **M** pace is faster than **E** pace but can occasionally replace part or all of an **E** run when conditions are good and you're feeling extra spry. Still, don't let **M** runs replace your **E** runs with regularity because you need the low-stress intensity afforded by **E**-pace running.

- Don't get carried away by pushing your **M** runs to an even faster pace—save that for a scheduled tempo run.

- Avoid doing **M** runs under adverse weather conditions or you might feel that you can't hold the pace for very long.

Peter Gilmore

Peter Gilmore was born in Santa Monica, California, where he participated in a variety of sports, including baseball, football, basketball, swimming, volleyball, surfing, and body boarding. Peter remembers watching the 1984 Olympic marathon as a seven-year-old and watching the New York City marathon with his mother whenever it was on TV. As a result of his early interest in watching major marathons and the experience of watching his mother compete in road races, Peter became personally involved in running and competed in his first race at age 12. His first breakthrough as a runner came in the 8th grade when he won a junior high cross country championship, breaking his school record in the process. As a 15-year-old, Peter ran a 10-second PR in the mile at the Los Angeles sectional semifinals, with a time of 4:23. His reaction to this accomplishment was to wonder "Why not 4:13 or 4:03? After all, I'm only 15 years old."

Photo courtesy of Peter Gilmore

After competing at Palisades High School, Peter moved on to University of California at Berkeley. In 1996, he competed in the World Junior Championships for Track and Field in Sydney, Australia, where he ran the 10,000 meters and discovered what it is like to race some really fast runners. Peter's initial running goals were to win L.A. city titles in track and cross country, but in the back of his mind lurked a desire to race in the Olympics and the major marathons that his mother had run—Boston, New York City, London, and Chicago. Following up on this desire proved to be a good move. Peter most recently placed 9th in the 2004 U.S. marathon Olympic Trials, recording his best time so far at that distance. I became acquainted with Peter during my 2002 sabbatical in Palo Alto, California, and began coaching him for the marathon.

Personal bests: 5,000m—14:04; 10,000m—28:57; 10 mile—47:41; marathon—2:15:44.

CHAPTER 7

Level 3: Threshold Training

The two types of threshold training that I discuss in this chapter are tempo runs and cruise intervals. Tempo runs—steady, moderately prolonged runs—have been around for some time, but runners and coaches define them differently. Cruise intervals are a series of repeated runs with a brief recovery between runs. I address the differences and similarities between tempo and cruise-interval workouts and explain the danger of trying to perform at a faster pace than is adequate for this type of training. Threshold workouts need to be run at the proper intensity (speed). The proper pace for tempo runs and cruise intervals is the same—a pace I call threshold (**T**) pace.

I introduced the term "cruise interval" to the running community in the 1980s. I had heard the term used by swimmers when I was involved in testing many of our national and Olympic team members. About the same time, Bertil Sjödin, a Swedish researcher and running coach, told me of the benefits of threshold training, both in the form of steady tempo runs and as interval sessions. So, the term that I borrowed from swimming was attached to the type of training that Sjödin told me about, and doing cruise intervals has since become a common type of training for runners.

Whether you're doing a tempo run or a set of cruise intervals, the proper pace for **T**-pace running is about 83 to 88 percent of $\dot{V}O_2$max, or 88 to 92 percent of $v\dot{V}O_2$max

Almost any runner can do a great workout now and then, but consistency is the key to productive training.

or maximum heart rate. **T**-pace running is one of the most productive types of training that distance runners can do. Training at this pace helps runners avoid overtraining and yields more satisfying workouts and better consistency. You can find your **T** pace and how it corresponds to your VDOT value in table 3.2 (page 52).

Some runners and coaches use tempo runs for the broader purpose of just going for a fairly prolonged steady, solid run—often, more for the psychological benefits (which can be considerable) than the physiological. With threshold-intensity running the physiological benefit is to improve endurance: the ability to endure a greater and greater intensity of effort for a longer and longer period of time. You might perform some (longer) tempo runs at an intensity slightly below threshold intensity, which offers a good opportunity to boost psychological endurance. Longer tempo runs that begin in the less intense area of the zone and progress to the higher end of the zone are accomplishing both the benefits of a longer tempo run and the benefits of true **T**-pace running.

Establishing Your Threshold Pace

You can establish your proper pace for threshold running fairly closely by running at a velocity that produces an elevated yet steady state of blood lactate accumulation. This pace is a little faster than a pace that you could maintain for two or more hours (marathon pace for most people) but slower than the pace you could maintain for 30 minutes (10K race pace for better runners). This pace is easy to discern because at the latter pace blood lactate continues to rise over the course of the run (that is, there's not a steady state of blood lactate accumulation). Also, at the former pace, blood lactate slowly drops after an initial rise or after any elevated lactate resulting from race surges (also not a steady state of blood lactate accumulation).

Most runners can figure that their threshold pace is equal to a pace they could race at for 50 to 60 minutes. In fact, for slower runners, threshold pace might actually be 10K race pace because they are taking nearly an hour to "race" this distance. *Intensity* of effort, not necessarily *distance* of running or racing, is what determines the degree of stress being put on the body's systems.

So, in the case of cruise intervals—a series of repeated workbouts at threshold pace, with brief rest breaks between workbouts—the pace remains the same, not faster; otherwise, blood lactate will gradually rise throughout the session. It's always tempting to run at a faster pace with cruise intervals than you run in a steady 20-minute tempo run because of the relative shortness of the runs and the brief breaks, which primarily reduce the mental stress of the workout. However, going faster isn't better for achieving the effects you want to achieve in threshold training, so this type of workout is a chance to benefit from a relatively low muscle–stress session.

You can accomplish more total mileage in a cruise-interval session than in a tempo-run session, and the brief rest periods can always be reduced to less than a minute, if you feel the session is too easy. Remember that the purpose of the workout is to stress lactate-clearance capability, not to overstress that capability. Let the ability to do more total mileage in a cruise interval session be the advantage of this type of session, and let the greater mental stress of the steady tempo run be the advantage of that type of session. By the way, I refer to threshold training as "comfortably hard" running. It shouldn't feel "hard," which is the pace of pure interval training.

Tempo Runs

Ideally, a tempo run is nothing more than a steady 20-minute run at **T** pace. Subjectively, the intensity of effort associated with **T**-pace running is comfortably hard. Again, your effort should be one that you could maintain for about an hour in a race.

Although the ideal duration of a steady threshold run is 20 minutes, your running time can vary somewhat to accommodate a particular course. For example, if your **T** pace is 6:00-mile pace, and you choose a three-mile course, this gives you an 18-minute tempo effort; or you might go four miles for a 24-minute tempo run. Of course, you could go exactly 20 minutes, using the mile markers to set proper pace, and stop between three and one-quarter and three and one-half miles. It's not a bad idea to do tempo runs on the track (or even a treadmill, now and then) so that you can closely control the pace.

Many coaches and runners do longer tempo runs at slower than true threshold pace, and this can yield positive results. Prolonged running at this relatively hard intensity builds a good sense of maintaining a strong pace for an extended period of time, and, as stated earlier, in some instances the demand can be as psychologically intense as a shorter run at true threshold pace. Also, some runners gradually build up the intensity of a longer "tempo" run until actually running at threshold pace. In any case, I believe in the benefits of tempo runs that are longer than 20 minutes and have designed two tables that alter the speed of the run as dictated by duration (see tables 7.1 and 7.2). Using these tables gives runners a better idea of what pace to expect of themselves when out on a tempo run that forces them to run slower than threshold pace and longer than the typical 20-minute duration. The adjusted paces are based on the natural dropoff in maintainable intensity as the duration of a steady run increases.

Table 7.1 shows the mile pace times for tempo runs lasting 20 to 60 minutes, and how much slower the pace is per mile (in seconds) than **T** pace is. Table 7.2 shows the pace times in kilometers. Both tables also show **M**-pace times and how much slower or faster it is per mile or kilometer than **T** pace is. If your VDOT falls between the displayed values, just add the appropriate number of seconds per mile or kilometer to your own **T** pace for the desired run duration.

Be sure to perform your tempo runs under desirable weather conditions and on relatively flat terrain with good footing because the goal of this workout is to maintain a steady intensity of effort for a prolonged period of time. Hills, rough footing, and wind all affect the ability to maintain a steady pace and interfere with achieving the purpose of the workout. You can monitor your heart rate, but a steady rhythm under constant conditions is what you want in a tempo run.

Possibly the biggest challenge in doing tempo runs is to hold the proper pace and resist turning your tempo run into a time trial. Remember that the proper pace is more beneficial than a faster (or slower) one. This is a good workout for practicing your ability to concentrate on a running task and keep in touch with how your body feels while running comfortably hard.

Begin a tempo workout with a good warm-up of at least 10 minutes of easy running and some light strides. Follow the tempo run with a cool-down, which should include some strides (four or five 20- to 40-second runs at about mile race pace). You'll be surprised how good you feel about 10 minutes after a tempo run.

My recommendation is that the quality portion of a session of cruise intervals should total at least 30 minutes and up to 10 percent of the week's total running distance or time, and that steady tempo runs should last 20 to 60 minutes, with pace adjustments as shown in tables 7.1 and 7.2.

Table 7.1 **Variations in Mile Tempo Pace Based on Run Duration (in Minutes)**

VDOT	20:00	25:00	30:00	35:00	40:00	45:00	50:00	55:00	60:00	M-pace 60:00
30	10:18	10:25 (+7)	10:31 (+13)	10:34 (+16)	10:37 (+19)	10:40 (+22)	10:43 (+25)	10:46 (+28)	10:50 (+32)	11:02 (+44)
35	9:07	9:13 (+6)	9:19 (+12)	9:22 (+15)	9:25 (+18)	9:28 (+21)	9:31 (+24)	9:34 (+27)	9:37 (+30)	9:46 (+39)
40	8:12	8:18 (+6)	8:23 (+11)	8:26 (+14)	8:29 (+17)	8:32 (+20)	8:34 (+22)	8:36 (+24)	8:38 (+26)	8:46 (+34)
45	7:25	7:31 (+6)	7:35 (+10)	7:38 (+13)	7:40 (+15)	7:42 (+17)	7:44 (+19)	7:46 (+21)	7:48 (+23)	7:57 (+32)
50	6:51	6:56 (+5)	7:00 (+9)	7:03 (+12)	7:05 (+14)	7:07 (+16)	7:09 (+18)	7:11 (+20)	7:13 (+22)	7:17 (+26)
55	6:20	6:25 (+5)	6:28 (+8)	6:31 (+11)	6:33 (+13)	6:35 (+15)	6:37 (+17)	6:39 (+19)	6:41 (+21)	6:42 (+22)
60	5:54	5:59 (+5)	6:01 (+7)	6:04 (+10)	6:06 (+12)	6:08 (+14)	6:10 (+16)	6:12 (+18)	6:15 (+21)	6:14 (+20)
65	5:32	5:37 (+5)	5:39 (+7)	5:41 (+9)	5:43 (+11)	5:45 (+13)	5:48 (+16)	5:50 (+18)	5:52 (+20)	5:49 (+17)
70	5:13	5:17 (+4)	5:19 (+6)	5:21 (+8)	5:23 (+10)	5:25 (+12)	5:28 (+15)	5:31 (+18)	5:32 (+19)	5:27 (+14)
75	4:56	5:00 (+4)	5:02 (+6)	5:04 (+8)	5:06 (+10)	5:08 (+12)	5:10 (+14)	5:11 (+15)	5:13 (+17)	5:08 (+12)
80	4:41	4:44 (+3)	4:46 (+5)	4:48 (+7)	4:50 (+9)	4:52 (+11)	4:53 (+12)	4:55 (+14)	4:57 (+16)	4:52 (+11)
85	4:27	4:30 (+3)	4:32 (+5)	4:34 (+7)	4:36 (+9)	4:38 (+11)	4:39 (+12)	4:41 (+14)	4:42 (+15)	4:37 (+10)

Table 7.2	**Variations in Kilometer Tempo Pace Based on Run Duration (in Minutes)**									
	T-pace									**M-pace**
VDOT	**20:00**	**25:00**	**30:00**	**35:00**	**40:00**	**45:00**	**50:00**	**55:00**	**60:00**	**60:00**
30	6:24	6:28 (+4)	6:32 (+8)	6:34 (+10)	6:36 (+12)	6:38 (+14)	6:40 (+16)	6:42 (+18)	6:44 (+20)	6:51 (+27)
35	5:40	5:44 (+4)	5:47 (+7)	5:49 (+9)	5:51 (+11)	5:53 (+13)	5:55 (+15)	5:57 (+17)	5:59 (+19)	6:04 (+24)
40	5:06	5:10 (+4)	5:13 (+7)	5:15 (+9)	5:17 (+11)	5:18 (+12)	5:20 (+14)	5:21 (+15)	5:22 (+16)	5:26 (+20)
45	4:38	4:42 (4)	4:44 (+6)	4:46 (+8)	4:47 (+9)	4:49 (+11)	4:50 (+12)	4:51 (+13)	4:52 (+14)	4:56 (+18)
50	4:15	4:18 (+3)	4:21 (+6)	4:22 (+7)	4:24 (+9)	4:25 (+10)	4:26 (+11)	4:27 (+12)	4:29 (+14)	4:31 (+16)
55	3:56	3:59 (+3)	4:01 (+5)	4:03 (+7)	4:04 (+8)	4:05 (+9)	4:07 (+11)	4:08 (+12)	4:09 (+13)	4:10 (+14)
60	3:40	3:43 (+3)	3:44 (+4)	3:46 (+6)	3:47 (+7)	3:49 (+9)	3:50 (+10)	3:51 (+11)	3:52 (+12)	3:52 (+12)
65	3:26	3:29 (+3)	3:30 (+4)	3:32 (+6)	3:33 (+7)	3:34 (+8)	3:36 (+10)	3:37 (+11)	3:38 (+12)	3:37 (+11)
70	3:14	3:16 (+2)	3:18 (+4)	3:19 (+5)	3:20 (+6)	3:21 (+7)	3:23 (+9)	3:25 (+11)	3:26 (+12)	3:23 (+9)
75	3:04	3:06 (+2)	3:08 (+4)	3:09 (+5)	3:10 (+6)	3:11 (+7)	3:13 (+9)	3:14 (+10)	3:15 (+11)	3:11 (+7)
80	2:54	2:56 (+2)	2:57 (+3)	2:58 (+4)	3:00 (+6)	3:01 (+7)	3:02 (+8)	3:03 (+9)	3:04 (+10)	3:01 (+7)
85	2:46	2:28 (+2)	2:49 (+3)	2:50 (+4)	2:52 (+6)	2:53 (+7)	2:54 (+8)	2:55 (+9)	2:55 (+9)	2:52 (+6)

Cruise Intervals

Cruise intervals are short-rest intervals performed at threshold pace. Here, because the duration of the individual runs within a cruise-interval session is relatively short, it's important to do each run at threshold pace. The typical duration of individual runs within a cruise-interval session varies from about 3 to 15 minutes, with 1 minute of recovery time following each 5 minutes of run time. For example, when doing cruise-interval miles the rest between runs is usually 1 minute; between 2-mile repeats, a 2-minute rest is appropriate.

The great advantage of the brief recoveries is that blood-lactate levels remain fairly constant, and the runner experiences threshold effort throughout the entire training session, which can last a fair bit longer than could be accomplished with a steady tempo run at threshold pace. Although it involves more **T**-pace running per workout than a tempo run does, a cruise-interval session is usually easier to do because the runner looks forward to the little breaks that come periodically throughout the workout.

BREATHING RHYTHMS

Most elite distance runners breathe with what's called a 2-2 rhythm—taking two steps (one with the right foot, one with the left foot) while breathing in, and two steps while breathing out. Most good runners take about 180 steps per minute (90 with each foot), so this gives them about 45 breaths per minute. This is an ideal rate because it gives you enough time for a substantial amount of air to be moved in and out of your lungs with each breath.

In the latter stages of an intense middle-distance race, 45 breaths per minute might not be enough. In this case, because you want to maintain some regular rhythm of breathing, the tendency is to shift to about 60 breaths per minute, which means either taking one step while breathing in and two while breathing out, or two in and one out. These would be referred to as 1-2 or 2-1 rhythms.

When you're not breathing particularly hard, you might use slower breathing rhythms, such as a 3-3 rhythm (three steps breathing in, three steps breathing out), which is often used during easy runs but which becomes stressful at **T** pace or faster. A 4-4 rhythm can also be used but isn't recommended because the depth of breathing consumes energy and the slowness of this rate often does a poor job of clearing CO_2 fast enough from the lungs. In an attempt to get more air into their lungs, runners often use a 1-1 rhythm to try to increase rate rather than depth of breathing. However, 1-1 breathing leads to very shallow breathing (more like panting) and isn't an efficient way to ventilate the lungs. I don't recommend a 1-1 pattern of breathing.

Actually, a runner can use different breathing rates in different ways, an important example being during a warm-up. Start your warm-up with a 4-4 rhythm, switch to 3-3 after a few minutes, and then to 2-2 for the remainder of the warm-up. This gives you something to focus on when going through an otherwise boring warm-up session.

You can also use your breathing rate to monitor your intensity of effort while running. You should be comfortable with a 3-3 pattern on an easy run, and maybe even a 4-4 pattern, if so desired. However, if 3-3 doesn't give you enough air on an easy run, then it's not an easy run. Slow down to where 3-3 is comfortable. You might prefer 2-2 on an easy run, but be able to go 3-3, if necessary, if for no other reason than to prove it's an easy run. On the other hand, 3-3 isn't fast enough to meet the demands of a distance race; the rhythm I recommend for distance is 2-2.

Knowledge of breathing rhythms can assist you in races for distance by helping you determine how fast to run up hills, for example. If you're trying to maintain a constant intensity while going up and down hills, focus on adjusting your speed so that the 2-2 rhythm feels equally demanding (or comfortable) during all terrain changes. This means slowing down on the rough terrain (or up hills) and being able to speed up going down hills.

Another time when knowledge of breathing rhythm comes in handy is when you get a side stitch. Usually stitches are aggravated by a fast, shallow breathing rate; a slower, deeper pattern can aid or eliminate a side stitch. Next time you get one of these sharp pains in your side or gut, try going to a 3-3 breathing rhythm and see if that helps.

About the only time a 1-1 rhythm might not be detrimental is during the final minute or so of a race. Keeping a 1-1 pattern for longer than a couple of minutes is usually counterproductive. In general, you'll use a 2-2 rhythm in most races, possibly switching to 2-1 the last third of the race. In a marathon, 2-2 should work well throughout the race.

Yet another time when knowledge of breathing patterns is of considerable aid is when you're first exposed to running at altitude. Let your typical rhythms guide you on easy runs, and on **T** runs in particular. If you usually use a 3-3 or 2-2 on these intensities, respectively, then adjust your speed of running at altitude to allow the same degree of discomfort as you normally experience at sea level. This is better than trying to reproduce the same speed of running you're used to at sea level.

During all types of training, the same principles apply. A 2-2 breathing rhythm is preferred for most quality training. Although you can use 3-3 on easy runs, I suggest using 2-2, just to be consistent. Further, 2-1 might be called for during the latter stages of an interval session in which workbouts (the repeated runs that make up a session of intervals) last several minutes each. It shouldn't be necessary to rely on a 2-1 rhythm during **T**-pace or **R**-pace work; in fact, the ability to avoid this faster pattern can be used to keep you from going too fast at times, particularly on a tempo run.

A typical cruise-interval workout might consist of 5 repeated miles at **T** pace, with one-minute recoveries. Another possibility is 8 or 10 repeated 1,000-meter runs at **T** pace with 30-second to one-minute recoveries. One-mile, 1,000-meter, 1,200-meter, 2,000-meter, and even 2-mile runs are pretty common distances to repeat in a cruise-interval workout. Slower runners usually select shorter distances, and in fact might find repeated 800s to be a good cruise-interval workout.

The total amount of quality running for a cruise-interval workout is up to about 10 percent of your current weekly mileage, with a maximum of 10 miles (15K) or one hour and a minimum of 4 miles (6 kilometers) or 30 minutes. A runner averaging 40 miles per week would do the 4-mile (30 minute) minimum; a 120-mile-per-week runner might do up to 10 miles (15K) or one hour of **T**-pace running in a session. I must admit that I have seen a couple of my elite marathoners total 15 miles at **T** pace in a single workout, but you have to be careful to build up gradually to that kind of total threshold stress.

I think that elite marathon runners are best suited for the upper mileage extremes, as opposed to the average runner, who might be well advised not to exceed 8 miles (13 kilometers) or about 50 minutes in a single cruise-interval session. I've found with several of the marathoners I've coached that mixing 8 miles of **T**-pace running with an hour (or up to 10 miles) of easy running in the same workout satisfies the needs of a long run and a threshold session. The idea behind this demanding workout is that the **T**-pace running forces the running muscles to use up glycogen stores more rapidly than they would in a steady, easy, long run. By the latter stages of the workout the feeling you get resembles the feeling during the final stages of a marathon race—but you haven't had to run so far. This is a pretty rugged workout, and I don't recommend that you do it weekly. You can find this type of workout in the marathon program presented in chapter 20.

Using Tempo Runs and Cruise Intervals

Although tempo runs and cruise intervals are designed for the same purpose (raising the lactate threshold, improving endurance), I recommend using both in a training regimen. The steady tempo runs are probably a better value for the time spent training because of the concentration factor—you must keep up a quality pace for a prolonged time. On the other hand, cruise intervals provide a break from the mental rigors of the tempo run and offer an opportunity to get more physical work done in a session.

A few words of caution regarding how often to repeat identical workouts and monitor progress in a particular type of threshold workout: It's human nature that runners often want to see progress in their workouts and sometimes try to perform a particular workout at faster and faster speeds over the course of a fairly short period of time. Trying to compete against yourself in this way is inadvisable. It doesn't conform to the principle of letting your body react and adjust to a particular type of stress before increasing the amount of stress (principle 3, page 10). It's better to perform the same workout quite a few times at the same speed, or until a race performance indicates that you've achieved a higher fitness level.

One of the best ways to monitor how your training is progressing is to see how much more easily you can perform a particular workout as time goes by. If what used to be a tough workout becomes not so tough after several weeks of training, then that's a great sign that your training is paying off in a positive way. At this point, you're usually ready for an increase in intensity or amount of training. In contrast, always trying to see if you can go faster in a workout that you have done before (the "always hurt as much as possible" technique) can be very misleading in trying to determine how much progress you're making. With this approach, you always hurt the same (or more), and you never get to experience doing a standard workout with diminishing discomfort. Doubts begin to set in as you ask yourself, "Am I really getting better or just learning to tolerate more pain?" If you often hurt badly in practice, a race won't be anything special; you should be able to take on more discomfort in a race than you do in daily training.

A more sophisticated way to monitor the degree of stress of a workout is to check heart rates or blood-lactate values at various points during the effort or during recovery. Relying on these more scientific means of keeping track of your progress, however, can prevent you from learning how to do a good job of it on your own. Whether or not you

The concentration developed by doing steady tempo runs pays off at race time.

use mechanical or electronic devices to monitor body responses, you should still learn to read your body's feelings and reactions to the types of workouts that you do.

Please remember not to run faster than the prescribed **T** pace when doing tempo and cruise-interval workouts. When you're having a good training day, it's not that tough to beat a previous time over a four-mile tempo course, and it's tempting to want to make each mile in a cruise-interval workout just a little faster than the previous one. It's very important, however, to let your ability, based on competitive efforts, determine your training intensities. When a workout begins to feel easier, use that feeling to support the idea that you're getting fitter. Then, prove that you are getting better in a race, not in a workout.

If you're in a prolonged phase of training, with no races scheduled, it's reasonable to increase training intensity without the supportive evidence of better competitive performances. In this case, a good rule of thumb is to increase VDOT one unit every four to six weeks. This is the same as improving your 5,000-meter race time by about 10 to 15 seconds, a substantial improvement in my opinion. If you're in a maintenance program, which is designed to require the least possible training stress that allows you to stay at a particular level of fitness (as is often the case in phase IV), there's no need to increase training intensity (VDOT) or distances. In this case, the best goal is to see how easy standard workouts can feel over time.

When setting up the phases of training, the placement of threshold training might vary in the overall order of the program, based on the individual involved and the event being trained for. Unlike **E** runs, which almost always fall in the earliest phase of a program, threshold training might be emphasized early, at the midpoint, or late in a runner's training schedule (see chapters 16 through 20).

Nicole Teter

Nicole Teter was born in San Diego but grew up farther north, in Redding, California. She played softball, volleyball, and basketball as a child and always had a desire to win. Her initial experience as a competitive runner was in the 5th grade when she ran the sprints; in the 6th grade, Nicole ran the 200 and 400 meter sprints at Junior Nationals. In her sophomore year at Shasta High School, Nicole's coach moved her to the 800 meters and also had her compete in cross country races; even though they "hurt too much," she felt the longer distances improved her strength. That first year as an 800-meter runner, she was 4th in the state 800-meter race. In her senior year of high school, she ran 2:05.61 and also won a silver medal at the Junior Pan Am Games. Throughout the 1990s, Nicole was unsettled and plagued by injuries, but she continued running times under 2:04 for the 800 meters.

In 2001 she moved to Palo Alto, California to begin running for the Farm Team and to have Frank Gagliano direct her training. Having tested Nicole in the lab and having logged hours watching Gagliano coach runners, I feel that this pairing is a perfect match of athlete and coach—and it has certainly paid off. In 2002 Nicole broke the American record for the 800 meters indoors with a time of 1:58.71 and realized for the first time that she could be competitive at the international level. Nicole has won two indoor and one outdoor national titles in the 800 meters and qualified for four U.S. world-championship teams, but she considers being on the starting line at the 2004 Olympic Games as her greatest moment in sport (so far).

Personal bests: 800m indoor—1:58.71 (AR); 800m outdoor—1:57.97; 1,500m—4:04.19 (and I have seen some outstanding 400m legs on relays)

© Empics

CHAPTER 8

Level 4: Interval Training

Of all the types of training, interval training takes on the greatest number of possible meanings, and it wouldn't be appropriate for me to try to accommodate them all. In fact, because of the many different meanings, I've chosen to define exactly what I mean by interval (**I**) training, or "$\dot{V}O_2$max interval (**I**) training," as I often refer to it. I use this definition because optimizing $\dot{V}O_2$max is, in my opinion, the greatest benefit of **I** training, especially when performed according to my description in this chapter. In this chapter I identify, and explain my reasoning behind, the ideal intensity for **I** training, the duration of individual workbouts, the optimal amount of recovery between workbouts, and some guidelines on how much total quality running is desirable for a session of intervals.

The idea of an interval session is to accumulate a good bit of time working at 95 to 100 percent $\dot{V}O_2$max. When running at proper **I** pace, your body takes about 2 minutes to reach the point where it's operating at maximum oxygen consumption (the purpose of the workout). If you run four 5-minute runs at this pace, and it takes 2 minutes to reach max in each run, then of your 20 minutes of hard running you've accumulated 12 minutes of running at $\dot{V}O_2$max, or **I** pace. In fact, you're pretty much guaranteed 12 minutes at max even if you completely recover between each of the 5-minute runs. On the other hand, if you run seven 3-minute runs at

Remember that the finish line is at the end of a race. Don't use up all your energy before reaching it.

interval pace, and it takes 2 minutes to reach max for each run, then you accumulate only 7 minutes at $\dot{V}O_2$max for the 21 minutes you've spent running hard.

Going a step further, if you run 20 one-minute runs at the same "hard" interval pace, and recover fully between each of the runs, then you would accumulate zero time at $\dot{V}O_2$max. It takes 2 minutes to reach max, and running hard for only 1 minute at a time won't allow that, so if you're running for only 1 minute at a time, you must reduce your recovery time so that you're not yet fully recovered before starting the next run. If you do this, then after several intervals you might reach $\dot{V}O_2$max in a matter of only 30 seconds or so, and over the course of completing 20 one-minute runs you might accumulate 10 minutes at $\dot{V}O_2$max. It's easy to understand why short workouts must be accompanied by even shorter recovery intervals in order to work at $\dot{V}O_2$max, and why the longer (3- to 5-minute) workouts are the ideal for stressing $\dot{V}O_2$max.

Performance in middle-distance races is enhanced by a phase of productive interval training.

On the other hand, the problem with working harder than the slowest pace that elicits $\dot{V}O_2$max, when the purpose of the session is to work *at* max, is that aerobically you can't work any harder, which means you're doing the extra work at the expense of anaerobic metabolism, and lactate accumulation begins to limit you as the workout progresses. Further, working at the harder-than-necessary intensity doesn't improve the aerobic mechanisms any more than working at the minimum max intensity does. The result is that the workout becomes more stressful and the benefits no greater—in fact, they could be less beneficial. If, for example, going too hard in early workbouts results in subsequent workbouts actually being slower than required to elicit $\dot{V}O_2$max, then the latter bouts won't be intense enough to be effective. Nothing's more frustrating than to work really hard in a training session and not get the desired, and deserved, benefits.

Although the duration of workbouts is important, when it comes to interval training, intensity (training pace) is even more important. This is because you can attain $\dot{V}O_2$max only when running at a particular intensity. You need to understand the difference between intensity and speed of running—*intensity* is the key word when stressing any physiological system. For example, if a running velocity (speed) of 300 meters per minute (5:20 mile pace) is associated with a runner's $\dot{V}O_2$max, it certainly wouldn't take that fast a speed to reach $\dot{V}O_2$max if running uphill, or into a wind, or at altitude. Under adverse conditions, intensity is clearly the better way to identify what pace elicits $\dot{V}O_2$max—be sure to consider this when doing your interval training.

Of course, it would be easy to say that all workbouts in an interval session should be "hard" and let it go at that. Certainly, if some surges within a fartlek session are meant to elicit $\dot{V}O_2$max, then the effort should be hard, but when it's possible to monitor the training pace, there's no need to run any faster than the minimum pace that produces $\dot{V}O_2$max. This last statement is worth additional consideration. Keep in mind that running at VO_2max is also associated with running at maximum heart rate. Now, suppose maximum HR is associated with a pace of 5:00 per mile; what HR will be associated with a 4:50 (or anything faster than 5:00) mile pace? Maximum, of course, or HRmax. So, this means that it's quite common to run faster than necessary, if you're looking at HRmax as an indicator of working at max.

The ideal intensity is the least stressful intensity that accomplishes what you want. In the case of interval training, ideal intensity is the lowest intensity that makes the cardiovascular system and aerobic metabolic mechanisms work as hard as they can. Keep in mind that under adverse conditions, the pace associated with the desired intensity might vary a fair bit.

Let me state that running a little less than 100 percent $\dot{V}O_2$max can still produce substantial conditioning benefits, thus I've identified the "**I** zone" as being from 95 to 100 percent $\dot{V}O_2$max (98 to 100 percent maximum heart rate).

Determining Interval Duration

Experience tells me (and researchers agree) that the optimal duration of individual workbouts in an interval session is between three and five minutes each. Consequently, I most often use mile and 1,200-meter intervals for men and 1,000-meter and

1,200-meter intervals for women to get the best results. Still, varying the durations of the workouts adds interest and helps minimize the mental stress of interval training. As in all types of training, there must be a balance in interval training between accomplishing the physiological and biomechanical goals of the training session and optimizing the psychological factors.

Interval intensity is demanding for anyone, so individual workouts in an interval workout are typically not over five minutes each. Going for longer than five minutes at a time leads to too great an accumulation of blood lactate, which usually ends up causing you to cut your workout short or run the last few intervals too slowly (which doesn't accomplish the purpose of the workout). At the other extreme, you can use workouts as short as 30 seconds, which is considered the lower boundary for the duration of workouts during a $\dot{V}O_2$max **I** workout. Again, with the shorter workouts, you also have to shorten recovery time to allow the body to reach $\dot{V}O_2$max within the workout.

As I've mentioned, five minutes is the usual recommended maximum duration for individual workouts in an interval session; this means that if your VDOT is less than 66, you shouldn't repeat miles or 1,600-meter runs in an interval workout (see page \bb\). In this case, proper **I** pace requires you to take longer than five minutes to complete a mile. For people who fall into this category (VDOT under 66), 1,200-meter or 1,000-meter runs are the longest distances that should be used for work intervals. Stay under the five-minute limit whenever possible.

Another option is to run strictly for time. Actually, five-minute runs are excellent for an interval session, regardless of how much distance you cover in this time. I used to call this type of interval training "nonstructured" because although you're timing the duration of each quality run, you're relying on feeling the degree of stress rather than going a set distance in a predetermined time. You can do the same type of thing with one-, two-, three-, or four-minute runs. Now I prefer to use the original Swedish term "fartlek" for these types of sessions.

Determining Recovery Time

The amount of recovery you should take between repeated runs in an interval session should be equal to, or a little less than, the time spent performing the preceding workout. For example, if you're doing 1,200-meter intervals in four minutes each, you should take up to four minutes of recovery time before the next 1,200 meters; 40-second intervals allow recoveries of no more than 40 seconds each. Generally, the longer the workouts, the less you need to concern yourself with recovery time being too brief.

Because the purpose of interval training is to stress your $\dot{V}O_2$max, you must spend time running at $\dot{V}O_2$max. As I've mentioned, a five-minute run does this well (see figure 8.1) because of the five minutes spent running you're spending two to get up to $\dot{V}O_2$max, and three at $\dot{V}O_2$max—a good return on your investment. That's why it doesn't matter much if recoveries after five-minute runs are a little longer than those that follow shorter intervals.

Figure 8.2 shows what happens when 400-meter workouts at 80 seconds each are used during an interval workout. Because a single run doesn't last long enough to allow

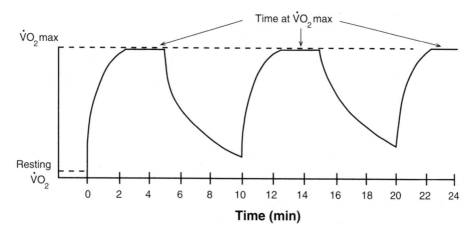

Figure 8.1 Interval running allows you to train at maximum aerobic capacity ($\dot{V}O_2$max) for a good portion of the workout while still getting necessary rest periods.

Adapted, by permission, from J. Karlsson, et al., 1970. *Energikraven vid Löpning.* Stockholm: Trygg, 39.

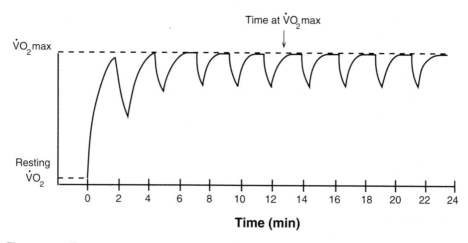

Figure 8.2 To reap the benefits of short interval training, the recovery periods must be kept even shorter.

Adapted, by permission, from J. Karlsson, et al., 1970. *Energikraven vid Löpning.* Stockholm: Trygg, 41.

your body to reach $\dot{V}O_2$max, the short recovery helps you to achieve $\dot{V}O_2$max more quickly in subsequent workouts. The short rest doesn't permit full recovery back to resting $\dot{V}O_2$, so with each new workout $\dot{V}O_2$max is reached more quickly than in earlier bouts or with longer recoveries. By repeating the short intervals and short recoveries over and over, you can accumulate a fair amount of time running at $\dot{V}O_2$max.

A good way to handle interval 400s is to start one every 2 minutes, which means that 80-second 400s allow for 40-second recoveries. (However, this doesn't work too well for runners who do interval 400s in 90 seconds or longer because they get so little recovery time that they have trouble running the 400s at the proper speed.) Interval 200s on a 1-minute send-off (starting a 200 every minute) are also good for variety.

FACING THE WIND

Of the many adverse weather conditions that runners face, probably the only one that every runner is confronted with at one time or another is wind—and if there's anything that interrupts training or racing more than wind, I have yet to meet it.

I consider myself fortunate to have coached for four years in Oklahoma, where you really learn to respect the wind. Wind is as much a part of running in Oklahoma as heat is in Florida or Arizona. You learn to work with the wind, and you learn to avoid it when you can. Avoiding the wind means running early in the morning or in the evening.

Here are some facts about wind that are important to runners:

- Wind generally moves heat away from the body, enhancing cooling. The exception is when you're running with a steady tailwind that's equal in velocity to your running speed, in which case removal of air surrounding the body is prevented. The result is a loss of heat dissipation and an increase in body temperature. This can be disastrous on a warm day but advantageous under cold conditions.

- Although headwinds can slow you down significantly, a tailwind of equal velocity won't speed you up to the same extent. Figure 8.3 shows the effect of wind on the aerobic demands of running.

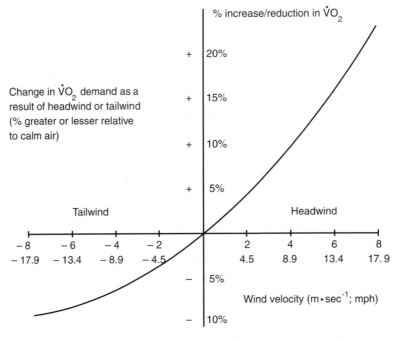

Figure 8.3 Change in oxygen consumption (VO2) demand as a result of a headwind or tailwind relative to calm air.

- Running behind another runner (drafting) is increasingly beneficial as wind velocity increases, and sometimes it's good to work with a competitor under windy conditions, sharing the duties of breaking the wind. This would be especially appropriate when both runners are trying for a particular time.

- Be careful in setting up workouts under different temperature conditions when you're not going around a track. On cold days, do your harder and faster running against the wind and your slower running with the wind. This way the cooling effect is kept short and is related to harder work, whereas recovery (slower running) can take advantage of the warmer tailwind. On warm days, do the opposite—run fast or hard with the wind, and run slowly against the cooling wind. This might not sound enjoyable, but it's better to spend more time being warm on a cold day and cool on a warm day than the other way around.

  This strategy for dealing with the cooling and warming effects of wind also applies to out-and-back steady runs. Start out against the wind on a cold day so that the trip home will be warmer. Running with a tailwind first on a cold day can lead to some really chilly conditions on the return run, particularly if you get sweaty on the way out. The opposite applies to runs in warm weather—go with the tailwind first and return against the cooling wind to negate the tendency to overheat later in the run.

Runners often ask, "What should I do during the recovery?" When performing **I**-pace training, it's best to use active recovery (easy running or jogging) because low-intensity activity helps to clear blood lactate and bring you to the next workout at a slightly elevated $\dot{V}O_2$, making the attainment of $\dot{V}O_2$max a little quicker. Jogging during recoveries also keeps muscles loose and flexible for the demanding runs yet to come.

Maintaining Proper Pacing

Be sure to maintain the proper pace during each quality run that makes up the **I** session, regardless of the duration of the individual workbouts. Many runners are surprised to learn that you shouldn't run interval 400s any faster than interval miles. Remember that the basic purpose of the workout is to boost your $\dot{V}O_2$max, not to convert you into a workout fanatic. Many runners try for a faster pace when doing shorter intervals, but it's better to save your speed for repetition workouts (described in chapter 9).

Running faster than v$\dot{V}O_2$max can't produce a greater aerobic involvement than running at v$\dot{V}O_2$max does. Remember that the stress of shorter intervals comes from shortening the recoveries, not from running faster. If you feel that interval 400s at **I** pace are too easy, shorten your recoveries, or use 1,000-meter instead of 400-meter workouts, but don't play with intensity. Please remember that you can introduce variety into your interval training by adjusting distances and recoveries. Don't introduce higher intensities into your workouts unless you're certain you've moved up in fitness. If you want to train faster, prove you're fit enough by racing faster first.

Setting Your Weekly Interval-Pace Training

The amount of quality running in an interval session should be up to 8 percent of weekly mileage, with a 6-mile or 10-kilometer maximum, or a 30-minute or 30-point limit as described in chapter 2. Even if you're logging 120-mile (200-kilometer) weeks, you shouldn't exceed the suggested cap, because $\dot{V}O_2$max intervals are without a doubt the most demanding training you can do. This is another reason you shouldn't go faster than prescribed during a workout—the excess speed might prevent you from accomplishing another quality workout on the day that you had planned.

The idea of holding interval mileage to a percentage of current weekly mileage is to prevent athletes with low training loads from performing interval sessions with others who are doing a lot more training. You should never ask a 20-mile-per-week runner to go through a 6-mile interval session with a 75-mile-per-week runner, even if they have the same **I** pace. They can run their workout together up to the point that the lower-mileage runner must drop out because of quality-training limits imposed by the lower total training stress. Six miles of running at **I** pace, plus warm-up, recovery, and cool-down running could easily add up to half of the lower-mileage runner's weekly total. That's just too much.

One of the nice things about interval training (and it's good to find something nice about intervals) is the variety of training sessions that you can do to accomplish the same purpose, which is to stress your $\dot{V}O_2$max. Keep in mind that the one aspect you shouldn't vary is the intensity, or speed, of the quality portion of an interval session, regardless of the length or duration of the workouts. The intensity (speed) of intervals should be changed only when race performances so dictate (or, if there's no race by which to judge improvement, only after four to six weeks of consistent training). If you do increase the stress of training, don't go over a one-unit VDOT increase, unless your races indicate that a larger increase is acceptable. If you're in a nonracing mode, refer to the same rule of thumb you use with threshold training—increase VDOT by one unit no more often than every fourth week of consistent training.

Not only can you change the makeup of an interval workout between one session and another, you can also vary the workouts within a single interval training session. For example, if your **I** pace is 268 meters per minute (6-minute mile pace or 90-second 400-meter pace) and you want to total 24 minutes (four miles) of quality running in an interval session, you could run six 2-minute runs with 1-minute recoveries, followed by eight 1-minute runs with 30-second recoveries, followed by eight 30-second runs with 15-second recoveries. All of the runs should be at 90-second 400-meter pace, so that

$\dot{V}O_2$max is stressed properly, and the recovery times should be equal to or less than the times of the related workbouts. The total session would last 36 minutes, with 24 minutes of **I**-pace running and 12 minutes of easy recovery running. In this particular workout, the feeling of stress should remain pretty constant as the workout progresses because the individual workbouts get shorter as the total amount of quality running accumulates.

Actually, you can make up almost any type of interval workout as long as you stick to the rules of interval training that I've set forth in this chapter and will summarize here.

- Run between 30 seconds and 5 minutes per workbout with 3 to 5 minutes being ideal.
- Stick to **I** pace for all aspects of quality running.
- Run easily during recoveries.
- Keep recovery periods equal to or shorter than the workbouts they follow.
- Let the quality portion of an interval session total up to 8 percent of your current weekly mileage (or weekly time spent running) with a nonnegotiable upper limit of 10 kilometers, or 30 minutes of running at **I** pace.

Perform an interval session with some thought about what the workout is going to accomplish for you in the long run. Intervals are challenging, but don't look at **I** pace as something you have to surpass. Consistent training is the key to success, and trying to set a record in an interval workout is not the best way to achieve consistency. Use the interval workout to meet your long-term goals with as little effort as possible; don't overtrain.

Heather Tanner

Heather Tanner was born in Baltimore, Maryland, and with a twin brother was always very active in her childhood days. As a high-school freshman in Ellicott City, Heather and her best friend gave cross country a try. The two of them quickly became the top two competitors on the team, even though they mostly just had fun and ran together in races. A family move to Alabama when she was a high school sophomore was unsettling for Heather, and she vented her frustration through running. This approach paid off, leading her to 13 individual state titles in track and cross country and to state records in both the mile and 2-mile.

Heather attended college at the University of North Carolina. During her junior year she moved to longer track races, and in her senior year she ran 16:33 and 34:21 for the 5,000 meters and 10,000 meters at the ACC conference meet. She went on to place 10th in the 10,000 meters at the NCAA national meet in 2000. Heather continued running at Stanford University, where she completed her master's degree in epidemiology. In 2001 she joined the Farm Team, and I became her coach. I have also tested her on numerous occasions in the lab. I feel compelled to say that Heather falls in a very unique category as an endurance athlete,

Photo courtesy of Heather Tanner

and I hope that we will be able to share her unusual test results with others through some future scientific publications. Heather is able to handle high mileage and considerable amounts of threshold running without undue stress, and she definitely feels that "there are no shortcuts to success." She was a member of the U.S. Chiba Ekiden team in 2002 and was selected for the U.S. team for the 2004 World Half-Marathon Championships. She looks forward to future success in long races and to being a high finisher in future Olympic marathon trials.

Personal bests: 10,000m—34:00 (33:36 road); 20K—1:11:42; 21K—1:15:51.

CHAPTER 9

Level 5:
Repetition Training

All the types of training I've detailed so far can be nicely identified by an intensity associated with a runner's VDOT value. Other types of training, however, are aimed more at anaerobic and biomechanical factors. Repetition (**R**) training is the major type of training whose purpose is not aerobic. The benefits of **R** training are associated more with mechanics and anaerobic metabolism than with aerobic factors.

The intensity of running reps usually puts considerable stress on the body to provide energy anaerobically, which in turn produces beneficial changes in anaerobic pathways, where fuel is converted to energy in the absence of adequate oxygen. Also, by practicing at **R** pace you learn to run more relaxed and faster, and race pace becomes more familiar and comfortable. In **R** training, you recruit the exact muscle fibers that you need for economical running. These are the muscle cells that allow you to run fast with minimal effort, minimal wasted movement, and minimal energy spent. Repetition workouts involve running at faster speeds, often at race pace or faster, while making sure that each workout is done with proper technique and adequate recovery.

In describing **R** training, one of my objectives is to improve the understanding of the various types of training that runners use. I like to separate **I** and **R** training based on the benefit a runner is trying to achieve (revisit chapter 2). In this chapter, I present the importance of

Sometimes picking up the pace in a race feels better than staying with the same pace; always try speeding up before you drop back from a tough pace.

recovery between **R** workbouts. I address the intensity and duration of the workbouts and the amount of quality running to do in an **R** session. I also introduce hill training and fartlek training, and give some important information about treadmill training.

So, how do you accomplish the benefits of **R** training? How do you become more comfortable, or more efficient, while running? The answer is by practicing the specific task as much as possible, avoiding undue fatigue. The easiest way to perform at a fairly fast pace for quite a while is to break the work time into shorter bouts of work. I once had 14 of my college cross country runners (9 men and 5 women) each run over 1,000 one-minute runs over a 14-day period. Two of my men averaged 322 meters per minute (5:00-mile pace) for over 250 miles (that's nearly ten 2:11 marathons in two weeks). They could do this because they always took at least four minutes of rest between each of the one-minute runs. It's questionable if a person could run 250 five-minute miles in that same period of time, but the shortness of the runs made the large number of miles at that average pace a possibility—and a reality. Interestingly, following this long repetition workout, only one of these runners suffered an injury (of short duration), and they all had good cross country seasons in the fall.

I'm certainly not proposing such an arduous way of achieving a large quantity of running at a pretty fast pace, or that such an amount of fast running is even desirable. But I am pointing out that with adequate recovery time a great deal of quality running can be accomplished, without losing good mechanics. If the recovery is not adequate, stress mounts, mechanics deteriorate, and the purpose of the training is destroyed.

This is **R** training—running relatively short workbouts with enough recovery time to allow each subsequent run to be just as efficient as the first run of the series. **R** training is also quite anaerobic in nature (especially compared with the other training intensities I've discussed), so it isn't necessarily a good approach to improving $\dot{V}O_2$max. Some runners and coaches get the impression that if 16×400 at 60 seconds each with four minutes of recovery between runs is good for you, then the same session with two-minute recoveries must be even better. This could be true if the two-minute breaks are long enough to let each subsequent run be done with equal efficiency and speed of running. However, if mechanics suffer because of a cut in recovery time, the purpose of the session is lost. Don't sacrifice the purpose of any workout; use recoveries wisely, taking more time when necessary. When you're doing reps, it's necessary to take more recovery time; when you're doing intervals, recovery time is important but is usually kept short rather than long.

Determining Recovery Time

Let me approach **R** training in a somewhat unusual manner: by considering the recovery periods first. This is a key difference among reps, intervals, and cruise intervals—the recovery activity and time for reps are not so structured. The type and amount of recovery following each workout is determined subjectively. Simply put, you recover until you feel you can perform the next run as well as you did the previous one. If you need five minutes to recover from a one-and-a-half-minute run, then take five minutes. Don't rush into the next rep feeling tired.

Some people use heart rates to determine how long recoveries should be, but I prefer to leave it up to the runner. The purpose of reps is to improve speed and economy, and the best way (almost the only way) to run fast and with good technique for repeated workouts is to be fully recovered from the previous run before starting the next. There are only two negative aspects of recovering too long between runs in an **R** session: You might become stiff, cold, and tense before embarking on your next fast rep, and the workout might take too long on a day when you're pressed for time.

During recovery periods between repetitions, do whatever helps you prepare to give your best effort when you resume running.

A guideline for planning **R** recoveries is to rest two to four times as long as you work; for example, you might need to follow a one-minute run with as much as a four-minute recovery period. At least part of the recovery should consist of easy running. Whatever brings you to the start of the next rep feeling ready to run at **R** pace is what's best for you for your recovery period. If that involves running, walking, or even some stretching, that's fine. In reps you should always feel you're ready to perform the next run as the best one of the series. If you reach a point at which resting four times longer than you're running is not enough rest, either you've had enough for that particular session or the pace has been too fast and you should slow it down for the next run.

Determining Repetition Pace

Another important difference between reps and intervals is that each **R** workout usually takes less than two minutes and is 600 meters or less in length (800-meter reps are acceptable for faster competitors). Shorter run times and longer recoveries are used for reps because **R** pace is faster than **I** pace. **R** pace is partly a function of the event you're training for. If your event of primary interest is 800 or 1,500 meters, then your reps will be faster than if you were training for a marathon. However, a marathon runner and a 1,500-meter runner might both be doing intervals and threshold runs at the same pace. In fact, the same runner might be doing intervals and threshold runs at the same pace, when preparing for different events, but this runner would let each event's duration dictate the pace of the reps. In addition to the normal **R** pace shown in the VDOT tables, I introduce a faster category ("**F**" pace) of reps for 800 and 1,500 runners in chapters 16 and 17.

Race Pace

It has become more and more clear to me that a variety of training paces can be set aside for repetition work. I've had runners enjoy considerable success concentrating on reps that are run about three seconds per 400 slower than their mile goal pace for the coming season. Another approach that I often advocate is to use current mile-race pace as rep pace. Actually, when you evaluate these two approaches—current mile-race pace and goal pace + 3 seconds per 400—you usually see that the two intensities are pretty similar, depending of course on your current state of fitness. In addition, there are times when running reps somewhat faster than race pace is also appropriate. This would certainly apply for 1,500 runners who also race the 800 and need familiarity with the shorter event's race pace.

For runners whose primary event of interest is 5,000 meters or longer, I prefer to set **R** pace at 6 seconds per 400 meters faster than current **I** pace. A 10K runner who races at 85-second pace per 400 meters (about 35:25 for the 10K) would have an **I** pace of 81 seconds per 400 meters. Because **I** pace is faster than race pace for this 10K runner, **R** pace would be about 6 seconds per 400 faster than the 81-second **I** pace—75 seconds per 400 meters. Table 3.2 (page 52) provides you with a basic **R** pace based on a standard relationship with **I**-pace training. It's certainly possible to experiment some with **R** intensities, but keep in mind the need for adequate recoveries and good mechanics.

Cruise Repetitions

"Cruise repetition" is my term for a modification of usual **R** running. A cruise-rep workout involves a series of runs performed at **T** pace for anyone preparing for races 10K or longer, or at **I** pace for runners preparing for races shorter than 10K. As opposed to the very brief recoveries used in cruise-interval workouts, in a cruise-rep workout, full recoveries are used between runs. Cruise reps are usually longer in duration than the two-minute limit for reps. It's typical to run 800s, 1,000s, or 1,200s in a cruise-rep work out (usually a total of two or three miles), allowing complete recovery between runs. Cruise reps aren't true reps by definition but are a relatively low-key set of reps at a comfortably hard pace. They're best used in the final days leading up to an important race because they provide some quality with minimal stress (because of the full recovery).

Hill Running

Hill running is a type of **R** training that involves intense, short uphill workbouts separated by relatively long recovery periods. Hill work produces some of the same benefits as reps, including better economy and the power that aids speed.

My preferred method of incorporating hill training into a program is to use a treadmill so that you can eliminate the downhill running that's generally part of a true hill session. (The downhill running between harder uphill runs can lead to a landing-shock injury if you're not careful). I provide more details on hill running in chapter 18, which covers cross country training.

Treadmill Training

I've been using treadmill workouts since 1960, when I first worked in a lab where a treadmill was available; it was also the year that I first started coaching runners at the collegiate level. I used to make up workouts that would just about stress me to the limit, in hopes of making a regular outdoor session seem easy in comparison. I also used to set up standard workouts on the treadmill that I could repeat during different times of the season to check my progress.

All these years of measuring $\dot{V}O_2$, HR, and blood lactate levels at different treadmill speeds and grades led to an interest in how I could use different combinations of speeds and grades to produce the demands of a variety of running paces on flat ground. This information is important because it allows you to create well-controlled workouts, even on a treadmill that won't go very fast, by adjusting the grade to impose the desired intensity.

Being able to set the desired pace on a treadmill allows you to concentrate on other things, such as good technique, breathing patterns, and leg cadence. One of the disadvantages of treadmill running is being unable to share a run with a partner. However, you can overcome this if you pick the right kind of workout. One of my favorites is to run a series of repeated 30-second or 1-minute runs at a pretty steep grade and slow speed with equal amounts of recovery between runs. This accommodates two people nicely—while one is resting, the other is running.

I've realized over the years that some injuries are not aggravated on a treadmill when running slowly up a steep grade, whereas a workout of the same intensity (stress) on the flat could exacerbate them. In a sense, graded treadmill running can be a specific type of cross-training (for those who cross-train in an attempt to avoid too much running) while still stressing physiological systems of importance.

As mentioned earlier, a big advantage of treadmill running is in the area of hill training. In overground training, hill work involves both going up and coming down. On the treadmill, it involves going up and then resting before going up again. There's none of the potentially damaging downhill stuff. This is particularly helpful for runners nursing a landing-shock injury.

Even downhill training (to prepare for the downhills of the Boston Marathon, for example) can be accomplished on a treadmill. Just jack up the rear support of the treadmill, lower it onto a solid block of wood, and you'll have to elevate the grade just to reach level running. I wouldn't try more than a 6 to 8 percent downhill grade for any training session because it's easy to run very fast, and the quads can take a beating; plus, recovery is slow from this training. I suggest setting up a fan so that the layer of hot air that inevitably builds up around your body when on a treadmill can be blown away and replaced with cooler, less humid air.

Equating Workout Intensities

Table 9.1 allows for using a wide variety of speeds and grades to accomplish desired training stresses. Be aware that any speed of running on a treadmill is slightly less demanding than it would be on a track or level road, yet because of the greater chance for heat build-up you might get an equal or even higher heart rate. To adjust for the lack of work that you would experience by running against a headwind, I advise adding a 1 to 2 percent grade (I prefer the 2 percent grade) to the treadmill; this also reduces landing shock slightly and is better than adjusting the workload by running faster than you would during overground running. Table 9.1 takes into account the need for a slight grade to equate treadmill running to overground running.

Table 9.1 shows the grade that, when applied to the miles per hour (mph) speed (shown at the top), will produce an effort equal to running at the mile pace shown in the left column. For example, a 6:11-mile effort could be accomplished by running at 6 mph on a 10.2 percent grade, 7 mph at a 7 percent grade, or 9.5 mph at a 2.3 percent grade. A 4:13-mile effort (63 seconds per 400 meters) could be done at 6 mph at a 21.2 percent grade, or any combination of values in that row ending with 12 mph at a 4.3 percent grade.

For **E**- and **M**-pace intensities, first determine your proper **E**- and **M**-pace mile or kilometer times from the VDOT tables (see tables 3.1 and 3.2), and then run for the desired or prescribed durations at the combination of speed and grade that achieves that intensity (from table 9.1). On different occasions, try different speed and grade combinations, but I suggest not going higher than about a 6 percent grade at these intensities

Table 9.1   **Treadmill Grades to Produce Specific Mile-Pace Efforts**

Mile effort	6.0	6.5	7.0	7.5	8.0	8.5	9.0	9.5	10.0	10.5	11.0	11.5	12.0
					Miles per hour								
9:19	2.9	1.9	--	--	--	--	--	--	--	--	--	--	--
8:15	4.8	3.5	2.5	--	--	--	--	--	--	--	--	--	--
7:24	6.6	5.2	4.0	3.0	2.2	--	--	--	--	--	--	--	--
6:44	8.4	6.8	5.5	4.4	3.5	2.6	--	--	--	--	--	--	--
6:11	10.2	8.5	7.0	5.8	4.7	3.8	3.0	2.3	--	--	--	--	--
5:43	12.1	10.1	8.5	7.2	6.0	5.0	4.1	3.3	2.6	2.0	--	--	--
5:19	13.9	11.8	10.0	8.5	7.3	6.2	5.2	4.3	3.6	2.9	2.3	--	--
4:59	15.7	13.4	11.5	9.9	8.5	7.3	6.3	5.4	4.6	3.8	3.2	2.6	2.0
4:42	17.5	15.1	13.0	11.3	9.8	8.5	7.4	6.4	5.5	4.7	4.0	3.4	2.8
4:27	19.4	16.8	14.5	12.7	11.1	9.7	8.5	7.4	6.5	5.6	4.9	4.2	3.6
4:13	21.2	18.4	16.0	14.1	12.4	10.9	9.6	8.5	7.5	6.6	5.7	5.0	4.3
4:01	23.0	20.0	17.5	15.4	13.6	12.1	10.7	9.5	8.5	7.5	6.6	5.8	5.1
3:51	24.8	21.7	19.0	16.8	14.9	13.2	11.8	10.5	9.4	8.4	7.5	6.6	5.9

For **T**-, **I**-, and **R**-pace workouts, first determine the proper pace (from the VDOT tables) that represents the training pace you want, then select an appropriate workout from the sessions provided in tables 9.2 a-c that gives you the total duration of quality running at the pace desired. I offer a variety of actual workouts (combinations of number of repeat runs and rest) that achieve the goal of the workout. Try different workouts on different occasions—either keep varying them or settle on one that you prefer for accomplishing your goal for a particular training session.

You also can add variety to treadmill workouts by making up some fartlek sessions in which you mix some **R**-pace running with **I**-pace and **T**-pace running. Remember to keep your rests following **T** pace to about one fifth of your run time; rests following **I**-pace runs should be about equal to or a little shorter than run time, and rests between **R**-pace runs should about double the run time.

Table 9.2*a*   **Threshold Treadmill Workouts**

Perform each of these workouts at your **T** pace or equivalent grade and speed combination. Warm up with a 10-minute easy run and a few 30-second strides.

Workouts	Minutes
Steady 20-min run	20
6 × 5 min with 1-min rests	30
3 × 10 min with 2-min rests	30
2 × 15 min with 3-min rests	30
8 × 5 min with 1-min rests	40
5 × 8 min with 1-min rests	40
4 × 10 min with 2-min rests	40
15 min with 3-min rest 2 × 10 min with 2-min rests 5 min	40
10 × 5 min with 1-min rests	50
5 × 10 min with 2-min rests	50
2 × 15 min with 3-min rests 2 × 10 min with 2-min rests	50
6 × 10 min with 2-min rests	60
4 × 15 min with 3-min rests	60
2 × 15 min with 3-min rests 2 × 10 min with 2-min rests 2 × 5 min with 1-min rests	60

Table 9.2*b* Interval Treadmill Workouts

Perform these at **I** pace or equivalent grade and speed combinations. Warm up with a 10-minute easy run and a few faster 30-second runs.

Workout	Minutes
4 × 3 min with 2-min rests	12
6 × 2 min with 1-min rests	12
1 min with 1-min rest 2 min with 2-min rest 2 × 3 min with 3-min rests 2 min with 2-min rest 1 min	12
5 × 3 min with 2-min rests	15
3 × 5 min with 4-min rests	15
1 min with 1-min rest 2 min with 1-min rest 3 min with 2-min rest 4 min with 3-min rest 3 min with 2-min rest 2 min	15
5 × 4 min with 3-min rests	20
4 × 5 min with 4-min rests	20
2 min with 1-min rest 3 min with 2-min rest 5 min with 4-min rest 5 min with 4-min rest 3 min with 2-min rest 2 min	20
5 × 5 min with 4-min rests	25
2 × 5 min with 4-min rests 2 × 4 min with 3-min rests 2 × 3 min with 2-min rests	24
3 min with 2-min rest 4 min with 3-min rest 2 × 5 min with 4-min rests 4 min with 3-min rest 3 min	24
6 × 5 min with 4-min rests	30
10 × 3 min with 2-min rests	30
1 min with 1-min rest 2 min with 1-min rest 3 min with 2-min rest 4 min with 4-min rest 2 × 5 min with 4-min rests 4 min with 3-min rest 3 min with 2-min rest 2 min with 1-min rest 1 min	30

Table 9.2*c* Repetition Treadmill Workouts

Perform these at **R** pace according to the training schedule you're using. Get a good warm-up with a 10-minute easy run and a few faster 30-second runs. Then try different speed and grade combinations that produce the intensity equal to your chosen repetition intensity.

Workout	Minutes
12 × 30 sec with 1- to 2-min rests	6
6 × 60 sec with 2- to 4-min rests	6
20 × 30 sec with 1- to 2-min rests	10
10 × 60 sec with 2- to 4-min rests	10
5 × (30 sec with 1-min rest + 30 sec with 2-min rest + 1 min with 30-sec rest)	10
12 × 60 sec with 2-min rests 8 × 30 sec with 1-min rests	16
16 × 60 sec with 2-min rests	16
8 × 30 sec with 1-min rests 8 × 60 sec with 2-min rests 8 × 30 sec with 1-min rests	16
40 × 30 sec with 1-min rests	20
20 × 60 sec with 2-min rests	20
8 × 30 sec with 1-min rests 12 × 60 sec with 2-min rests 8 × 30 sec with 1-min rests	20

| Table 9.3 | **Conversion of Miles Per Hour (mph) and Meters Per Minute (M/min) on Treadmill to Mile Pace Times** | | | | | | | |

Mph	Mile	M/min	Mph	Mile	M/min	Mph	Mile	M/min
6.0	10:00	161	8.1	7:24	217	10.1	5:56	271
6.1	9:50	164	8.2	7:19	220	10.2	5:53	274
6.2	9:41	166	8.3	7:14	223	10.3	5:49	276
6.3	9:31	169	8.4	7:09	225	10.4	5:46	279
6.4	9:22	172	8.5	7:04	228	10.5	5:43	282
6.5	9:14	174	8.6	6:59	231	10.6	5:40	284
6.6	9:05	177	8.7	6:54	233	10.7	5:36	287
6.7	8:57	180	8.8	6:49	236	10.8	5:33	290
6.8	8:49	182	8.9	6:44	239	10.9	5:30	292
6.9	8:42	185	9.0	6:40	241	11.0	5:27	295
7.0	8:34	188	9.1	6:36	244	11.1	5:24	298
7.1	8:27	190	9.2	6:31	247	11.2	5:21	300
7.2	8:20	193	9.3	6:27	249	11.3	5:19	303
7.3	8:13	196	9.4	6:23	252	11.4	5:16	306
7.4	8:06	198	9.5	6:19	255	11.5	5:13	308
7.5	8:00	201	9.6	6:15	257	11.6	5:10	311
7.6	7:54	204	9.7	6:11	260	11.7	5:08	314
7.7	7:48	207	9.8	6:07	263	11.8	5:05	317
7.8	7:42	209	9.9	6:04	266	11.9	5:02	319
7.9	7:36	212	10.0	6:00	268	12.0	5:00	322
8.0	7.30	215						

Calibrating Your Treadmill

If you train on the same treadmill regularly, you might want to determine the accuracy of the speedometer by measuring the running belt length to the nearest centimeter and then timing 10 revolutions (while running on the treadmill) to determine how fast you're actually running in meters per minute. Then use table 9.3 to identify your mph and pace per mile.

Fartlek

Another type of training that can involve **R** running is fartlek (pronounced "fart-lake"), a Swedish term translated as "speed play." Fartlek workouts mix several types of running—easy running, hills, reps, and even **I**- and **T**-pace bouts—into one session.

There can be long fartlek sessions or short ones, hard ones or easy ones, depending on what you want to accomplish. Keep in mind the purpose of the session. If a fartlek workout is planned as an easy day, don't let it become a hard day just because aspects of the session lend themselves to getting into a race (with someone else or with yourself).

A type of fartlek session that works well, especially if you don't have known distances to cover or a watch to keep time, is to count steps as you run. Run 10 steps (counting one foot, not both) then jog 10, run 20 and jog 20, run 30 and jog 30, and so on up to running 100 and jogging 100 (or more if you wish). Then descend by 10s until you run and jog 10 steps again. This is a good workout when you feel lethargic but want to get in some decent running. In this workout, there's no pressure to achieve certain splits, and the nature of the workout gets you going at a pretty good pace. A more specific fartlek workout might include the following sequence:

- An easy warm-up of 10 to 15 minutes
- 3 × 1 mile at **T** pace with 1-minute rests between
- 3 × 1,000 at **I** pace with 3-minute recovery jogs
- 3 × 400 at **R** pace with 3-minute jogs
- 3 × 200 at **R** pace with 200-meter jogs
- Easy 10- to 15-minute cool-down

Setting Your Weekly Repetition-Pace Training

The amount of quality running in a true **R** session should be up to 5 percent of your current weekly mileage, with an upper limit of 5 miles or 8,000 meters. For example, a 5K runner who is running 60 miles per week and whose **R** pace is 70 seconds per 400 meters might run as many as 12 × 400 meters at 70 seconds each, or 24 × 200 meters at 35 seconds each, or some combination of 200s and 400s that totals 3 miles (5 percent of 60). On the other hand, 5 percent of 100 weekly miles would be 5 miles of reps, which could be okay but might be a bit demanding and, because recovery time is relatively long, this could be a very time-consuming workout—which is why I recommend an upper limit of 5 miles or 8,000 meters. Runners who base their training on duration rather than mileage should use a 3 percent rule (3 percent of weekly total running time) but should not do more than 20 minutes at **R** pace in any single training session. Please keep in mind that the 5 percent or 5-mile (or 20-minute) figure represents an upper limit for reps and need not be the required amount. After some experience with the point system (chapter 2), you might also want to set a point total that applies to rep sessions.

Repetitions are pretty intense for many runners and often leave them dead-legged and without much of a kick for races. This is true particularly during a phase of training when reps are emphasized, such as during phase III of a program that relies heavily on reps (for 800- and 1,500-meter runners, in particular). When going into a period of important competitions, you can minimize true **R**-pace running in favor of cruise reps, or you can cut back by almost 50 percent on the total amount of quality running at **R** pace. Surprisingly, cruise reps seem to aid the development of a kick, and for some runners they produce greater speed than the faster reps do. Before trying the more demanding reps, I recommend using cruise reps for a season, especially if you're a young runner or a beginner. Chapter 4 discusses how to plot out a season of training, and part IV presents specific training programs.

A good measure of a successful workout that involves **R** running is that you end the workout feeling that you've accomplished some relatively fast, quality running and that you could have continued a little longer without struggling with the pace. Being in control of the pace you're setting is the key to successful **R** training.

Alan Culpepper

© Claus Andersen

Alan Culpepper was born in Ft. Worth, Texas, where as a youngster he participated in basketball, baseball, soccer, rock climbing, and skiing. He started running at age 12 and realized early on that he had unique abilities; success in training spurred him to pursue the sport further. As is often the case with beginners, Alan's first interests in running were cross country and the shorter distance events of 800 and 1,500 meters. In his quest to continue improving his personal bests, Alan ran at Coronado High School in El Paso, Texas. He was successful enough as a high school runner to believe that he was capable of performing at the national and international level, and therefore set the lofty goals of making World Championship and Olympic Teams.

Alan's running achievements during college at the University of Colorado and since graduation have certainly substantiated his early belief in his capabilities. In 1996 he was NCAA Champion in the 5,000 meters, an event he also won at the U.S. nationals in 2002. He won U.S. national track titles in the 10,000 meters in 1999 and 2003; during those same years he was the U.S. 12K cross country national champion. In addition to these accomplishments, Alan made the U.S. World Cross Country team in 1999 and made four World Track and Field Championship Teams between 1997 and 2003. His most recent accomplishments have come in the marathon, with a first-place finish in the 2004 U.S. Olympic Trials and a solid 12th place finish in the Athens Olympic marathon.

Personal bests: 1,500m—3:37.66; mile—3:55.1; 3,000m—7:47.6; 5,000m—13:27.5; 10,000m—27:33.9; marathon—2:09:41.

CHAPTER 10

Supplemental Training

In this chapter I want to discuss some types of nonrunning training that can benefit runners and explain how to use this training throughout the season and during any time off from running, whether planned or because of injury or illness. When I say "supplemental training," I'm referring to any type of activity (physical or mental) that runners perform in addition to the running portion of their training program. The expected outcomes of supplemental training include the following:

- An increase in the amount or quality of running that can be performed
- A decrease in the chance of injury during running
- Maintenance of fitness level, even during an injury or illness

One of the most important aspects of reaching your potential as a runner is consistency—the ability to train regularly for extended periods with few setbacks along the way. Thus, part of my coaching philosophy is that training must be rewarding and safe enough that my athletes can and will stay with it long enough to find out how good they truly are. Plenty of runners can endure some pretty strenuous training sessions, but if their training isn't progressive and consistent, disappointments mount along the way. In the worst cases, hard training and lost

Avoiding injury should be one of the primary goals of a good training program.

time caused by lack of consistency lead to a loss of interest, and what might have been a great running career is side-tracked.

There's no doubt that over the years I've been coaching, my most successful runners have included nonrunning activities as a regular part of their training program. I encourage all runners to set aside regular time for supplemental activities; doing so can be the edge you need to move up to the next level of fitness and performance. Many runners include stretching as part of their daily routine, and some might even overemphasize flexibility. Maybe more time spent on developing power and mental toughness (related to proper race tactics and good technique) would serve many runners better than working on increased flexibility. Certainly, deep-water running and using an elliptical trainer have considerably aided many injured runners and should even be considered by noninjured runners as a way to augment their aerobic conditioning. Running specificity, of course, is still of utmost importance, but if supplemental training increases a runner's resistance to injury, it's time well spent.

Although supplemental training likely provides more in the way of injury prevention than direct running benefit, any training you do that allows you to do more running, without injury, also provides you with a better chance of converting that additional running into improvements in performance. So, think of time you spend strengthening and stretching as time well spent, time that will lead to less downtime and more quality time running.

One might argue that it doesn't really matter *why* you get better, as long as you *do* get better. But I think it's important for runners to understand the factors that directly and indirectly affect their performances. One thing to keep in mind is that just because some weight loss or type of supplemental training leads to an improvement in running performance, this doesn't necessarily mean that more weight loss or more training will result in further improvement. More is not always better (e.g., adding more mileage to your training program doesn't always produce positive results; sometimes the result is an injury that causes a long setback). There are limits to how much weight or body fat you should lose and to how much cross-training you should undertake. The goal of any competitive runner should be to produce better race results, not to become super lean or develop a bodybuilder's physique.

Training the Mind

Many books and publications out there relate to the benefits of mental training. I don't pretend to be a specialist in this area. What I use with my athletes comes from coaching clinics and international conferences I present at and attend. But my former sport, modern pentathlon, probably demands as much in terms of mental readiness as any sport does. The pentathlete must be able to switch from a state of extreme mental alertness for fencing, to extreme tranquility for shooting, then to a state of aggressiveness for the swim, alertness for the ride on an unfamiliar horse, and back to aggressiveness for the final running event.

For distance runners, the mental task is often less complicated but no less important. Possibly the single best statement that applies to the mental approach to running training and racing is "focus on the task at hand." Sometimes that means calming yourself while you "float" through a particular workout or segment of a race, and sometimes it means calling on all the physical energy you can muster to get the job done.

One popular method of mental training is to mentally relive positive running experiences and think of disappointments only long enough to imagine how you could have changed them to make them successful. Visualizing how you want to get the job done and how events will unfold, while still being ready for the unexpected, usually provides for a state of strong mental readiness before a serious run or race. Take an optimistic attitude toward your successes *(I believe in myself and my ability)* and your failures *(a failure is temporary and doesn't reflect my true abilities)*. Try to set aside some time before all races to go through the race in your mind, imagining how you'll feel as you run and how you'll respond to the unexpected. With practice, you'll be able to think through even long races in a short period of time, possibly within seconds as you approach the start.

© Human Kinetics

Visualization is an effective way to create a confident mind-set and to achieve your desired mental state.

Enhancing Flexibility

When you train, you want it to count. Be sure what you're doing is beneficial and not just adding unproductive activity to your training program. This goes for both your regular training and anything supplemental that you do. Proof that what you're doing is beneficial can come in two ways. First, your normal training loads and intensities will feel easier, and second, your race performances will improve. If these changes aren't happening, then over time you should question if what you're doing is really worthwhile.

The first thing to ask anyone who offers a quick (or even a not so quick) fix for problems you're having or who suggests a guaranteed performance boost is, "Can you give me some hard evidence to support your claims?" I learned this while working at Athletics West. People often contacted me to sing the praises of some great training device or powerful pill that they wanted Alberto Salazar or Joan Benoit or Mary Slaney to try out, claiming that using the product would improve performance. When I gave them my "show me the evidence" line, their answer was usually, "Well, that's what we want you to do for us." I guess I was supposed to do their job for them, using proven running stars as guinea pigs.

However, with some types of supplemental training, such as stretching, trial and error is the only way to discover what works for you. When you do decide to try a new approach in your training, give the method a fair trial—something on the order of four to six weeks. Don't just try a few days of flexibility training, feel no difference in your performance, and give up on stretching. If something is worth trying at all, it's worth giving a fair shot.

A good approach when choosing which stretching exercises to include in your program is to think of the areas of your body that have given you some trouble in your running career. Have you had tightness or soreness in your iliotibial band? Have your calves or Achilles tendons bothered you on occasion? Do you sometimes suffer from tight hamstrings? Once you've determined the parts of your body that might benefit most from flexibility training, choose some stretches and set aside a few minutes daily for stretching. Try to give this training as much priority as you give your running. No, you won't spend nearly as much time stretching as you do running, but the benefits of flexibility exercises come with far less time commitment—just make sure it's serious time.

As is true of all illnesses and injuries, prevention is far better than treatment after the fact, so don't wait until you have a problem to start a flexibility program. On the other hand, it's not always best to start stretching a problem area when you start having pain in that area—it can be counterproductive to stretch a sore tendon or muscle. If you have a prolonged injury or one that doesn't seem to be healing itself with time off, seek professional help.

The best time for serious stretching is after you've warmed up your muscles with about 10 minutes of easy running, which increases blood flow and muscle temperatures. If an injury prevents you from running, then work into your stretching exercises gradually and involve walking or other types of total body movement during and between exercises to warm up the muscles and keep them warm. If you have an injury that significantly reduces the amount of running you can do, this might be a great time to get serious about flexibility exercises and other types of supplemental training. Just check with your doctor or trainer beforehand.

Strengthening Muscles

Normally, it's a good idea to include some strengthening exercises in your weekly training program. For a beginning runner, gaining strength might be as important as running itself, and for an experienced runner these kind of exercises might make the difference in whether or not you reach some lofty goals.

In case you're wondering, my recommendation to include strengthening exercises in your overall training program is not a contradiction of training principle 2, which deals with specificity of training (chapter 1), because I'm not saying to *replace* running with strengthening exercises but rather to *add* them to your running program. If you perform them correctly, the least these exercises will do for you is prevent some injuries, whereas in the best-case scenario, they'll allow you (through additional resistance to injury and better toned muscles) the ability to do more quality running, which is usually a positive thing for a distance runner. As with a stretching regimen, work into strengthening exercises easily. Gradually build to the point to which you're spending 15 to 30 minutes with your chosen exercises, three days a week.

I'll always remember my exercise physiology professor, P.O. Åstrand, telling us that in schools in Sweden almost every sportsman relies on a solid trunk from which the extremities and various muscles function. It's true that well-toned abdominal muscles and strong back muscles serve athletes well. With this in mind, I encourage my runners to perform exercises that strengthen their trunk muscles. I also recommend knee extensions (that involve only the final 15 to 20 degrees of extension) and hamstring curls because they provide additional medial quad and hamstring strengthening, which can help prevent knee problems. I also like exercises that can be done without equipment, such as push-ups, chin-ups, light uphill bounding, abdominal crunches, and burpees (going from a standing to a squat position, to a front push-up position, back to squat position, and returning to standing), which can be done using both hands or first one hand and then the other. One of the main benefits of these exercises is that they give you better control over your body, better balance, and better running economy (you spend less energy to run faster).

Often the best way to include some strengthening exercises in your overall program is to set up a circuit or series of exercises to go through three times a week, moving from station to station at set intervals of time or number of repetitions. A good circuit involves 7 to 10 stations with some stretching, strengthening of several different muscle groups, and even aerobic activity. For example, you might set up a circuit that starts with a station for push-ups, followed by one for hamstring curls, one for chin-ups, then rope jumping, short jogging, burpees, stretching exercises, sit-ups (or abdominal curls from a hanging chin-up position), knee extensions, and finally, straight arm and leg raises while lying face down on the ground. After you complete one circuit, you return to the start and begin the cycle again.

If you're a coach working with many athletes, a good way to approach a circuit routine is to devote a certain amount of time at each station and continue that station's exercise until the time is up; then have athletes move to the next station. This way everyone is moving from one station to the next at the same time. Another approach is to set a number of repeats of each exercise to do at each station, and when that number has been completed, it's time to move to the next station. Allocate time for easier stations (rope jumping, stretching, and jogging, for example), but limit the more demanding activities by number of repetitions (for example, one half the maximum number the athlete can do or one half the maximum he or she can do in one minute). An advantage of this latter method is that athletes work relative to their ability level and don't spend the same amount of time at each station. When you use this individualized approach, you can help motivate your athletes by timing them (once a week) on how long it takes to complete their three circuits. Every few weeks, record each athlete's new "max" efforts, which will change the number of repeats he or she does at each station and give him or her a new standard to try to beat. I've found that athletes' times usually improve dramatically.

When creating circuit stations, avoid stressing the same muscle groups at consecutive stations, and vary the type of activity being performed (strength, flexibility, aerobic, and so on). You might even want to include a run that lasts a minute or two as part of the circuit, though usually you can save this for more experienced runners. I've included a sample circuit in table 10.1. Before starting this routine, you first need to determine a maximum performance for push-ups, chin-ups, hamstring curls, and knee extensions, as well as the maximum number of sit-ups (or abdominal crunches or bar-hanging knees-to-chest roll-ups) that can be performed in one minute.

Table 10.1 **Example of a Circuit-Training Routine**

Station	Activity	Work load or time at station
1	Push-up	One-half max
2	Hamstring curl	10 × at one-half max
3	Knee extension	10 × at one-half max
4	Chin-up	One-half max
5	Jump rope	50 reps
6	Flexibility work	Pick an activity and do for 2 min
7	Sit-up, curl-up, or crunch	One-half of 1-min max
8	Burpee (1 or 2 handed)	20 reps
9	Run	Can be short or fast, easy or relatively hard
10	Back flex (arms overhead)	30 reps

Make three complete circuits of the 10 stations. Time the three reps of the circuit once each week and establish new maxes every third or fourth week.

Cross-Training

Cross-training refers to nonrunning activities used in place of running within a running training program. Although some runners might never need to cross-train, some might occasionally find it beneficial; still others might depend on cross-training as part of their regular week's training plan. Activities that help an athlete ward off or recover from injury are the ones most useful to cross-train. Hiking, swimming, water running, cycling, cross-country skiing, and using an elliptical trainer all qualify, as does anything else that can benefit a runner's body and mind as he or she becomes better prepared for racing.

Some people think that supplemental nonrunning activities can help prepare runners for competition better than a program of only running can. In my view, this can be true, but mainly for runners who can spend only a small amount of time actually running and for those who suffer regular setbacks when they try to undertake a high-volume, or high-intensity, running program.

Unfortunately, more running doesn't always keep you injury free, and if cross-training permits harder running training through reducing injuries, then select supplemental activities are well worth the effort. Through trial and error and scientific research, we're always learning more about training, and it might be true that some nonrunning activities can produce future running breakthroughs. In any case, I believe improvements in running through cross-training are much more likely when the cross-training enables runners to run more intensely, more effectively, or with less physical and emotional stress.

I'm sometimes asked by runners, "How much running does my cross-training correspond to?" One way in which you can at least identify the intensity of your cross-training is to monitor your heart rate while performing a cross-training activity. Because you're not running and may or may not be involving muscles of the lower extremities, I suggest the following: If your legs are involved, such as in cycling, water running, cross-country skiing, and the like, count the time spent at the desired heart rates as equal to two thirds of that amount of time spent running. With other types of cross-training, such as swimming, figure time spent as being equal to half that time spent running. Use the point tables in chapter 2 to figure points earned for time spent at relative heart rates.

If a runner can be reasonable about nutrition and not lose anything psychologically while waiting for an injury to heal, I think it's accurate to say that cross-training during a layoff prevents some of the fitness decay associated with the same amount of time off with no cross-training.

Taking Unplanned Time Off

There are certainly benefits to be gained from cross-training during times when you're not able to run, such as while you're injured. In the pages that follow I discuss these benefits as well as how to deal with unplanned setbacks and avoid future setbacks. I also talk about ways to plot a return to normal training and how to rearrange an interrupted season. Note that I discuss planned breaks from training toward the end of chapter 4.

CHANGES IN BODY COMPOSITION

Another way in which cross-training can benefit running is by producing a loss of excess body mass. The extra activity associated with cross-training burns calories, and there's no doubt that the loss of nonessential body fat results in better race performances, even in the absence of improved fitness. It's hard to tell, however, how much of improved running performance can be traced to a leaner frame rather than the fact that quality training can be carried out more effectively with a slimmer body. I want to emphasize that becoming too lean or overly conscious of body fat can be quite detrimental to a quality training program. Losing unneeded body fat is one matter—losing body mass for the sake of weighing less is another. Doing this can be counterproductive and even lead to a runner's downfall. When losing weight involves a loss of useful muscle mass, performance will suffer because of a lowered $\dot{V}O_2$max. Less muscle mass means less work can be performed and thus less oxygen consumed.

An important factor relating to $\dot{V}O_2$max that we should acknowledge is that there are two general components associated with aerobic power. The central component is the delivery of blood and oxygen to the exercising muscles. The other, peripheral, component involves how well the exercising muscles can use the delivered oxygen for turning fuel into useful energy. In addition, the actions the running muscles perform as they support the body and move it forward all lead to improved muscle fitness to better perform these actions.

When you have an injury that reduces or temporarily prevents your running muscles and their associated peripheral aerobic components from experiencing beneficial training stress, then a detraining of these important components occurs. When this happens, performing supplemental or cross-training exercises (such as swimming, rowing, and cycling) that might stress the central delivery system is really doing only half the job required for optimal running benefits. That is, the specific peripheral factors are neglected.

Coming back from time off running following an injury, even if you've diligently performed cross-training activities the entire time, sometimes leads to additional injury. Although the central system has remained fit, the muscles, connective tissue, and other peripheral factors haven't received much stress, which makes them susceptible to new injuries or overuse. I say more about returning from setbacks later in this chapter.

Maintain a Positive Attitude

Although runners fear setbacks and are often reluctant to take breaks from running, I like to look at the bright side of time off. As I discuss in chapter 4, breaks can be beneficial to runners in terms of their overall development; this includes unplanned breaks and setbacks caused by injury or illness. A break gives both the body and the mind a rest.

© Empics

| Even elite competitors such as Kelly Holmes sometimes find themselves sidelined by injury.

Often a setback benefits runners because of the determination factor. Setbacks sometimes make runners determined to prove that great things were just about to happen before their training was rudely interrupted. What serious runner hasn't been on a roll, only to have his or her training suddenly curtailed by a setback? Injuries are an inevitable part of distance runners' careers. But they're not always as bad as they're made out to be.

It's best to look at setbacks optimistically; try to view them as career prolongers. As a setback-induced break ends, a runner's enthusiasm for running is renewed, and he or she now knows more about what kinds of training is and isn't stressful to his or her body. Wiser, better rested, and more determined, the runner is actually in position to have a longer career because of the imposed break.

Setbacks can be terribly disappointing, but they also have a way of keeping us hungry. Temporary training stalemates can actually rekindle competitive fires, revitalize worn and tired body parts, and minimize the chance of burnout that occurs more often in other sports.

Many women runners consider pregnancy a setback to their continuous training (especially at a high intensity), but this time off from training might also be a
blessing in disguise. Consider the behavioral changes that most women make during
pregnancy—they tend to make sure they get enough rest, they undergo less training
stress, and they generally eat better. In fact, you could say pregnancy leads to improved
health, which often leads to improved athletic performance. It's little wonder that
many female runners run personal-best times after they fully resume training following the birth of a child.

Log the Specifics

Unlike contact sports, in which it's normal to know just how and when an injury
occurred, runners are quite often unable to relate an injury to a specific incident.
An injury is often the result of overstressing an imperfection in the body, such as a
leg length discrepancy or a tendency toward overpronation. Many running injuries
simply progress slowly over time. This is why you should record your daily training in
a logbook—so you can see the trends or events that lead to every setback.

In addition to noting the time, duration, distance, weather, and other stats about
a run that you want to keep in your log, each daily entry should include a record of
anything physically unusual you experience, categorized by the parts of the body in
which they occur—knee, ankle, foot, hip, hamstring, midsection. This way you'll know
the date that you first noticed signs of a possible injury as well as the exact day that
you think the injury occurred. You should also note what you think caused the injury,
or at least the training, competition, accident, or incident that you associate with it.
Finally, from the day you recognize an injury to the day it has healed, keep track of
what you do to treat the problem and how well the treatment has worked.

This information might help you handle (or even prevent) future injuries. You'll
have a permanent record, for instance, of what helped you alleviate pain in your
knee or soreness in your Achilles. Some injuries vanish after a couple of weeks of
rest; others disappear even while training continues. Along with telling you how your
body responded to various injuries, your logbook might also save you worry, time, and
money, if in the future a similar injury should happen again.

Of the 26 elite distance runners I tested in the late 1960s (and again 25 years later),
the runner who had the best results in his $\dot{V}O_2$max (76 ml $\cdot$ kg^{-1} $\cdot$ min^{-1}) in his 25-year
follow-up test was a 47-year-old who had recorded nearly 100 setbacks over the years.
This runner had done a magnificent job of learning to rest when he needed to and had
become a highly successful masters competitor, lending credence to the notion that
setbacks, when documented and cared for, might even lengthen a running career.

Let Experience Guide You

It's always a little scary when an injury occurs for the first time, but most running injuries do respond to treatment, and many can be prevented. A trip or two to a doctor
might be necessary for a first-time injury, but the treatment (unless it's a prescription)
might be something you can do yourself in the future, especially if you responded well

the first time and have written down the details of the treatment or rehabilitation in your logbook.

In many cases, a good selection of strengthening and stretching exercises can work wonders in clearing up injuries and preventing them from recurring. If you find that with a few exercises you're able to remedy or prevent an injury in one leg, you should use the same exercises on the other leg. Many runners I've coached who were prone to knee pain had their problem corrected by faithfully doing some final 10- to 15-degree knee extensions with moderate resistance. Other runners have cleared up hamstring problems by doing regular hamstring curls.

I don't profess to be an expert when it comes to ailments and injuries. I'll leave that to trained specialists in sports medicine. I will say that I think all runners can do themselves a favor by learning to keep in touch with their bodies rather than always relying on someone else to do it for them. I can say the same thing about nutrition and training. A competent sport nutritionist can be a great asset, as can a qualified coach, but it's usually up to you to use their teachings in a way that brings you success and satisfaction.

My approach regarding injury and illness is rather cautious. As you have probably realized by now, I strongly believe in the "ounce of prevention" philosophy. I think that it's more productive to spend time and effort on identifying optimal injury preventing training instead of identifying overtraining after the fact, which usually receives a great deal of attention. It sometimes seems that the goal of many training programs is to strive for a state of excess training. With some coaches the attitude seems to be, "May the strongest survive—and let the others find another sport." The sad part of this attitude is that it discourages many potentially outstanding runners at a time when they're not physically ready for the stress being imposed. Instead of shooting for signs of fatigue and physical stress, you should strive for improved performance. If improved performances result from easier training and a healthier, stronger body, then I'm not disappointed that my training program didn't produce the magical signs of overtraining.

Take Care of Injuries

Don't take injuries lightly because even the slightest injury can become a major problem. It's not at all unusual for a little ankle pain in one leg to cause a slight limp during running. Continued favoring of one leg can easily put enough extra stress on the other leg that a new, more serious injury occurs in the "good" side of the body—in the hip or knee, for example. It's never a good idea to try to hobble through an injury, even if it seems like one that will clear up soon. The danger of causing a second injury by running with a limp is just too great.

When overuse injuries occur, a runner can't just continue training as usual. Something has to be changed. It might be a matter of reducing mileage or intensity of training; it might involve adding some stretching and strengthening exercises to the overall program; or it might mean putting corrective devices in one (or both) of your running shoes. Get to know your own body (or, if you're a coach, the bodies of the runners you coach), and take care to avoid risky situations.

No matter how careful and thoughtful you are about your training, injuries will occasionally occur. One of the key aspects of dealing successfully with an injury is making sure you don't return to your normal amount and intensity of training or competition too quickly. My first rule in this regard is not to run a race after an injury until you've done at least one high-quality workout to prove that you're capable of handling the physical demands of race-intensity stress. In other words, don't use a race to test your recovery.

One approach that I've found works well in dealing with what appears to be an injury is to go for an easy run and notice what happens:

- Does the injury discomfort decrease the farther you go?
- Does the discomfort stay the same as you progress in the run?
- Does the discomfort increase the farther you go?

If you answer yes to the third question, it's time to terminate the run and either seek medical advice or take some days off before trying again. If you answer yes to the first or second questions (the discomfort gets no worse as you run farther), then continue trying easy runs every day and gently stretching or strengthening the area. Compare the daily responses as you did in the initial trial run—is the discomfort getting better each day, staying the same, or getting worse? If it's getting worse, take time off or get medical advice. My point here is that some "injuries" are not really injuries. They might just be muscle soreness, in which case some running might not do any harm—in fact, running might accelerate the healing process. When an injury is showing little or no sign of clearing up after several days, don't mess with it—get some professional advice. A few days off might save you many days of frustration if you continue to aggravate an injury that needs rest.

I suppose if you're running a season-ending championship, you might reasonably choose to chance running with a minor injury, especially if you know you'll have plenty of rehabilitation time following the race. But in most cases it's far preferable to bypass competitions in favor of full recovery from an injury or illness, especially if doing so gives someone else an opportunity to participate. I'm forever grateful to an Olympic teammate in 1956 who was our national champion but who suffered an injury just before the Olympics. His pulling out gave me (as the team's alternate) the opportunity to be in my first international competition, the Olympic Games, and I performed well enough to win a team silver medal. That success led to my staying with the sport and most certainly was the main reason I was able to compete in another Olympics (where I won a team bronze medal) and three World Championships (another bronze medal), and to twice win the individual United States National Championship.

Avoid Hypertraining

When a setback is the result of overtraining (what I call hypertraining—I hope you never have to experience this firsthand), you can hasten your recovery to normal status by being kind to yourself. Don't subject yourself to additional physical or emotional stress. For me, as a coach, the easiest way to detect hypertraining is by knowing my athletes, each and every one of them.

Here's how I look for hypertraining. When a runner is progressing through a season of training, he or she has scheduled gradual increases in amount and intensity of running every few weeks. These increases in training stress should be associated with better performances and should produce no greater subjective stress than earlier increases to loads and intensities did. If training is increased and the runner doesn't show some positive results within three or four weeks, and if test workouts don't go favorably, then I'd say it's time to back off, or at least make some serious assessments of current training—this runner is training too hard for the results that are being realized.

I call this kind of overwork "hypertraining" because it corresponds to the definition of hyperventilation perfectly. Hyperventilation means ventilating (breathing) more air than is necessary to do the job at hand. Hypertraining means training harder than is needed to perform at a level that could be attained with less training. Obviously, it's better to train less and still get the same performances.

If you think you might be hypertraining, try the following four-step program. Try each step, in order, until you find one that works.

1. Back off in your training by lowering total mileage, which will decrease the amount of quality work accordingly, per the rules that designate 10 percent of weekly mileage at threshold pace, 8 percent at interval pace, and 5 percent at repetition pace (see chapters 7, 8, and 9, respectively).

2. Cut out all quality training for a week or two and treat yourself as if you were recovering from an injury. At this point you're already stressed out from subpar races or evaluation sessions, so don't do anything that might add to your mental fatigue.

3. Try maintaining your weekly mileage for a couple of weeks, but switch to a different quality emphasis (usually abandon interval training in favor of threshold or repetition training).

4. Give the same program one more try for a couple of weeks without any changes.

Unless experience tells you that a particular approach works best for you, I recommend trying these four steps in the order listed. Usually the first step produces positive results within a week or two. I suggest a 20 percent drop in mileage as a starting point. You might have to cut back even more, particularly if you're on a high-mileage program.

I hope that one of these options, or a variation, does the job. If none works and you continue to feel poorly, it's time for a thorough medical checkup and probably a prolonged break of several weeks from training. But don't worry. No matter how long you're away from running, once you get back into it, all cares about the hypertraining will be forgotten. Just make sure that you learned a valuable lesson the first time around.

One last reminder about training load as it relates to reaching competitive fitness and the likelihood of experiencing a setback caused by a general lack of desire as a result of hypertraining (or injury or illness, for that matter): Figure 10.1 shows two response curves related to changes in training stress in the form of greater training volume, greater training intensity, or both. The upper curve (curve a) illustrates how competitive fitness responds to increases in training stress, showing that diminishing returns ensue. Curve b, which is a reverse image of curve a, depicts the possibility of a setback as training stress increases. It shows that the chance of a setback increases with repeated increases in training stress.

Note that setbacks are few until you reach a fairly high training load. However, at some critical point, further increases in training are accompanied by a rapidly rising chance of a setback. At what amount of training a setback actually happens among a group of runners varies, and in addition to being associated with both amount and intensity (collectively referred to as "training stress"), a setback is probably also a function of how rapidly you try to increase that stress. What might be intolerable this season could be fine next year. Steady, consistent, thoughtful training is always the answer.

Notice that in figure 10.1 there's an area of training, shown by a shaded box, that represents the ideal training window for any runner. In this window, about 95 percent of all possible benefits will be realized, with a low chance of setbacks. This is where the bulk of your training should take place, year in and year out. To reach outstanding performances, you might have to venture to the right of this window, but only for a few weeks at a time. This provides the extra seconds of improvement that might make the difference between making an Olympic team and staying at home, but it also carries with it an increased risk of a setback—you can't stay out there too long. The logging of intensity points (introduced in chapter 2) might help you avoid introducing too much quality training too soon or too fast into a season's program.

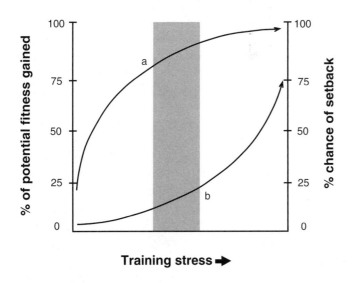

Figure 10.1 Comparison of increase in fitness level caused by increased training (curve a) to chance of setback caused by increased stress from training (curve b).

Dealing With Setbacks Due to Illness

When we think about setbacks caused by illness rather than injury, colds are probably on the top of our list. It's rare for a cross country team to get through a fall season without the top seven runners coming down with a total of seven colds.

The types of training least suited for runners suffering from colds and nagging illnesses are intervals and threshold training. I make a point of not including either of these types of stress in an ill runner's schedule. First of all, $\dot{V}O_2max$ (interval) training and threshold workouts represent the kinds of training that require good conditions to produce good results. Runners seldom feel good when they're sick. Second, and more important, stressful exercise of a somewhat prolonged nature might transform a relatively minor illness into something more serious. When athletes are sick they should put their strength into returning to normal health and not try to satisfy the requirements of a rigorous training schedule. Races and demanding workouts should be postponed for a while.

Just as academics should be the primary focus of high school and college runners, good health should take precedence over training at all levels of athletic endeavor. It's not bad for an athlete in a nonendurance sport to practice some skills during certain illnesses, but endurance athletes can't afford to train as usual when their health is abnormal. That said, I've found that steady, easy runs and short repetition sessions, with a heavy emphasis on full recoveries during the rep workout, can usually be performed adequately when a runner has a nonserious illness.

My college runners hate to miss normal training and do everything possible to avoid illness. However, when they are sick, they often get good results from doing a reduced schedule of easy runs and 15 to 20 × 200 meters about three seconds faster than their current 5K race pace with full recoveries. In fact, sometimes they feel that they're getting a better deal by being sick and backing off the harder training for a while. Mentally, they're good at accepting the alteration in training and are enthusiastic about returning to a normal running schedule.

If an athlete needs to train less because of an illness, his or her competition must also be cut out at this time. Of course if a doctor gives medical clearance, I'll permit a runner with a certain illness to compete in a national championship or another very important competition, but it's neither consistent nor fair to let sick runners compete in lesser meets when they're avoiding demanding training sessions for a while. A coach must consider the effect his or her decisions have on the rest of the team; consistency is critical in building team morale. Furthermore, replacing one of the team's better, yet ill, runners with another athlete might be the very opportunity this "backup" runner needs to experience a breakthrough in performance.

With serious illnesses, including all those that require a doctor's care or a prescription or that involve a fever, athletes shouldn't train without a doctor's support and knowledge. The same thing is true when an athlete feels bad enough to want time off, despite a lack of any particular symptoms. Again, it's far better to take some time off, although it might not be absolutely necessary, than it is to train or race under inappropriate conditions. To many athletes and coaches, injuries and illnesses seem to last forever, but once they've cleared up things get back to normal quite quickly. Revisit chapter 4 for recommendations about returning to training after a break or setback.

Here are some final thoughts to consider about supplemental training.

- Avoid working parts of the body where extra muscle mass is extra weight to carry without benefit.
- Use supplemental exercise to strengthen a weak area where increased running might cause an injury.
- Increase the stress of supplemental training no more often than every third week.
- Don't limit supplemental training to times when you can't run; such training can be useful throughout your running program. But don't ever sacrifice valuable running time to perform supplemental training.
- Exercising specific parts of the body that are stressed by running provides a good foundation for the task of running.

Bolota Asmerom

Bolota Asmerom was born in Eritrea, an independent state in Africa, where he wrestled and played soccer and basketball before taking up running at the age of 15. He became a competitive runner because he found the "physical, emotional, and psychological experiences very exciting." After just one year in the sport, he beat his brother Yonathan in a mile race, with a time of 4:19, an accomplishment that convinced Bolota that he was capable of competing at a national and international level. He set his goal at being able to compete with the best in the world, in fact, at becoming number one in the world. Bolota attended McAteer high school in San Francisco, California.

During his college years at the University of California at Berkeley, Bolota was Pac 10 champion and second at NCAA nationals in the 5,000 meters. He also made the Eritrean Olympic Team in the 5,000 meters for the Sydney Olympics, and was on World Indoor championship teams in the 3,000 meters in 2003 and 2004. At U.S. Indoor Nationals, Bolota placed in the top three in 2002, 2003, and 2004. He followed these performances with a third place finish at the 2004 U.S. Olympic Trials in the 5,000-meter distance. I became acquainted with Bolota during my sabbatical in Palo Alto, California, and my vision of him as a runner is someone with a smooth stride who can change speed without any apparent effort.

Personal bests: 800m—1:49; 1,500m—3:41; mile: 3:59; 3,000m—7:48; 5,000m—13:26.

Photo courtesy of Bolota Asmerom

PART III

Training for Fitness

M y approach to the task of helping anyone interested in becoming a runner is to provide a series of training plans, each designed to help runners interested in different levels of proficiency in the sport. I've given the different plans identifying colors, with a white plan designed for the true beginner. Once the white plan has been successfully completed, a runner can move into the second level, the red plan. Following the red plan are blue and then gold plans, designed for more advanced running. Note that when I say *advanced* I don't necessarily mean elite in terms of running times. Rather, I mean to identify as advanced runners those runners who have put a good deal of effort and experience into their running. Their race times might not be outstanding, but their training is solid, and their fitness is certainly advanced. Runners who complete the gold plan (even those who complete the blue plan) will be far more fit than most people in our society.

Each program is designed to allow participants to reach a particular level of aerobic fitness. Having been involved in physical education and fitness throughout the years that I've been coaching runners, it has become clear to me that fitness is not something you can bank for later in life—it's an ongoing proposition. The benefits of regular physical activity are many, from fighting disease and obesity, to lowering medical costs, to just plain making people feel better in life. If some non-elite runners feel better about themselves after following one or more of the plans in this part of the book, my effort has been well worthwhile. Those who get through the blue or gold training programs will have reached a very high level of fitness, and if they so choose will be prepared to take on some competitive running, for which they can train further by reading and applying the information in part IV.

CHAPTER 11

White Starting Plan

Several factors have motivated me to develop and write about a running program for people who want either to get started running with no previous experience or to re-engage with running after being away from it for a prolonged time. One of these factors is that I was exposed to an outstanding fitness program when I was in high school. My high school required physical education classes an hour every day of the week for all four years. Students were exposed to a wide variety of activities and games and, through these, I learned to embrace fitness as a necessary part of growing up. One result of our excellent program was that three of us in the same graduating class participated in the same Olympic Games just six years after graduating from high school—not because we'd been sport stars but because we'd become very physically fit.

Second, I later studied and taught in Sweden and was truly impressed with the fitness of the young students I taught there, especially compared with what I've seen in the United States and elsewhere. My students took their health and fitness levels seriously, and I'd like to see the rest of the world follow suit. A third reason I've become interested in providing this starter–runner training program is that for several years I've been involved with helping the Leukemia and Lymphoma Society's Team in Training Program prepare average citizens for a marathon run. Finally, I've conducted research showing

Until you have tried running, you will never know how enjoyable it can be.

the rapid benefits of getting involved in regular aerobic exercise, and I'd like very much to make running more inviting to anyone who's interested in improving health and aerobic fitness.

Newcomers to any exercise program should have a doctor's clearance before getting involved in physical activity, and they should be free of injury and illness when first striking out on the program. I also recommend that new runners seek professional advice about proper apparel and footwear before embarking on a running program. You can get professional advice at any reputable local running specialty store.

White Level I—**Weeks 1 Through 4**

Day	Workout	Time running/total time
1	5-min walk 10 × (1 min **E** pace with 1-min walk) 5-min walk	10/30 min
2	If you train this day, do the same as prescribed for day 1.	10/30 min
3	5-min walk 7 × (2 min **E** pace with 1-min walk) 4-min walk	14/30 min
4	If you train this day, do the same as prescribed for day 3.	14/30 min
5	5-min walk 6 × (1 min **E** pace with 30-sec walk) 8 × (30 sec **E** pace with 1-min walk) 4-min walk	10/30 min
6	If you train this day, do the same as prescribed for day 5.	10/30 min
7	If you train this day, do the same as prescribed for day 1.	10/30 min

White Level II—**Weeks 5 Through 8**

Day	Workout	Time running/total time
1	3 min **E** pace 3-min walk 10 × (2 min **E** pace with 1-min walk) 4-min walk	23/40 min
2	If you train today, do the same as prescribed for day 1.	23/40 min
3	3 min **E** pace 3-min walk 6 × (3 min **E** pace with 2-min walk) 4-min walk	21/40 min
4	If you train today, do the same as prescribed for day 3.	21/40 min
5	3 min **E** pace 3-min walk 20 × (1 min **E** pace with 30-sec walk) 4-min walk	23/40 min
6	If you train today, do the same as prescribed for day 5.	23/40 min
7	If you train today, do the same as prescribed for day 1.	23/40 min

I've designed the basic white plan so that participants don't have to run every day and are free to pick the days that best suit their schedule, as long as they commit to at least three days of running each week. The plan requires a minimum of 90 minutes per week and builds up to a minimum of 2 hours 15 minutes or a maximum of 5 hours of training per week. It's designed for those who want to start a running program for the first time or to return to running after a lengthy time away from the sport. This plan is for beginners who may or may not want to use it as preparation for future, more advanced training. Anyone who has been running, even on a sporadic basis,

White Level III—**Weeks 9 Through 12**

Day	Workout	Time running/total time
1	10 min **E** pace 3-min walk 10 min **E** pace 3-min walk 10 min **E** pace 4-min walk	30/40 min
2	If you train today, do the same as prescribed for day 1.	30/40 min
3	2-min walk 4 × (8 min **E** pace with 1-min walk) 2-min walk	32/40 min
4	If you train today, do the same as prescribed for day 3.	32/40 min
5 **or** 6	5-min walk 20 min **E** pace 5-min walk 10 min **E** pace 5-min walk	30/45 min
6	See day 5 above. If done on day 5, rest on day 6.	0/0 min
7	If anything today, just a 30-min walk	0/30 min

White Level IV—**Weeks 13 Through 16**

Day	Workout	Time running/total time
1	30 min **E** pace 6 strides 6 min **E** pace	36/45 min
2	If you train today, do the same as prescribed for day 1.	36/45 min
3	10 min **E** pace 5 strides 10 min **E** pace 5 strides 10 min **E** pace	30/45 min
4	If you train today, do the same as prescribed for day 3.	30/45 min
5 **or** 6	Same as day 1	36/45 min
6	See day 5 above. If done on day 5, rest on day 6.	0/0 min
7	If anything today, just a 30 min walk	0/30 min

might find that the starting level of the white plan doesn't challenge them enough. If this is the case, move ahead to the more advanced levels of the white plan, or even progress to the red plan, which is designed for runners who are beyond the demands of the white plan.

The white plan lasts 16 weeks, broken into 4-week segments: levels I, II, III, and IV. The tables highlight each level's training plan. After a few months of following this white plan, participants will have achieved a moderate level of fitness. Along with adhering to this basic running plan, it's a good idea to include some stretching and strengthening exercises two or three days each week.

In these tables, you'll notice in the right-hand column two numbers separated by a slash. The first number indicates the total number of minutes of actual running for that day, and the second number is the total number of minutes in that day's workout. You'll recall that **E** runs are easy runs or jogging; strides are 20- to 30-second quick, light runs with 1-minute rests between each.

The workouts in the shaded boxes indicate the three basic workouts for that week. I typically indicate day 1 as a Sunday, but you can assign any day of the week as your day 1. Throughout the white program, follow this schedule for which days to train:

If training three days a week, train on any three days, but no two days in a row.

If training four days a week, train on days 1, 3, 5, and 7 or days 1, 2, 4, and 6.

If training five days a week, train on days 1, 3, 4, 6, and 7.

You may change the number of training days at any time.

Once you've completed the 16 weeks, you've finished the white training program. If you're satisfied with the amount of training you're now doing, simply continue repeating the level IV schedule; if level IV doesn't suit you, you can also pick any of the other training sessions in any of the four training levels and continue repeating those sessions. If you want to progress to a more demanding training program, follow the red plan, presented in chapter 12. Although the white plan prepares you for some short road races, the red plan prepares you better for race participation.

CHAPTER 12

Red Intermediate Plan

The red plan is designed for runners who have completed level IV of the white plan (see chapter 11) or who have recently run regularly for a few months. This program prepares a runner for satisfactory success in recreational track or road races up to about 10 miles. Plan to train at least four days every week in the red plan, and for best results try for five or more days. The average weekly mileage for the red plan falls between 20 and 35 miles, or about three to five hours of running each week.

If you've decided to skip the white plan and start with the red plan, I suggest that you read through the white plan to get a feel for what's being asked of starting runners and to verify that you belong in the red program. You might also want to read through the blue plan (chapter 13) to see if you think you're up to that level of training. Any time you're in doubt about which program you belong in, go with the less demanding one until you've spent several weeks in the same program. In some cases, you might just need to move up a level or two within the program you've started with; other times, you might be justified to move on up to the next, more demanding, program.

I don't recommend using this red plan to prepare for completing a marathon; however, the plan could be a good one to follow prior to engaging in a marathon-training program that involves some longer training runs. If you're a beginner planning to run a marathon, work

Running is a good beginning to improved fitness; training is the next step up.

first through the white plan, and then through this plan, before moving on to more serious marathon preparation, as described in chapter 20. This will ensure that you've achieved the proper base to run a marathon safely and reduce your risk of injury.

This red plan is designed for a minimum of four days of training each week, with the four basic workout days shown in the shaded boxes in the tables. The amount of time you can expect to take to perform each day's workout is also shown in the column to the right of each workout. If you're training four days a week, don't train more than two days in row. If you're training five days a week, don't train more than three days in a row. The tables that follow detail the four levels of the program.

Red Level I—**Weeks 1 Through 4**

Day	Workout	Time
1	30 min **E** pace 6 strides	40 min
2	If you run today, repeat day 1 workout.	40 min
3	10 min **E** pace 3 × (1 mile **T** pace with 1-min rest) 10 min **E** pace	40 min
4	If you run today, repeat day 1 workout.	40 min
5	10 min **E** pace 6 × (1,000m **T** pace with 1-min rest) 10 min **E** pace	50 min
6	If you run today, repeat day 1 workout.	40 min
7	40 min or 6 miles (whichever is less) **L** run (steady **E** pace)	40 min

Red Level II—**Weeks 5 Through 8**

Day	Workout	Time
1	30 min **E** pace 6 strides	40 min
2	If you run today, repeat day 1 workout.	40 min
3	10 min **E** pace 2 mile **T** pace 2-min rest 1 mile **T** pace 10 min **E** pace	45 min
4	If you run today, repeat day 1 workout.	40 min
5	10 min **E** pace 2 × (1 mile **T** pace with 1-min rest + 1,000m **T** pace with 1-min rest) 10 min **E** pace	45 min
6	If you run today, repeat day 1 workout.	40 min
7	40 to 50 min **L** run (steady **E** pace)	40-50 min

As you use the workout tables, remember that **E** = easy run, in which strides are 20- to 30-second quick, light runs with 1 minute of rest between each; **L** = long run, which is at **E** pace; **T** = threshold-pace running (comfortably hard); and **I** = interval pace, which is "hard": a speed at which you could race for two to three miles. With recent race or timed performances, use the VDOT tables (see chapter 3) to identify exact paces for your **I** and **T** running (**E** pace is also shown). If no race times are available, let 6 minutes of comfortably hard running approximate each mile, or 4 minutes of comfortably hard running approximate 1,000 meters of **T**-pace running. This is not to say you'll necessarily be covering a mile in 6 minutes or 1,000 meters in 4 minutes, but by using these approximations you'll subject yourself to the same amount of time running as runners of that ability level would be doing.

Red Level III—**Weeks 9 Through 12**

Day	Workout	Time
1	30 min **E** pace 6 strides	40 min
2	If you run today, repeat day 1 workout.	40 min
3	10 min **E** pace 6 strides 5 × (3 min **I** pace with 2 min **E** pace rest) 10 min **E** pace	50 min
4	If you run today, repeat day 1 workout.	40 min
5	10 min **E** pace 3 miles or 20 min **T** pace (whichever is less) 10 min **E** pace	40 min
6	If you run today, repeat day 1 workout.	40 min
7	40 to 50 min **L** run (steady **E** pace)	40-50 min

Red Level IV—**Weeks 13 Through 16**

Day	Workout	Time
1	30 min **E** pace 8 strides	40 min
2	If you run today, repeat day 1 workout.	40 min
3	10 min **E** pace 4 strides 2 × (5 min **I** pace + 3 min **E** pace + 3 min **I** pace + 3 min **E** pace) 10 min **E** pace	50 min
4	If you run today, repeat day 1 workout.	40 min
5	10 min **E** pace 6 strides 2 × (2 mile **T** pace with 2 min rest) 10 min **E** pace	50 min
6	If you run today, repeat day 1 workout.	40 min
7	40 to 50 min **L** run (steady **E** pace)	40-50 min

Having completed the red plan, you'll be in quite good shape, certainly fit enough to run in some races; you will also have experienced what's involved in running at **E**-, **T**-, and **I**-pace intensities and have learned how to incorporate strides into a program. After completing the red plan, you might want to take a break from a structured program and just run for several weeks. In other words, you might choose to drop the intervals and threshold runs and just go for regular steady runs of a variety of durations and, possibly, intensities.

At the end of the red plan, you can opt for a period of steady, less-structured runs; take a break from running; or move right on to the more challenging blue plan.

Even a total break from running might be an option. If you do take a break from running, it's a good idea to do some steady, easy runs for several weeks before jumping back into a structured program that involves quality days, as you experienced in the red program. Review the section in chapter 4 about coming back from breaks in training.

For runners who want to continue to even more demanding training, the red plan has prepared you for progressing to the blue plan, presented in chapter 13.

CHAPTER 13

Blue Advanced Plan

The blue plan is for runners who have completed level IV of the red plan (chapter 12) or who have considerable running experience, including some races at some time in their career. Runners following this plan will train five to seven days a week, with the possibility of some days that include two runs in the same day (if necessary) to reach desired weekly mileage totals. For this plan, typical weekly mileage ranges from 40 to 52 miles (about 4 hours and 30 minutes to 7 hours and 15 minutes) of running. Rearrange your schedule to include at least two easy days of running prior to any races (drop one quality training day these weeks).

Because the blue plan is designed for at least five days of training each week, the five basic workout days in the tables are denoted by the shaded boxes. In addition, days 3 and 6 are listed as possible additional training days; you can add one or both of these days (or not) to any of the weeks of training, as desired.

As has been the system throughout the book, in the tables **E** = easy run, in which strides are 20- to 30-second quick, light runs with 1-minute rests; **L** = long run, which is at **E** pace; **T** = threshold pace (comfortably hard running or from VDOT tables in chapter 3); **I** = interval pace, "hard" and at a speed that could be raced for two to three miles (or from the VDOT tables in chapter 3); and **R** = rep pace, which is approximately your *current* mile race pace (or see VDOT tables in chapter 3). Recovery time

Experiencing different types of training lets you appreciate what elite athletes take for granted.

with **R** runs is at least an equal distance of **E**-pace running, or walking and **E**-pace running. As you can see, runners doing the blue plan should get to know the VDOT tables presented in chapter 3; these tables take the guesswork out of determining the proper training paces for **T**, **I**, and **R** workouts.

Blue Level I—**Weeks 1 Through 4**

Day	Workout	Time
1	60 min **E** pace (1 or 2 runs to total 60 min)	60 min
2	10 min **E** pace 8 × (400m **R** pace with 400m **E** pace to recover) 10 min **E** pace	50 min
3	If you run today, repeat day 1 workout.	60 min
4	30 to 45 min **E** pace 8 strides	40-50 min
5	15 min **E** pace 4 × (1,200m **I** pace with 4 min **E** pace to recover) 15 min **E** pace	60-65 min
6	If you run today, repeat day 4 workout.	40-50 min
7	60 to 90 min **L** run (steady **E** pace)	60-90 min

Blue Level II—**Weeks 5 Through 8**

Day	Workout	Time
1	60 min **E** pace (1 or 2 runs to total 60 min)	60 min
2	15 min **E** pace 4 × (2 × 200m **R** pace with 200m **E** pace + 1 × 400m **R** pace with 400m **E** pace to recover) 15 min **E** pace	60 min
3	If you run today, repeat day 1 workout.	60 min
4	30 to 45 min **E** pace 8 strides	40-50 min
5	15 min **E** pace 20 min **T** pace 4 strides 15 min **E** pace	60 min
6	If you run today, repeat day 4 workout.	40-50 min
7	60 to 90 min **L** run (steady **E** pace)	60-90 min

After completing the blue plan, you're well versed in how to carry out a variety of workouts and should feel perfectly comfortable running in races of different distances and intensities. However, the distance of the long runs in this plan is still not adequate for taking on a marathon; if your goal is to run a marathon, you should follow a regular marathon-training schedule, such as the ones described in chapter 20. Also, if you decide to begin a training program geared toward racing a certain distance, check the other chapters in part IV for programs to progress to after completing the blue program.

Blue Level III—**Weeks 9 Through 12**

Day	Workout	Time
1	60 min **E** pace	60 min
2	15 min **E** pace 6 strides 6 × (400m **R** pace with 400m **E** pace + 200m **R** pace with 200m **E** pace to recover) 15 min **E** pace	75-80 min
3	If you run today, run 30 min **E** pace + 6 strides.	40 min
4	30 to 45 min **E** pace 8 strides	40-50 min
5	15 min **E** pace 5 × (1,000m **I** pace with 3 min **E** pace to recover) 15 min **E** pace	65 min
6	If you run today, repeat day 4 workout.	40-50 min
7	60 to 90 min **L** run (steady **E** pace)	60-90 min

Blue Level IV—**Weeks 13 Through 16**

Day	Workout	Time
1	60 min **E** pace	60 min
2	15 min **E** pace 3 × (1,000 m **T** pace with 1-min rest) 3 × (800m **I** pace with 2-min rest) 15 min **E** pace	60 min
3	If you run today, run 30 min **E** pace.	30 min
4	30 to 45 min **E** pace 6 strides	40-50 min
5	15 min **E** pace 2 × (200m **R** pace with 200m **E** pace to recover) 3 × (1,000m **T** pace with 1-min rest) 2 × (200m **R** pace with 200m **E** pace to recover) 15 min **E** pace	50-55 min
6	If you run today, repeat day 4 workout.	40-50 min
7	60 to 90 min **L** run (steady **E** pace)	60-90 min

If the blue plan proves to be more demanding than you expected or are willing to maintain, consider returning to the red plan (chapter 12) and trying a "break" phase of steady easy running as your schedule and motivation allow—or even take several weeks off as a complete break from running for a while. If you do choose to take a break and later return to running, review the information in chapter 4 on how to return to running after a break, so you won't risk taking on too much too soon.

The demanding blue plan may leave you feeling ready for a return to the red plan, a brief break from running, or the increased challenge and structure of the gold plan.

For those of you who want a greater challenge than you've found in the blue plan, or if you want to reach a higher level of running fitness, try the gold plan presented in chapter 14. I doubt that many readers will be willing to take on this advanced training plan—and those who do might want to target their training to a certain distance, using one of the plans in part IV. That said, the gold plan is a good choice for many competitive runners who want a structured program to follow—something a little different from their normal training.

CHAPTER 14

Gold Elite Plan

The gold plan is designed for runners who have completed level IV of the blue plan (chapter 13) or who have considerable experience and time for training as a runner and want to be prepared for competitive efforts at a variety of distances. Runners who follow this plan should train six or seven days a week and might also train twice on some days (to meet weekly mileage or duration goals). Weekly mileage will be in the 60- to 75-mile range, or about 7 hours and 20 minutes to 9 hours and 40 minutes. Although you can use the gold plan to prepare for a marathon, I recommend using the 18-week marathon program presented in chapter 20.

In the gold plan, six workouts are scheduled for each week (noted in the shaded boxes of the tables that follow). You can do some of these workouts by running twice in the same day or by running a single longer session. Day 4 is indicated as an optional run day, but it could be switched with any other day. I usually indicate Sunday as day 1, but you may choose any day as day 1 and go from there. Of course, in addition to the running time indicated in each table for each day, you'll need additional time for stretching, changing clothes, showering, traveling to a training site, if necessary, and so forth, so be sure to account for all of this time in your commitment to training.

Achieving a level of fitness that few others reach produces a feeling of euphoria that few others ever experience.

Whenever a race is scheduled, take three **E** days prior to the race and one **E** day for each 3,000 meters of race distance, after each race (for example, follow a 10K race with 3 easy days). Try to make a **T**-pace day the last quality day of training before each race. Drop any other quality days within three days of races.

Gold Level I—**Weeks 1 Through 4**

Day	Workout	Time
1	75 min **E** pace (in 1 or 2 runs)	75 min
2	20 min **E** pace 10 × (400m **R** pace with 3 min **E** pace to recover) 10 min **E** pace	70 to 75 min
3	60 min **E** pace (in 1 or 2 runs) 6 strides	65 to 70 min
4	If you run today, repeat day 3 workout.	65 to 70 min
5	20 min **E** pace 6 strides 20 min **T** pace 6 strides	50 to 60 min
6	60 min **E** pace	60 min
7	120 min **L** (**E** pace)	120 min

Gold Level II—**Weeks 5 Through 8**

Day	Workout	Time
1	75 min **E** pace (in 1 or 2 runs)	75 min
2	20 min **E** pace 5 × (1,000m **I** pace with 3 min **E** pace to recover) 20 min **E** pace	75 min
3	1 or 2 × 30 to 40 min **E** pace (in 1 or 2 runs) 6 strides	30-80 min
4	If you run today, repeat day 3 workout.	30-80 min
5	20 min **E** pace 6 strides 2 × (10 × 200m **R** pace with 1 min **E** pace); 10 min **E** pace after each set	85-90 min
6	60 min **E** pace (in 1 or 2 runs)	60 min
7	120 min **L** (**E** pace)	120 min

Unless you're a serious, competitive runner, the gold plan is a demanding program to follow. It offers a variety of training intensities and is not designed for any particular race distance. This plan should prepare you well for most race distances, but to follow a more specific race program, I recommend those offered in the final chapters of this book.

Gold Level III—**Weeks 9 Through 12**

Day	Workout	Time
1	75 min **E** pace (in 1 or 2 runs)	75 min
2	20 min **E** pace 6 strides 5 × (4 min **I** pace with 3 min **E** pace to recover) 20 min **E** pace	80 min
3	75 min **E** pace (in 1 or 2 runs)	75 min
4	If you run today, repeat day 3 workout.	75 min
5	20 min **E** pace 5 × (6 min **T** pace with 1-min rest) 6 strides 10 min **E** pace	65-70 min
6	60 min **E** pace (in 1 or 2 runs)	60 min
7	120 min **L** (**E** pace)	120 min

Gold Level IV—**Weeks 13 Through 16**

Day	Workout	Time
1	75 min **E** pace (in 2 runs)	75 min
2	20 min **E** pace 4 × (200m **R** pace with 200m **E** pace to recover) 3 × (1,000m **I** pace with 3 min **E** pace to recover) 4 × (200m **R** pace with 200m **E** pace to recover) 10 min **E** pace	65 min
3	75 min **E** pace (in 1 or 2 runs)	75 min
4	If you run today, repeat day 3 workout.	75 min
5	20 min **E** pace 6 × (1,000m **T** pace with 1-min rest) 6 strides 20 min **E** pace	75 min
6	60 min **E** pace (in 1 or 2 runs)	60 min
7	120 min **L** (**E** pace)	120 min

Certainly, a runner who has completed the gold plan will be capable of handling any type of sound running training that he or she might choose to follow. If this plan is too demanding to maintain, then move back to a less demanding plan, select favorite parts of any of the plans to follow on a regular basis, or take a break from running for a while. If you do take time off, read through chapter 4 when you return for guidelines on returning to running after a break.

PART IV

Training for Racing

For many people who run, competition is the last thing on their minds. These runners enjoy the many good things they feel and receive from regular running. Some of these noncompetitors become very knowledgeable about training and racing but choose not to be competitive themselves. This is perfectly legitimate, in my opinion. Just as millions of people read about one topic or another without becoming actively involved in what they're studying, many people want to read about running, training, and competing without ever taking a competitive step themselves.

There's a lot to be learned about training and competing in regard to sports in general, simply by reading about training and competing in running. Certainly, a great deal of my knowledge about training and athletic competition comes from learning about the body in general and about how athletes in other sports prepare themselves mentally, physically, and competitively.

© Rob Tringali/SportsChrome

This fourth part of the book deals with competition and training programs and is primarily for runners who want to test themselves against others, against the clock, or against their own expectations. These runners might be newcomers (perhaps just starting out on a high school team or having worked through one or two of the programs provided in part III) or seasoned competitors looking for a new or more structured approach to training. In addition to the events covered in the first edition of my book—1,500 to 3,000 meters; 5 to 15 kilometers; and half-marathon and marathon—all of which I've upgraded here, I've added a chapter for 800-meter specialists and a separate chapter on cross country running.

I present this material in hopes that competitors in other sports or noncompetitive runners might learn a little more about competing. I address such issues as what races to run and how often to run. I also describe final race preparation, including prerace meals, what to wear, prerace warm-ups, and predicting your time (even for races you've never run before). Finally, I provide suggestions about race tactics and what to think about when running a race.

Think of racing as completely separate from training. Unfortunately, some runners find this difficult to accept and do. Training prepares the mind and the body to run in races, but it takes some serious racing to become good at racing. Think of racing as a completely different type of training (just as doing threshold runs is different if you've never done them before); it might take several attempts to get the true value of the new experiences. Just as racing at altitude when you're accustomed to sea level, or racing your first 5K after some seasons as a 1,500-meter runner, presents a new challenge, so does racing for a runner who has trained well but who lacks race experience. Remember that training benefits and strengthens body systems; racing is your chance to challenge these systems. Don't let your training limit your ability to race. That might sound like a strange statement, but some runners can separate training and racing and race beyond what their training would seem to indicate they can do. I wish all runners could do that!

In these chapters I've tried to provide for a little more flexibility as to when quality days can be included in a weekly schedule, which has been a concern of some high school coaches who often have competition schedules that demand their participation on certain days of the week. A final addition that might be of use to some coaches and runners are training intensity tables that allow you to go directly from a recent performance to training paces without having to refer to the VDOT tables in chapter 3.

CHAPTER 15

Preparing for Competition

The idea of competition is to compete. I'm sure that someone has said this before, but I'll restate it to get us in the proper frame of mind. Competition is a special part of the sport of running. It's fine to plan some competitions as part of an overall training program, but each competition is important and must be taken seriously. The purpose of competing is to achieve a specific goal or performance. You should know exactly why you're running each race, just as you should know the purpose of every workout you complete. Improving your ability to hold a fast pace, sticking with a group of tough competitors for a prolonged period, helping to build confidence in your kick, learning patience, and aiding the development of a physiological or mental attribute that's beneficial to your long-term development as a runner are all reasons why you run races. Of course, there are more obvious reasons as well: to win a championship, to qualify for a championship, or to win an award.

The goal of competition doesn't have to be to discover how fast you can race a particular distance, although that's often the case. Your goal might be to try a new tactic in a competitive setting. For example, you might be a runner who goes out too fast in the early part of a race and ends up paying the price later. If so, your goal for an upcoming competition might be to set a more cautious early pace. You might strive for as even a pace as possible, or you might attempt to run negative splits (i.e., run progressively faster throughout the race).

Run with your head the first two thirds of a race and with your heart the final third.

Define Your Competitive Goals

Maybe your goal for the race is to stay with a particular competitor or pace as long as you can. This goal might help you overcome a fear of certain competitors or of running a particular pace. For example, you might decide to run to at least the two-mile mark of a 5K race with a teammate or competitor whose pace you know has always been faster than yours has. This goal provides a greater opportunity for success than one to simply beat this person to the finish line; the confidence you develop also provides a stepping-stone to reach a new goal. An equally valid goal might be to go out more cautiously than usual, conceding your competitors a better first mile, and then to run the last part of the race as fast or faster than any of them.

Select goals that boost your confidence in your ability to compete. It's discouraging to always fail because you set unrealistic goals. It's also not difficult to set yourself up (or to set up an athlete you're coaching) for failure in a race. Set goals that are challenging but that allow for success.

Even current world-record holders will continuously fail if their prerace goal is always to improve on their times. There were many failures along the road to breaking the 4-minute barrier in the mile run, just as women failed many times before breaking 2 hours and 20 minutes in the marathon. Certainly, there are many marathoners whose goal to break 3 hours is never achieved. The same thing happens in the game of golf, where the goal for thousands of weekend golfers is to break 100. I often wonder how success rates might vary if the goal were to run with good technique for the duration of a race, or to make each iron shot a smooth and artful effort, rather than worrying about the final outcome.

Just as the idea of competing is to achieve a specific goal or performance, the idea behind goal setting is to establish a goal that has a decent chance of being attained. It's unrealistic for everyone entered in a cross country

© Claus Andersen

Top competitors such as Amy Rudolph have specific goals but accept that a race in which they don't beat their previous record time can still be extremely successful.

race or road race to have first place as a goal, but the chance of achieving the goal of a team victory is much improved if each runner on the team achieves his or her own realistic personal goal for the race.

It's fine for an aspiring, inexperienced runner to enter a long race or a marathon with the main goal being to test his or her ability to consume fluids at a certain rate. Fluid consumption can make or break a marathoner, so learning to take in fluids at an adequate rate is a crucial part of eventually achieving a good time in a marathon.

I don't want to leave anyone with the impression that you must set goals that you'll always achieve. Losing can sometimes be more valuable than winning, and setting tough goals for races might mean not reaching your goals now and then. If you make an honest evaluation of why you failed on these occasions, you might benefit even more than if you had achieved your goal.

Strength comes from the confidence of winning and from learning to accept and evaluate losses. Sometimes it takes an overenthusiastic approach to a race to really test yourself and find out just where your current limits are. So, take a positive attitude toward victory and toward defeat, but also try to tip the scales a little so there are more personal wins than losses.

Most competitive runners, particularly those involved with school teams, are faced with three important questions:

1. Which race should I run?
2. When is the right time to run races of different lengths?
3. How often should I race a particular distance?

Which Races When

When you're involved in a season full of races, it's a good idea to vary your race distance, but you should also repeat the same distance often enough to let yourself use what you learn in one race for improvement the next time around. This works better for shorter races (up to about 5K) than for longer ones—obviously, you don't run several marathons a few weeks apart to benefit from what you learned in the first one.

Have a plan in setting up your races. For example, a runner who's planning to race a 10K at the end of the season might want to be in good enough shape to run a qualifying time early in the season. Once the qualifying time is achieved, he or she can then concentrate on training and running shorter races for the bulk of the season before returning to another 10K. A panicky feeling can set in when, late in the season, you find yourself not yet qualified for the championship event for which you're peaking.

One plan many runners use is to race longer and shorter than their favorite distance early in the season, and then run several races at the preferred distance toward the end of the season. There are a couple of reasons for racing over and under a specific distance. First, underdistance racing helps your running economy and gives you confidence in being able to handle the race pace of the longer race. Racing 5Ks helps make 10K pace feel easier, and 1,500s make 3,000 and 5,000 races feel mechanically more comfortable. If your running mechanics don't feel manageable, a race usually seems longer than it really is. On the other hand, overdistance racing can also help you, because the important (shorter) race can be viewed as passing more quickly, and you're thus more willing to endure the greater race intensity associated with the shorter race.

Whether it's best to choose shorter or longer races as tune-up events depends on the individual runner, the conditions of the race, and the competition. You might need an ego boost, and you might be able to win or set a personal best (PB) by racing a particular distance (a shorter distance, for example), whereas going longer might put you in a tougher field of competitors or in a race where your PB is currently out of reach.

It might be unusually warm or windy, and a longer race would present too many problems to achieve success. Adverse conditions, although not ideal as far as time is concerned, might present the perfect ego boost if the conditions are to your liking or suited to your strengths. A good "mudder" on a wet, sloppy cross country course might profit considerably against some very good runners who don't do so well under those conditions. The same can hold true for an altitude runner or a good heat runner going against competitors who might be great but who aren't ready for the race conditions they're facing that day.

When conditions don't dictate much, as is usually the case for indoor races, then the competitors and the race distance are the two factors of most importance. You might want tough competition for a particular race, so you pick the race with the best field of competitors. If the level of competition is irrelevant, then you pick the race distance that will help you most in your preparation for later in the season, when performance is more important.

All things being equal, I normally favor shorter-distance tune-up races throughout the season to prepare my runners for later season championship races at their ideal distance—but there are always exceptions. A particular runner might be stronger over longer distances and the benefits of success in a longer race might outweigh the benefits of the fast-paced tune-up afforded by the shorter race.

Some runners like to vary race distances every meet; others stay with the same distance for several consecutive meets. Typically, I suggest racing the same distance a couple of times in a row because learning can take place more effectively. Especially for beginners, there's usually something to be learned from a race, and it's nice to turn right around and repeat the same distance in the next meet and put into practice what you picked up in the race before. Of course, a 10K, because of its longer distance, is not a race you want to repeat often, but early in the season it might not be a bad idea to run a couple of 10Ks fairly close together. In the case of shorter races, try repeating the same race a few times, then leave that race for a while before returning to it again later on. An understanding coach is particularly valuable in helping determine race distances and frequency.

How Often

How often to race is of major concern to most coaches and runners. Many novice runners benefit by racing shorter distances (800 to 3,000 meters) even weekly for a couple of months; they learn to race and improve performance by doing just that. However, it's not advisable to race 5K and 10K races nearly as often (only two or three in a season) because you can't recover as fast from these longer races, and they can force you to cut back more on your training. Veterans don't need as much race experience to feel comfortable racing. The better runners like to have confidence that they're ready for their best performance, and this can come from specific workouts, races, or a combination of the two.

Runners who are part of a school or college team usually have a fuller race schedule than club runners do, so school runners and their coaches must select races that complement their progress toward end-of-the-season championships. I had some very surprising responses to my question about how many races the elite runners ran in their year leading up to the 1968 Olympics. The average was 36, with one respondent indicating he'd run 80 races over the year. Of course, the latter runner was a college runner who sometimes ran meets like the Texas or Drake Relays in which he raced four or five times in a two- or three-day period. Still, 80 races is a lot in one year, and they must be considered carefully.

Fit races into your training schedule. For runners who have control of, or confidence in, their coach's selection of races, the important thing to keep in mind is how each race complements the season's overall program. When I plot a runner's season program, I first note how many weeks are available for training (see chapter 4), then I plug in the dates when we anticipate or learn of various races. This allows us to pick the type of training that the races will complement and vice versa. And always remember to answer the all-important questions for each race as you plan your racing schedule: Why am I running this race? What will it do for me? If you don't have good, practical answers for these questions, why run the race?

Prepare for Your Races

I've talked about race selection; I turn now to preparation for a race. There are some differences between preparing for midseason races and end-of-season championships. First, let's deal with the similarities between these two types of races. You must have a plan for any race yet be able to alter your plan if the situation demands (because of weather or the tactics of other competitors, for example).

Sleep

Adequate sleep is an important consideration before any race, and the simplest approach here is consistency. Get into a sleep routine in training and stick with it as closely as possible. Try to avoid situations in which shorter nights of sleep are compensated by longer nights. If you're routinely well rested, a short night's sleep on the night before a race will have no effect on performance. Several nights of poor rest might ruin a performance, but a single night rarely has a detrimental effect.

Meals

Consistency again is the key with daily meals and nutrition as well as with prerace and preworkout meals and snacks. Paying attention to good nutrition for a few days before a race might help a little but will never make up for weeks of inadequate nutrition.

Another important consideration is eating before competition. Like warm-ups and race tactics, when and what to eat is an individual matter but should be based on sound principles.

Some runners have problems running with food in their stomachs; others do well eating shortly before a race or strenuous workout. I once saw a guy at the Indoor Nationals consume a hot dog and a soft drink just 30 minutes before his second race of the meet (the two-mile run). When asked about the last-minute food consumption, he said, "I run with my legs, not with my stomach." He won the race.

In contrast to this approach was a runner I coached who couldn't eat anything within eight hours of a race or he would lose it all, either during or following the race. Another runner, whom I did not coach, told me that his stomach had been uncomfortable for two days prior to a 10K road race he'd entered, and that he'd eaten absolutely nothing for the 36 hours leading up to the race—in which he set a PB. Because of his unexpected success, from that day on, he always fasted 36 hours before running a longer race.

Do what works best for you. As a starting point as you figure this out, I suggest that you consume little or no food for three to four hours before any race. Leading up to that time period, eat food with lots of carbohydrates, such as bread, bagels, pancakes, rice, and pasta—all foods that most runners tolerate well on race day or leading up to race day. Some runners like some protein and even some fat, as in eggs, pastries, and meat, but this type of food is usually consumed a little further ahead of race time than carbohydrate foods are. Be moderate. "Practice" is another good word. Experiment with various foods before some training sessions and races of lesser importance, and then do what works best for you in competitions that are more important.

Drink water with your prerace meals because it's quickly absorbed. But many modern-day sports drinks also have ideal rates of absorption. Avoid large amounts of sweet foods because more fluid is retained in the stomach to aid in dilution of the sugars, which makes you feel bloated. Consume most of your water or sports drink four to eight hours before race time, and try to stay well hydrated right up to race time, though not to the point that you have to use the bathroom every 10 minutes.

Get in the habit of drinking and eating some carbohydrates in the four hour period following training sessions and races. Consume small amounts of food and drink about every 30 minutes during this time, at a rate of about 2 grams of carbohydrate per kilogram of body weight per hour. This speeds up the replenishment of depleted glycogen stores, a particularly desirable process following long races. The longer the race or training session, the more important this postexercise practice becomes.

Shoes

Contrary to popular belief, it's not always true that the lighter the shoe, the more economical the running. The effectiveness of running shoes is a function of both shoe weight and design, not just one factor or the other. The choice of which shoe to use is further complicated by individual running style. Stride length and rate play a role in running economy, as does the way each runner's feet strike the ground. Some runners use less energy with one type of foot plant, whereas others do best with a different technique. It's a case of individual makeup interacting with various combinations of stride rate, stride length, shoe type, and foot strike, in addition to the surface you're running on. There's no one right way that suits everyone. Just as different coaches and runners relate differently, different techniques suit various runners in different ways.

The materials used in various parts of shoe midsoles and the composition and design of outsoles also affect running economy. Plus, the surface over which the athlete is running becomes a factor. A very light shoe with poor cushioning might be a relatively "costly" shoe, especially for a rear-foot runner (a runner whose feet first strike the ground with their heels, or rear of the foot). This would be particularly true on a hard surface, such as a road.

Barefoot running produces poor economy for most runners on a hard road (or treadmill) but might be the most economical way to go on a forgiving synthetic track. Barefoot running on the proper surface would probably produce the best race times. This is because the runner would be using the lightest possible footwear (none at all), and the cushioning characteristics of the track surface eliminate the need for a midsole between the runner's foot and the ground. Of course, potential problems accompany barefoot running, but the fact remains that what's on your feet, and the surface on which your feet are landing and from which they're pushing off, are important factors in running economy.

Training and Racing Shoes

I'm convinced that some training should be done in racing shoes, for two reasons:

1. Each type of shoe has its own economy characteristics, and to take full advantage of these characteristics you must do some actual training in the shoes.
2. Each type of shoe has its own mechanical characteristics, and it can be disastrous never to train under the conditions that you'll face in a race.

It's hard to document how many injuries have resulted from wearing "new" shoes in a race, shoes that fit and function differently from those used in practice. To never wear racing shoes in practice is like never training at race pace. It's always risky to let any conditions of a race be completely foreign to you, and that includes wearing shoes whose effects on your economy and your feet are unpredictable. Of course, when you find a shoe model that suits you well, it's a good idea to have more than one pair of the same shoes. Also, make sure that you've broken in each pair with some easy miles and race-pace quality work in them before you use them in a race.

Spikes and Orthotics

Some runners wonder whether to wear orthotics during races, and some question the value of wearing spikes in longer track races. I've performed research regarding both of these issues and have found that with good traction (which is a function of the running surface and shoe outsole material), spikes are no more economical than racing flats, provided shoe weight and cushioning characteristics don't differ. In other words, putting spikes on the bottom of your shoes won't necessarily help in longer races, such as 5,000 and 10,000 meters. Of course, on slippery footing, as is often the case in cross country races, or on a wet track, spikes are usually advantageous.

The problem, of course, is to find flats that fit like spikes and have the same biomechanical characteristics in terms of resiliency and shock absorbency. Because there's no real advantage or disadvantage from an energy demand standpoint in longer races (such as the 5,000- or 10,000-meter track races), it makes sense that the athlete would select what's most comfortable and provides the most confidence. On a flat indoor track, someone could make the argument that it's better not to wear spikes so that the rotation that takes place on the sharp turns is between the shoe and the track rather than between the foot and the shoe, or within the ankle itself.

Many runners are concerned about wearing orthotics during races. Because a function of these devices is to provide you with better mechanics, the increased cost of carrying the extra weight should be counteracted by the decreased cost of running with better mechanics. On the average, this seems to be the case. However, under racing conditions, some people are more economical with their orthotics, whereas others see their economy worsen when orthotics are used. Of course, there are different kinds of orthotics, and racing shoes might require a different pair than training shoes. If you feel better racing without orthotics, I suggest asking the doctor who provided them if racing without them would be of any consequence. If it's okay to race without the orthotics, be certain to do some training in your racing shoes without orthotics before the actual race.

Clothing

In regard to clothing and performance, I suggest wearing the least amount of clothes necessary to maintain comfort. Being overdressed typically leads to dehydration and overheating, and can even cause you to become chilled under certain conditions. The latter case is likely if you're running in cold weather at a hard pace and then must slow down, or if you're running in cold weather with a tailwind and must turn into a headwind. In both situations the moisture on and around your body can become a chilling or even a freezing layer of coolant.

In general, increased weight or increased restriction of clothing increases the cost of running. However, according to some extensive tests I've conducted in the lab, flexible tights don't affect economy. Further, we found no difference in cost of running based on the design of tights being used. Because the weight and restrictiveness of modern materials don't affect economy, one could argue under the right conditions they could actually improve economy. If the tights allow the runner to be more relaxed and comfortable while running, they might indeed lower the cost of running.

I should point out that with the great variety of tights available, one sort or another could affect running economy negatively. It's best to use the lightest, least restrictive pair that adequately warm the legs under the given conditions. It might even take more than one pair or more than one style to meet all conditions, and don't wear tights in a race if you haven't used them first during some quality training sessions in which you've tested their comfort.

It's easier to dress for various degrees of cold than for the heat, because wearing layers of clothes works very well. It's not wise to wear one heavy garment that might feel nice when you start your run, but gets too hot later and can't be shed because of

insufficient clothing under it. Learn to know what's necessary for runs under different temperatures and wind conditions. A windbreaker required when running into a
cold wind can be taken off and tied around the waist on the way home when a tailwind
provides a warmer surrounding blanket of air. Hats and mittens (mittens are much
better than gloves when it's really cold) are other items that are nice to wear early in
a run but that you can get rid of later, if you get too warm.

Quality Training

When you perform a quality workout, say a set of 1,000-meter intervals, you repeat a
given task at a specific intensity with a certain amount of rest. You expect a particular
sense of discomfort and satisfaction. If you've been following a good running program,
you can expect that this workout will be as fast as ever but with less discomfort and a
quicker recovery, as weeks go by.

Similarly, midseason races give you a chance to see where you are in terms of race
fitness. You might plan a particular pace to see how that affects you, or you might see
how fast you can go in an all-out attempt. In any case, you'll have some plan in mind,
and you'll then follow that plan and analyze the result.

In a championship race, on the other hand (barring setbacks along the way), you
have every reason to believe that this will be your best race of the season, or maybe
even of your life. You've done the training and tapering necessary for success. The
important difference is rest. For a championship race, or series of races, you're in
a mode of final-quality training designed to let your body take advantage of all the
stress it has been through during the season. This is a time to reflect on the many
great training sessions you've completed, the successful races you've run, and the joy
associated with a good, hard-run race. Take advantage!

Tapering

As I mentioned in chapter 4, I believe in phases of training, each designed to prepare
you for what comes next. In keeping with this philosophy, the final-quality phase of
training (phase IV) before an important race must include those things that best prepare you for the race. When applicable, this is the time to get in the proper time zone,
in the proper environmental conditions, and into training that allows for maintenance
of earned race attributes. It's also the time for optimal performance and sharpening
of qualities you need for a successful race—part of which is achieved by tapering.

Recent research on tapering agrees on some points but suggests considerable variability in another area. The main points of agreement are that a taper should include
a reduction in the total amount of work and in the amount of quality training, but
maintenance of normal intensity in the work you do. An important point regarding this
quality factor is that you don't maintain the normal amount of quality—you maintain
normal speed with a comparable reduction in the amount of quality running. This
is a good opportunity to follow the suggested guidelines I've presented in chapters
7, 8, and 9 about how much of different types of running to include in your weekly
program. For example, I've suggested that the quality portion of an interval session

shouldn't exceed 8 percent of your week's total mileage. During a taper you can follow this same rule of thumb because as you reduce your total mileage you also reduce how much quality running you do (because it's a percentage of the lower total mileage). Another way to look at how much to reduce quality training is to cut it by the same relative percentage that you cut your weekly mileage. In general, your mileage (and relative amount of quality running) will be reduced during phase IV of a typical four-phase program.

Part of the idea about cutting back on training, and not losing any fitness, brings us back to training principle 7—ease of maintenance—which indicates that maintaining a fitness level is easier than achieving it in the first place. Basically just cutting back on what you're doing, in terms of amount, allows you to keep the fitness you have and still become more rested and feel better prepared to extend yourself in a race situation.

The aspect of tapering on which there's less agreement is how long the taper should be. There have been studies that suggest taper periods of as little as four or five days and others that say you need three or more weeks. Part of the difference in taper time is related to the event you're preparing for, some depends on how hard and how long you've been training, and there are also individual differences and preferences to consider.

I tend to believe that programs for 800- and 1,500-meter events, the shorter distance events, which typically switch from more medium-speed quality to faster training during the final phase of training, are actually tapering in terms of total mileage when they move to their final phase of training, so a taper in terms of amount is usually put into place a good number of weeks (often six to eight weeks) before the most important race(s). On the other hand, marathon runners may wait until the final four or five weeks to introduce a serious drop in mileage.

© Empics

Taking time to rest and reflect upon your accomplishments during the final-quality phase will pay off on race day.

Runners who haven't reached a particularly high level of training might be better off with very little taper because they're often still making weekly improvements and there's no reason to believe that tapering will produce any better results than continued solid training will.

The shorter the taper phase, the less opportunity for any final sharpening races, which vary in importance among individuals based on race distance, past experience, and length of season, for example. The final taper period is not a good time to put the body under new stresses, which could cause uncertain results. It's tempting during a period of lesser mileage to want to do everything faster than usual, but this is not the best strategy. Chances are that most runners would be happy with a 1 or 2 percent improvement in performance over what has already been accomplished (a 1 percent improvement is about two to three seconds in a 1,500-meter or mile race and about one to two and a half minutes in a marathon time). Of course, the slower your race times are, the greater the time drop that is associated with a 1 percent change. In the final analysis, coming up with the taper that best fits any particular runner requires trying different approaches, as does finding the best warm-up for a race. Stick with the basic idea of decreasing total work and total quality running during phase IV training, while maintaining normal intensity of the quality running that you do.

Establish a Race-Day Routine

On occasion, you might have to attend to some prerace matters a day or more ahead of a race, and it's always wise to get ready for each race well ahead of time. Have all possible pairs of shoes (and lengths of spikes, if used) packed and ready for each competition. Have a competition kit or bag that is always ready well before departing for a race. This kit should have shoes, uniforms, spare clothing (including appropriate clothing for a postrace awards ceremony), and something to drink and eat. Don't forget any food or fluids to be used before and during the race itself. Depending on the weather and location of the competition, other items might also be required, such as soap, a towel, a padlock for a locker, and a stopwatch. Take whatever you think you might need.

Probably the most important items are racing shoes and any required uniforms, which you should have in your carry-on bag if flying to a competition. Consider an additional uniform in case the first one doesn't fit right or gets wet or sweaty before the start of the race (it's usually best to put on your competition uniform after completing your warm-up). Marathoners allowed to provide their own fluids must consider water bottles, marking pens for their bottles, their drinks of choice, and where to place the drinks on the course.

In cross country racing, some runners prefer particular kinds of shoes or lengths of spikes. Always have both racing spikes and flats for cross country races. Rapidly changing course conditions can alter the type of footwear that is appropriate for a particular course.

I well remember a young runner who realized when he took off his warm-up suit just before a cross country race that he had no shorts on. Another time I watched a

Cross country racers must be prepared for an assortment of conditions.

runner take his shorts off along with his warm-up pants just as he was getting ready to take the baton for his (anchor) leg of a sprint relay. A teammate handed him his shorts, but it was too late, so he ran with his shorts in one hand and the baton in the other, right through the finish line and out of the stadium. He won the race, but I never did hear if he was disqualified for not wearing a proper uniform during his leg of the relay.

Before Warming Up

Before discussing the common prerace warm-up, let me first encourage the practice of a light morning run on the day of a race. This is usually a run of about 20 to 30 minutes, performed some time in the morning before a midday or afternoon race. During cross country season, when races are typically run before noon, you do this easy run early enough that you can still follow it with a light meal. The advantages of this are that it gets you up and going (rather than sleeping late or just sitting around worrying about your race) and allows for a refreshing shower and light meal well ahead of race time.

During the last hour or so before a race, regardless of the importance of the race, keep to your set routine. This helps in two ways. First, a good warm-up and mental attitude prepare you for competing at your best. Second, if you have a good routine to follow in less important races, then you can concentrate on the same routine before more important competitions, when many runners get nervous and don't know what to do when the chips are down.

To break a runner from relying on good luck charms, I try to set up a certain success situation and then find a way to hide the runner's "secret victory socks." If you can be victorious once in the absence of a good luck item, chances of future success without it are improved. The day will come when you forget or lose your good luck charm, and if that day happens to be at the Olympic Trials, well, that's really bad luck.

Warming Up

The term "warm-up" is misleading because warming up the muscles is only part of the process. In fact, "prerace preparation" might better describe what a runner goes through during the 30 to 60 minutes before a race starts. Whatever you call it, this is a time to prepare yourself physically and mentally for the task ahead.

Just as you experiment with different types of training, you should try out different prerace warm-ups. One approach is to think about some good, quality training sessions you've had and how you felt at different stages of those workouts. Recall a workout that involved repeating some 800s, 1,000s, or 1,200s, with a designated recovery between each bout of the workout. How did you feel during various repeated runs? Was the first one the easiest? The second, or the third? Sometimes it's even the last one that feels best (probably because it's the last one).

In a series of repeated runs, you'll often find a second or third run to be more comfortable than the first or the first couple. Think about this. If this applies to you, then consider this when warming up for a race. In other words, don't be afraid to put in some pretty solid running not too long before the start of a competitive effort if you find that works for you.

Many of the successful distance runners I've coached end their warm-up with an 800- or 1,000-meter run at about threshold pace. Others prefer a couple of repeated 400s at about interval pace with two minutes of recovery between them. In either case, this tune-up works quite well if the somewhat demanding part of the warm-up is completed 15 to 20 minutes before the race. I've seen cases in which such a warm-up ended 30 minutes before race time and yet the race went very well. This is good to remember in the event that a race doesn't start as scheduled.

Trying a demanding, prolonged run as part of a prerace warm-up often takes a little courage, but don't wait until your most important race of the year to try it out. Give it a fair trial in some less important races, and if it's successful, use it with confidence when it really counts.

The same principle of trying a particular prerace warm-up for lesser races applies to every type of warm-up. Always practice a new method in training and in meets of lesser importance so that you'll know what works best for you.

Many coaches like to have the whole team warm up at the same time and the same pace; this may look nice and encourage team cohesiveness, but it might not be best for the individuals on the team. In general, the same principles apply to warming up as to racing and training. If you're a coach, accommodate individual differences, and, to encourage team spirit, spend some time explaining the reasons why different strategies work best for different people.

Components of a Warm-Up

The following are some general characteristics of effective warm-ups.

Elevating muscle temperature. Muscular activity (involving the muscles that will do the running) improves performance through a slight elevation of muscle temperature. However, more than a degree or two of increase in muscle temperature can lead to a worse performance, especially if the weather is very warm or humid and the race is long (more than a mile).

In warm conditions, wearing a warm-up suit is not a good idea. One of a distance runner's greatest enemies is heat, and there's no need to accelerate body heating by overdressing before a race. If the weather is warm enough to feel comfortable sitting around without a warm-up suit on, then it's too warm to wear one during a warm-up routine.

Stretching. Stretching following the bulk of warm-up activity prepares the body for efficient movement and offers additional time to mentally prepare for the race. Try to avoid doing more stretching than usual during regular training because this will likely produce some muscle soreness in subsequent days. This is particularly undesirable if an athlete does more than the usual amount of stretching during preparation for a preliminary race, which can result in unwanted muscle soreness just in time for the finals, which might be contested a day or two later.

Quality running. Quality running, such as some quick strides or more prolonged threshold- or interval-intensity running, prepares your body for the task ahead. You not only get a feeling for the race pace, your fuel sources are made readily available, and your physiological systems are prepared for high-intensity operation. For most race distances, you want to stimulate carbohydrate metabolism (as compared to fat oxidation), and higher-intensity running accomplishes this. An exception for many people might be warming up for a marathon race, where race pace uses a combination of fat and carbohydrate for fuel, and carbohydrate sparing is a desirable goal. The reason for avoiding a high-intensity warm-up for long races is that the faster you run, the more your body selects carbohydrate for fuel, and you want to save as much of your available carbohydrate as possible for the race itself. Some easy running and stretching is usually adequate for long races.

Mental preparation. Runners are very different when it comes to getting mentally prepared for a race. I've had athletes who want me to talk to them almost constantly during the final minutes before a race; others would rather not even make eye contact for over an hour beforehand. I actually prefer the latter approach for my athletes because it indicates they can make their final preparation without me, so when the day comes that I'm not with them, they'll fare just fine on their own.

Some runners need to avoid thinking about their race, whereas others seem to thrive on almost constant visualization of how the race will proceed from start to finish.

Whatever time is afforded for mental preparation should be fit into the overall prerace routine so that it doesn't detract from other equally important aspects of preparing for the race (such as having your shoes on in time, your race number pinned in place, your proper racing uniform on, and your warm-up completed).

If you find it beneficial to go through some last-minute mental preparation, make a point of reviewing only positive thoughts. Don't think of mistakes of past races, advantages opponents might have had in previous encounters, or how awful you felt at the four-mile mark of your last 10K race. Visualize how you'll perform, how you'll adjust to midrace surprises, how you'll just let your legs carry you over the ground, as if some outside force is picking up each leg for you as you float over the ground. Have a plan for the race that's flexible enough to change if circumstances require it.

Try to go in to every race with confidence that you can achieve a particular performance but with a certain amount of anxiety about how well you might really be able to do. Great performances come at the most unexpected times and seldom arrive when they're intensely preplanned.

Remember during your prerace preparation that a race is a serious yet enjoyable expression of your ability to do something that you very much look forward to doing. The preparation for a championship race varies mainly in the groundwork preceding a less important race and in the training leading up to race day. Midseason races are important tests of where you are during various stages of training; championship races are a test of how fast you've become as the result of a season of training. You typically rest for a midseason race as you would for an important workout, whereas you give championship races special attention during the final-quality phase of training.

Warm-Ups to Try

The following are some prerace warm-ups that you can experiment with at different times to determine which works best for various races and environmental conditions. You may use some of these to prepare for quality training sessions as well.

Plan your total warm-up time carefully, with the critical factor being when the warm-up session will end relative to the start of the race. Remember that one idea behind a warm-up is to elevate the temperature of the exercising muscles, so have adequate clothing available for maintaining warmth between the end of the warm-up and the start of the race (or training session). If a race gets delayed after the warm-up has been terminated, add a few more strides or some more easy running until a short time before the race.

Easy running. This warm-up involves only easy running, with the possibility of adding a few strides and some stretching at the end. The amount of running can vary significantly, from as little as 5 to 10 minutes to several miles. Complete the warm-up 5 to 10 minutes before the start of the race. Do any stretching following at least some, if not all, of the running. Easy running warm-ups are a good idea before very long races, where race intensity is not particularly fast; before a second or third race in a track meet in which you're competing in more than one event; and when you haven't been training very long or hard for the race ahead of you.

Easy running plus strides or light repetitions. This is a variation of the easy running warm-up, the difference being that either during or following the easy run portion, you engage in a series of strides (usually from 3 or 4 to as many as 10 or 12). Strides are relatively fast runs lasting between 10 and 40 seconds each. Stride speed is about the pace you would race 1,500 meters or 1 mile. Fast strides might also be incorporated into this warm-up for additional speed. Fast strides are close to 800-meter race pace and are used as part of a warm-up for shorter races in which the starting pace must be fast. Understand that strides and even fast strides aren't sprints but are comfortably fast runs controlled and performed with light, quick leg turnover, rather than long, powerful strides. Take 20 to 60 seconds of recovery—either walking or easy running—between each stride. Try to have completed all of the strides about 10 minutes before race time. Some runners prefer doing their strides in racing shoes; others use their training flats and change to racing shoes during their final minutes of recovery and stretching, just before the race starts.

Easy–hard–easy running. With this warm-up, start off with one or two miles of easy running, some stretching, a few strides, and then a solid 3-minute run at about threshold (**T**) pace. There should be about 15 to 20 minutes of relaxation time after the **T** run before the start of the race itself. During the final relaxation period, you should do some easy running, typically to get yourself over to the area of the start in time to make final preparations. A variation of the single 3-minute run would be two 2-minute **T** runs, which would end 15 to 20 minutes before race time. This warm-up might seem demanding, and is somewhat intimidating, but if you reflect back on some training sessions composed of several long intervals or cruise intervals, you might remember that you typically start feeling better after the first, second, or even third workbout of the session. This warm-up is worth trying in a couple of low-key races before using it in an important competition.

Deena Kastor exudes confidence on the track and on the roads.

© Claus Anderson

Race-pace running. The race-pace warm-up often works best for shorter and medium-distance races, when you want to get a feel for the pace at which you would like to start the race. Following some easy running, stretching, and strides, run 200 or 400 meters a couple of times at the pace that you want to run the first 400 meters of the race. Usually it's better to run 2×400 meters or 2 to 3×200 meters (or a couple of 200s followed by a 400) than it is to run a single one of these runs. Take a full recovery between runs. During the race-pace warm-up, try to imagine being in the race with people around you, and imagine how easy and comfortable the pace will be once the race begins. Fall into a normal 2-2 breathing pattern at the start of the warm-up, and wear your racing shoes and racing uniform (weather permitting) in order to mimic race conditions as closely as possible. Time the warm-up so that you have about 10 minutes of full recovery before the start of the race.

Accelerations. This is similar to the easy run plus strides warm-up, except that this warm-up involves a brief easy run followed by a series of strides of increasing velocity. In this warm-up, the strides make up the bulk of the prerace preparation, so pay attention to how they're going. For instance, run each stride over the same stretch of ground and note the time that you take to perform each stride. Without making a conscious effort to lengthen your stride or to speed up, let each stride be a little faster than the previous one. This usually happens automatically, and it's nice to see yourself getting faster and faster with no additional effort as the warm-up progresses.

A variation of the timed strides is to count 30 or 40 right-foot steps as you do the strides and see how far this number of steps takes you. Count the same number of right footfalls for each stride, and notice that you're going farther each time as you loosen up and warm up, and as you fall into a good running rhythm. Once you've started to repeat the same number of steps (or to run the same time) for the same distance, you can figure the warm-up is complete.

Usually it takes about five or six strides to feel ready, but on occasion you might need 10 or more minutes of striding to get the feeling you want. Always take a good recovery after each stride so that you feel as rested for the new stride as you did for the previous one. Allow about 10 minutes after the last stride for making final race preparations. Because you aren't running a particular distance in a particular time, it's not imperative that you wear racing shoes during this warm-up. However, if you want to get a true feel for the opening pace of the race, you might want to throw in a timed run in racing shoes. An acceleration warm-up often works well for people who are entered in more than one event in a meet, and for runners who regularly include a set of strides in their daily training schedule.

Be aware that warm-ups that include fast short runs as the major part of the warm-up (or the final part of the warm-up) can lead to going out faster than desired in the race, unless race pace coincides with the final stride pace.

The Moment of Truth

A race is your expression of your ability to perform in a particular setting. Whether you're running against time or against an opponent, you're out there all alone, calling on all your ability, all the energy you've developed through weeks, months, years of training, and all the mental toughness and motivation you've gained through previous competitions and good coaching. The goal of all this is to achieve some predesignated time or place. The best that can happen is that you exceed your prerace expectations; the worst that can happen (in most cases) is that you don't meet your expectations. Look for a lesson that each particular race offers, and log that experience in a positive way. With a negative result, remember the race in terms of how you could have run it differently for a more desirable outcome. With a positive result, remember how it felt and how various aspects of the race were run.

It's usually better to finish a race saying, "I probably could have run a little faster if I'd been up a little farther in the early stages," rather than, "I wonder how much better I would have run if I hadn't gone out so fast and died." Most mistakes in a race are made in the first two minutes, perhaps in the very first minute. Going out too slowly during the first minute or two of a race won't necessarily cause the rest of the race to be too slow. But going out too quickly can produce a pace that's too slow for the rest of the race. Going out 10 seconds too fast in the first 400 meters of a 5K race can lead to losing a few seconds in each 400 thereafter. So, you might gain 10 seconds and lose 30, for a net loss of 20 seconds. On the other hand, giving away 5 seconds in the first 400 meters of a 5K will probably produce no loss the rest of the way. In this case, you lose a total of 5 seconds, and you'll undoubtedly find yourself passing many runners during the middle and later stages of the race (and it's much more enjoyable to be the passer than the "passee").

Keep the Intensity Even

Some runners are good front-runners and thrive on being in the lead; others do better staying behind the leader and letting others set the pace. In either case, most runners are better off running even-intensity races and settling down somewhere in the pack of leaders. I prefer to use the term "even-intensity" rather than "even-paced" in reference to what I consider the best approach to most distance races. Conditions such as wind, footing, and hills can alter a pace, even when the effort or intensity is constant. Changing the intensity of effort is costly, whereas changing pace might not be if you're doing so because of external factors. On a track, particularly an indoor track where wind never plays a role, pace and intensity often become one and the same.

If you realize that you've gone out faster than you wanted to, don't slow down abruptly—just relax, concentrate on the task at hand, and let the pace slow down on its own. The exception is in a marathon or other long race when you need to make adjustments as soon as you realize the problem. As a tip, if you can't hold a 2-2 breathing rhythm during the first two-thirds of a race (see page 116), your early pace is probably too fast.

Concentrate on Your Own Actions

Concentrate on what you're doing, not on what's going on around you. I've had some Olympic runners tell me that if they hear lap times, they know they aren't adequately focused on the task at hand. For young runners, there's a lot to be learned from getting splits at various stages of a race, but a well-trained veteran should be able to feel how the race is going. Of course, when a particular time is the goal of a race, splits might be a necessity and other aspects of the race can be ignored (including competitors in some cases).

When things get really tough in a race, you might have to think about running just one lap at a time, or just to a particular place on a cross country or road course. I once had a young runner set a 30-second PB in a two-mile race during which I had encouraged him by saying, "Just work on this next lap." After the race I asked him if that advice had helped, and his reply was that one lap at a time was too much to think about: "All I could think about was the next step." If that's what it takes, then that's what needs to be done.

Stay Relaxed Through Discomfort

When discomfort occurs, don't shift your thoughts to how much of the race is remaining. Concentrate on what you're doing and on being as relaxed as possible. Before a long race (particularly cross country races), I remind my runners that if they find themselves feeling lousy as they run alongside a group of other runners, they should realize that those around them must be feeling at least as terrible or they would be ahead of my runners.

Some runners, and probably even some coaches, feel that dropping out of a race is an absolute no-no. I agree that it's not a great idea, particularly if dropping out is associated with not wanting to keep going when it starts to hurt. However, there are some legitimate times when abandoning a race is acceptable. One is when you've sustained an injury, and continuing to race might cause complications or additional injury. Another legitimate time is when an illness or existing health problem, such as exercise-induced asthma, turns a race into a struggle for survival.

I've known people to run through a bad stitch to avoid dropping out of a race, only to aggravate the stitch to such a degree that training is curtailed for several weeks or even months. It's better to abandon the race than to put your future health in jeopardy. Incidentally, if you feel a stitch (a stabbing pain in the abdomen) coming on, make a conscious effort to take slower, deeper breaths (3-3 is usually a helpful pattern). Rapid, shallow breathing often aggravates a side stitch. Usually stitches on the right side are most troublesome.

A note to those who might consider dropping out of a cross country race—never assume anything. A runner who's struggling along as the sixth runner on a team, well back in the pack and feeling pretty dejected and worthless to the team, might decide to drop out. The runner often justifies this by saying, "I'm not scoring in our top five, so my place won't affect the scoring anyway." Moments after the runner drops out, one of the top five runners on the same team steps into a hole and is forced out of the race by injury. Not having the sixth runner as a backup becomes a major factor in the team scoring, and if there's no seventh runner, the team is completely out of the team race.

Feeling sorry for yourself is not a good reason to drop out of a race. On the other hand, avoiding a major setback that could occur if you continue in a race can be a legitimate reason to stop running.

When Struggling . . . Speed Up!

A race tactic that began as a joke, but which has merit, is one that I came up with when I was coaching in South America in the 1960s. One of my runners was a young mountain boy who was running a tough 5,000-meter race after having won a good 1,500-meter race earlier in the day. About seven or eight laps into the 5,000-meter he was 20 seconds behind the leaders, and as he ran by me, he asked if he could drop out. The next time he ran by, I told him that if he could run ahead and catch the leaders, then he could drop out. He took me at my word, and over the next two and a half laps, he did catch the leaders, but instead of dropping out he ran with them and then outkicked them for the win.

Another way of looking at a race is to stay with your competitors until you can't stay with them any longer—and then pass them. It's worth a try. Often in a long race, the unvarying pace gets you down, and you simply need a change. Most runners don't consider changing to a faster pace, but they should. Always try a pace increase before deciding to let the pace drop; you might find that you feel better.

If things keep going better than you expected in a race, you might begin to realize that you're better than you thought you were. Enjoy the fact that everything is clicking. There's no need to slow down just to satisfy some preconceived idea of how fast the pace should be. Usually a runner will know in the first few minutes of a race how things are going to go, so use that early assessment to make your adjustments.

Use the Two Thirds Tactic

A good tactic is to be in your desired finishing position two thirds of the way into the race. Arrive at that point as if it were the finish. Not many races change drastically (aside from a few position changes after runners' kicks) during the final third of a race. If you aren't with the lead pack in a mile race by the 1,200-meter mark, things aren't in your favor for being with the leaders at the finish. In a 10K, working your way up to a desired place of finish by the four-mile mark is a sound tactic, but waiting much longer makes your job a tougher one.

The same applies to reaching a time goal. Try for an even or negative-split race two thirds or three quarters of the way through the race, with the idea of being on pace at that point. Being on pace for the first 400 meters of a 5,000-meter race is nothing, and being much ahead of pace might spell disaster. Often, runners say something like, "I was right on pace at the mile (of a two-mile race, for example), but I couldn't hold the pace the second mile." Actually, in such a case, the runner might have been out in 70 seconds for the first 400 meters, then ran 76-, 77-, and 77-second 400s to arrive at the mile mark at 5:00 (just what he or she wanted for the first mile). But the pace was not a 5:00 pace at the mile; it was 5:08 pace, based on the two 77-second laps. The runner would be likely to run the second mile in over 5:00, if that was the pace going into the second mile.

Maybe the right way to think about pace is to think in terms of speed per 200 or 400 meters (or per kilometer or mile in longer races). Don't think of arriving at distance markers in a certain time because this can lead to disappointing results. If, for example, your goal is to run 3,200 meters in 12:00 on an indoor track, then the appropriate pace is 45 seconds per 200 meters, or 90 seconds per 400 meters. If the first 200 is 43 seconds, forget that lap and try for the desired 45 on the next lap. If a lap goes slower than 45, make an immediate adjustment to get back on pace. On the other hand, if 44- or 43-second laps come without undue stress, just relax and let each lap take care of itself, trying for 45 seconds but accepting a faster pace if it comes easily.

Avoid Obstacles and the Wind

Try to avoid traffic and confrontations during a race. It can be costly to be pushing and shoving other runners and having to run around them during a race. If you like to start out conservatively, then do just that; start at an easy pace and most of the jostling will be in front of you. By the time you've settled into your pace and are ready to move past all the runners who chose to fight each other in the first couple of minutes, most of them won't be in a mood to challenge you.

On the track, once you're comfortable running at your desired pace, do your best not to lose that rhythm, even if it means moving outside other runners around the curve. It's more costly to slow down and drop behind a runner around the curve and then have to accelerate on the straight than it is to maintain pace and move out a little. Running to the outside of another runner around the curve actually means you're going faster than your competition, and once you reach the straight your momentum will carry you by without the need to accelerate.

Likewise, headwinds are extremely costly (and tailwinds never make up for what you lose going against the same wind). When you're racing at 6:00-mile pace (3:45 per kilometer), you're creating a headwind of 10 miles per hour (mph), or 16 kilometers per hour, even if there's no wind blowing. Remember that the maximum allowable tailwind for a sprint or horizontal jump is 2.0 meters per second, less than half of the headwind created by running in calm air at 6:00 pace. Imagine the effort required to run against a 15-mph headwind, which is created in calm air when running at 4:00 mile pace.

With this in mind, it's easy to understand how damaging an additional wind of 10 or 15 mph can be. The fact is, the energy required to run a 6:00 mile against a fairly strong headwind (about 15 mph) is the same amount of energy as required to run at 5:00 pace in calm air. A headwind means a slower pace, and any runner who fails to heed this fact is flirting with disaster.

The same thing applies to leading or following in a distance race. Drafting off another runner can reduce the cost of the task a great deal. Unless you're considerably better than any of your opponents, trying to lead a 10K race all the way is almost certain to produce disappointment.

––––––––––––

Racing is the ultimate expression of a runner's ability, training, and motivation. A race should be thought out, prepared for, and performed with determined intensity. Analyze the results of every race you run, and use these data to adjust your training and tactics in future competitions.

CHAPTER 16

800 Meters

The 800 meters is a special event in that it requires true speed as well as endurance, which poses a problem for many coaches and runners. The tendency of high school and many collegiate coaches is to consider the 800 meters a fast, short-distance event for runners inclined to be distance oriented, and it's viewed as a long, "endurance" event by the 400-meter types. We simply need to recall the powerful Cuban, Alberto Juantorena, 1976 Olympic champion in both the 400 and 800 meters, and Peter Snell of New Zealand, 1964 Olympic champion in both the 800 and 1,500 meters, to understand why there's often concern over how to train best for the 800. Snell was very much endurance trained, whereas Juantorena was a speed-trained 800 runner. I doubt anyone would question Juantorena's endurance, however, because he had to qualify through many rounds in his quest for his double victory. Nor can they question Snell's speed, especially later in a tough 800 or 1,500 meters.

Jim Ryun (former world-record holder in both the mile and 880 yards) was probably a more endurance-trained runner, but he did include a fair bit of speed training in his overall program. Ryun also included strength training in his program, as did Joaquim Cruz (1984 Olympic champion in the 800 meters), who opted for circuit training, whereas Ryun included weights and some pool work in his training program.

Racing fast can be fun, racing hard is demanding, but racing fast and hard is a real discomfort.

In keeping with my physiological belief that you train the systems that are important in each event, I have to conclude that the ideal 800-meter runner is someone with good speed who's willing to do some much-needed specific endurance training. Also, because there's a solid aerobic component to 800-meter racing, there must be time set aside for basic foundation work. My suggested training program to include all that's required for the 800 meters takes me back to my usual four phases of training (see chapter 4). In the current chapter, I include two timetables to help differentiate training paces for 400- to 800-meter specialists and for 800- to 1,500-meter specialists.

Phase I

In addition to the usual easy and steady running typical of all distance programs, the 800-meter runner's phase I should include a concerted effort to make strength training a regular part of the program. Schedule three sessions of this supplemental training per week in the initial stages of training, and then cut back to two sessions per week when you begin more stressful running (as in phase III). Thirty minutes is sufficient for each supplemental training session, and what you perform during this time can vary considerably and still yield the desired results. The important thing is to work on core strength, which can take the form of weight training, circuit training, or simple body-resistance work (sit-ups, crunches, chin-ups, push-ups, bar dips, and so forth). Review chapter 10 for more information on supplemental training.

How much time you set aside for phase I depends partly on how many weeks you feel you have for the entire season ahead. Some high school runners might not have more than a few weeks available; some might be coming off a season in another sport and have little time to prepare for the competitive track season. On the other hand, more advanced runners might be able to set aside a couple of months for this initial phase of running. The important thing is to have an overall plan for the season in which each phase builds on the previous phase and the final phase takes advantage of your individual strengths. See table 16.1 for details on the 800-meter training plan.

Phase II

Each of the six weeks in this phase has two or three scheduled quality sessions (Q1, Q2, and Q3), one long (**L**) run, and three or four **E** days. You should also continue supplemental training three days each week. If you have a race during this phase of training, then let the race day replace one of the quality sessions (though preferably not the Q1 session). Try to schedule Q1 on Monday or Tuesday, Q2 on Wednesday or Thursday, and Q3 on Saturday (when there's no weekend race).

Table 16.1 **800-Meter Training Plan**

Phase	Week	Workouts		
I*	1-3	6 or 7 days each week **E** pace + 3 or 4 days of supplemental training (see chapter 10)		
	4-6	6 or 7 days each week **E** pace. Include one **L** run (25% of week's total mileage or 1.5 hours, whichever is less). Add 6 to 8 strides to at least four **E** runs per week. Do 3 or 4 days each week of supplemental training.		
		Q1 workout	**Q2 workout**	**Q3 workout**
II	7	1 to 2 miles **E** pace + 4 × (200m **R** pace with 1- to 2-min recovery jogs) + 4 to 6 × (400m **R** pace with 2- to 3-min jogs) + 4 × (200m **R** pace with 1- to 2-min jogs) + 1 to 2 miles **E** pace	1 to 2 miles **E** pace + 4 to 5 × (1 mile **T** pace with 1-min rests) + 1 to 2 miles **E** pace	1 to 2 miles **E** pace and race *or* 4 × (200m **R** with 1- to 2-min jogs) + 4 × (1,000m **T** pace with 1-min recoveries) + 4 × (200m **R** pace with 1- to 2-min jogs) + 1 to 2 miles **E** pace
	8	1 to 2 miles **E** pace + 4 × (200m **R** pace with 1- to 2-min jogs) + 2 × (400m **R** pace with 2- to 3-min jogs) + 1 × (600m **R** pace with 4-min jog) + 2 × (400m **R** pace with 2- to 3- min jogs) + 4 × (200m **R** pace with 1- to 2-min jogs) + 1 to 2 miles **E** pace	1 to 2 miles **E** pace + 3 to 4 miles (or 20 min) at steady **T** pace + 1 to 2 miles **E** pace	1 to 2 miles **E** pace and race *or* 6 × (200m **R** pace with 1- to 2-min jogs) + 1,000m **I** pace and 3-min jog + 1 mile **T** pace with 1-min rest + 6 × (200m **R** pace with 1- to 2-min jogs) + 1 to 2 miles **E** pace
	9	1 to 2 miles **E** pace + 4 × (200m **R** pace with 1- to 2-min recovery jogs) + 4 to 6 × (400m **R** pace with 2- to 3-min jogs) + 4 × (200m **R** pace with 1- to 2-min jogs) + 1 to 2 miles **E** pace	1 to 2 miles **E** pace + 4 to 5 × (1 mile **T** pace with 1-min rests) + 1 to 2 miles **E** pace	1 to 2 miles **E** pace and race *or* 4 × (200m **R** pace with 1- to 2-min jogs) + 4 × (1,000m **T** with 1-min recoveries) + 4 × (200m **R** with 1- to 2-min jogs) + 1 to 2 miles **E** pace
	10	1 to 2 miles **E** pace + 4 × (200m **R** pace with 1- to 2-min jogs) + 2 × (400m **R** pace with 2- to 3-min jogs) + 1 × (600m **R** pace with 4-min jogs) + 2 × (400m **R** pace with 2- to 3-min jogs) + 4 × (200m **R** pace with 1- to 2-min jogs) + 1 to 2 miles **E** pace	1 to 2 miles **E** pace + 3 to 4 miles (or 20 min) steady **T** pace + 1 to 2 miles **E** pace	1 to 2 miles **E** pace and race *or* 6 × (200m **R** pace with 1- to 2-min jogs) + 1,000m **I** pace with 3-min jog + 1 mile **T** pace with 1-min rest + 6 × (200m **R** pace with 1- to 2-min jogs) + 1 to 2 miles **E** pace

(continued)

Table 16.1 **800-Meter Training Plan**

(continued)

Phase	Week	Workouts		
		Q1 workout	**Q2 workout**	**Q3 workout**
II	11	1 to 2 miles **E** pace + 4 × (200m **R** pace with 1- to 2-min recovery jogs) + 4 to 6 × (400m **R** pace with 2- to 3-min jogs) + 4 × (200 **R** pace with 1- to 2-min jogs) + 1 to 2 miles **E** pace	1 to 2 miles **E** pace + 4 to 5 × (1 mile **T** pace with 1-min rests) + 1 to 2 miles **E** pace	1 to 2 miles **E** pace and race *or* 4 × (200 **R pace** with 1- to 2-min jogs) + 4 × (1,000m **T** pace with 1-min recoveries) + 4 × (200m **R** pace with 1- to 2-min jogs) + 1 to 2 miles **E** pace
	12	1 to 2 miles **E** pace + 4 × (200m **R** pace with 1- to 2-min jogs) + 2 × (400m **R** pace with 2- to 3-min jogs) + 1 × (600m **R** pace with 4-min jog) + 2 × (400m **R** pace with 2- to 3-min jogs) + 4 × (200m **R** pace with 1- to 2-min jogs) + 1 to 2 miles **E** pace	1 to 2 miles **E** pace + 3 to 4 miles (or 20 min) steady **T** pace + 1 to 2 miles **E** pace	1 to 2 miles **E** pace and race *or* 6 × (200m **R** pace with 1- to 2-min jogs) + 1,000m **I** pace and 3-min jog + 1 mile **T** pace with 1-min rest + 6 × (200m **R** pace with 1- to 2-min jogs) + 1 to 2 miles **E** pace
III	13	1 to 2 miles **E** pace + 4 strides + 6 to 8 × (1,000m at **I** pace with 2-to 3-min recovery jogs) + 1 to 2 miles **E** pace The sum of **I** pace shouldn't be more than 8% of the week's mileage.	1 to 2 miles **E** pace + 4 strides + 1 × (600m **R** pace with 5-min jog) + 2 × (400m **F** pace with 4-min jogs) + 1 × (600m **F** pace with 5-min jog) + 2 × (300m **F** pace with 3-min jogs) + 4 × (200m **R** pace with 200m jogs) + 1 mile **E** pace	—
	14	1 to 2 miles at **E** pace 4 strides + 2 × (1,200m at **I** pace with 4-min jogs) + 3 × (1,000m at **I** pace with 3-min jogs) + 4 × (800m at **I** pace with 2-min jogs) + 1 to 2 miles at **E** pace	1 to 2 miles at **E** pace 4 strides + 2 × (600m at **R** pace with 600m jogs) + 3 × (400m at **R** pace with 400m jogs) + 4 × (300m at **R** pace with 400-m jogs) + 6 × (200m at **F** pace with 200m jogs) 1 mile at **E** pace	—

Table 16.1   **800-Meter Training Plan**

Phase	Week	Workouts		
		Q1 workout	**Q2 workout**	**Q3 workout**
III	15	1 to 2 miles **E** pace + 4 strides + 6 to 8 × (1,000m **I** pace with 2- to 3-min recovery jogs) + 1 to 2 miles **E** pace. The sum of **I** pace shouldn't be more than 8% of the week's mileage.	1 to 2 miles **E** pace + 4 strides + 1 × (600m **R** pace with 5-min jog) + 2 × (400m **F** pace with 4-min jogs) + 1 × (600m **F** pace with 5-min jog) + 2 × (300m **F** pace with 3-min jogs) + 4 × (200m **R** pace with 200m jogs) + 1 mile **E** pace	—
	16	1 to 2 miles **E** pace + 4 strides + 2 to 4 × (1,200m **I** pace with 4-min jogs) + 2 to 4 × (800m **I** pace with 2-min jogs) + 1 mile **E** pace. The sum of **I** pace shouldn't be more than 8% of the week's mileage.	1 to 2 miles **E** pace + 4 strides + 2 × (200m **R** pace with 200m jogs) + 1 × (800m **R** pace with 800m jog) + 1 × (600m **F** pace with 5-min jog) + 1 × (400m **F** pace with 4-min jog) + 1 × (300m **F** pace with 200m jog) + 1 to 2 miles **E** pace	
	17	1 to 2 miles **E** pace + 4 strides + 6 to 8 × (1,000m at **I** pace with 2- to 3-min recovery jogs) + 1 to 2 miles **E** pace. Sum of **I** pace should not be more than 8% of week's mileage.	1 to 2 miles **E** pace + 4 strides + 1 × (600m **R** pace with 5-min jog) + 2 × (400m **F** pace with 4-min jogs) + 1 × (600m **F** pace with 5-min jog) + 2 × (300m **F** pace with 3-min jogs) + 4 × (200m **R** pace with 200m jogs) + 1 mile **E** pace	—
	18	1 to 2 miles **E** pace + 4 strides + 2 to 4 × (1,200m pace with 4-min jogs) + 2 to 4 × (800m **I** pace with 2-min jogs) + 1 mile **E** pace. The sum of **I** pace shouldn't be more than 8% of the week's mileage.	1 to 2 miles **E** pace + 4 strides + 2 × (200m **R** pace with 200m jogs) + 1 × (800m **R** pace with 800m jog) + 1 × (600m **F** pace with 5-min jog) + 1 × (400m **F** pace with 4-min jog) + 1 × (300m **F** pace) + 1 to 2 miles **E** pace	
IV	19- 21	1 to 2 miles **E** pace + 4 × (200m **R** pace) + 1 × (600m **R** pace with 5-min jog) + 1 × (600m **F** pace , 8-min jog) + 1 × (600m **F** pace, 6-min jog) + 2 × (300m **F** pace with 3-min jogs) + 1 to 2 miles **E** pace	Good warm-up and race + 4 to 6 × (200m **R** or **F** pace) or 3 × (1,000m **T** pace with 1-min rests) + 2 to 3 × (1,000m **I** pace with 2-min jogs) + 3 × (400m **F** pace with 3-min jogs)+ 1 to 2 miles **E** pace	

(continued)

Table 16.1 **800-Meter Training Plan**

(continued)

Phase	Week	Workouts		
		Q1 workout	Q2 workout	Q3 workout
IV	22-24	1 to 2 miles **E** pace + 2 × (200m **R** pace with 200m jogs) + 2 × (200m **F** pace with 200m jogs) + 1 × (800m **R** pace with 5-min jog) + 1 × (600m **F** pace with 6-min jog) + 1 × (400m **F** pace with 4-min jog) + 1 × (300m **F** pace with 3-min jog) + 1 × (200m **F** pace) + 1 to 2 miles **E** pace	Good warm-up and race + 4 to 6 × (200m **R** or **F** pace) *or* 2 to 3 × (400m **F** pace with 4-min jogs) + 3 to 4 × (300m **F** pace with 3-min jogs) + 2 miles **E** pace	

* If you have 8 weeks available for phase I, still split the phase in half: Weeks 1-4 and weeks 5-8.

For **R** training phase II, refer to tables 16.2 on pages 208 to 209 and 16.3 on pages 210 to 211 for pacing information. These modified VDOT tables are based on your current, or estimated, 800-meter race ability and on the type of 800-meter runner you are—whether a 400- to 800-meter type or an 800- to 1,500-meter type. While the VDOT tables in chapter 3 are more appropriate for training if your primary event of interest is 1,500 meters or longer, tables 16.2 and 16.3 are more applicable for runners who specialize in the 800. Table 16.2 covers 400- to 800-meter runners, and table 16.3 covers 800- to 1,500-meter runners. These new tables allow runners to go directly from performance to training speeds without first going to VDOT.

Stick with tables 16.2 and 16.3 for determining **R**, **I**, **T**, and **E** paces for all of phase II. Use the same intensities for at least three or four weeks, even if a better performance suggests a faster set of training paces. You can also use hills in place of **R**-paced workouts.

Phase III

Each week is to have one **L** run (on Saturday if there's no race). Include two quality days—Monday and Thursday if there's no Saturday race, or Monday and Wednesday when there is a Saturday race, which would make a third quality day for that week. Follow any race-day sessions with 4 × 200 at **R** pace. This phase of training is the most demanding and is designed to prepare you for the fast (though not so prolonged) training to come in phase IV. There will be some solid interval (**I**) training, and the rep sessions will include both fast reps (**F**) and pace reps (**R**). Continue supplemental training on two of the remaining **E** days each week, with at least two days between supplemental sessions. Also, do six or eight strides following two of the **E** runs each week.

Use the appropriate training pace table for identifying your training intensities, based on your current 800-meter race ability. Notice that some rep work is at **F** pace and some at **R** pace. It's better now to do the rep training on the track and depart from the hill training (if you've been doing hills up to now). Perform supplemental training a couple of times each week, but avoid doing supplemental work two or three days before an important race.

Phase IV

Each of the six weeks of this phase should have two quality sessions and five **E** days, two of which should include 4 to 6 × 200 at **F** or **R** pace. Also, one **E** day can be a moderately long run, though not as long as you were doing during the previous phases of training. Limit your supplemental training to stretching after workouts and some light abdominal, back, and upper-arm work (two days a week). When there's a race, arrange to have at least two (three for more important races) **E** days before the race day. So, during race weeks, do your Q1 workout on Tuesday, 6 × 200 at **F** pace on Wednesday, 4 × 200 at **R** pace on Friday, and 4 to 6 × 200 at **F** pace after the race, which is the Q2 workout for the week.

| Forego supplemental work and train easy in the days just before a big race.

Table 16.2 Training Paces for 400- to 800-Meter Specialists

Current ability 800	F (fast, race pace reps)				R (pace reps)				
	200	300	400	600	200	300	400	600	800
1:42	:25	:38	:51	1:16	:29	:44	:59	1:28	1:58
1:44	:26	:39	:52	1:18	:30	:45	:60	1:30	2:00
1:46	:26	:39	:53	1:19	:30	:45	:61	1:31	2:02
1:48	:27	:40	:54	1:21	:31	:46	:62	1:33	2:04
1:50	:27	:41	:55	1:22	:31	:47	:63	1:34	2:06
1:52	:28	:42	:56	1:24	:32	:48	:64	1:36	2:08
1:54	:28	:43	:57	1:26	:32	:48	:65	1:37	2:10
1:56	:29	:44	:58	1:28	:33	:49	:66	1:39	2:12
1:58	:29	:44	:59	1:29	:33	:50	:67	1:40	2:14
2:00	:30	:45	:60	1:30	:34	:51	:68	1:42	2:16
2:02	:30	:45	:61	1:31	:34	:51	:69	1:43	2:18
2:04	:31	:47	:62	1:34	:35	:53	:70	1:46	2:20
2:06	:31	:47	:63	1:35	:35	:53	:71	1:47	2:22
2:08	:32	:48	:64	1:36	:36	:54	:72	1:48	2:24
2:10	:32	:48	:65	1:37	:36	:54	:73	1:49	2:26
2:12	:33	:49	:66	1:39	:37	:55	:74	1:51	2:28
2:14	:33	:50	:67	1:40	:37	:56	:75	1:52	2:30
2:16	:34	:51	:68	1:42	:38	:57	:76	1:54	2:32
2:18	:34	:52	:69	1:44	:38	:57	:77	1:55	2:34
2:20	:35	:53	:70	1:46	:39	:58	:78	1:57	2:36
2:22	:35	:53	:71	1:47	:39	:59	:79	1:58	2:38
2:24	:36	:54	:72	1:48	:40	:60	:80	2:00	2:40
2:26	:36	:55	:73	1:50	:40	:61	:81	2:02	2:42
2:28	:37	:56	:74	1:52	:41	:62	:82	2:04	2:44
2:30	:37	:57	:75	1:53	:41	:63	:83	2:06	2:46
2:32	:38	:57	:76	1:54	:42	:63	:84	2:07	2:48
2:34	:38	:57	:77	1:55	:42	:64	:85	2:08	2:50
2:36	:39	:58	:78	1:57	:43	:65	:86	2:10	2:52
2:38	:39	:59	:79	1:58	:43	:65	:87	2:11	2:54
2:40	:40	:60	:80	2:00	:44	:66	:88	2:12	2:56
2:42	:40	:61	:81	2:02	:44	:67	:89	2:14	2:58
2:44	:41	:62	:82	2:04	:45	:68	:90	2:16	3:00
2:46	:41	:62	:83	2:05	:45	:68	:91	2:17	3:02
2:48	:42	:63	:84	2:06	:46	:69	:92	2:18	3:04
2:50	:42	:63	:85	2:07	:46	:69	:93	2:19	3:06
2:52	:43	:64	:86	2:09	:47	:70	:94	2:20	3:08
2:54	:43	:65	:87	2:10	:47	:71	:95	2:22	3:10
2:56	:44	:66	:88	2:12	:48	:72	:96	2:24	3:12
2:58	:44	:67	:89	2:14	:48	:73	:97	2:26	3:14
3:00	:45	:68	:90	2:16	:49	:74	:98	2:28	3:16
3:02	:45	:69	:91	2:17	:49	:74	:99	2:29	3:18
3:04	:46	:70	:92	2:19	:50	:75	1:40	2:30	3:20
3:06	:46	:70	:93	2:20	:50	:75	1:41	2:31	3:22
3:08	:47	:71	:94	2:21	:51	:76	1:42	2:33	3:24
3:10	:47	:72	:95	2:22	:51	:77	1:43	2:34	3:26

Table 16.2 **Training Paces for 400- to 800-Meter Specialists**

I (intervals)			T (threshold)		E (easy)	
400	**1,000**	**1,600**	**1,000**	**1,600**	**Mile**	**Kilometer**
:69	2:53	4:36	3:18	5:16	6:06-6:36	3:47-4:06
:70	2:55	4:40	3:20	5:20	6:10-6:40	3:50-4:08
:71	2:58	4:44	3:23	5:24	6:14-6:44	3:53-4:12
:72	3:00	4:48	3:25	5:28	6:18-6:48	3:55-4:14
:73	3:02	4:52	3:27	5:32	6:22-6:52	3:57-4:16
:74	3:05	4:56	3:30	5:36	6:26-6:56	4:00-4:18
:75	3:08	5:00	3:33	5:40	6:30-7:00	4:02-4:21
:76	3:10	5:04	3:35	5:44	6:34-7:04	4:05-4:24
:77	3:13	5:08	3:38	5:48	6:38-7:08	4:07-4:26
:78	3:15	5:12	3:40	5:52	6:42-7:12	4:10-4:28
:79	3:18	5:16	3:43	5:56	6:46-7:16	4:12-4:31
:80	3:20	5:20	3:45	6:00	6:50-7:20	4:15-4:33
:81	3:23	5:24	3:48	6:04	6:54-7:24	4:17-4:36
:82	3:25	5:28	3:50	6:08	6:58-7:28	4:20-4:38
:83	3:27	5:32	3:52	6:12	7:02-7:32	4:22-4:41
:84	3:30	5:36	3:55	6:16	7:06-7:36	4:25-4:43
:85	3:33	5:40	3:58	6:20	7:10-7:40	4:27-4:46
:86	3:35	5:44	4:00	6:24	7:14-7:44	4:30-4:48
:87	3:38	5:48	4:03	6:28	7:18-7:48	4:32-4:51
:88	3:40	5:52	4:05	6:32	7:22-7:52	4:35-4:53
:89	3:43	5:56	4:08	6:36	7:26-7:56	4:37-4:56
:90	3:45	6:00	4:10	6:40	7:30-8:00	4:40-4:58
:91	3:48	6:04	4:13	6:44	7:34-8:04	4:42-5:00
:92	3:50	6:08	4:15	6:48	7:38-8:08	4:45-5:03
:93	3:53	6:12	4:18	6:52	7:42-8:12	4:47-5:05
:94	3:55	6:16	4:20	6:56	7:46-8:16	4:50-5:08
:95	3:58	6:20	4:23	7:00	7:50-8:20	4:52-5:11
:96	4:00	6:24	4:25	7:04	7:54-8:24	4:54-5:13
:97	4:03	6:28	4:28	7:08	7:58-8:28	4:57-5:15
:98	4:05	6:32	4:30	7:12	8:02-8:32	5:00-5:18
:99	4:08	6:36	4:33	7:16	8:06-8:36	5:02-5:21
1:40	4:10	6:40	4:35	7:20	8:10-8:40	5:04-5:23
1:41	4:13	6:44	4:38	7:24	8:14-8:44	5:07-5:26
1:42	4:15	6:48	4:40	7:28	8:18-8:48	5:10-5:28
1:43	4:18	6:52	4:43	7:32	8:22-8:52	5:12-5:31
1:44	4:20	6:56	4:45	7:36	8:26-8:56	5:14-5:33
1:45	4:23	7:00	4:48	7:40	8:30-9:00	5:17-5:36
1:46	4:25	7:04	4:50	7:44	8:34-9:04	5:20-5:38
1:47	4:28	7:08	4:53	7:48	8:38-9:08	5:22-5:41
1:48	4:30	7:12	4:55	7:52	8:42-9:12	5:24-5:43
1:49	4:33	7:16	4:58	7:56	8:46-9:16	5:27-5:46
1:50	4:35	7:20	5:00	8:00	8:50-9:20	5:30-5:48
1:51	4:37	7:24	5:02	8:04	8:54-9:24	5:32-5:50
1:52	4:40	7:28	5:05	8:08	8:58-9:28	5:35-5:52
1:53	4:43	7:32	5:08	8:12	9:02-9:32	5:37-5:55

Table 16.3 Training Paces for 800- to 1500-Meter Specialists

Current ability 800	F (fast, race pace reps)				R (pace reps)				
	200	300	400	600	200	300	400	600	800
1:42	:25	:38	:51	1:16	:29	:44	:59	1:27	1:58
1:44	:26	:39	:52	1:18	:30	:45	:60	1:30	2:00
1:46	:26	:39	:53	1:19	:30	:45	:61	1:31	2:02
1:48	:27	:40	:54	1:21	:31	:46	:62	1:33	2:04
1:50	:27	:41	:55	1:22	:31	:47	:63	1:34	2:06
1:52	:28	:42	:56	1:24	:32	:48	:64	1:36	2:08
1:54	:28	:42	:57	1:25	:32	:48	:65	1:37	2:10
1:56	:29	:43	:58	1:27	:33	:49	:66	1:39	2:12
1:58	:29	:44	:59	1:28	:33	:50	:67	1:40	2:14
2:00	:30	:45	:60	1:30	:34	:51	:68	1:42	2:16
2:02	:30	:45	:61	1:31	:34	:51	:69	1:43	2:18
2:04	:31	:46	:62	1:33	:35	:52	:70	1:45	2:20
2:06	:31	:47	:63	1:34	:35	:53	:71	1:46	2:22
2:08	:32	:48	:64	1:36	:36	:54	:72	1:48	2:24
2:10	:32	:48	:65	1:37	:36	:54	:73	1:49	2:26
2:12	:33	:49	:66	1:39	:37	:55	:74	1:51	2:28
2:14	:33	:50	:67	1:40	:37	:56	:75	1:52	2:30
2:16	:34	:51	:68	1:42	:38	:57	:76	1:54	2:32
2:18	:34	:51	:69	1:43	:38	:57	:77	1:55	2:34
2:20	:35	:52	:70	1:45	:39	:58	:78	1:57	2:36
2:22	:35	:53	:71	1:46	:39	:59	:79	1:58	2:38
2:24	:36	:54	:72	1:48	:40	:60	:80	2:00	2:40
2:26	:36	:55	:73	1:50	:40	:61	:81	2:02	2:42
2:28	:37	:56	:74	1:52	:41	:62	:82	2:04	2:44
2:30	:37	:56	:75	1:53	:41	:62	:83	2:05	2:46
2:32	:38	:57	:76	1:54	:42	:63	:84	2:06	2:48
2:34	:38	:58	:77	1:56	:42	:63	:85	2:07	2:50
2:36	:39	:59	:78	1:58	:43	:64	:86	2:09	2:52
2:38	:39	:59	:79	1:59	:43	:65	:87	2:10	2:54
2:40	:40	:60	:80	2:00	:44	:66	:88	2:12	2:56
2:42	:40	:61	:81	2:02	:44	:67	:89	2:14	2:58
2:44	:41	:62	:82	2:04	:45	:68	:90	2:16	3:00
2:46	:41	:62	:83	2:05	:45	:68	:91	2:17	3:02
2:48	:42	:63	:84	2:06	:46	:69	:92	2:18	3:04
2:50	:42	:64	:85	2:08	:46	:70	:93	2:20	3:06
2:52	:43	:65	:86	2:10	:47	:71	:94	2:22	3:08
2:54	:43	:65	:87	2:11	:47	:72	:95	2:24	3:10
2:56	:44	:66	:88	2:12	:48	:72	:96	2:25	3:12
2:58	:44	:67	:89	2:14	:48	:73	:97	2:26	3:14
3:00	:45	:68	:90	2:16	:49	:74	:98	2:28	3:16
3:02	:45	:68	:91	2:17	:49	:74	:99	2:29	3:18
3:04	:46	:69	:92	2:18	:50	:75	1:40	2:30	3:20
3:06	:46	:70	:93	2:20	:50	:76	1:41	2:32	3:22
3:08	:47	:71	:94	2:22	:51	:77	1:42	2:34	3:24
3:10	:47	:71	:95	2:23	:51	:77	1:43	2:35	3:26

Table 16.3 **Training Paces for 800- to 1500-Meter Specialists**

I (intervals)			T (threshold)		E (easy)	
400	**1,000**	**1,600**	**1,000**	**1,600**	**Mile**	**Kilometer**
:67	2:47	4:28	3:07	5:00	5:58-6:28	3:42-4:01
:68	2:50	4:32	3:10	5:04	6:02-6:32	3:44-4:03
:69	2:52	4:36	3:12	5:08	6:06-6:36	3:47-4:06
:70	2:55	4:40	3:15	5:12	6:10-6:40	3:50-4:09
:71	2:57	4:44	3:17	5:16	6:14-6:44	3:53-4:12
:72	3:00	4:48	3:20	5:20	6:18-6:48	3:55-4:14
:73	3:02	4:52	3:22	5:24	6:22-6:52	3:57-4:16
:74	3:05	4:56	3:25	5:28	6:26-6:56	4:00-4:18
:75	3:07	5:00	3:27	5:32	6:30-7:00	4:02-4:21
:76	3:10	5:04	3:30	5:36	6:34-7:04	4:05-4:23
:77	3:12	5:08	3:32	5:40	6:38-7:08	4:07-4:26
:78	3:15	5:12	3:35	5:44	6:42-7:12	4:10-4:28
:79	3:17	5:16	3:37	5:48	6:46-7:16	4:12-4:31
:80	3:20	5:20	3:40	5:52	6:50-7:20	4:15-4:33
:81	3:22	5:24	3:42	5:56	6:54-7:24	4:17-4:36
:82	3:25	5:28	3:45	6:00	6:58-7:28	4:20-4:38
:83	3:27	5:32	3:47	6:04	7:02-7:32	4:22-4:40
:84	3:30	5:36	3:50	6:08	7:06-7:36	4:25-4:43
:85	3:32	5:40	3:52	6:12	7:10-7:40	4:27-4:45
:86	3:35	5:44	3:55	6:16	7:14-7:44	4:29-4:48
:87	3:37	5:48	3:57	6:20	7:18-7:48	4:32-4:51
:88	3:40	5:52	4:00	6:24	7:22-7:52	4:35-4:53
:89	3:43	5:56	4:03	6:28	7:26-7:56	4:37-4:56
:90	3:45	6:00	4:05	6:32	7:30-8:00	4:40-4:58
:91	3:48	6:04	4:08	6:36	7:34-8:04	4:42-5:00
:92	3:50	6:08	4:10	6:40	7:38-8:08	4:44-5:02
:93	3:53	6:12	4:13	6:44	7:42-8:12	4:47-5:05
:94	3:55	6:16	4:15	6:48	7:46-8:16	4:50-5:08
:95	3:58	6:20	4:18	6:52	7:50-8:20	4:52-5:10
:96	4:00	6:24	4:20	6:56	7:54-8:24	4:55-5:12
:97	4:03	6:28	4:23	7:00	7:58-8:28	4:57-5:15
:98	4:05	6:32	4:25	7:04	8:02-8:32	5:00-5:17
:99	4:08	6:36	4:28	7:08	8:06-8:36	5:02-5:20
1:40	4:10	6:40	4:30	7:12	8:10-8:40	5:04-5:23
1:41	4:12	6:44	4:32	7:16	8:14-8:44	5:07-5:26
1:42	4:15	6:48	4:35	7:20	8:18-8:48	5:10-5:28
1:43	4:18	6:52	4:38	7:24	8:22-8:52	5:12-5:31
1:44	4:20	6:56	4:40	7:28	8:26-8:56	5:14-5:33
1:45	4:23	7:00	4:43	7:32	8:30-9:00	5:17-5:36
1:46	4:25	7:04	4:45	7:36	8:34-9:04	5:20-5:38
1:47	4:28	7:08	4:48	7:40	8:38-9:08	5:22-5:41
1:48	4:30	7:12	4:50	7:44	8:42-9:12	5:25-5:44
1:49	4:33	7:16	4:53	7:48	8:46-9:16	5:27-5:46
1:50	4:35	7:20	4:55	7:52	8:50-9:20	5:30-5:48
1:51	4:38	7:24	4:58	7:56	8:54-9:24	5:32-5:50

Racing the 800 meters is a special event for several reasons. It requires both endurance and speed, it's brief enough that there's little room for tactical errors, and it often demands several rounds of competition that put considerable physical and mental stress on the runner.

CHAPTER 17

1,500 to 3,000 Meters

In keeping with my approach toward the physiological demands of training and racing distance events, I feel that it's appropriate to plan training sessions based on the duration of time you're racing rather than on the distance you're racing. For example, an elite runner concentrating on racing the 5,000-meter distance is training for a race that will last about 13 to 15 minutes, the same duration a less-gifted or beginning runner might spend racing 3,000 meters and not much beyond the time spent racing a one-mile distance for some runners. You should gear your training toward racing for a particular duration of time, such as 4 minutes, 15 minutes, 30 minutes, or a few hours, as opposed to a particular distance. That said, then runners at a stage of fitness or ability that would suggest they race 3,000 meters slower than about 12 or 13 minutes might want to follow the 5,000-meter training plan described in chapter 19. On the other hand, I think a better approach for these same runners might be to train for and more often race the 1,500 meters because the shorter, faster race is often a better preparation for a somewhat longer race.

Add to the time and distance dilemma the fact that different runners have different physiological (and psychological) makeups, and it's no wonder that a particular coach's training system works well for one athlete and not so well for another. One of the greatest mistakes we can make in training beginner runners is to throw them

Whether you view a race as a day off from training or as a test, treat every race seriously and with respect.

into a program currently used by a successful star athlete. If we do this, we're asking one runner to fit someone else's mold. Different individuals need different training programs. It's silly to think that all milers should train the same because they're training for the same distance.

In this chapter I present some ideas and sample training phases and workouts that are based on a 24-week season; these phases and workouts are geared toward preparing runners to race durations of time that rely heavily on both aerobic and anaerobic energy sources. I call these races "intense distance events" or "speed distance events," and they cover races that last from 3 and a half to 13 minutes (usually between 1,500 meters and 2 miles).

I've included two 24-week training plans (plans A and B) that you can use if you're planning to train and race 1,500 to 3,000 meters (see tables 17.1 and 17.2). Plan A is geared more toward controlled track workouts, and plan B is a little less structured, with more workouts using subjective training intensities rather than timed distances. Look over the two plans and pick the one that suits you better. What I think I do best is to identify the types of training and training intensities that meet the needs of different body systems. I also suggest some logical order of training that suits most people, but the best mix of ingredients is an individual matter that can be identified and finalized only through many seasons of training. Hang onto the positives you gain from each season's training, and set aside the negatives (though don't be too quick to discard the negatives altogether). If you don't have 24 weeks for your season, refer to chapter 4 for suggestions.

Approaching 1,500- to 3,000-Meter Training

The approach to training for these races is to learn to get out well but with as little effort as needed to stay with the pace you want. This is followed by a conscious effort to increase the effort during the middle portion of the race and eventually to shift into an even faster, more anaerobic finish.

To accomplish this, you need to train for speed, economy, and aerobic power. Races that last between about 4 and 13 minutes are won with speed, but a high aerobic capacity allows for some control in the middle of the race and provides a strong base and recovery system that facilitates optimal anaerobic training. There's a definite need for steady, comfortable distance runs, for demanding intervals, and for a variety of repetition-type workouts. Threshold training becomes an extension of easy runs and allows for light quality training that you can mix with reduced amounts of faster running.

You must learn to run fast and still be in control of your mechanics; run fast and not strain; run fast and still feel you have another gear when you need it. This is when having a high aerobic capacity pays off. It means saving anaerobic reserves as your final gear, rather than having to call on them to maintain the intensity of the midrace pace.

In the following pages I describe each phase's focus for the A and B plans. Tables 17.1 and 17.2 detail the workouts for each week of each plan. Phase I of each plan is identical. It's possible to make some switches between the two plans, but only do so within the same type of workout (just exchange **T**-pace, **R**-pace or **I**-pace workouts in one plan with the same type of workout from the other plan if you wish—but don't switch an **I** workout for a **T** session, for example).

Phase I

In a four-phase program, phase I—weeks 1 through 6 in a 24-week program—is set aside for foundation work and injury prevention, for building up to the point of being able to take on more formal quality training. For the first 3 weeks of this phase, do only steady, easy running. Runners with a solid background of base training who have maintained a reasonably good level of fitness may run twice a day. However, if you're returning from a period of no running, limit single runs to about 30 minutes each. Also, review the information in chapter 4 on returning to running after a planned time off.

After the first three weeks of steady running, add five or six strides to each of the daily easy runs, four days each week. Also, starting with week four, you can increase your mileage and add a long run once a week. Be sure to follow mileage rules when increasing your distance, though. Increase weekly mileage up to 10 miles (or about one hour) per week, but do this no more often than every third week.

Phase II

In phase II, or weeks 7 through 12, some quality running is added to the program and mileage might still be increasing, depending on the time and desire of the runner. It's a good idea to record at the top of the program you follow (and in your training log) your weekly mileage and the types of training you're emphasizing. Note that "Hard" efforts don't mean a timed distance but are meant to be a subjective intensity that approximates 3,000 to 5,000 race effort. If hill training is possible, substitute 30 seconds of uphill running for the **R**-pace 200s and 1-minute uphill runs for the **R**-pace 400s.

Beginning with phase II, you may use a VDOT value (see tables 3.1 and 3.2) to help you set your training intensities. When you haven't recently run a race, you can estimate a current race performance to establish an initial VDOT. Another possibility is to use an early **T** run to estimate a starting VDOT, using table 3.2. I've also included an additional table that uses current 1,500-meter race performances to set training paces for the training programs in this chapter (see table 17.3).

For plan A, each week has two or three quality days of training. In addition to these quality days, include one long (**L**) run and three or four easy (**E**) days as well as supplemental training three days each week. In the event that you have a competition scheduled during this phase, use that competition day to replace one of the quality sessions. However, keep in mind that it's best not to sacrifice Q1 because this is usually the primary training scheduled for this phase.

When a week has three quality days, it's usually best to schedule Q1 on Monday, Q2 on Wednesday or Thursday, and Q3 on Friday or Saturday. With only two quality days in a week, schedule Q1 for Monday or Tuesday and Q2 for Thursday or Friday. Always get in a good warm-up before the quality workout sessions and end each session with a cool-down run and stretching. Finally, consider doing some or all of the repetition-paced intensity runs (including fast reps, **R** and **F**) on hills, ignoring the paces indicated, but simply running for equivalent periods of time on the uphill portions.

Table 17.1 **1,500- to 3,000-Meter Training Plan A**

Phase	Week	Workouts		
I	1-3	6 or 7 days each week at **E** pace + 3 or 4 days each week of supplemental training (see chapter 10)		
	4-6	6 or 7 days each week E pace. Include one L run (25% of the week's total mileage or 1.5 hours, whichever is less). Add 6 to 8 strides to at least four E runs per week. Do 3 or 4 days each week of supplemental training.		
		Q1 workout	**Q2 workout**	**Q3 workout**
II	7	Sets of 2 × (200m **R** pace with 200m jogs to recover + 1 × 400m **R** pace with 400m jog to recover) The sum of **R** pace should total 3 to 5% of the week's mileage but not over 5 miles.	Sets of 800m or 1,000m **I** pace with 2-min recovery jogs The sum of **I** pace should be no more than 8% of the week's total mileage.	6 to 10 × (1,000m **T** pace with 1-min rests) The sum of **T** pace should be no more than 8% of the week's total mileage.
	8	3 to 5 × (2 × 200m **R** pace with 200m jogs + 1 × 800m **R** pace with 800m jog)	20-min at steady **T** pace + 4 to 6 × (200m **R** pace with 200m jogs)	—
	9	Sets of (2 × 200m **R** pace with 200m jogs to recover + 1 × 400m at **R** pace with 400m jog to recover) The sum of **R** pace should total 3 to 5% of the week's mileage but not over 5 miles.	Sets of 800 or 1,000m at **I** pace with 2-min recovery jog The sum of **I** pace should be no more than 8% of the week's total mileage.	6 to 10 × (1,000m **T** pace with 1-min rest) The sum of **T** pace should be no more than 8% of the week's total mileage.
	10	3 to 5 × (2 × 200m **R** pace with 200m jogs + 1 × 800m **R** pace with 800m jog)	40-min tempo run (use your VDOT and table 7.1 or 7.2 to figure your adjusted tempo pace) + 4 × (200m **R** pace with 200m jogs)	—
	11	Sets of (2 × 200m **R** pace with 200m jogs to recover + 1 × 400m **R** pace with 400m jog to recover) The sum of **R** pace should total 3 to 5% of the week's mileage but not over 5 miles.	3 to 5 × (2 min hard, 1 min **E;** 1 min hard, 30 sec **E;** 30 sec hard, 30 sec **E**) The sum of hard running should be the lesser of 10K and 8% of the week's total mileage.	6 to 10 × (1,000m **T** pace with 1-min rests) The sum of **T** pace should be no more than 8% of the week's total mileage.

Table 17.1 **1,500- to 3,000-Meter Training Plan A**

Phase	Week	Workouts		
		Q1 workout	**Q2 workout**	**Q3 workout**
II	12	3 to 5 × (2 × 200m **R** pace with 200m jogs + 1 × 800m **R** pace with 800m jog)	20 min steady **T** pace + 4 to 6 × (200m **R** pace with 200m jogs)	–
III	13	Sets of (1,000m, 1,200m, miles **I** pace or 4 to 5 min of hard running) with 3-min recovery jogs The sum of the sets should be the lesser of 10K and 8% of the week's total mileage.	Sets of (2 × 1,000m or 2 × 1-mile **T** pace with 1-min rest + 4 × 200m **R** pace with 200m jogs) The sum of **T** pace should be no more than 8% of the week's total mileage. If you race this week, drop Q2 and replace Q2 with Q3.	2 × (600m **R + 3** sec pace with 600m jogs) + 3 × (400m **R** pace with 400m jogs) + 4 × (300m **R** pace – 1 sec with 300m jogs) + 6 × (200m **F** pace with 200m jogs)
	14	Sets of (1,000m, 1,200m, miles **I** pace or 4 to 5 min of hard running) with 3-min recovery jogs. The sum of sets should be the lesser of 10K and 8% of the week's total mileage.	Sets of (2 × 1,000m or 2 × 1-mile **T** pace with 1-min rest + 4 × 200m **R** pace with 200m jogs). The sum of **T** pace should be no more than 8% of the week's total mileage.	Race *or* 3 to 5 × (1 × 800m **R** pace with 800m jog + 2 × 400m **R** pace with 400m jogs + 4 × 200m **R** pace with 200m jogs). The sum of **R** pace should not go over 5% of the week's total mileage.
	15	3 to 5 × (2 min hard, 1 min **E** + 1 min hard, 30 sec **E** + 30 sec hard, 30 sec **E**). The sum of sets should be the lesser of 10K and 8% of the week's total mileage.	8 to 10 × (400m **R** pace with 1-min rests) (Don't start too fast—this is tough.)	
	16	Sets of (1,000m, 1,200m, or miles **I** pace or 4 to 5 min of hard running) with 3-min recovery jogs The sum of sets should be the lesser of 10K and 8% of the week's total mileage.	Sets of (2 × 1,000m or 2 × 1-mile **T** pace with 1-min rest + 4 × 200m **R** pace with 200m jogs). The sum of **T** pace should be no more than 8% of the week's total mileage.	Race *or* 2 × (600m **R + 3** sec pace with 600m jogs) + 3 × (400m **R** pace with 400m jogs) + 4 × (300m **R – 1** sec pace with 300m jogs) + 6 × (200m at **F** pace with 200m jogs)

(continued)

Table 17.1 **1,500- to 3,000-Meter Training Plan A**

(continued)

Phase	Week	Q1 workout	Q2 workout	Q3 workout
			Workouts	
III	17	Sets of 800 or 1,000m **I** pace with 2-min recovery jogs. The sum of **I** pace should be no more than 8% of the week's total mileage.	Sets of (2 × 1,000m or 2 × 1-mile **T** pace with 1-min rest + 4 × 200m **R** pace with 200m jogs). The sum of **T** pace should be no more than 8% of the week's total mileage.	**Race** *or* 2 to 3 × (1 × 800m **R** pace with 800m jog + 2 × 400m **R** pace with 400m jogs + 4 × 200m **R** pace with 200m jogs) The sum of **R**-pace running should not go over 5% of the week's total mileage.
	18	Sets of 800 or 1,000m **I** pace with 2-min recovery jogs The sum of **I** pace should be no more than 8% of week' total mileage	8 to 10 × (400m **R** pace with 1-min rests) (Don't start too fast—this is tough.)	—
IV	19	Sets of (2 × 200m **F** pace with 200- to 400m jogs to recover + 1 × 400m **F** pace with 600-800m jog to recover). The sum of **F** pace should be the lesser of 3,200m and 5% of the week's total mileage.	3 × (2 × 200m **R** pace with 200m jogs + 5 to 6 min **T** pace)	Race or Sets of (2 × 200m **R** pace with 200m jogs + 1-mile **T** pace + 200m **F** pace + 400m jog) to total 20-25 min **T** pace
	20	2 to 3 × (2 × 200m **R** pace with 200m jogs + 1 × 800m **R** pace with 800m jog + 300m **F** pace + 800m jog)	3 × (5 to 6 min **T** pace + 200m **R** pace + 200m **E** pace + 200m **F** pace + 400m **E** pace)	Race *or* 2 × (600m **R + 3** sec pace with 600m jogs) + 3 × (400m **R** pace with 400m jogs) + 4 × (300m **R − 1** sec pace with 300m jogs) + 6 × (200m **F** pace with 200m jogs)
	21	Sets of (2 × 200m **F** pace with 200 to 400m jogs to recover + 1 × 400m **F** pace with 600-800m jog to recover). The sum of **F** pace should be the lesser of 3,200m and 5% of the week's total mileage.	3 × (5 to 6 min **T** pace + 200m **R** pace + 200m **E** pace + 200m **F** pace + 400m **E** pace)	Race *or* Sets of (2 × 200m **R** pace with 200m jogs + 1-mile **T** pace + 200m **F** pace + 400m jog) to total 20-25 min at **T** pace

Table 17.1   **1,500- to 3,000-Meter Training Plan A**

Phase	Week	Workouts		
		Q1 workout	**Q2 workout**	**Q3 workout**
IV	22	3 to 5 × (2 × 200m **R** pace with 200m jogs + 1 × 800m **R** pace with 800m jog + 300m **F** pace + 800m jog)	Race *or* 2 × (600m **R + 3** sec pace with 600m jogs) + 3 × (400m **R** pace with 400m jogs) + 4 × (300m **R − 1** sec pace with 300m jogs) + 6 × (200m **F** pace with 200m jogs)	—
	23	Sets of (2 × 200m **F** pace with 200 to 400m jogs to recover + 1 × 400m **F** pace with 600 to 800m jog to recover). The sum of **F** pace running should be the lesser of 3,200m or 5% of the week's total mileage.	3 × (2 × 200m **R** pace with 200m jogs + 5 to 6min **T** pace + 400 jog)	Sets of (2 × 200m **R** pace with 200m jogs + 1-mile **T** pace + 200m **F** pace +400m jog) to total 20-25 min at **T** pace
	24	3 × (2 × 200m **R** pace with 200m jogs + 5 to 6 min **T** pace + 400m jog)	Race *or* Sets of (2 × 200m **R** pace with 200m jogs + 1 mile **T** pace + 200m **F** pace +400m jog) to total 20-25 min at **T** pace	—

Table 17.2   **1,500- to 3,000-Meter Training Plan B**

Phase	Week	Workouts		
I	1-3	6 or 7 days each week at **E** pace 3 or 4 days each week of supplemental training (see chapter 10)		
	4-6	6 or 7 days each week at **E** pace. Include one **L** run (25% of the week's total mileage or 1.5 hours, whichever is less). Add 6 to 8 strides to at least four **E** runs per week. Do 3 or 4 days each week of supplemental training		
		Q1 workout	**Q2 workout**	**Q3 workout**
II	7	Sets of 400m **R** pace with 400m recovery jogs The sum of the sets should be the lesser of 4 miles and 5% of the week's mileage with 400m recovery jogs.	Sets of 3-min runs or 1,000m **I** pace with 3-min jogs for recovery The sum of **I** pace should be lesser of 8K and 8% of the week's total mileage.	20- to 40-min **tempo** run (use your VDOT and table 7.1 or 7.2 to figure your adjusted tempo pace)
	8	4 to 8 × (200m **R** pace with 200m recovery jogs) + 2 to 4 × (400m **R** pace with 400m jogs) + 1 × (800m **R** pace with 800m jog) + 2 to 4 × (400m **R** pace with 400m jogs) + 4 to 8 × (200m **R** pace with 200m jogs)	3 × (1,000-1,600m **T** pace with 1-min rests + 4 × 400m **R** pace with 400m jogs) + 1 × 1,600m **T** pace	—
	9	Sets of 400m **R** pace with 400m jogs The sum of **R** pace should total the lesser of 3 miles and 5% of the week's mileage.	2 × 4 min **I** pace with 3-min jogs 3 × 3 min **I** pace with 2-min jogs 2 to 4 × 2 min **I** pace with 1-min jogs	30- to 40-min **tempo** run (use your VDOT and table 7.1 or 7.2 to figure your adjusted tempo pace)
	10	4 to 8 × (200m **R** pace with 200m recovery jogs) + 2 to 4 × (400m **R** pace with 400m jogs) + 1 × (800m **R** pace with 800m jog) + 2 to 4 × (400m **R** pace with 400m jogs) + 4 to 8 × (200m **R** pace with 200m jogs)	2 × (10 min **T** pace with 2-min rest) + 2 × (1,000m or 3-min runs **I** pace with 2-min jogs) + 2 × (400m **R** pace with 400m jogs) + 2 × (200m **R** pace with 200m jogs)	—
	11	3 × (400m **R** pace with 400m jogs) + 3 × (800m **R** pace with 800m jogs) + 6 × (200m **R** pace with 200m jogs)	2 × (10-min **T** pace with 2-min rest) + 2 × (1,000m or 3-min runs **I** pace with 2-min jogs) + 2 × (400m **R** pace with 400m jogs) + 2 × (200m **R** pace with 200m jogs)	Sets of 3-min runs or 1,000m **I** pace with 3-min jogs The sum of **I** runs should total the lesser of 8K and 8% of the week's mileage.

Table 17.2 **1,500- to 3,000-Meter Training Plan B**

Phase	Week	Workouts		
		Q1 workout	**Q2 workout**	**Q3 workout**
II	12	3 × 400m **R** pace with 400m jogs + 3 × 800m **R** pace with 800m jogs + 6 × 200m **R** pace with 200m jogs	2 × 10-min **T** pace with 2-min rest + 2 × 1,000m (or 3-min runs) **I** pace with 2-min jogs + 2 × 400m **R** pace with 400m jogs + 2 × 200m **R** pace with 200m jogs	—
III*	13	4 × 2 min **I** pace with 1-min jogs + 6 × 1 min **I** pace with 30-sec jogs + 8 × 30 sec **I** pace with 30-sec jogs	Lesser of 5 × 5-min or 5 × 1 mile **T** with 1-min rests	Race _or_ Sets of 400m **R** pace with 400m recovery jogs The sum of **R** pace is the lesser of 4 miles and 5% of the week's total mileage. If you're racing one event, add 6 to 8 × 200m **R** pace with 200m jogs after the race.
	14	Sets of 3-min runs or 1,000m **I** pace with 3-min jogs The sum of the sets is the lesser of 10K and 8% of the week's mileage.	20- to 40-min tempo run (use your VDOT and table 7.1 or 7.2 to figure your adjusted tempo pace)	Race _or_ Sets of 400m **R** pace with 400m recovery jogs (Sum of **R** pace lesser of 4 miles and 5% of the week's total mileage If you are racing one event, add 6 to 8 × (200m **R** pace with 200m jogs) after the race
	15	4 to 6 × (1,200m or miles **I** pace with 4-min recovery jogs)	3 × (1,000m to 1,600m **T** pace with 1-min rests) + 4 × (400m **R** pace with 400m jogs) + 1 × 1,600m **T** pace	Race _or_ 3 miles **T** pace, 3-min rest + 2 miles **T** pace, 2-min rest + 1 mile **T** pace If you are racing one event, add 6 to 8 × (200m **R** pace with 200m jogs) after the race
	16	2 × (4 min **I** pace with 3-min jogs) + 3 × (3 min **I** pace with 2-min jogs) + 2 to 4 × (2 min **I** pace with 1-min jogs)	3 × (400m **R** pace with 400m jogs) + 3 × (800m **R** pace with 800m jogs) + 6 × (200m **F** pace with 200-400m jogs)	Race _or_ 3 × (1,000 to 1,600m **T** pace with 1-min rests) + 4 × (400m **R** pace with 400m jogs) + 1 × 1,600m **T** pace If you are racing one event, add 6 to 8 × (200m **R** pace with 200m jogs) after the race

(continued)

Table 17.2 1,500- to 3,000-Meter Training Plan B

(continued)

Phase	Week	Workouts		
		Q1 workout	**Q2 workout**	**Q3 workout**
III*	17	Sets of 400m at **R** pace with 400m recovery jogs to total the lesser of 4 miles and 5% of the week's total mileage.	Sets of 800m at **I** pace with 400m recovery jogs to total the lesser of 4 miles and 8% of the week's total mileage	Race *or* 30 to 40-min tempo run (use your VDOT and table 7.1 or 7.2 to figure your adjusted tempo pace) If you're racing one event, add 6 to 8 × (200m at **R** pace with 200m jogs) after the race.
	18	4 to 6 × (1,200m or mile at **I** pace with 4-min recovery jogs)	3 × (1,000 to 1,600m at **T** pace with 1-min rests) + 4 × (400m **R** pace with 400m jogs) + 1 × 1,600m at **T** pace	Race *or* Lesser of 5 × (5-min and 5 × 1 mile at **T** pace with 1-min rests) If you're racing one event, add 6 to 8 × (200m at **R** pace with 200m jogs) after the race.
IV**	19	3 × (800m at **R** pace, 200m jog + 200m at **R** pace, 200m jog + 200m at **F** pace, 800m jog)	2 to 3 × (1,000 to 1,600m **T** pace with 1-min rests) + 2 × (400m **R** pace with 400m jogs) + 4 × (200m **F** pace with 400m jogs)	Race *or* 2 or 3 × (4 × 200m **R** pace with 200m jogs + 1 × 1,000m **T** pace with 2-min rest + 2 × 200m **F** pace with 400m jogs) If you're racing one event, add 6 to 8 × (200m **R** pace with 200m jogs) after the race.
	20	2 to 3 × (800m at **R** pace with 800m jog + 400m **R** pace with 400m jog + 2 × 200m **F** pace with 400m jog)	2 to 3 × (1,000 to 1,600m **T** pace with 1-min rests) + 2 × (400m **R** pace with 400m jogs) + 4 × (200m **F** pace with 400m jogs)	**Race** *or* 2 or 3 × (4 × 200m **R** pace with 200m jogs + 1 × 1,000m **T** pace with 2-min rest + 2 × 200m **F** pace with 400m jogs) If you're racing one event, add 6 to 8 × (200m **R** pace with 200m jogs) after the race.

* If during phase III Q3 is a Friday race, do Q1 on Monday and Q2 on Tuesday or Wednesday; if Q3 is a Saturday race, do Q1 on Monday and Q2 on Wednesday. If there's a midweek race, skip Q2.

** If during phase IV Q3 is a Friday race, do Q1 on Tuesday, skip Q2, and make Q3 race day. If Q3 is a Saturday race, do Q1 on Monday and two sets of Q2 on Wednesday. If the Saturday race is important, do Q1 on Tuesday and skip Q2 for the week.

Table 17.2 **1,500- to 3,000-Meter Training Plan B**

Phase	Week	Workouts		
		Q1 workout	**Q2 workout**	**Q3 workout**
IV**	21	2 to 3 × (800m **R** pace with 200m jog + 200m **R** pace with 200m jog + 200m **F** pace with 800m jog)	2 to 3 × (1,000 to 1,600m **T** pace with 1-min rests) + 2 × (400m **R** pace with 400m jogs) + 4 × (200m **F** pace with 400m jogs)	**Race** *or* 2 or 3 × (4 × 200m **R** pace with 200m jogs + 1 × 1,000m **T** pace with 2-min rest + 2 × 200m **F** pace with 400m jogs) If you're racing one event, add 6 to 8 × (200m **R** pace with 200m jogs) after the race.
	22	2 to 3 × (800m at **R** pace with 800m jog + 400m at **R** pace with 400m jog + 2 × 200m at **F** pace with 400m jog)	Race *or* 2 to 3 sets of (4 × 200m at **R** pace with 200m jogs + 1 × 1,000m at **T** pace with 2-min rest + 2 × 200m at **F** pace with 400m jogs) If you're racing one event, add 6 to 8 × (200m at **R** pace with 200m jogs) after the race.	—
	23	3 × (800m at **R** pace with 200m jog + 200m at **R** pace with 200m jog + 200m at **F** pace with 800m jog)	Race *or* 2 to 3 sets of (4 × 200m at **R** pace with 200m jogs + 1 × 1,000m at **T** pace with 2-min rest + 2 × 200m at **F** pace with 400m jogs) If you're racing one event, add 6 to 8 × (200m at **R** pace with 200m jogs) after the race	—
	24	2 to 3 × (1,000 to 1,600m **T** pace with 1-min rests) + 2 × (400m **R** pace with 400m jogs) + 4 × (200m **F** pace with 400m jogs)	**Race** *(Friday and Saturday)*	

** If during phase IV Q3 is a Friday race, do Q1 on Tuesday, skip Q2, and make Q3 race day. If Q3 is a Saturday race, do Q1 on Monday and two sets of Q2 on Wednesday. If the Saturday race is important, do Q1 on Tuesday and skip Q2 for the week.

Hicham El Guerrouj, known as the prince of middle distance, has held the world 1,500-meter record countless times.

See table 17.3 (page 226) for **E, T, I, R,** and **F** paces, or refer to the VDOT tables and use the prescribed **E, T,** and **I** paces and **R** in place of both the **R** and **F** paces in table 17.3.

Phase III

Typically, phase III is the toughest phase of any training program. The first phases have prepared your body for what's ahead, and you're now fit enough to enter some races, which will help identify your current VDOT.

Some runners who compete on a school team find themselves facing a midweek race as well as a race the following Saturday. If you have a race on Tuesday, consider Tuesday and Wednesday as two midweek quality days, with the possibility of some additional light interval training worked in following the Tuesday race. Of course, the training session scheduled for Tuesday must be adjusted or eliminated altogether in favor of the race. Wednesday's session remains as scheduled. With a Wednesday race, follow a Monday–Wednesday quality-day schedule, perhaps adding some light interval training after Wednesday's race. With no midweek race, use Monday and Wednesday as the two early-week quality days. As I've indicated in the previous chapter on 800-meter training, I prefer identifying quality days of training for each week, which you can work in where they fit best.

Saturdays are set aside for a solid quality session, which often might be a race. If you do have a Saturday race on the schedule, it might be possible to add a reduced version of the quality session after the race (possibly one set); you can run at least some 200s as part of a postrace cool-down. If you have no races during this phase, just follow the training sessions as outlined. Total mileage should *not* increase during this phase; the training itself is demanding enough without introducing an additional stress of more mileage.

Phase IV

Set up the final quality phase of the intense distance program to take advantage of your strengths and previous training and racing experiences. The key components of this phase should be adequate rest and recovery from workouts, quality training (of limited volume), well-chosen races, and possibly a drop in overall weekly mileage. The toughest physical work is behind you, and improved performances will come as a result of what you've already done. Don't increase your training stress during this phase. Just do quality workouts with minimal effort and put your energy into high-quality races.

It's still fine to get in two quality days (Q1 and Q2) prior to a Saturday race (which also is considered a quality day), but if the race is a particularly important one (a championship race or a qualifier) limit your quality training to one quality session (eliminate whichever quality workout you feel is most stressful) and schedule that one good session for Tuesday. In the six-week plan, consider four approaches to arranging quality days leading up to a Saturday race:

- Monday–Wednesday quality days (the standard approach)
- Tuesday–Wednesday quality days, which allow a slightly longer recovery from a previous weekend's race
- Monday–Tuesday quality days, which provide an additional easy day before a Saturday race, when the previous week's work requires little recovery
- Tuesday as the only quality day, when the coming race is of particular importance

Follow Sunday runs with a few light and quick 200s. Easy-day 200s should never be sprints; 800-meter race pace is the fastest they need to be, and always with adequate recoveries to feel good for the next run. Be particularly careful not to increase or decrease the intensity of your training in the final weeks of the season. The best taper approach is usually to cut back on the amount of training you do (amount of quality and total mileage) but not on the speed of training.

Table 17.3 Training Paces for 1,500- to 3,000-Meter Runners

Current ability 1,500	F (Fast reps)				R (Pace reps)				
	200	300	400	600	200	300	400	600	800
3:26	:25	:38	:51	1:16	:27	:41	:55	1:22	1:50
3:30	:26	:39	:52	1:18	:28	:42	:56	1:24	1:52
3:34	:26	:39	:53	1:19	:28	:43	:57	1:25	1:54
3:38	:27	:40	:54	1:21	:29	:44	:58	1:27	1:56
3:42	:27	:41	:55	1:22	:29	:44	:59	1:29	1:58
3:46	:28	:42	:56	1:24	:30	:45	:60	1:30	2:01
3:50	:29	:43	:57	1:26	:31	:46	:61	1:32	2:03
3:54	:29	:44	:58	1:28	:31	:47	:62	1:34	2:05
3:58	:30	:45	:60	1:30	:32	:48	:64	1:35	2:08
4:02	:30	:45	:61	1:31	:32	:48	:65	1:37	2:10
4:06	:31	:46	:62	1:32	:33	:49	:66	1:38	2:12
4:10	:31	:47	:63	1:34	:33	:50	:67	1:40	2:14
4:14	:32	:48	:64	1:36	:34	:51	:68	1:42	2:16
4:18	:32	:48	:65	1:37	:34	:51	:69	1:43	2:18
4:22	:33	:49	:66	1:39	:35	:52	:70	1:45	2:20
4:26	:33	:50	:67	1:40	:35	:53	:71	1:46	2:22
4:30	:34	:51	:68	1:42	:36	:54	:72	1:48	2:24
4:34	:34	:52	:69	1:44	:36	:55	:73	1:50	2:26
4:38	:35	:53	:70	1:46	:37	:56	:74	1:52	2:28
4:42	:35	:53	:71	1:47	:37	:56	:75	1:53	2:30
4:46	:36	:54	:72	1:48	:38	:57	:76	1:54	2:33
4:50	:36	:55	:73	1:50	:38	:58	:77	1:56	2:35
4:54	:37	:56	:74	1:52	:39	:59	:78	1:58	2:37
4:58	:37	:56	:75	1:53	:39	:59	:79	1:59	2:39
5:02	:38	:57	:76	1:54	:40	:60	:80	2:01	2:41
5:06	:39	:58	:78	1:56	:41	:61	:82	2:03	2:44
5:10	:39	:59	:79	1:58	:41	:62	:83	2:04	2:46
5:14	:40	:60	:80	2:00	:42	:63	:84	2:06	2:48
5:18	:40	:61	:81	2:02	:42	:64	:85	2:08	2:50
5:22	:41	:62	:82	2:04	:43	:65	:86	2:10	2:52
5:26	:41	:62	:83	2:05	:43	:65	:87	2:11	2:54
5:30	:42	:63	:84	2:06	:44	:66	:88	2:12	2:56
5:34	:42	:64	:85	2:08	:44	:67	:89	2:14	2:58
5:38	:43	:65	:86	2:10	:45	:67	:90	2:15	3:00
5:42	:43	:66	:87	2:12	:45	:68	:91	2:16	3:02
5:46	:44	:66	:88	2:13	:46	:69	:92	2:18	3:04
5:50	:44	:67	:89	2:14	:46	:70	:93	2:20	3:06
5:54	:45	:68	:90	2:16	:47	:71	:94	2:22	3:08
5:58	:45	:69	:92	2:18	:47	:72	:95	2:24	3:10
6:02	:46	:70	:93	2:20	:48	:72	:96	2:25	3:12

Table 17.3 **Training Paces for 1,500- to 3,000-Meter Runners**

I (Intervals)			T (Threshold		E (Easy)	
400	1,000	1,600	1,000	Mile	Mile	Kilometer
:61	2:33	4:04	2:49	4:32	5:34-6:04	3:27-3:46
:62	2:35	4:08	2:51	4:36	5:38-6:08	3:29-3:48
:63	2:37	4:12	2:54	4:40	5:42-6:12	3:33-3:52
:64	2:39	4:16	2:56	4:45	5:46-6:16	3:35-3:54
:65	2:42	4:20	2:59	4:50	5:50-6:20	3:38-3:57
:66	2:45	4:24	3:02	4:55	5:55-6:25	3:41-4:00
:67	2:48	4:28	3:06	5:00	6:00-6:30	3:44-4:03
:68	2:50	4:32	3:08	5:02	6:06-6:35	3:47-4:06
:70	2:55	4:40	3:13	5:11	6:14-6:44	3:53-4:12
:71	2:58	4:44	3:16	5:15	6:18-6:48	3:55-4:14
:72	3:00	4:48	3:18	5:19	6:22-6:52	3:57-4:16
:73	3:03	4:52	3:21	5:23	6:26-6:56	4:00-4:18
:74	3:05	4:56	3:24	5:28	6:30-7:00	4:02-4:21
:75	3:08	5:00	3:27	5:33	6:35-7:05	4:05-4:25
:76	3:10	5:04	3:30	5:38	6:40-7:10	4:08-4:28
:77	3:13	5:08	3:34	5:43	6:45-7:15	4:12-4:31
:78	3:15	5:12	3:37	5:48	6:50-7:20	4:15-4:33
:79	3:18	5:16	3:40	5:52	6:55-7:25	4:18-4:37
:80	3:20	5:20	3:43	5:57	7:00-7:30	4:21-4:40
:81	3:23	5:24	3:45	6:02	7:05-7:35	4:24-4:43
:82	3:25	5:28	3:48	6:07	7:10-7:40	4:27-4:46
:83	3:28	5:32	3:51	6:12	7:15-7:45	4:30-4:49
:84	3:30	5:36	3:54	6:17	7:20-7:50	4:33-4:52
:85	3:33	5:40	3:56	6:21	7:25-7:55	4:36-4:55
:86	3:35	5:44	3:59	6:25	7:30-8:00	4:40-4:58
:88	3:40	5:52	4:04	6:33	7:35-8:05	4:43-5:01
:89	3:43	5:56	4:07	6:38	7:40-8:10	4:46-5:04
:90	3:45	6:00	4:10	6:42	7:45-8:15	4:49-5:07
:91	3:48	6:04	4:12	6:46	7:50-8:20	4:52-5:11
:92	3:50	6:08	4:15	6:50	7:55-8:25	4:55-5:14
:93	3:53	6:12	4:17	6:54	8:00-8:30	4:58-5:16
:94	3:55	6:16	4:20	6:58	8:04-8:34	5:01-5:19
:95	3:58	6:20	4:22	7:02	8:08-8:38	5:03-5:21
:96	4:00	6:24	4:25	7:06	8:12-8:42	5:06-5:24
:97	4:03	6:28	4:27	7:10	8:15-8:45	5:08-5:27
:98	4:05	6:32	4:30	7:15	8:20-8:50	5:11-5:30
:99	4:08	6:36	4:33	7:19	8:24-8:54	5:13-5:32
1:40	4:10	6:40	4:35	7:23	8:28-8:58	5:16-5:35
1:42	4:15	6:48	4:40	7:31	8:35-9:05	5:19-5:38
1:43	4:18	6:52	4:43	7:35	8:40-9:10	5:22-5:42

———————————

There's no doubt that some runners in speed distance events rely more on endurance than others do, and this is where being able to read your reactions to various types of training (or having a coach who can do that for you) really pays off. This is also why it takes years to develop your full potential in these events. You spend some seasons developing one aspect of your talent, and you spend other seasons recognizing the approaches that aren't right for you. Each individual runner must experiment to find the proper mix of training ingredients.

CHAPTER 18

Cross Country

Many readers of my first edition requested that this new edition include a chapter on training programs specifically for cross country runners. Because I want to provide training that applies to a wide variety of runners, it's a challenge to include information that pertains mainly to those athletes whose primary interest is racing cross country, where race distances vary from 4,000 meters or less to 12,000 meters. These different distances call for different kinds of training. Runners who race distances that demand 15 to 20 minutes might do well to follow a 5,000-meter training schedule. On the other hand, those who race distances between 6K and 12K often find a 10K program more to their liking. After considering all this, I've included in this chapter what I think is a good progression of types of training that runners can add to or deduct from, depending on their experience, fitness level, and race distance of primary interest.

Certainly, some runners who race 6K and 8K distances might benefit more from the 5K program than the 10K program. A good approach for these runners might be to try one approach in one season and the other in the next. A main concern might be what events are of primary interest in the upcoming track season. If your main interest is track, let cross country training help prepare you for track. If cross country is more important to you, follow the plan you feel best prepares you for competing

A win on the track is not easy to achieve, but a win in cross country is a rare treat.

during the cross country season, and use the track season to improve on weaknesses so that you enter the next cross country season well prepared.

Phase I

In general, I strongly recommend that cross country runners do a prolonged initial phase of steady, easy running. Experienced runners are familiar with this base-building stage and usually have a good feel for how much time they should dedicate to this type of early-season preparation. Beginners should do a minimum of four weeks of steady, easy running. More is often better, if possible, but many high school programs don't allow for more. In many cases, high school coaches are faced with a number of raw beginners each year, with limited time for base building before competitions begin. Returning runners on high school teams should be encouraged to spend much of the summer getting in their foundation work. When possible, it's best to perform much of this foundation running over rolling terrain and on dirt or grass footing, which is what you face on most cross country courses.

The running during this phase should all be easy (**E**) running, with drills and stretching every day. Increase weekly mileage every third week by 7 to 10 miles (40 to 60 minutes). First-time runners might have to begin with no more than 30 minutes of easy running, broken into shorter runs of 2 to 5 minutes each and separated by a few minutes of walking to recover. These beginners might spend three or more weeks of this phase building up to being able to run steadily for 30 minutes. More experienced runners, and beginners who have more than four weeks available for this phase, should try to gradually increase their weekly mileage to a point at which they're accomplishing about two thirds of the maximum weekly total mileage they plan to reach for the season.

Phase II

The second phase of the cross country program is for adjusting to some faster running and hill running, but with controlled stress. By "controlled stress" I mean working hard for short periods of time within a workout, with a relatively prolonged recovery between repeated runs. This is a great time to introduce some hill work into the program, and—in keeping with my basic philosophy that some time should be spent on quick, light turnover early in a season—I recommend a phase of running that provides for this before getting into the more prolonged, stressful workouts of phase III.

Hills

Hill running provides some of the same benefits as repetition training (see chapter 9). In fact, when you analyze what you're doing during a hill session and during a rep session, they're quite similar indeed. You're typically working at a rather high intensity (running uphill or doing reps on the flat) for a relatively short period, followed by a recovery break that's longer than the workbout that it follows (returning downhill or doing easy jogging between fast rep runs). Uphill running is also good for strengthening areas of the hips and legs, which leads to improved running economy. In fact, you can argue that hill training is an important ingredient of early-season training even for distance runners whose primary interest is track competition. Hill training specifically (and cross country training in general) provides a solid preparation in terms of strength and variability for distance runners whose sights are set on good track performances.

Hilly terrain requires that you make an adjustment for proper training (especially **T** training), but once you learn to monitor intensity properly, your running speed will vary as you go up and down, and the effort can remain constant—this is the goal of a tempo run. A heart rate monitor can be useful when you're trying to maintain a constant effort over undulating terrain; otherwise, it can be mentally demanding to sustain intensity of effort when you're being constantly confronted by hills of different grades and sizes. With hills, you can also incorporate a good variety of workouts into your **R** training—uphills for greater strength and economy, and downhills (preferably gradual, grassy slopes rather than steep and hard surfaced) for speed and additional economy development.

Hills can also offer a nice variation of **I** training. By running over a rolling course at a fairly constant pace, you can use the uphills to stress $\dot{V}O_2$max intensity, whereas the downhills and flats work well for recovery. By selecting different courses, you can vary the high-intensity portion of the workout, using brief periods or longer workbouts of several minutes each.

For faster downhill runs, look for some relatively long (one minute to several minutes duration), gradually sloping hills on which you can maintain good speed with minimal effort.

Cross Country Surfaces

In keeping with the principle of specificity of training, as much cross country training as possible, including **I** training, should be performed on softer, cross country surfaces. Look for good, even grass areas or dirt hills to run on. However, uphill running is one instance when being on a hard (even road) surface is not so bad because running uphill reduces the landing shock typically associated with hard surfaces. Just make sure that on the return downhill runs you find a more gradual slope, or else lighten your pace, because downhill running on hard surfaces is particularly stressful and puts you at risk of injury. I've always thought that uphill running on a treadmill is the ideal way to hill train because you get the uphill running and eliminate the downhills—you can simply hop off the treadmill for your recovery breaks and back on again for the next hill run (see chapter 9 for details about treadmill running).

Some runners run in environments that are mostly slow going, such as over sand, grass, gravel roads, or rocky trails. These runners must adjust to the lack of good footing that's conducive to faster training. Residents of such slow-footing environments learn to be strength runners; they also develop good resistance to injuries because they're constantly twisting and turning their feet.

FLATLANDERS' CHALLENGE

For runners who have no hills available, the challenge is to come up with other ways to vary the demands of your workouts. One advantage flatlanders have is that no matter what course they design for training or for testing themselves, they can always make legitimate time comparisons in order to monitor their fitness. They can easily have "controlled variety" in their workouts.

Unless they're training for a race that's over a particularly hilly course, I don't think that flat-terrain runners need to be concerned about having no hills available. Flat-terrain residents should think of themselves as "finesse" runners. Proper intensity of effort is associated with a slightly faster pace than you'd use if you were always going over hills. The result is that a steady fast pace becomes comfortable and isn't unusual come race time.

Because there's nothing particularly challenging about the terrain facing flatlanders, runners learn to be tough within the intensity of the workouts. Tempo runs can be controlled, and by selecting longer workbouts (three to five minutes each) in interval sessions, runners can simulate the constant prolonged demands of racing.

Whereas hill runners learn to deal with constant changes in intensity, flatlanders learn to deal with unrelenting intensity without the occasional break afforded by downhills. Of course, a flatlander might have other ways to make a workout demanding, such as using sand, soft grass, or other types of rough footing in training sessions.

Because poor footing affects running economy (the amount of energy required to run any particular speed) by increasing the cost of running, a runner need not go as fast to be stressing the body to the same degree as he or she would be with a faster pace on better footing. Here's where learning to read your body becomes important. When a workout calls for a particular relative intensity of effort (as is the case in threshold, marathon-pace, and interval workouts), the pace can be slower on poor footing and still meet the physiological requirements of the workout.

If you run regularly in slow-footing environments, you might have to use track work more than other distance runners, particularly for repetitions. But during cross country season it's better to find an area where you can have some smooth, fast footing so that you can practice the mechanics you'll use in races on good footing. Nothing's more frustrating than to be in great shape but to lack the speed to finish well or stay with a pace that's a little too fast just because your training conditions prevented quality repetition work. Under such conditions, it's also useful to do some of your faster running on a treadmill. If you have a treadmill that goes fast enough to match your desired **R** pace, take advantage. If your treadmill doesn't go fast enough, consider adding 5 percent to the grade for each minute per mile faster than your treadmill allows. This grade accommodation won't match the speed but will make the workload equal to what you want from your **R** pace. It definitely gives the impression of having gone faster than the actual speed indicates. A couple of these sessions per week will work wonders for your speed development, and using a grade of 5 percent or greater will help prepare you for racing on hilly cross country courses.

A more concrete way of identifying proper intensity is to learn what heart rates correspond to various intensities on a flat, dry course and then let your heart rate rather than your running speed guide you when you're running on poor footing, just as you would do on undulating terrain. An even better way to monitor threshold intensity is to use a lactate analyzer (these are becoming easier for average runners to find). Percentages of both maximum heart rate and predetermined blood-lactate values can be used effectively when terrain or weather conditions affect normal running economy. Always try to use your perceived feeling of your training to help determine to what degree a workout is stressing you.

During phase II, you can continue to increase your weekly mileage or total training time by about 10 miles or one hour every third week. It would be nice if each runner had six weeks available for this phase of training, but for programs with a limited season, I believe at least three weeks can be of considerable benefit. For high school runners and certainly for college runners, it's best if this phase is accomplished over the summer, before school starts.

Throughout phase II, **E** days help you accomplish your desired weekly total mileage or hourly duration, which means that there might be some **E** days that involve no running. **E** runs are also used as a warm-up or cool-down on quality days (shaded in table 18.1).

Table 18.1 **Phase II—Cross Country Prerace Season (3 to 6 weeks)**

Day	Workout
1	**L** run (lesser of 25% of week's mileage and 2 hours)
2	**E** pace 30 minutes or more as needed + 6 to 8 × (20-sec strides) + Circuit training drills (3 circuits)
3 Q1	2 miles **E** pace + 6 × (1 min uphill with 3-min jogs) *or* 6 × (400m at **R** pace with 400m jogs) + 8 × (30 sec uphill with 2-min jogs) *or* 8 × (200m at **R** pace with 200m jogs) + 2 miles **E** pace
4	**E** pace 30 minutes or more as needed + 6 to 8 × (20-sec strides) + Circuit training drills (3 circuits)
5	**E** pace 30 minutes or more as needed + 6 to 8 × (20-sec strides) + Circuit training drills (2 circuits)
6 Q2	2 miles **E** pace + 4 × (30 sec uphill with 2-min jogs) *or* 4 × (200m at **R** pace with 200m jogs) + 8 × (1 min uphill with 3-min jogs) *or* 8 × (400 at **R** pace with 400m jogs) + 2 miles **E** pace
7	**E** run 30 minutes or more as needed + 6 to 8 × (20-sec strides) + Circuit training drills 2 circuits

It's certainly possible to increase, or decrease in some instances, the amount of warm-up or cool-down to suit individual runners of differing levels of fitness. Strides are quick, light runs (but not sprinting) at about mile race pace. Drills can include calisthenics, hurdle drills, circuit training (see chapter 10), and the like.

Phase III

When I think of the real quality training associated with the cross country season, I think of long intervals and threshold running, which take place during phase III of the overall program. This is also the phase of the season during which it's most important to train over typical cross country terrain. The specificity-of-training principle is again at play here; do most of your cross country training—solid, longer intervals and tempo runs—over soft footing and hills of varying difficulty.

When you have a home course regularly accessible to you, it might be a good idea to mark off some accurate distances to use for your workouts. The main advantage in running over measured distances is that you can compare your progress over the weeks of the season (and future seasons). I believe you can realize great benefits from work that's *not* based on timed runs over known distances, but it's always encouraging to see that you can do your familiar runs more comfortably as time passes. Possibly the best of both worlds is to do some workouts in which you run hard for a set time (with no concern about how far you get), and other times run known distances for time to check on your progression. In my view, it's a better measure of improved fitness when you feel better doing the same workout a couple weeks apart than it is to run a faster workout just to prove to yourself that you've improved. When the same performance starts feeling easier, you know it's time to increase the stress of your workout.

I discourage increasing weekly mileage during this phase of training. Peak mileage for the season has already been reached, and now it's time to focus on quality training. Increasing amount and intensity at the same time might be introducing too much additional stress at once, particularly for runners in high school or college programs.

For coaches and runners who use my VDOT tables during cross country season, I offer the following advice: Try to get an early-season performance on the course on which you'll be training (maybe hold an alumni or intrasquad time trial) and use the corresponding VDOT value for intervals and threshold runs over the next few weeks. With a race run over the same course, you can adjust the VDOT values according to the latest effort; in the absence of a race over the same course, it's usually safe to increase the VDOT value by one unit every three to four weeks. Another approach is to subjectively evaluate the various courses you race on (look at the average times of known runners on different courses to make an educated guess about the amount of time you might run slower or faster than you would on your training course) and look up the respective VDOT value, using the adjusted time. If you do some of your training on a road or track (not ideal during cross country season), I usually figure about 10 seconds per mile slower on flat grass than track or road and then subjectively add more time for any hills you have to deal with. Using the adjusted times can give you a reasonable idea of the VDOT value to use for training. As long as your training is going well, with no injury or illness setbacks, the one unit of VDOT increase every third week is a pretty safe rule to go by.

You'll notice that in phase III there are Q1 and Q2 workouts on consecutive days. I think this can work well for many programs. This plan provides two low-stress days after a previous Saturday race and two low-stress days before the upcoming Saturday race. For runners who have to compete in a midweek race in addition to a Saturday race, the midweek race can replace either Q1 or Q2 (it's probably best to eliminate Q1 and keep Q2). I find that the consecutive-day approach is good for some runners because it holds them back a little from going harder than they should, knowing that the next day or the previous day is also of good quality. An easy day between quality days works better when the previous Saturday's race is not too demanding (which is more often the case during track season).

I've indicated phase III as a three- to six-week block of training because I think in three weeks you can reap considerable benefits from the type of training involved—plus, three weeks is often all high school programs can afford to set aside in their

© Human Kinetics

Adjust the amount of time spent doing phase III training to fit the needs of the individual runner as well as the school calendar.

brief season. When phases I and II can be done during the summer, or with a long enough season, then a full six weeks can be set aside for this more demanding phase of training. If you're a coach working with beginners (often the case in high school programs), the most important phases of training are I and IV. With luck, you'll have at least four weeks for phase I and three weeks for phase II before you have to make a decision on what to do with the remaining weeks of the season. With only a few weeks left after attending to phases I and II, it would be better to skip phase III and spend the final weeks on phase IV or V. For beginning runners, you need to determine what approach is best for the future development of each individual. Many times, what's best in the long run is not what would produce the best immediate results in terms of race performance.

You'll notice in table 18.2 (the phase III program) that some workouts are different for female and male runners on some days. This is because typical training paces are slower for females; doing fewer repeats of a certain distance will result in spending as much time at the designated quality pace as males will in doing more repeats. In places where the intensity of running is indicated as "hard," this is meant to approximate interval (**I**) pace, which is subjectively "hard." You can always interchange two, three, four, and five-minute runs with timed distances of 800s, 1,000s, 1,200s, and so on—or whatever distance is best represented by the designated time for the runner involved. A race is listed as a typical day 7 event, but if there's not a race that day, an additional Q3 workout is recommended.

Table 18.2 **Phase III—Cross Country Early Season (3 to 6 weeks)**

Day	Workout
1	**L** run (lesser of 25% of week's mileage and 2 hours)
2	**E** run 30 minutes or more as needed + 8 × (20-second stride) + Circuit training drills (3 circuits)
3 Q1	2 miles **E** pace + 6 (female) or 8 (male) × (1,000 **I** pace with 3-min jog) *or* 6 (female) or 8 (male) × (3-min hard running with 3-min jog) + 2 miles **E** pace
4 Q2	2 miles **E** pace Total 5 miles (female) or 7 miles (male) of cruise intervals at **T** pace with short rests (5:1 work:rest ratio) or steady 30-40 minute tempo run with pace adjusted for duration 2 miles **E** pace
5	**E** run as needed to meet weekly mileage 6 × (20-sec stride) + Circuit training drills (3 circuits)
6	**E** run as needed to meet weekly mileage
7 Q3	Race *or* 3 × (800 **I** pace with 1-min jog) *or* 4 × (2-min hard with 1-min jog) + 5 × (400 at **I** pace with 30-sec jog) *or* 6 × (1-min hard with 30-sec jog) + 10 × (200 at **I** pace with 30-sec jog) *or* 10 × (30-sec hard) with 30-sec jog) + 2 miles **E** pace

Phases IV and V: Competition Phases

Phases IV and V could be lumped together into a single training phase, but, as is often the case in a cross country season, there's a span of time during which weekly competitions occur, and this is followed by a final few weeks of qualifying and championship races. Thus, I present a phase IV, which applies to the competitive season, and a separate phase V, designed for runners who want to be more rested for a qualifier or season-ending competition.

As you'll see in table 18.3, phase IV includes a fartlek Q1 early in the week (it could be day 2 or 3) designed to maintain previously acquired benefits of both **R** and **I** training, in addition to some **T**-pace running, all without increasing the overall stress of training. Later in each week is a Q2 session designed to total about 30 minutes of running cruise intervals at **T** pace (could be a steady 30-minute "tempo" run at the appropriate pace dictated by the duration of the run—see pages 114 to 115 on adjusted tempo pace). When the goal of a training session is to accumulate a specific amount of time (or distance) of running at **T** pace, runners should experiment with different combinations of distances or durations of running. For example, to total six miles of

Table 18.3 Phase IV—Cross Country Competitive Season (3 weeks)

Day	Workout
1	**L** run (20% of week's mileage but not over 2 hours)
2 Q1	Fartlek session = 2 miles **E** pace + 4 × (30 sec fast running with 1-min jog) + 3 × (800m **I** pace with 2-min jog) + 4 × (1,000m **T** pace with 1-min rest) + 2 miles **E** pace
3	**E** run 30 minutes or more as needed + 6 × (20-sec stride) + Circuit training drills (3 circuits)
4 Q2	2 miles **E** pace + Total 4 miles (female) or 6 miles (male) of cruise intervals **T** pace with short rests (5:1 work:rest ratio) + 6 × (200m **R** pace with 200 jogs) + 1 mile **E** pace
5	**E** run as needed for weekly mileage + 6 × (20-sec stride) + Circuit training drills (2 circuits—fewer than usual)
6	**E** run 20 minutes or more as needed
7 Q3	Race *or* Circuit training drills (2 circuits) + 4 miles **E** pace + 8 × (200m **R** pace with 200m jogs) + 2 × (5 min **T** pace with 2-min rest) + 2 miles **E** (more if needed for week's mileage total)

T running, you might do three 2-milers; a 3-miler, a 2-miler, and a 1-miler; or even six 1-milers. Regarding recovery time following different durations of **T** running, a simple rule is to rest 1 minute for each 5 or 6 minutes or each mile of running. Follow a 3-mile run with 3 minutes of rest, a 2-mile run with 2 minutes of rest, and so on. If there happens to be a week in this competitive phase of training in which there's no race, then I've recommended a Q3 session at the end of the week.

In phase V (table 18.4), the time during which qualifying or championship races are held, I think it's best to restrict quality training to one Q1 session, followed by a few reps the next day and a couple of **E** days prior to the race. Be sure to maintain your normal pace when doing reps in this phase—don't try to go faster than usual. There's always a tendency to want to go faster than usual in these final days or weeks of a season, but the time for faster-than-usual running is during the race, not in training.

Review the section on warming up for races in chapter 15. Try different approaches throughout the season to see what works best for you. My preferred approach is to add a steady **T**-pace run (of about 3 minutes) to earlier easy running and strides; time this run so it terminates about 10 minutes before the start of the race.

Table 18.4 **Phase V—Cross Country Championship Season (3 weeks)**

Day	Workout
1	**L** run (Lesser of 20% of week's mileage and 60 to 90 min)
2	**E** run 30 minutes or more as needed 6 × (30-sec stride) Stretching + 1 circuit of drills
3 Q1	2 miles **E** pace 4 × (30-sec stride) 4 (female) or 5 (male) × (I mile at **T** pace with 2-min rest) 2 miles **E** pace
4	**E** run 30 minutes or more as needed 6 × (200m at **R** pace with 200m jog)
5	**E** run 20-40 minutes
6	**E** run 20-30 minutes
7 Q2	Race *or* 2 miles **T** pace + 1 × 1,000 **I** pace with 3-min jog + 1 × 400m **R** pace with 400-m jog + 4 × 200m **R** pace with 200-m jogs

After the final race of the season, runners should do a couple of weeks of easy running. With track season looming ahead, runners involved in track should take advantage of what they've accomplished during the cross country season and plan their track training based on their current level of fitness.

———————————

Cross country is often a young runner's introduction to organized and competitive running. Every attempt should be made to ensure that those who test their resolve against others and the terrain come away from this initial experience with a positive attitude. There's no telling how many young people have given cross country running a try only to be discouraged or driven away because of an injury or being overstressed. It's the responsibility of coaches to provide a training environment that holds the attention of young runners long enough to let them discover the benefits of being fit and feeling the joy of training and competing among friends. Cross country offers both individual and team opportunities and can be a great introduction to fitness and athletic competition.

CHAPTER 19

5 to 15 Kilometers

I've referred to the shorter distance events as intense, and that they are. When you get into the medium-long events, the term "intense" often gives way to just plain "hard." Racing the 5K through 15K distances can be cruel and often fatiguing in many senses of the word. To prepare for these distances, you must train your aerobic capacity and lactate threshold to their maximum capabilities. This means solid foundation work, a strong emphasis on interval training, and spending enough time on repetitions and threshold runs that speeds close to your aerobic capacity become pleasant—or at least acceptable.

Within the category of medium distances, in terms of time spent racing, about 13 to 15 minutes is the lower limit for men and women, respectively, and races that take about one hour or a little longer constitute the upper limit. Race distances range from 5,000 meters for better runners and 3,000 meters for less developed runners to the half-marathon for elite runners and to at least 10,000 meters for slower competitive runners.

As with the programs for the other distances, the sample training program I present here is set up for a 24-week season and geared for preparing you to race distances that are demanding in both intensity and duration. Some 5K runners might respond better to training for a shorter race and should thus consider the information presented in chapter 17. The schedule presented here

The biggest mistakes you can make in a distance race are in the first minute.

should provide a solid base for enduring both the physical and mental demands of racing any medium-distance event. You can lengthen or shorten the schedule based on your time constraints by following the suggestions presented in chapter 4. In addition, training outlined in this chapter might be also suitable for cross country preparation, but I suggest that you examine chapter 18 before deciding which approach is more attractive to you.

Each of the categories of distance races I discuss in chapters 16 through 20 has its own way of attempting to make the runner's training stressful. With the intense, shorter-distance events presented in chapters 16 and 17, the stress comes primarily from a steadily increasing rise in blood-lactate concentration that challenges your ability to fight off the urge to give in to its unmerciful attack on your running muscles.

In the case of the medium-distance races covered in this chapter, the enemy is total body fatigue. It's often hard to pinpoint the exact spot of discomfort (probably because it's everywhere). During these races, the degree of discomfort doesn't always get progressively worse throughout the race, and your challenge is to learn to deal with a consistent feeling of overall stress.

In setting up for a season of training for medium-distance races, you'll want to spend plenty of time developing a powerful aerobic system. However, this doesn't mean there's no place for repetition training. On the contrary, reps lead not only to speed development but also to improvements in running economy, which in turn helps raise the lactate threshold to a faster running pace. In a sense, reps make any given running speed more acceptable for longer periods of time. The secret to a good training program for medium-distance events is knowing when to do the various types of training and how much of them to do.

Phase I

Phase I training—weeks 1 through 6 in a 24-week program—is the same for runners preparing for any race distance, at least regarding the *type* of running you need to do (see table 19.1). The shorter-distance specialists might not get in as much mileage as those gearing up to race medium- or longer-distance events, but all runners need to take it pretty easy in terms of intensity throughout this phase. Phase I is for easy running, stretching, strengthening exercises, and getting back into the habit of regular, daily training after a layoff.

As for the shorter-distance runners who run 3,000-meter races or less, I prescribe nothing but steady, easy running for the first three weeks of this phase; for medium-distance specialists, weeks four through six can have a longer run and some strides thrown into the weekly plan. Remember that you shouldn't increase mileage more often than every third week, and a long (**L**) run shouldn't be longer than 25 percent of the week's total mileage.

Phase II

The early quality, phase II (weeks 7 through 12) program for runners keying on medium-distance events is a time for adjusting to quality running (see table 19.1). Repetition (**R**) workouts are important because they allow an adjustment to faster running. But with full recoveries between quality runs in a workout, reps feel relatively comfortable and make for good, light, and quick leg turnover. Throughout this phase, you can increase weekly mileage up to 10 miles every third week.

During this phase, threshold (**T**) runs are introduced, along with days of reps; interval (**I**) sessions are added at the end of each week. You could run an occasional low-key race in place of a weekend interval session. In addition, I suggest replacing a threshold session with a marathon-pace (**M**) run of about one-hour duration every other week or so. See chapters 3 and 6 regarding **M** running and proper pace.

Each week has two or three quality days of training, one long (**L**) run, and three or four easy (**E**) days. In addition, continue supplemental training three days per week. In the event that a competition is scheduled during this phase, one of the quality sessions is replaced by the race. But it's best not to sacrifice Q1 because this is usually the primary type of training scheduled for this phase. If a competition day involves minimal stress, consider also running six to eight rep 200s following the race. When a week has three quality days, it's usually best to schedule Q1 on Monday, Q2 on Wednesday or Thursday, and Q3 on Friday or Saturday. With only two quality days in a week, schedule Q1 for Monday or Tuesday and Q2 for Thursday or Friday. Always get in a good warm-up for quality sessions and end these sessions with a cool-down run and stretching. See table 19.2 (which shows training paces associated with the race times listed) for **E, T, I,** and **R** paces, or use the VDOT **E, T, I,** and **R** paces from chapter 3 (see table 3.2).

Phase III

Weeks 13 through 18, phase III, is the most stressful phase of a medium-distance runner's program. It's possible to increase weekly mileage slightly (not more than 10 miles every third week), but mileage is not the main stress during this phase. The main emphasis is on long intervals (**I** training). A few races or some light fartlek sessions are also added on weekends (see table 19.1).

The other type of quality training that receives a fair bit of emphasis during this phase is threshold (**T**) training, both of the steady, tempo type and longer sets of cruise intervals. As you did in phase II, consider replacing a **T** run with an **M** run now and then. Keep in mind that races that last from about 12 to 30 minutes produce most of the same benefits reaped from a good interval session, so occasional races of this duration can replace the late-week interval sessions planned for nonrace weeks.

Each week is scheduled to have three quality days, with the most important being Q1, near the beginning of each week. Some weeks, Q3 might be a race. Each week should also have one **L** run. The remaining days are **E** days (one or more runs per day—unless you need a day off now and then, which is an **E** day). Remember that **E**

Table 19.1 **5K to 15K Training Plan**

Phase	Week	Workouts		
I	1-3	7 days each week at **E** pace (enough to reach your weekly mileage goal; see chapters 4 and 5 3 or 4 days each week of supplemental training (see chapter 10)		
	4-6	7 days each week at **E** pace. Include one **L** run (25% of week's total mileage or 1.5 hours, whichever is less). Add 6 to 8 strides to at least four **E** runs per week. Do 3 or 4 days each week of supplemental training		
		Q1 workout	**Q2 workout**	**Q3 workout**
II	7	5 to 6 × (2 × 200m **R** pace with 200m recovery jogs + 1 × 400m **R** pace with 400m jog)	5 to 6 × (1 mile **T** pace with 1-min rests)	Sets of (2 min hard [**I**] pace, 1-min jog + 1 min hard [**I**] pace, 30-sec jog + 30 sec hard [**I**] pace, 30-sec jog) The sum of **I** pace should be 8% of the week's total mileage or 10K, whichever is less. Hard [**I**] pace means to run at **I** pace or to run equally hard if not a measured distance.
	8	10 to 12 × (400m **R** pace with 400m jogs) The sum of **R** pace should total no more than 5% of the week's mileage.	40-min **T** pace (use your VDOT and table 7.1 or 7.2 to figure your adjusted tempo pace)	–
	9	4 × (200m **R** pace with 200m jogs) + 2 × (400m **R** pace with 400m jogs) + 1 × (800m **R** pace with 800m jog) + 2 × (400m **R** pace with 400m jogs) + 4 × (200m **R** pace with 200m jogs)	3 × (2-mile or 10 to 12 min at **T** pace with 2-min rests)	5 to 6 × (3-min hard or 800, 1,000, or 1,200m **I** pace with 3-min recovery jogs) Stay under 8% of the week's total mileage at **I** pace.
	10	4 × (200m **R** pace with 200m jog + 200m **R** pace with 400m jog + 800m **R** pace with 400m jog)	40-min **T** pace (use your VDOT and table 7.1 or 7.2 to figure your adjusted tempo pace)	–
	11	10 to 12 × (400m **R** pace with 400m jogs) The sum of **R** pace should total no more than 5% of the week's mileage.	15-min or 3-mile **T** pace, + 3-min **E** pace + 10-min or 2-mile **T** pace, + 2-min **E** pace + 5-min or 1-mile **T** pace	Sets of (2 min hard [**I**] pace, 1-min jog + 1 min hard [**I**] pace, 30-sec jog + 30 sec hard [**I**] pace, 30-sec jog) The sum of **I** pace should be 8% of the week's total mileage or 10K, whichever is less.

Table 19.1 **5K to 15K Training Plan**

Phase	Week	Workouts		
		Q1 workout	**Q2 workout**	**Q3 workout**
II	12	4 × (200m **R** pace with 200m jog + 200m **R** pace with 400m jog + 800m **R** pace with 400m jog)	45 min steady **T** pace (use your VDOT and table 7.1 or 7.2 to figure your adjusted tempo pace) *or* 20 min or 4 miles **T** pace, + 4 min **E** pace + 15 min or 3 miles **T** pace, + 3 min **E** pace + 10 min or 2 miles **T** pace, + 2 min at **E** pace + 5 min or 1 mile **T** pace 20 min or 4 miles means to do whatever distance **T** pace will take 20 min, which is about 4 miles for better runners.	—
III	13	Sets of 4 to 5 min hard (or 1,200m or 1 mile) **I** pace with 3- to 4-min recovery jogs The sum of the workout should be the lesser of 10K and 8% of the week's total mileage.	3 × (2-mile or 10 to 12 min **T** pace with 2-min rests)	Race *or* Sets of (2 min hard [**I**] pace + 1-min jog + 1 min hard [**I**] pace + 30-sec jog + 30 sec hard [**I**] pace + 30-sec jog) The sum of **I** pace should be 8% of the week's total mileage or 10K, whichever is less.
	14	Sets of 4 to 5 min hard (or 1,200m or 1 mile) **I** pace with 3- to 4-min recovery jogs The sum of the workout should be the lesser of 10K and 8% of the week's total mileage.	40 min **T** pace (use your VDOT and table 7.1 or 7.2 to figure your adjusted tempo pace)	Race *or* 10 to 12 × (400m **R** pace with 400m jogs) The sum of **R** running should be under 5% of the week's total mileage.
	15	Sets of (2 min hard [**I**] pace + 1-min jog + 1-min hard [**I**] pace + 30-sec jog + 30-sec hard [**I**] pace + 30-sec jog) The sum of **I** pace should be 8% of the week's total mileage or 10K, whichever is less.	3 to 5 × (2 miles or 10 min **T** pace with 2-min rests)	Race *or* 4 × (200m **R** pace with 200m jogs) + 3 × (1,000m **I** pace with 2-min jogs) + 2 × (400m **R** pace with 400m jogs)

(continued)

Table 19.1 **5K to 15K Training Plan**

(continued)

Phase	Week	Workouts		
		Q1 workout	**Q2 workout**	**Q3 workout**
III	16	3 × (1 mile or 1,200m) **I** pace with 4-min recovery jogs + 3 × (1,000 or 800m) **I** pace with 2-min jogs	15 min or 3 miles **T** pace + 3 min **E** pace + 10 min or 2 miles **T** pace + 2 min **E** pace + 5 min or 1 mile at **T** pace	Race *or* 4 × (200m **R** pace with 200m jogs) + 2 × (400m **R** pace with 400m jogs) + 1 × (800m **R** pace with 800m jog) + 2 × (400m **R** pace with 400m jogs) + 4 × (200m **R** pace with 200m jogs)
	17	Sets of 4 to 5 min hard (or 1,200m or 1 mile) **I** pace with 3- to 4-min recovery jogs The sum of the workout should be the lesser of 10K and 8% of the week's total mileage.	7 to 10 × (1 mile or 5 min) **T** pace with 1-min rests	Race *or* Sets of 4 to 5 min hard (or 1,200m or 1 mile) **I** pace with 3- to 4-min recovery jogs The sum of the workout should be the lesser of 10K and 8% of the week's total mileage.
	18	Sets of 4 to 5 min hard (or 1,200m or 1 mile) **I** pace) with 3- to 4-min recovery jogs The sum of the workout should be the lesser of 10K and 8% of the week's total mileage.	20 min or 4 miles **T** pace + 4 min at **E** pace + 15 min or 3 miles **T** pace + 3 min **E** pace + 10 min or 2 miles **T** pace + 2 min **E** pace + 5 min or 1 mile **T** pace	Race *or* 10 to 12 × (400m **R** pace with 400m jogs) The sum of **R** running should be under 5% of the week's total mileage.
IV Plan A	19	3 × (2 miles **T** pace with 2-min rests)	4 × (1,000m to 1 mile **T** pace with 1 min rests) + 2 × (1,000m at **I** pace with 3-min jogs) + 4 × (200m at **R** pace with 200m jogs)	Race *or* Sets of (2 min hard [**I**] pace + 1-min jog + 1 min hard [**I**] pace + 30-sec jog + 30 sec hard [**I**] pace + 30-sec jog) The sum of **I** pace should be 8% of the week's total mileage or 10K, whichever is less.

Table 19.1   **5K to 15K Training Plan**

Phase	Week	Workouts		
		Q1 workout	**Q2 workout**	**Q3 workout**
IV Plan A	20	20 min at steady **T** pace + 4 × (200m at **R** pace with 200m jogs)	4 × (1,000m to 1 mile **T** pace with 3-min jogs) + 6 × (200m **R** pace with 200m jogs) + 2-mile acceleration run Note: an acceleration run is a run that starts out very slow and increases the pace 5 sec per 400m (the last 400m should be about interval pace).	Race *or* 4 to 5 × (3-min run at about **I** pace with 3-min recovery jogs)
	21	40 min **T** pace (use your VDOT and table 7.1 or 7.2 to figure your adjusted tempo pace)	Race *or* Sets of (2 min hard [**I**] pace + 1-min jog + 1 min hard [**I**] pace + 30-sec jog + 30 sec hard [**I**] pace + 30-sec jog) The sum of **I** pace should be 8% of the week's total mileage or 10K, whichever is less.	—
	22	3 × (2 miles **T** pace with 2-min rests) *or* 6 × (1 mile **T** pace with 1-min rests)	4 × (200m **R** pace with 200m jogs) + 3 × (1,000m **I** pace with 2-min jogs) + 2 × (400m **R** pace with 400m jogs)	Race *or* 4 × (1,000m to 1 mile **T** pace with 1-min rests) + 2 × (1,000m **I** pace with 3-min jogs) + 4 × (200m **R** pace with 200m jogs)
	23	30 min **T** pace (use your VDOT and table 7.1 or 7.2 to figure your adjusted tempo pace)	4 × (200m **R** pace with 200m jogs) + 3 × (1,000m **I** pace with 2-min jogs) + 2 × (400m **R** pace with 400m jogs)	Race *or* 4 × (1,000m to 1 mile **T** pace with 3-min jogs) + 6 × (200m **R** pace with 200m jogs) + 2-mile acceleration run Note: an acceleration run is a run that starts out very slow and increases the pace 5 sec per 400m (the last 400m should be about interval pace).
	24	4 to 5 × (1 mile **T** pace with 2-min recovery jogs) + 4 × (200m **R** pace with 200m jogs)	Race	—

(continued)

Table 19.1 **5K to 15K Training Plan**

(continued)

Phase	Week	Q1 workout	Q2 workout	Q3 workout
IV **Plan B**	19	2 × (2 miles **T** pace with 2-min jogs) + 3 × (800m **I** pace with 2-min jogs) + 3 × (400m **R** pace with 400m jogs) Don't go too fast on the interval 800s—do **I** pace.	Race *or* 4 × (200m **R** pace with 200m jogs) + 4 × (1,000m **I** with 2-min jogs) + 2 × (400m **R** pace with 400m jogs)	—
	20	20 min **T** pace 3 × 400m **R** pace with 400m jogs 2 × 1 mile **T** pace with 1-min rest	Race *or* 6 × (200m **R** pace with 200m jogs) 3 × (1,000m **I** pace with 2-min jogs) 3 × (400m **R** pace with 400m jogs)	—
	21	2 × (2-mile **T** pace with 2-min jogs) + 1 × (800m **I** pace with 2-min jog) + 2 × (400m **R** pace with 400m jogs) + 2 miles **T** pace	Race *or* 45-min **T pace** (use your VDOT and table 7.1 or 7.2 to figure your adjusted tempo pace) + 6 × (200m **R** pace with 200m jogs)	—
	22	4 × (200m **R** pace with 200m jogs) + 2 × (400m **R** pace with 400m jogs) + 3 × (1-mile **T** pace with 1-min rests) + 1 × 1,000m pace + 400m jog + 4 × (200m **R** pace with 200m jogs)	Race *or* 5 to 6 × (1,000m **I** pace with 3-min recovery jogs) + 4 × (200m **R** pace with 200m jogs)	—
	23	4 × (1 mile **T** pace with 2-min jogs) + 6 × (200m **R** pace with 200m jogs) + 1 mile at **T** pace	Race *or* 40 min **T** pace (use your VDOT and table 7.1 or 7.2 to figure your adjusted tempo pace) + 4 × (200m **R** pace with 200m jogs)	—
	24	4 × (1,200m **T** pace with 2-min jogs) + 4 × (200m **R** pace with 200m jogs)	**Race** *(Friday and Saturday)*	

days can be anything from more than one run on that day to not running at all, if a rest is warranted. The important thing about **E** days is that the intensity of running is comfortable. Use **E** days to maintain your desired weekly mileage totals. Adding a few strides to the middle—or the end—of easy runs is always a good idea.

If you have a demanding race on a weekend, then the next week's quality workouts should follow the Tuesday–Wednesday format. Without a weekend race, you could go with Monday and Wednesday quality days the following week. If you don't have a weekend race, you might consider alternating weeks of three and two quality runs. If you decide on this approach (and if I've indicated three quality days in a week in which you prefer just two quality days), eliminate the Q2 session in the week and try to schedule the two remaining quality days for either Monday and Thursday or Tuesday and Friday. In the event that a race is scheduled during this phase, one of the quality sessions is replaced by the race.

When a week has three quality days, it's usually best to schedule Q1 on Monday, Q2 on Wednesday or Thursday, and Q3 on Friday or Saturday. With only two quality days in a week, schedule Q1 for Monday or Tuesday and Q2 for Thursday or Friday.

Phase IV

Phase IV—weeks 19 through 24—is the final phase of the season's program and should be viewed as a high-performance phase. Clearly, the toughest days should be races, not training sessions. The long runs become a little less long, and the quality sessions become a little less strenuous, by reducing *how much* quality running you do in a session. The highly structured, long-interval workouts of primary concern during phase III are now dropped. However, some fartlek sessions, which include some interval work, are included (see table 19.1).

As is true of any final phase of training, now isn't the time for experimentation; stick with familiar types of training that produce good quality with limited stress. Your total weekly mileage will probably drop somewhat, particularly if you have reached high weekly totals. Usually, runners who have been running more than 50 miles per week will benefit from cutting back by about 20 percent, but those who haven't reached the 50-mile total can usually stay at their current load and do just fine. This is an individual matter—some elite runners can maintain high mileage levels and still produce top performances in races. But this is definitely something you'll want to monitor and log carefully (consider using the point system in chapter 2). You can then use the information about how you feel and perform under different approaches to set up your training plan for next season.

During weeks of less important races, it's okay to get in two moderate quality days prior to race day, but when races are more important, one early-week quality day is sufficient. I advise allowing one easy recovery day for each 3,000 meters of distance raced, and this might dictate whether more than one quality day can be included in a week of training. It's also best to allow three or four easy days (that include four to six light strides) before a championship race.

Table 19.2 Training Paces for 5K to 15K Runners

Current race ability			R (rep pace)			I (intervals)			
5,000	10K	Marathon	200	400	800	400	1,000	1,200	1,600
12:45	26:33	2:02:19	:27	:55	1:52	:61	2:34	3:05	4:04
12:53	26:49	2:03:35	:27	:55	1:53	:61	2:36	3:06	4:08
13:01	27:06	2:04:52	:28	:56	1:54	:62	2:37	3:08	4:10
13:09	27:23	2:06:12	:28	:57	1:55	:63	2:38	3:10	4:12
13:18	27:40	2:07:33	:29	:58	1:56	:64	2:40	3:12	4:16
13:26	27:58	2:08:56	:29	:58	1:57	:64	2:41	3:13	4:18
13:35	28:16	2:10:22	:29	:59	1:58	:65	2:43	3:15	4:20
13:44	28:34	2:11:49	:30	:60	2:00	:66	2:45	3:18	4:24
13:53	28:53	2:13:18	:30	:61	2:02	:67	2:48	3:21	4:28
14:03	29:13	2:14:50	:30	:61	2:03	:67	2:49	3:22	4:30
14:13	29:33	2:16:24	:31	:62	2:05	:68	2:50	3:24	4:32
14:23	29:53	2:18:01	:31	:63	2:06	:69	2:53	3:27	4:36
14:33	30:15	2:19:40	:32	:64	2:08	:70	2:55	3:30	4:40
14:44	30:36	2:21:21	:32	:64	2:10	:70	2:56	3:31	4:42
14:55	30:59	2:23:05	:32	:65	2:11	:71	2:58	3:33	4:44
15:06	31:21	2:24:52	:33	:66	2:12	:72	3:00	3:36	4:48
15:17	31:45	2:26:42	:33	:67	2:14	:73	3:02	3:39	4:52
15:29	32:09	2:28:35	:34	:68	2:16	:74	3:05	3:42	4:56
15:41	32:34	2:30:31	:34	:69	2:18	:75	3:07	3:45	5:00
15:54	33:00	2:32:31	:35	:70	2:20	:76	3:10	3:48	5:04
16:07	33:26	2:34:33	:35	:71	2:22	:77	3:13	3:51	5:08
16:20	33:54	2:36:40	:36	:72	2:24	:78	3:15	3:54	5:12
16:33	34:22	2:38:50	:36	:73	2:26	:79	3:18	3:57	5:16
16:48	34:50	2:41:03	:37	:74	2:28	:80	3:20	4:00	5:20
17:02	35:20	2:43:21	:37	:75	2:30	:81	3:22	4:03	5:24
17:17	35:51	2:45:43	:38	:76	2:32	:82	3:25	4:06	5:28
17:32	36:23	2:48:10	:38	:77	2:34	:83	3:27	4:09	5:32
17:48	36:56	2:50:40	:39	:78	2:36	:84	3:30	4:12	5:36
18:05	37:30	2:53:16	:39	:79	2:38	:85	3:33	4:15	5:40
18:22	38:05	2:55:57	:40	:81	2:42	:87	3:37	4:20	5:48
18:39	38:41	2:58:43	:41	:82	2:44	:88	3:40	4:24	5:52
18:57	39:19	3:01:35	:41	:83	2:46	:89	3:43	4:27	5:56
19:16	39:58	3:04:32	:42	:85	2:50	:91	3:48	4:33	6:04
19:36	40:38	3:07:35	:43	:86	2:52	:92	3:50	4:36	6:08
19:56	41:20	3:10:45	:44	:88	2:56	:94	3:55	4:42	6:16
20:17	42:04	3:14:02	:44	:89	2:58	:95	3:58	4:45	6:20
20:39	42:49	3:17:25	:45	:91	3:02	:97	4:03	4:51	6:28
21:01	43:35	3:20:56	:46	:92	3:04	:98	4:05	4:54	6:32
21:25	44:24	3:24:35	:47	:94	3:08	1:40	4:10	5:00	6:40
21:49	45:15	3:28:23	:48	:96	3:12	1:42	4:15	5:06	6:48
22:14	46:08	3:32:19	:49	:98	3:16	1:44	4:20	5:12	6:56
22:41	47:03	3:36:24	:50	1:40	3:20	1:46	4:25	5:18	7:04
23:08	48:00	3:40:39	:51	1:42	3:24	1:48	4:30	5:24	7:12
23:37	49:00	3:45:05	:52	1:44	3:28	1:50	4:35	5:30	7:20
24:07	50:03	3:49:42	:53	1:46	3:32	1:52	4:40	5:36	7:28
24:38	51:08	3:54:30	:54	1:48	3:36	1:54	4:45	5:42	7:36
25:11	52:17	3:59:31	:55	1:51	3:42	1:57	4:53	5:51	7:48

Table 19.2 **Training Paces for 5K to 15K Runners**

T (threshold)			M (marathon)		E (easy)	
400	1,000	Mile	Mile	Kilometer	Mile	Kilometer
:67	2:48	4:30	4:39	2:53	5:34-6:04	3:27-3:46
:68	2:50	4:32	4:42	2:55	5:38-6:08	3:29-3:48
:68	2:51	4:35	4:45	2:57	5:40-6:10	3:31-3:50
:69	2:53	4:38	4:48	2:59	5:42-6:12	3:33-3:52
:70	2:54	4:41	4:51	3:01	5:46-6:16	3:35-3:54
:70	2:56	4:44	4:55	3:03	5:48-6:18	3:36-3:55
:71	2:58	4:46	4:58	3:05	5:50-6:20	3:38-3:57
:72	3:00	4:50	5:01	3:07	5:54-6:24	3:40-3:59
:73	3:02	4:53	5:05	3:09	5:58-6:28	3:42-4:01
:73	3:04	4:56	5:08	3:11	6:00-6:30	3:44-4:03
:74	3:06	4:59	5:12	3:14	6:02-6:32	3:45-4:04
:75	3:08	5:02	5:15	3:16	6:06-6:36	3:47-4:06
:76	3:10	5:06	5:19	3:18	6:10-6:40	3:50-4:08
:77	3:12	5:09	5:23	3:21	6:12-6:42	3:51-4:10
:78	3:14	5:13	5:27	3:23	6:14-6:44	3:53-4:12
:79	3:17	5:16	5:31	3:25	6:18-6:48	3:55-4:14
:80	3:20	5:20	5:35	3:28	6:22-6:52	3:57-4:16
:80	3:21	5:24	5:40	3:31	6:26-6:56	4:00-4:18
:81	3:24	5:28	5:44	3:34	6:30-7:00	4:02-4:21
:82	3:26	5:32	5:49	3:37	6:34-7:04	4:05-4:24
:83	3:29	5:36	5:53	3:39	6:38-7:08	4:07-4:26
:84	3:32	5:41	5:58	3:42	6:42-7:12	4:10-4:28
:85	3:34	5:45	6:03	3:45	6:46-7:16	4:12-4:31
:87	3:36	5:50	6:08	3:48	6:50-7:20	4:15-4:33
:88	3:40	5:55	6:13	3:52	6:54-7:24	4:17-4:36
:89	3:43	5:59	6:19	3:55	6:58-7:28	4:20-4:38
:90	3:46	6:04	6:24	3:58	7:02-7:32	4:22-4:41
:92	3:50	6:10	6:30	4:02	7:06-7:36	4:25-4:43
:93	3:53	6:15	6:36	4:06	7:10-7:40	4:27-4:46
:95	3:58	6:23	6:42	4:10	7:18-7:48	4:32-4:51
:96	4:01	6:27	6:49	4:14	7:22-7:52	4:35-4:53
:97	4:04	6:32	6:55	4:18	7:26-7:56	4:37-4:56
:99	4:09	6:40	7:02	4:22	7:34-8:04	4:42-5:00
1:40	4:11	6:44	7:09	4:26	7:38-8:08	4:45-5:03
1:42	4:16	6:52	7:16	4:31	7:46-8:16	4:50-5:08
1:44	4:20	6:57	7:24	4:35	7:50-8:20	4:52-5:11
1:46	4:25	7:05	7:31	4:40	7:58-8:28	4:57-5:15
1:47	4:27	7:10	7:39	4:45	8:04-8:34	5:01-5:19
1:49	4:33	7:18	7:48	4:50	8:12-8:42	5:06-5:24
1:51	4:38	7:26	7:56	4:56	8:20-8:50	5:11-5:30
1:53	4:43	7:34	8:05	5:01	8:28-9:00	5:16-5:35
1:55	4:48	7:43	8:15	5:07	8:36-9:06	5:21-5:40
1:57	4:53	7:51	8:24	5:13	8:45-9:15	5:26-5:45
1:59	5:00	8:00	8:35	5:20	8:53-9:23	5:31-5:50
2:01	5:04	8:08	8:45	5:26	9:00-9:30	5:36-5:55
2:03	5:08	8:16	8:56	5:33	9:10-9-40	5:42-6:00
2:07	5:17	8:30	9:08	5:40	9:20-9:50	5:48-6:06

When doing two quality days prior to a Saturday race, Tuesday and Wednesday might be best if the previous Saturday was also a race day, but Monday–Wednesday works well if there was no race the previous week. Either Monday-only or Tuesday-only quality days are advisable before a championship race. If you're dropping one of two quality workouts indicated on the training plan, keep the one that you feel better about at this time of the season.

Table 19.1 shows two options for phase IV training. In plan A, you'll find some weeks with two and some weeks with three quality sessions, which might be a little more than you need or want to do. Plan B prescribes only two quality days each week, even if there's a race, which is considered a quality day. If you wish, you can also pick from either plan for phase IV, selecting the weeks or workouts that suit you best.

Monitor your own performances to determine whether to cut back your final mileage during the final phase of training or maintain your current load.

Total mileage may be reduced a little during phase IV, especially if you have been at a relatively high-mileage phase III. There might be workouts you have performed during an earlier phase that you found to your liking; if so, feel free to make a substitution now and then. However, this phase should not be as strenuous as phase III was, so don't eliminate what seems to be too easy a session for one you like because it's harder.

Keep a long run in most weeks, but realize that even the distance of your long runs might be cut a little short (stay under the 25 percent of total weekly mileage rule or maximum of two hours, whichever is less). Perform some strides on at least a couple **E** days each week, and maintain some light involvement in supplemental training (but cut that back some also). Phase IV is a time to race well and feel you're getting stronger each day. Try to give yourself three **E** days before important races, and remember to recover well from any races before taking on your next stressful workout.

The races covered in this chapter are probably the most popular distances for runners beyond their school years. They last long enough that you can get into a nice pace for the bulk of the race, yet they're short enough that the intensity of effort is not particularly enjoyable. That so many runners compete in these races is testimony to the dedication that serious runners share. The quotation at the beginning of the chapter ("the biggest mistakes you can make in a race are in the first minute") definitely pertains to races of 5 to 15K distances. Still, races at this distance usually turn out well if you abide by my quote at the start of chapter 15, which I'll restate here in an expanded version: "Run with your head during the first two thirds of a medium-distance race, with a goal of arriving at the point at which you want to be positioned for your finishing drive—then race the rest of the way with your heart."

CHAPTER 20

Half-Marathon and Marathon

What separates the marathon (and other long races that take more than an hour to run) from shorter distances is that you run the bulk of the race below your lactate threshold. This means several things:

- You won't build up much lactic acid, and unless the duration of the race has taken its toll on the supply of carbohydrate fuel and thus reduced your body's ability to produce lactic acid, the accumulation of lactic acid is limited to brief stages of the race (such as the early and final minutes).

- You normally won't suffer from local muscular stress (as often occurs during a 5K or 10K race).

- Ventilation is relatively comfortable throughout the race.

- If you monitor your heart rate, it won't be at a max value, as it is in shorter races.

In addition, longer races place a considerable demand on carbohydrate fuel supply, body temperature mechanisms, and the maintenance of adequate body fluids—all of which can affect race performance. Fatigue appears in a more subtle way than in shorter races; it's sometimes difficult to accept that while you're racing at relatively comfortable intensities, the urge to slow down can still raise its ugly head.

No one is unbeatable, and the fence protecting the seemingly invincible is more fragile than it may appear.

It's not valid to say that training for all distance races beyond 15K requires the same training schedule, and I would vary my approach based on the specific event in question. It's difficult to prescribe a generalized training program for the half-marathon because elite runners race this distance in about an hour, which is about how long it takes slower runners to run a 10K. In fact, elite runners can easily finish a full marathon in the time it takes slower runners to cross the finish line of a half-marathon. For this reason, I don't present a half-marathon schedule. Instead I propose that elite runners should basically train for a 10K and be willing to hang in there for an hour in the race. Intervals and threshold training are great ways to prepare for just such a race. In fact, a half-marathon could be considered as the ultimate test of lactate threshold—the intensity that can be maintained for just about one hour.

On the other hand, for runners out there racing a half-marathon for a couple of hours, many stresses are the same as they would face in a marathon—heat and dehydration, to mention a couple—so following a marathon training schedule might be the best way to go. Just think of yourself as an elite marathoner and prepare accordingly. One- to two-hour runs, threshold runs followed by one-hour steady efforts, and a solid phase of some intervals will prepare you well for a two-hour race. As is true for the fastest half-marathoners, slower runners need to spend time maximizing their lactate threshold. A relatively nice thing about the half-marathon is that the amount of work you do is within the body's ability to perform primarily on carbohydrates as fuel. The associated danger with this is that the intensity of effort you need for a half-marathon can put you over your lactate threshold, forcing you to unexpectedly drop off your pace. The half-marathon, then, can be relatively enjoyable or very demanding.

However, the full marathon distance seems to attract the most attention, and for this reason the training plans I present in this chapter are aimed at the entire marathon distance. Because of the seemingly unlimited number of approaches to preparing for a marathon (and there are many valid approaches because of the range of reasons people run marathons), I provide three different training plans: two 24-week schedules (program A and an elite program) for seasoned and elite marathoners, respectively, and an 18-week total plan for first-time marathoners who just want to complete a marathon.

Predicting Race Performances

It's useful to have a reliable predicting table (table 3.1, for example) available to you when training for marathons, particularly if it's been a while since you ran one (if indeed you've ever run one). By looking up a recent time for a more familiar race distance (10K, for example), you can fairly well predict how fast you can expect to run a marathon (or almost any other race distance, for that matter). Naturally, a performance in a longer race (20K or half-marathon) is a better predictor of marathon ability than is a shorter race, such as a 5K. However, this isn't always the case, because you might have performed more 5K races recently than you have longer races, and under a variety of conditions,. In this case the information provided by your 5K times might better predict your current fitness under conditions anticipated in the upcoming marathon.

Let me offer a word of caution about predicting times. When a table equates times, indicating that a 19:57 5K equals a 3:10:49 marathon, for example (see table 3.1), this doesn't necessarily mean that by breaking 20:00 in a 5K you'll run a sub-3:11 marathon. What it means is that these two performances are equal, and that with reasonable mileage and marathon training under your belt, you could expect to run a 3:11 marathon if you recently ran a 20:00 5K under conditions and terrain similar to the marathon.

Keep in mind that some runners might never achieve some of their predicted times, no matter how hard they train. Some individuals are physiologically designed to race better over shorter distances, whereas others are better at longer races. Actually, runners at lower levels of performance—those not aspiring to being Olympians or national champions—will probably have an easier time reaching times predicted over a variety of distances than elite competitors do. This is because the elite have found their absolute best event through years of dedicated training and racing experiences.

Program A

Program A is for runners who like a typical marathon approach. I've designed this program to work for any amount of mileage—you simply pick the highest (peak) mileage that you plan to hit over the course of the program and determine each week's mileage from there. This program doesn't contain a formal repetition phase and includes typical marathon-specific training throughout all three quality phases (II, III, and IV). First-time marathoners with a good background in running might find that this program suits them well.

When training for longer races, your body must learn to take advantage of available fuel sources, develop a strong aerobic profile, be able to replace diminishing body fluids, and maintain an optimal temperature. It's also important to have a well-planned taper leading up to a long-distance race-because a runner doesn't run as many long races as short ones over a year's time, and a mistake in a long race seems to have farther-reaching effects than a mistake has in a shorter race.

Phase I

The first phase of a program geared toward a marathon or other long-distance race can often last longer than the usually recommended six weeks. This is because some marathoners want to spend a long period of time building up mileage before launching into quality training. If only a few weeks have passed since you performed serious training, then six weeks might be adequate for phase I. But if you're moving into marathon training for the first time or if you're returning to marathon training after a long layoff, you might want to spend as much as two or three months just running and building up mileage to a point where you feel you've built a solid base.

Regardless of the duration of this first phase of training, your emphasis is to get comfortable with steady, easy running and with some runs of an hour or more. It's also a good idea to add some strides to the program after three or four weeks of steady, easy runs so that moving into quality workouts won't be a great shock to your body. Remember that you should add mileage to the overall program no more than every third week. When you do increase mileage, don't add more than 10 miles, or about one hour of weekly running, to your previous weekly total. When building up to a long-distance race, progress gradually and thoughtfully to avoid injury. In most cases, you're training for a race several months down the road, which makes an interruption for an injury all the more disappointing.

If you manage to get beyond about 50 miles per week, you should probably start running twice a day most days of the week rather than increasing your single daily runs to longer and longer distances. Two-a-day runs take more time out of your day, but they're also less stressful. Still, you will eventually get into some regular long (**L**) runs that provide as much continuous stress as you'll need in any given week. Phase I is set up for two three-week blocks, but they could just as easily be four-week blocks—or even longer if you have lots of time before your marathon or need more time to build your base of training. Table 20.1 shows the program A training plan.

The fourth column in table 20.1 indicates a fraction of your peak weekly mileage to total that week, and another column indicates how many weeks are remaining before the race. Remember from earlier chapters that **E** = easy running, **L** = long run at **E** pace, **T** = threshold-pace running, **M** = marathon-pace running, **I** = interval-pace running, and "hard" = running at the subjective feel experienced in a race that lasts about 10 to 15 minutes. Better runners of either gender should consider 5 to 6 minutes equivalent to 1 mile of running, 10 to 12 minutes equivalent to 2-mile runs, and 15 to 20 minutes equivalent to 3-mile runs. Slower runners are better off going by time or using adjusted distances to correspond to the times indicated. In addition to using the VDOT tables (3.1 and 3.2 in chapter 3), you can use table 19.2 (chapter 19) to identify proper training paces.

Phase II

It's during phase II of a long-distance program that you prepare your body for the most strenuous phase III training that's ahead. This means adding some quality sessions to the previous steady, easy runs that made up the bulk of phase I training. In the following program, if you want to allow more than six weeks for any of the last three phases of training, you can extend by a week or more any of the three phases by repeating any of the weeks that particularly appealed to you. I don't recommend repeating two demanding weeks back to back.

Some runners like to include hill running in their marathon build-up, and this is the phase where that fits best. However, you'll also notice that formal repetition training isn't introduced into this A program; strides are the fastest running you'll do. This means that you'll need to accomplish any hill training as part of interval sessions or incorporate hills into some of the longer runs. Or, you could add some short, steep, but slow treadmill hill sessions (say, 10 × one-minute runs with one-minute rests) into any week of phase II or III training, even on an easy (**E**) day of training. It's useful to include some hill running throughout your training season if the marathon course that you'll be running is hilly. Even downhill running can be beneficial if the course you'll race has long downhills. Always be careful to progress gradually in your downhill training to avoid imposing too much landing shock on your feet, legs, hips, and back.

Notice in table 20.1 that quality days (Q1 and Q2) are listed for each week, with Q1 typically on Saturday or Sunday and Q2 three or four days later. Always warm up before moving into the quality portion of quality workouts. Also cool down following each quality session.

Phase III

As is true with all of my training programs, phase III is the most demanding. This is because of an increase in mileage, longer threshold workouts, and more demanding marathon-pace (**M**) workouts and long runs that involve threshold-pace (**T**) running.

Many runners have opportunities to run a variety of shorter (medium-distance) races, and fitting these into your training scheme is important. The general rule is to allow three **E** days of running before any race, and at least three **E** days after a race before you take on another quality-training session. I recommend not running more than two races during this six-week phase.

When you do have a race, drop one of the scheduled quality training sessions for that week. You can either drop the Q1 quality session or the midweek quality session and replace it with the next Q1 session scheduled on the day of the race. Avoid dropping the **M** runs, unless a scheduled race is a half-marathon, in which case you can race at marathon pace, thus accomplishing two things at once (see table 20.1 for details). Of course, if the race is an important (all-out) effort, then your training session will simply have to be sacrificed.

Phase IV

Phase IV is the final quality phase and should be less stressful than the previous phase of training. As you progress through phase IV you should feel stronger and start looking forward to your upcoming long race. You might begin thinking that you're not training hard enough or that you're starting to get out of shape. This is often the feeling you get when you have been doing demanding workouts at interval pace or demanding mixtures of threshold and long runs. Actually, runners doing program A will be continuing with training similar to what they did in the previous phase, but they should be feeling better now, primarily because they're more accustomed to the type of training they're doing, and mileage is coming down.

There's still time for one or two competitions during this phase, but choose them carefully. A good guideline to follow is that any secondary race you do during this phase shouldn't be longer than half the distance of the upcoming important race, and less if raced during the final four weeks. For one of these secondary races, you might want to enter a marathon race and complete only part of it, as you perform one of your **M** training sessions. If you do enter a race you don't plan to complete, still enter officially and be considerate of the officials and the runners who will continue after you've stopped.

Table 20.1 **Marathon Training Plan A**

Phase	Week	Weeks left before race	Fraction of peak mileage	Workouts	
I	1-3	24-22		7 days of at least 30 min **E** pace; do more than 30 min if you already have a base established	
	4-6	21-19		1 day of **L** run; 25% of week's total mileage or 2.5 hours, whichever is less 6 days of 30 min or more **E** pace; after 2 or 3 of the **E** runs, add 6 to 8 × 20- to 30-sec strides	
				Q1 workout	**Q2 workout**
II	7	18	0.80	**L** run; 2 hours or 25% of week's total mileage, whichever is less	Sets of 4-min **hard** with 3-min recovery jogs to total 8% of week's mileage or 10K, whichever is less
	8	17	0.80	20 min **E** pace + 20 min **T** pace (or 40 min **T** pace + adjustment per Table 7.1 or 7.2) + 20 min **E** pace	Sets of 4-min **hard** with 3-min recovery jogs to total 8% of week's mileage or 10K, whichever is less
	9	16	0.70	2 miles **E** pace + 5 × (5 to 6 min **T** pace with 1-min rests) + 1 hour **E** pace	Sets of 1,000m, 1,200m, or miles **I** pace, with 3-, 4- or 5-min recovery jogs to total lesser of 6% weekly mileage and 8K
	10	15	0.90	**L** run; 2.5 hours or 25% of week's total miles, whichever is less	Sets of 1,000m, 1,200m, or miles **I** pace, with 3-, 4- or 5-min recovery jogs to total lesser of 6% of weekly mileage and 8K
	11	14	0.90	2 miles **E** pace + 2 × (10 to 12 min at **T** pace with 2-min rests) + 1 hr **E** pace	2 miles **E** pace Sets of 5 min **hard** with 3- to 5-min jogs to total 10K or 8% of week's mileage, whichever is less
	12	13	0.70	2 miles **E** pace + 6 × (5 to 6 min at **T** pace with 1-min rests) + 2 miles **E** pace	Sets of 1,000m, 1,200m, or miles at **I** pace, with 3-, 4- or 5-min recovery jogs to total lesser of 8% of weekly mileage and 10km
III*	13	12	1.00	**L** run; 2.5 hours or 25% of week's total mileage, whichever is less	2 miles **E** pace + 4 × (10 to 12 min **T** pace with 2-min rests) + 2 miles **E** pace
	14	11	0.90	2 miles **E** pace + 4 × (5 to 6 min **T** pace with 1-min rests) + 1 hr **E** pace + 15 to 20 min **T** pace + 2 miles **E** pace	2 miles **E** pace + 4 × (1 mile **T** pace with 1-min rest)+ 5 min **E** pace + 3 × (1 mile **T** pace with 1-min rest) + 2 miles **E** pace

Table 20.1 **Marathon Training Plan A**

Phase	Week	Weeks left before race	Fraction of peak mileage	Workouts	
				Q1 workout	**Q2 workout**
III*	15	10	0.80	2 miles **E** + 12 to 13 miles or 100 min **M** pace (whichever is less) + 2 miles **E** pace	2 miles **E** pace + 2 × (15 to 20 min **T** pace with 3-min rests) + 10 to 12 min **T** pace + 2 miles **E** pace
	16	9	1.00	**L** run; 2.5 hours or 25% of week's total mileage, whichever is less	2 miles **E** pace + 20 min **T** pace + 10 min **E** pace + 20 min **T** pace + 2 miles **E** pace
	17	8	0.90	2 miles **E** pace + 2 × (10 to 12 min **T** pace with 2-min rest) + 10 miles or 80 min (whichever is less) **E** pace + 15 to 20 min **T** pace + 2 miles **E** pace	2 miles **E** pace + 8 × 5 to 6 min **T** pace with 30-sec rests + 2 miles **E** pace
	18	7	0.70	2 miles **E** pace + 2 hours or 15 miles **M** pace (whichever is less) + 2 miles **E** pace	2 miles **E** pace + 4 × (10 to 12 min **T** pace with 2-min rests) + 2 miles at **E** pace
IV	19	6	1.00	**L** run; 22 miles or 2.5 hours, whichever is less	2 × (20 min **E** pace + 20 min **T** pace) + 2 miles **E** pace
	20	5	0.80	2 miles **E** pace + 4 × (5 to 6 min **T** pace with 1-min rests) + 10 miles or 80-min **E** pace (whichever is less) + 4 × (5 to 6 min **T** pace with 1-min rests) + 2 miles **E** pace	1 hour **E** pace + 6 × (5 to 6 min **T** pace with 1-min rests) + 15 min **E** pace
	21	4	0.70	**L** run; 22 miles or 2.5 hours, whichever is less	2 × (35 to 40 min **E** pace + 15 to 20 min at **T** pace) + 2 miles at **E** pace
	22	3	0.70	2 miles **E** pace + 15 miles or 2.5 hours **M** pace (whichever is less) + 2 miles **E** pace	2 × (20 min **E** pace + 15 to 20 min **T** pace) + 2 miles at **E** pace
	23	2	0.60	2 miles **E** pace + 2 × (10 to 15 min **T** pace with 3-min rest) + 30 to 45 min **E** pace	2 × (35 to 40 min **E** pace +15 to 20 min **T** pace) + 2 miles **E** pace

(continued)

Table 20.1 **Marathon Training Plan A**

(continued)

Phase	Week	Weeks left before race	Fraction of peak mileage	Workouts
IV	24	1		7 days out: 1.5 hour **E** pace
				6 days out: 1 hour **E** pace + 4 to 6 strides
				5 days out: 2 miles **E** pace + 4 × (1,200m at **T** pace with 2-min rests) + 2 miles at **E** pace
				4 days out: 40 to 50 min **E** pace + 4 to 6 strides
				3 days out: 30 min **E** pace + 4 strides
				2 days out: 0 to 30 min **E** pace
				1 day out: 30 min **E** pace

* Consider a change in VDOT training paces at this point if indicated by performance.

Note: All other days for phases II through IV are **E**-pace runs of sufficient mileage to reach each week's mileage goal. After two or three of the **E** runs, add six to eight × 20- to 30-second strides.

Adapted by permission from *Runner's World Magazine*. Copyrighted 1996. Rodale Press Inc., all rights reserved.

Probably the best approach to adding a race to your schedule is to drop one of your scheduled quality workouts in favor of the race. This might mean switching other quality sessions around some. Try to avoid dropping the same type of training session every time you have a race. Always remember to give yourself three easy days before any race and three or more days after the race, or one easy day for every 3K of race distance that the race involves (up to seven days after a half-marathon).

Be especially attentive to the final weeks of this phase IV schedule; if you follow the taper carefully, you should have a satisfying race.

Elite Program

The elite program groups what would normally be called phases II through IV into one continuous 18-week phase. This plan is set up to steadily increase (over the final 18 weeks leading up to a marathon) the various types of stress being imposed on the runner rather than changing which system is being stressed during different periods of time.

Phase I

Spend at least six weeks in phase I (see table 20.2); however, extend this phase to as many weeks as you feel you have available as you move into the final 18 weeks leading up to the marathon you plan to run. Completing this phase should bring you into the final 18 weeks having reached nearly the maximum amount of mileage you would like to designate as your season's "peak" weekly mileage (the greatest amount of mileage you feel is realistic for any single week—but it must be an amount you could repeat for several weeks). Be reasonable in building your weekly mileage to the level you achieve in this phase of training. It might happen that you'll do some quicker runs in training and be encouraged to enter a couple of races, but the main goal of this phase is to prepare you for the final serious 18 weeks of training that bring you into your marathon in peak shape.

Phases II Through IV—Continuous Phase

The final 18 weeks of this program are designed for serious runners who have completed at least two levels of the gold plan (see chapter 14) or the first phase of this elite program. This marathon program expects runners to train every day, with only occasional days off, if necessary. Runners who have a good background and recent weekly mileage in the 90s (150 kilometers) or more should feel free to begin this program with anywhere from 12 to 18 weeks to go to their target marathon. A solid build-up period of good weekly mileage followed by the 18-week schedule as described is ideal.

Also, as with program A, if you want to allow more than 18 weeks for the last phase(s) of training, you can extend the program by a week or more by repeating any of the weeks of training that particularly appealed to you—as long as you don't repeat two demanding weeks back to back.

Use table 19.2 (pages 250-251) or tables 3.1 and 3.2 to establish your training paces for the workouts in this phase. It's best to use race times from the previous six to eight weeks, or those that represent your current degree of fitness, to set appropriate paces.

Each week in this phase is designed to include two quality days: one scheduled for a Sunday, or marathon race day (Q1), and the other scheduled for midweek (Q2), which will typically be Wednesday or Thursday. All other days are easy running, made up of one or two sessions, with the goal of using these days to accumulate your weekly mileage (or point) goal. On the day after Q1, add six strides to the end of one of your easy runs, and two days before the next Q1, add eight strides to your (or one of your) easy runs.

Any weekend that you run a race during this schedule, be sure to do the previous Q2 three or four days before the race and drop the Q1 scheduled for the weekend of the race. Try to rearrange the Q1 sessions so that you don't miss the same type of Q1 workout on more than one occasion.

The distances shown for different types of training are designed with elite runners in mind; slower marathoners should use time-of-running values instead of distances. If you follow this time approach, consider each mile of **E** running to be about 6 minutes and each mile at **M** to be worth 5 minutes of running at your own marathon pace. Also, figure each mile of **T**-pace running to equal 4-1/2 to 5 minutes at your **T**-pace. When doing **I**-pace running, consider 1000s to demand about 3 minutes of hard running and miles to demand about 4:30 each (at your appropriate **I** pace). Select distances that approximate the respective periods of time at the proper intensities.

Before you begin this phase, settle on the greatest total weekly mileage you think is reasonable and designate that as your "peak" mileage. The fourth column of table 20.2 designates the fraction of "peak" mileage to total that week. For example, if you pick 120 as your peak mileage, then 0.8 peak = 96 miles for that week.

Table 20.2 **Elite Training Plan**

Phase	Week	Weeks left before race	Fraction of peak mileage	Q1 workout	Q2 workout
A	1-3	24-22		7 days of at least 30 min **E** pace; do more than 30 min if you already have a base established	
	4-6	21-19		1 day of **L** run; 25% of week's total mileage or 2.5 hours, whichever is less 6 days of 30 min or more **E** pace; after 2 or 3 of the **E** runs, add 6 to 8 × 20- to 30-sec strides	
II– IV	7	18	0.80	2 miles (or 12 min) **E** pace + 6 miles (or 30 min) **M** pace + 1 mile (or 4:45) **T** pace + 5 miles (or 25 min) **M** pace + 1 mile (or 4:45) **T** pace + 1 mile (or 4:45) **M** pace + 2 miles (or 12 min) **E** pace	2 miles (or 12 min) **E** pace + 8 miles (or 40 min) **T** pace (adjusted per table 7.1 or 7.2) + 2 miles (or 12 min) **E** pace
	8	17	0.80	2 miles **E** pace + 3 miles **T** pace + 1 hour **E** pace + 3 miles **T** pace + 2 miles **E** pace	2 miles **E** pace + 5 × (1,000m **I** pace with 2 min jogs) + 6 × (400 **R** pace with 3 min **E** pace) + 2 miles **E** pace
	9	16	0.70	18 miles steady **E** pace	2 miles **E** pace + 4 miles **T** pace + 4 min **E** pace + 3 miles **T** pace + 3 min **E** pace + 2 miles **T** pace + 2 min **E** pace + 1 mile **T** pace + 2 miles **E** pace
	10	15	0.90	2 miles **E** pace + 8 miles **M** pace + 1 mile **T** pace + 4 miles **M** pace + 1 mile **T** pace + 2 miles **M** pace + 2 miles **E** pace	2 miles **E** pace + 8 miles **T** pace (adjusted as per table 7.1 or 7.2) + 2 miles **E** pace
	11	14	0.90	2 miles **E** pace + 2 × (2 miles **T** pace with 2-min rest) + 1 hr **E** pace + 3 miles **T** pace + 2 miles **E** pace	2 miles at **E** pace 8 × (1000 or 5 × 1mile **I** pace with 2 or 4 min **E** pace) + 2 miles **E** pace
	12	13	0.70	20 miles steady **E** pace	2 miles **E** pace + 10 miles steady **T** pace (adjusted as per table 7.1 or 7.2) 2 miles **E** pace

Table 20.2 **Elite Training Plan**

Phase	Week	Weeks left before race	Fraction of peak mileage	Q1 workout	Q2 workout
II–IV	13	12*	1.00	4 miles **E** pace + 8 miles **M** pace + 1 mile **T** pace + 6 miles **M** pace + 1 mile **T** pace + 2 miles **E** pace	2 miles **E** pace + 4 miles **T** pace + 4 min **E** pace + 3 miles **T** pace + 3 min **E** pace + 2 miles **T** pace + 2 min **E** pace + 1 mile **T** pace + 2 miles **E** pace
	14	11	0.90	2 miles **E** pace + 4 miles **T** pace + 10 miles **E** pace + 2 × (2 miles **T** pace with 2-min rests) + 2 miles **E** pace	2 miles **E** pace + 6 × (1,000m or 4 × 1 mile **I** pace with 2 or 4 min **E** pace) + 4 × (400 **R** pace with 3 min **E** pace) + 2 miles **E** pace
	15	10	0.80	20 miles steady **E** pace	2 miles **E** pace + 10 miles steady **T** (adjusted per table 7.1 or 7.2) + 2 miles E pace
	16	9	1.00	6 miles **E** pace + 2 × (6 miles **M** pace + 1 mile **T** pace) + 2 miles **E** pace	2 miles **E** pace + 5 miles **T** pace + 5 min **E** pace + 4 miles **T** pace + 4 min **E** pace + 3 miles **T** pace + 3 min **E** pace + 1 mile **T** pace + 2 miles **E** pace
	17	8	0.90	2 miles **E** pace + 4 miles **T** pace + 10 miles **E** pace + 4 miles **T** pace + 2 miles **E** pace	2 miles at **E** pace + 3 × (1 mile **I** pace with 4 min **E** pace) + 3 × (1,000m **I** pace with 2 min **E** pace) + 2 miles **E** pace
	18	7	0.70	22 miles steady **E** pace	2 miles **E** pace + 8 miles steady **T** pace (adjusted per table 7.1 or 7.2) + 2 miles **E** pace

(continued)

Table 20.2   **Elite Training Plan**

(continued)

Phase	Week	Weeks left before race	Fraction of peak mileage	Q1 workout	Q2 workout
II–IV	19	6*	1.00	8 miles **E** pace + 8 miles **M** pace + 1 mile **T** pace + 4 miles **M** pace + 1 mile **T** pace + 1 mile **M** pace	2 miles **E** pace + 5 miles **T** pace + 5 min **E** pace + 4 miles **T** pace + 4 min **E** pace + 3 miles **T** pace + 3 min **E** pace + 2 miles **T** pace + 2 min **E** pace + 1 mile **T** pace + 2 miles **E** pace
	20	5	0.80	2 miles **E** pace + 4 miles **T** pace + 10 miles **E** pace + 4 miles **T** pace + 2 miles **E** pace	2 miles **E** pace + 6 × (1,000m **I** pace with 2 min **E** pace) + 4 × (400 **R** pace with 3 min **E** pace) + 2 miles **E** pace
	21	4	.070	22 miles steady **E** pace	2 miles **E** pace + 3 × (1mile **T** pace with 1 min **E** pace) + 3 × (1,000m **I** pace with 2 min **E** pace) + 3 × (400 **R** pace with 3 min **E** pace) + 2 miles **E** pace
	22	3	0.70	6 miles **E** pace + 2 × (6 miles **M** pace +1 mile **T** pace) + 2 miles **E** pace	2 miles **E** pace + 4 × (2 miles **T** pace with 2 min **E** pace) + 2 miles **E** pace
	23	2	0.60	2 miles **E** pace + 3 × (2 miles **T** pace with 2 min **E** pace) + 10 miles **E** pace	2 miles **E** pace + 3 × (2 miles **T** pace with 2 min **E** pace) + 2 miles **E** pace
	24	1		7 days to race (Q1): 90 min **E** pace 6 days to race: 60 min **E** pace + 4 to 6 strides	5 days to race (Q2): 2 miles **E** pace + 4 × 1,200m at **T** pace with 2 min **E** pace + 2 miles **E** pace 4 days to race: 30 to 50 min **E** pace + 4 to 6 strides 3 days to race: 20 to 30 min **E** pace + 4 strides 2 days to race: 0 to 20 min **E** pace 1 day to race: 20 to 30 min **E** pace

*At these two points you might want to increase your VDOT (by one unit each or as dictated by a race).

Program for Completing a Marathon

A growing number of runners want to experience the satisfaction of running a marathon, often with the goal of just completing the distance and feeling the joy associated with preparing for and participating in such an event. Sometimes serious and more hardcore runners feel their turf is being invaded by slower, less-serious runners, who have no intention of running fast. But I'd never discourage anyone from training for or attempting a marathon, regardless of how slowly they might run it. For one thing, many of these "slower" runners are highly motivated, having dedicated their marathon experience to a friend or loved one unable to share in the run. In addition, anyone who gets involved in a serious physical exercise program has my respect and support. In a country where the norm is overeating and underexercising, the more people who get involved in some regular exercise, the better it is for everyone.

For this reason, I offer a training program for those who seriously want to complete a marathon but who have only 18 weeks to engage in an optimal training program. In fact, the availability of time is so often a factor for these runners that many find it useful to learn how to make the very most of what time they have. Or, some people have plenty of time in each day for training but not enough days or weeks prior to the marathon they've committed to. These "short-season" runners present a special problem for a coach because runners who have lots of time on a daily basis but not enough weeks for building mileage gradually are good candidates for trying to do too much too fast and overstressing themselves.

Elite and serious runners of the marathon run to achieve the best possible performance; now many less advanced runners pursue different, but laudable, marathon goals of their own.

One of the first things that these runners whose goal is just to complete the run must accomplish is to convince themselves that they can achieve their goal without having to do the same type of training that the elite runners do. To successfully finish your first marathon, you don't need to include 20-plus mile runs in your training program. Easy runs, some **M** runs, and some slightly faster runs will serve you well.

With the goal of finishing your first marathon, you're focusing on training for just this one race, so you can do with or without the typical phases of training that include repetition running or interval sessions. If your time is limited and you've had little or no background in running, you'll first need to learn how to spend time on your feet. This might mean interspersing some walking with your running. If so, consider time spent walking as quality time that you can use for taking in fluids, or just to grab a few minutes of needed rest before you continue running again.

Here are a few guidelines to set the stage for the formal training program that follows.

1. Set a realistic "peak" amount of weekly mileage, an amount that will represent the greatest mileage accumulated in any single week, over the entire training program. If you haven't been running prior to starting the program, your daily training shouldn't exceed 30 minutes of running, and 30 minutes total running might even have to be broken into a number of brief runs, separated by a minute or two of walking. Every three weeks, increase your total weekly mileage by about 5 to 8 miles (or 10 to 15 miles every 6 weeks). Runners in this category will probably have to settle for a peak mileage of 40 or fewer. If you start the marathon schedule with some regular running behind you, limit your increases in weekly mileage to every third week, and limit them to between 5 and 10 miles at a time. You should reach your peak mileage three to six weeks before the marathon you're training for.

2. Without any races to establish a VDOT for your own training intensities, train subjectively—**E** and **L** runs should be easy and conversational. **T** running is meant to be comfortably hard. If **M** is the pace you'll shoot for in your race, it should be a pace midway between **E** and **T** pace. Breathing should *never* be stressful in **E, L, or M** intensities. If you enter a race or two during the training season, use the resulting VDOT to accurately set your training intensities (using tables 3.1 and 3.2 or table 19.2).

3. If you already have some races to establish a VDOT value, use that VDOT for at least four weeks before letting a better race performance increase your VDOT. If training is going well, but you don't race, feel free to increase VDOT by one unit after four to six weeks of consistent training.

4. Always breathe with a 2-2 rhythm (two steps breathing in and two steps breathing out), and learn to take at least 180 steps each minute (90 steps per foot) by using short, light, quick steps, rather than long bounding strides.

5. Practice drinking on **L** and **M** runs.

6. Have more than one pair of shoes that you're comfortable wearing for long runs and plan to use one of those in the marathon race. You might have to buy

a few pairs of shoes during the season, so stick with a model that suits you well, and make sure the shoes you race in are in good shape and have seen you through a few long runs.

Phase I

As in the other programs presented in this book, phase I of this program is devoted to building your resistance to injury and getting into the habit of running (see table 20.3).

Phase II

Phase II is a good time to get consistent in your training—running as many days per week as can you can fit in without undue stress. In table 20.3 the fraction of peak mileage values for each numbered week of training refers to the amount of mileage for that coming week. You must first establish a peak amount of weekly mileage for the season. The decimal portion of that peak is then set for the week in question. For example, if 40 miles will be the greatest (peak) mileage for any week this season, then $0.90 \times 40 = 36$ miles for that week.

For runners with little or no running background, **T**-paced sessions (comfortably hard running in which your breathing doesn't feel overly stressed) might best be kept to the appropriate subjective intensity for designated periods of time, rather than trying to run a specific distance for time (unless you've been able to establish a VDOT from a recent race). The duration of a **T** run could be as long as a steady 20 minutes, or you might run several 5- to 10-minute runs with a rest of 1 or 2 minutes between each, with a goal of totaling 30 minutes of **T**-pace running in a single session of training. **T** runs will work wonders toward making your **M** and easy **L** runs feel more within your capability.

Perform the **M**-pace run in the sixth week of this phase at a pace that you feel is appropriate for the marathon you'll be running. Most beginners have little idea of what that pace should be, but if you've had any experience with long runs and **T** runs, then just think of **M** pace as being between **L** and **T** in intensity. For a true beginner, there might not be much difference between **L** and **M** runs, but the idea of including some **M** runs in your training program is to go into the training session with a mindset that this run is a preview of what you plan to do in your marathon. Practice drinking at **M** pace; make every effort to imagine you're in the middle of the marathon itself.

On your nonquality days (see table 20.3), perform **E**-pace runs that allow you to reach your peak mileage for the week. Follow two of your weekly **E** sessions with 5 to 6 × 20- to 30-second strides.

If you have the opportunity to jump into a few road races during your buildup to a marathon, do it—preferably during the second phase of your training. If you do run a race, arrange your training to allow for at least two easy days of running before and three easy days after any races. This might mean dropping a quality-training day for a race day.

Table 20.3 **Training Program for Runners Who Want to Complete a Marathon**

Phase	Week	Weeks left before race	Fraction of peak mileage	Workouts	
I	1-3	16-18		7 days of at least 30 min **E** pace; break up each 30-min run with walking, if necessary; do more than 30 min if you already have a base established. An **E** day might be one run, two runs, or even *no* running, if you feel the need for complete rest. The amount of running totaled on an **E** day is however much you need to reach weekly mileage goals.	
	4-6	13-15		1 day of **L** run; no more than 25 to 33% of week's total mileage 6 days of 30 min or more **E** pace; after 2 to 3 of the **E** runs, add 5 to 6 × 20- to 30-sec strides.	
				Q1 workout	**Q2 workout**
II	7	12	0.80	**L** run; 2.5 hours or 25 to 30% of week's total miles, whichever is less	20- to 30-min **T** pace run. You can break this into two or three 10- to 15-min runs with 1-min rests between.
	8	11	0.80	**L** run; 2.5 hours or 25 to 30% of week's total mileage, whichever is less	20- to 30-min **T**-pace run. You can break this into two or three 10- to 15-min runs with 1-min rests between.
	9	10	0.70	2 **E**-pace runs to total 25 to 30% of week's total mileage, whichever is less	20- to 30-min **T**-pace run. You can break this into two or three 10- to 15-min runs with 1-min rests between.
	10	9	0.90	**L** run; 2.5 hours or 25 to 30% of week's total mileage, whichever is less	20-to 30-min **T**-pace run. You can break this into two or three 10- to 15-min runs with 1-min rests between.
	11	8	0.90	**L** run; 2.5 hours or 25 to 30% of week's total mileage, whichever is less	20-to 30-min **T**-pace run. You can break this into two or three 10- to 15-min runs with 1-min rests between.
	12	7	0.70	**M** run; lesser of 12 miles or 2 hours plus 5 to 6 20- to 30-sec strides with 1-min rests	20-to 30-min **T**-pace run. You can break this into two or three 10 to 15 min runs with 1-min rests between. *or* **L** run; 2.5 hours or 25 to 30% of week's total miles, whichever is less

(continued)

Table 20.3 **Training Program for Runners Who Want to Complete a Marathon**

Phase	Week	Weeks left before race	Fraction of peak mileage	Workouts	
				Q1 workout	Q2 workout
III	13	6	1.00	3 × (5 to 6 min at **T** pace with 1-min rests) + 60-min **E** pace + 2 to 3 × (5 to 6 min **T** pace with 1-min rests)	2 × (10 to 12 min **T** pace with 2-min rest) + 60 to 90 min **E** pace
	14	5	0.90	2-1/2 hours or 15 miles **M** (projected marathon race) pace, whichever is less	2 × (10 to 12 min **T** pace with 2-min rest) + 60 to 90 min **E** pa
	15	4	1.00	25% of week's total or 2-1/2 hours **L** run; if you're planning to run slower than 4 hours in a marathon, don't run more than 18 miles	2 × (10 to 12 min **T** pace with 2-min rest) + 60 to 90 mi
	16	3	0.80	3 × (5 to 6 min **T** pace with 1-min rests) + 60-min **E** pace 2 to 3 × (5 to 6 min **T** pace with 1-min rests)	2 × (10 to 12 min **T** pace with 2-min rest) + 60 to 90 min at **E** pace
	17	2	0.80	2 hours or 12 miles **M** pace, whichever is less	2 miles **E** pace + 20 to 30 min **T** pace (in 5- to 10-min bouts)
	18	1		2 **E**-pace runs to total 25 to 30% of week's total mileage, whichever is less	2 miles **E** pace + 20 to 30 min **T** pace (in 5- to 10-min bouts)

Note: All other days for phases II and III are **E**-pace runs of sufficient mileage to reach the week's mileage goal. After two or three of the **E** runs each week, add 5 to 6 × 20- to 30-second strides.

Phase III

Phase III is the final phase of this beginner's program. Your long runs will take quite a bit of time, typically in the two to two-and-a-half-hour range, so I suggest doing these early in the day, preferably about the same time of day that you'll be racing your marathon. If by four weeks prior to your marathon you can't complete the lesser of 15 miles or 2 and a half hours of steady running at your projected marathon pace, change your plans and start looking for a marathon a little further in the future until you can meet that goal.

When doing your quality sessions (**T**, **M**, and combinations of these), run during good weather conditions, if possible. It can be discouraging to try to accomplish a quality session under adverse conditions—heat, strong winds—when you're particularly tired or not feeling well. This might even mean juggling some quality sessions around a bit, but try not to make a habit of dropping or switching the order of training any more often than necessary, and never try to make up for a missed session by increasing the stress of another session. A day missed here or there is far more acceptable than overstressing yourself in an attempt to make up for a missed workout. Your primary goal must be to arrive at the start of your marathon in good health and good spirits.

Of course, any nonquality session is an **E**-pace run to help you reach your weekly mileage needs. Follow a couple of these **E** runs each week with 5 to 6 × 20- to 30-second strides.

If you run part of a longer race (as a training run), have someone meet you when you have completed your run so that you don't get stuck out in the middle of nowhere when your time is up. Also, remember that you will feel better in the actual marathon race than in a training run (even if part of a race), because you'll be more rested and mentally prepared for the full distance when the time comes.

Even when runners follow the same sets of basic training principles and have the same goals in mind, there are many different ways to accomplish these goals. No one has all the answers to what the best training program is, and there probably isn't one best program that applies to everyone—what works well for one runner might not work well at all for another.

By committing yourself to a well-designed training plan, and with proper nutrition and rest, you'll be amazed at how enjoyable (at least, rewarding) a marathon, or similar long-distance race, can be. In fact, running just for the fun of it is a great activity. I hope that running gives you the enjoyment and satisfaction in life that it has given to me.

Appendix A: Pace Table

This table shows times at various distances when running at the same pace.

400	1,000 m	Mile	3,000 m	5,000 m	10,000 m	15K	10 mile	20K	Half-marathon	Marathon
50	2:05	3:21	6:15	10:25	20:50	31:15	33:31	41:40	43:57	1:27:54
51	2:07	3:25	6:22	10:37	21:15	31:52	34:12	42:30	44:50	1:29:40
52	2:10	3:29	6:30	10:50	21:40	32:30	34:52	43:20	45:42	1:31:25
53	2:12	3:33	6:37	11:02	22:05	33:07	35:32	44:10	46:35	1:33:10
54	2:15	3:37	6:45	11:15	22:30	33:45	36:12	45:00	47:28	1:34:56
55	2:17	3:41	6:52	11:27	22:55	34:22	36:53	45:50	48:21	1:36:41
56	2:20	3:45	7:00	11:40	23:20	35:00	37:33	46:40	49:13	1:38:27
57	2:22	3:49	7:07	11:52	23:45	35:37	38:13	47:30	50:06	1:40:12
58	2:25	3:53	7:15	12:05	24:10	36:15	38:53	48:20	50:59	1:41:58
59	2:27	3:57	7:22	12:17	24:35	36:52	39:33	49:10	51:52	1:43:43
60	2:30	4:01	7:30	12:30	25:00	37:30	40:14	50:00	52:44	1:45:29
61	2:32	4:05	7:37	12:42	25:25	38:07	40:54	50:50	53:37	1:47:14
62	2:35	4:09	7:45	12:55	25:50	38:45	41:34	51:40	54:30	1:49:00
63	2:37	4:13	7:52	13:07	26:15	39:22	42:14	52:30	55:23	1:50:45
64	2:40	4:17	8:00	13:20	26:40	40:00	42:55	53:20	56:15	1:52:31
65	2:42	4:21	8:07	13:32	27:05	40:37	43:35	54:10	57:08	1:54:16
66	2:45	4:25	8:15	13:45	27:30	41:15	44:15	55:00	58:01	1:56:02
67	2:47	4:29	8:22	13:57	27:55	41:52	44:55	55:50	58:54	1:57:47
68	2:50	4:33	8:30	14:10	28:20	42:30	45:36	56:40	59:46	1:59:33
69	2:52	4:37	8:37	14:22	28:45	43:07	46:16	57:30	1:00:39	2:01:18
70	2:55	4:41	8:45	14:35	29:10	43:45	46:56	58:20	1:01:32	2:03:04
71	2:57	4:45	8:52	14:47	29:35	44:22	47:36	59:10	1:02:24	2:04:49
72	3:00	4:49	9:00	15:00	30:00	45:00	48:16	1:00:00	1:03:17	2:06:35
73	3:02	4:53	9:07	15:12	30:25	45:37	48:57	1:00:50	1:04:10	2:08:20
74	3:05	4:57	9:15	15:25	30:50	46:15	49:37	1:01:04	1:05:03	2:10:06
75	3:07	5:01	9:22	15:37	31:15	46:52	50:17	1:02:30	1:05:55	2:11:51
76	3:10	5:05	9:30	15:50	31:40	47:30	50:57	1:03:20	1:06:48	2:13:37
77	3:12	5:10	9:37	16:02	32:05	48:07	51:38	1:04:10	1:07:41	2:15:22
78	3:15	5:14	9:45	16:15	32:30	48:45	52:18	1:05:00	1:08:34	2:17:08
79	3:17	5:18	9:52	16:27	32:55	49:22	52:58	1:05:50	1:09:26	2:18:53
80	3:20	5:22	10:00	16:40	33:20	50:00	53:38	1:06:40	1:10:19	2:20:39
81	3:22	5:26	10:07	16:52	33:45	50:37	54:19	1:07:30	1:11:12	2:22:24
82	3:25	5:30	10:15	17:05	34:10	51:15	54:59	1:08:20	1:12:05	2:24:10
83	3:27	5:34	10:22	17:17	34:35	51:52	55:39	1:09:10	1:12:57	2:25:55
84	3:30	5:38	10:30	17:30	35:00	52:30	56:19	1:10:00	1:13:50	2:27:41

(continued)

400	1,000 m	Mile	3,000 m	5,000 m	10,000 m	15K	10 mile	20K	Half- marathon	Marathon
85	3:32	5:42	10:37	17:42	35:25	53:07	57:00	1:10:50	1:14:43	2:29:26
86	3:35	5:46	10:45	17:55	35:50	53:45	57:40	1:11:40	1:15:36	2:31:12
87	3:37	5:50	10:52	18:07	36:15	54:22	58:20	1:12:30	1:16:28	2:32:57
88	3:40	5:54	11:00	18:20	36:40	55:00	59:00	1:13:20	1:17:21	2:34:43
89	3:42	5:58	11:07	18:32	37:05	55:37	59:40	1:14:10	1:18:14	2:36:28
90	3:45	6:02	11:15	18:45	37:30	56:15	1:00:21	1:15:00	1:19:07	2:38:14
91	3:47	6:06	11:22	18:57	37:55	56:52	1:01:01	1:15:50	1:19:59	2:39:59
92	3:50	6:10	11:30	19:10	38:20	57:30	1:01:41	1:16:40	1:20:52	2:41:45
93	3:52	6:14	11:37	19:22	38:45	58:07	1:02:21	1:17:30	1:21:45	2:43:30
94	3:55	6:18	11:45	19:35	39:10	58:45	1:03:02	1:18:20	1:22:38	2:45:16
95	3:57	6:22	11:52	19:47	39:35	59:22	1:03:42	1:19:10	1:23:30	2:47:01
96	4:00	6:26	12:00	20:00	40:00	1:00:00	1:04:22	1:20:00	1:24:23	2:48:47
97	4:02	6:30	12:07	20:12	40:25	1:00:37	1:05:02	1:20:50	1:25:16	2:50:32
98	4:05	6:34	12:15	20:25	40:50	1:01:15	1:15:43	1:21:40	1:26:09	2:52:18
99	4:07	6:38	12:22	20:37	41:15	1:01:52	1:16:23	1:22:30	1:27:01	2:54:03
1:40	4:10	6:42	12:30	20:50	41:40	1:02:30	1:07:03	1:23:20	1:27:54	2:55:48
1:41	4:12	6:46	12:37	21:02	42:05	1:03:07	1:07:43	1:24:10	1:28:47	2:57:34
1:42	4:15	6:50	12:45	21:15	42:30	1:03:45	1:08:23	1:25:00	1:29:40	2:59:20
1:43	4:17	6:54	12:52	21:27	42:55	1:04:22	1:09:04	1:25:50	1:30:32	3:01:05
1:44	4:20	6:58	13:00	21:40	43:20	1:05:00	1:09:44	1:26:40	1:31:25	3:02:50
1:45	4:22	7:02	13:07	21:52	43:45	1:05:37	1:10:24	1:27:30	1:32:18	3:04:36
1:46	4:25	7:06	13:15	22:05	44:10	1:06:15	1:11:04	1:28:20	1:33:11	3:06:22
1:47	4:27	7:10	13:22	22:17	44:35	1:06:52	1:11:45	1:29:10	1:34:03	3:08:07
1:48	4:30	7:14	13:30	22:30	45:00	1:07:30	1:12:25	1:30:00	1:34:56	3:09:52
1:49	4:32	7:18	13:37	22:42	45:25	1:08:07	1:13:05	1:30:50	1:35:49	3:11:38
1:50	4:35	7:22	13:45	22:55	45:50	1:08:45	1:13:45	1:31:40	1:36:42	3:13:24
1:51	4:37	7:26	13:52	23:07	46:15	1:09:22	1:14:26	1:32:30	1:37:34	3:15:09
1:52	4:40	7:30	14:00	23:20	46:40	1:10:00	1:15:06	1:33:20	1:38:27	3:16:54
1:53	4:42	7:34	14:07	23:32	47:05	1:10:37	1:15:46	1:34:10	1:39:20	3:18:40
1:54	4:45	7:38	14:15	23:45	47:30	1:11:15	1:16:26	1:35:00	1:40:12	3:20:25
1:55	4:47	7:42	14:22	23:57	47:55	1:11:52	1:17:07	1:35:50	1:41:05	3:22:11
1:56	4:50	7:46	14:30	24:10	48:20	1:12:30	1:17:47	1:36:40	1:41:58	3:23:56
1:57	4:52	7:50	14:37	24:22	48:45	1:13:07	1:18:27	1:37:30	1:42:51	3:25:42
1:58	4:55	7:54	14:45	24:35	49:10	1:13:45	1:19:07	1:38:20	1:43:43	3:27:27
1:59	4:57	7:58	15:52	24:47	49:35	1:14:22	1:19:48	1:39:10	1:44:36	3:29:13
2:00	5:00	8:02	15:00	25:00	50:00	1:15:00	1:20:28	1:40:00	1:45:29	3:30:58
2:01	5:02	8:06	15:07	25:12	50:25	1:15:37	1:21:08	1:40:50	1:46:22	3:32:44
2:02	5:05	8:10	15:15	25:25	50:50	1:16:15	1:21:48	1:41:40	1:47:14	3:34:29
2:03	5:07	8:14	15:22	25:37	51:15	1:16:52	1:22:28	1:42:30	1:48:07	3:36:15
2:04	5:10	8:19	15:30	25:50	51:40	1:17:30	1:23:09	1:43:20	1:49:00	3:38:00
2:05	5:12	8:23	15:37	26:02	52:05	1:18:07	1:23:49	1:44:10	1:49:53	3:39:46

400	1,000 m	Mile	3,000 m	5,000 m	10,000 m	15K	10 mile	20K	Half-marathon	Marathon
2:06	5:15	8:26	15:45	26:15	52:30	1:18:45	1:24:29	1:45:00	1:50:45	3:41:31
2:07	5:17	8:31	15:52	26:27	52:55	1:19:22	1:25:09	1:45:50	1:51:38	3:43:17
2:08	5:20	8:35	16:00	26:40	53:20	1:20:00	1:25:50	1:46:40	1:52:31	3:45:02
2:09	5:22	8:39	16:07	26:52	53:45	1:20:37	1:26:30	1:47:30	1:53:24	3:46:48
2:10	5:25	8:43	16:15	27:05	54:10	1:21:15	1:27:10	1:48:20	1:54:16	3:48:33
2:11	5:27	8:47	16:22	27:17	54:35	1:21:52	1:27:50	1:49:10	1:55:09	3:50:19
2:12	5:30	8:51	16:30	27:30	55:00	1:22:30	1:28:31	1:50:00	1:56:02	3:52:04
2:13	5:32	8:55	16:37	27:42	55:25	1:23:07	1:29:11	1:50:50	1:56:55	3:53:50
2:14	5:35	8:59	16:45	27:55	55:50	1:23:45	1:29:51	1:51:40	1:57:47	3:55:35
2:15	5:37	9:03	16:52	28:07	56:15	1:24:20	1:30:31	1:52:30	1:58:40	3:57:20
2:16	5:40	9:07	17:00	28:20	56:40	1:25:00	1:31:11	1:53:20	1:59:33	3:59:06
2:17	5:42	9:11	17:07	28:32	57:05	1:25:37	1:31:52	1:54:10	2:00:26	4:00:52
2:18	5:45	9:15	17:15	28:45	57:30	1:26:15	1:32:32	1:55:00	2:01:18	4:02:37
2:19	5:47	9:19	17:22	28:57	57:55	1:26:52	1:33:12	1:55:50	2:02:11	4:04:22
2:20	5:50	9:23	17:30	29:10	58:20	1:27:30	1:33:52	1:56:40	2:03:04	4:06:08
2:21	5:52	9:27	17:37	29:22	58:45	1:28:07	1:34:33	1:57:30	2:03:57	4:07:54
2:22	5:55	9:31	17:45	29:35	59:10	1:28:45	1:35:13	1:58:20	2:04:49	4:09:39
2:23	5:57	9:35	17:52	29:47	59:35	1:29:22	1:35:53	1:59:10	2:05:42	4:11:24
2:24	6:00	9:39	18:00	30:00	1:00:00	1:30:00	1:36:33	2:00:00	2:06:35	4:13:10
2:25	6:02	9:43	18:07	30:12	1:00:25	1:30:37	1:37:14	2:00:50	2:07:27	4:14:55
2:26	6:05	9:47	18:15	30:25	1:00:50	1:31:15	1:37:54	2:01:40	2:08:20	4:16:41
2:27	6:07	9:51	18:22	30:37	1:01:15	1:31:52	1:38:34	2:02:30	2:09:13	4:18:26
2:28	6:10	9:55	18:30	30:50	1:01:40	1:32:30	1:39:14	2:03:20	2:10:06	4:20:12
2:29	6:12	9:59	18:37	31:02	1:02:05	1:33:07	1:39:55	2:04:10	2:10:58	4:21:57
2:30	6:15	10:03	18:45	31:15	1:02:30	1:13:45	1:40:35	2:05:00	2:11:51	4:23:43

Appendix B:
$\dot{V}O_2$ Testing Protocol

The following is suggested protocol for testing runners for max and submax values of $\dot{V}O_2$ (economy), heart rate, and max blood lactate.

Treadmill

1. Identify current or estimated current 10K race time and convert this time into mph and meters per minute velocities and consider this your fastest sub-max test velocity.

2. Identify the velocity from the following list of velocities (m/min) that most closely approximates the velocity (in meters per minute) from step 1 above: 150, 170, 190, 210, 230, 250, 270, 290, 310, 330, 350, 370, (20 m/min increments).

3. Start the first (slowest) submax test at the velocity that is 3 velocities slower than the fastest submax test velocity identified above. This is your slowest or beginning velocity.

4. Run 5-minute submax runs at progressively faster velocities, starting with your beginning velocity and making your fastest submax velocity your fourth test. Monitor heart rate and $\dot{V}O_2$ during the final 90 seconds of each submax run and average the data for this period of time. Upon completion of each submax run take the necessary blood sample for blood-lactate determination. Plan about two minutes rest time between the submax test runs (at least get the blood lactate reading prior to starting the next run).

5. If the fourth velocity is clearly not very demanding, (blood lactate below about 3.8 or heart rate not greater than 90% of a known max, for example), you may move to the next faster velocity for a fifth submax test. If the third submax velocity is clearly too demanding to allow for a fourth submax run, (blood lactate over 4.0, very near max heart rate), then do not perform the fourth submax run.

6. After about a four- or five- minute break following the final sub-max test, run the max test, all at a constant velocity which is equal to the velocity used in the final submax test (but not faster than 330 m/min), as follows: two minutes at 0 percent grade and add a 1 percent grade to the treadmill each subsequent minute until the test is terminated.

7. Starting just before the end of the third minute, and during the final 10 seconds of each subsequent minute, ask the runner if he or she is able to go 1 more minute. If the answer is "yes" (with a thumbs up hand signal), add 1 percent to the grade, and continue with this same procedure until test termination. If the answer is "no" (horizontal waving of the hand), ask if 30 more seconds is

possible. If the answer to this is "yes," continue 30 more seconds and terminate the test. If the answer is "no," terminate the test immediately.

8. Monitor $\dot{V}O_2$ and heart rate throughout the max test (or if bags of expired air are collected, start collection at the end of the third minute and collect consecutive 30- to 45-second bags until the test is terminated).

9. Consider $\dot{V}O_2$max as the average of the two consecutive bag collections (or three consecutive 20-second or two consecutive 30-second readouts on an on-line system) that give the highest $\dot{V}O_2$ value. Once you determine the time frame that is recognized as the max value, use this same time frame to identify max expired ventilation, or $\dot{V}_E$ ($\dot{V}_E$ associated with $\dot{V}O_2$max), respiratory exchange ration (R), heart rate, and any other values of interest. Two to three minutes after the termination of the max test, the lab technician should take the blood sample that will determine blood lactate associated with $\dot{V}O_2$max (not necessarily max lactate as the test was not a high-intensity anaerobic effort).

Overground

Use a golf cart or car driven beside the runner to make collections. This is very difficult so you should have a driver who has practiced driving at these speeds with a runner running beside. A golf cart is preferable to a car if available.

1. Use the same treadmill method to determine test velocities and the starting velocity, as described in step 2 of the treadmill protocol, above.

2. For submax data, run a 1600-meter test, running at a constant velocity throughout the test. Give times every 100 or 200 meters to control velocity.

3. Collect expired-air samples for 60 to 90 seconds during the final 60 to 90 seconds of each sub-max run. If not able to monitor heart rate during the run, take a 10-second HR immediately at termination of each run, and take a blood sample for lactate values immediately at the end of each run. Take two to three minutes rest between submax runs and four to five minutes rest prior to the max test.

4. At the end of each submax run a decision must be made regarding the need for an additional submax run.

5. The max run is a 2000-meter run with the first 400 meters run at a comfortable pace (a good bit slower than 10K race pace).

6. The next 1200 meters are run at 5K race pace or a little faster, and the final 400 meters are run as fast as possible.

7. Collect 30 to 45 second expired-air samples, starting at the end of the third total lap of running and continuing to the termination of the test. Average the two consecutive bags that produce the highest $\dot{V}O_2$ and use the associated $\dot{V}_E$, HR and R values to be expressed as $\dot{V}_E$, HR and R at $\dot{V}O_2$max. Two to three minutes after the termination of the max test, the lab technician should take a blood sample to determine lactate associated with $\dot{V}O_2$max.

Index

Note: The italicized *f* and *t* following page numbers refer to figures and tables, respectively.

About the Author

Jack Daniels grew up in the San Francisco Bay Area, and upon failing at high school baseball tryouts, turned to swimming, a sport he stayed with through his undergraduate college days at the University of Montana, where he also competed on the ROTC rifle team. During an Army tour of duty in Korea, Daniels qualified for the All-Army Championships in triathlon (pistol shooting, swimming, and running), which led to assignment with the U.S. Modern Pentathlon Team in San Antonio, Texas. Five months after learning to ride horses over a cross country course and to fence with an epée (the additional sports added to run, swim, and shoot, that make up the modern pentathlon), he qualified as alternate on the Melbourne Olympic Team. When a riding accident took the top American out of the competition, Daniels was substituted in his place and won a Silver Team Medal in the 1956 Olympics. Daniels went on to twice win the U.S. national title and to compete in three world championships (including a Bronze team medal)·

Upon leaving the Army, Daniels moved to Sweden, where he studied sport at the Royal Gymnastic and Sport High School and continued pentathlon training. He won another team medal (Bronze) in the 1960 Rome Olympics. As result of his weakness in pentathlon running, Daniels decided to dedicate his time to studying the science of distance running and left swim coaching to become a track and field coach, an endeavor he has pursued over a 45-year period.

After four years coaching at Oklahoma City University and a year as national coach of Peru, Daniels returned to college and earned his PhD in exercise physiology from the University of Wisconsin. During the summers he conducted altitude research with many of the country's greatest athletes of that era and was altitude consultant to the 1968 Olympic track and field team in Mexico City.

Daniels was men's distance coach at the University of Texas for three years then started and directed the women's track and cross country teams at Texas for several years, and in summers worked for Sport Canada. The latter position culminated with a job as color commentator for CBC during the Montreal Olympics. He left Texas to spend six years with Nike, in New Hampshire and Eugene, Oregon, where he ran research projects and tested Athletics West distance runners.

After having success coaching a couple of elite marathoners, the urge to coach full time sent Daniels to the State University of New York at Cortland, where in a 12-year period his distance runners won 8 NCAA Division III national team titles (7 in cross country). He also coached 30 individual national champions and 130 All-Americans at SUNY Cortland. In 2000, Daniels was named NCAA Division III women's cross country coach of the 20th century. Most recently he has become involved in coaching some members of the Nike Farm Team and in coaching the "Chasquis," a group of marathoners in Peru. He is proud of his many research and coaching accomplishments, but his fondest memories are of time he has spent with his wife, Nancy, and their two girls, Audra and Sarah, to whom he refers as "The real joys in my life."